S0-AHZ-841

DK EYEWITNESS
ENCYCLOPEDIA OF
EVERYTHING

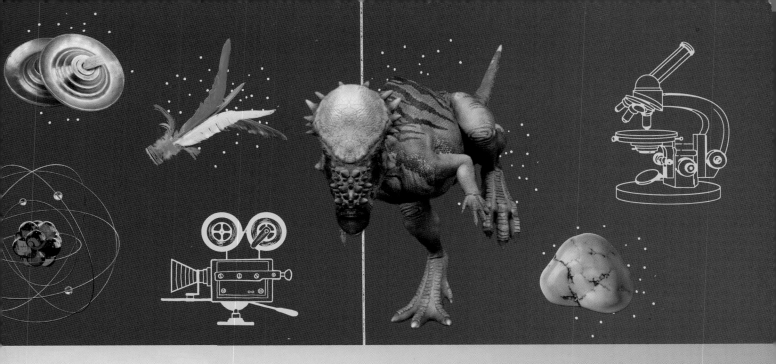

DK EYEWITNESS
ENCYCLOPEDIA OF
EVERYTHING

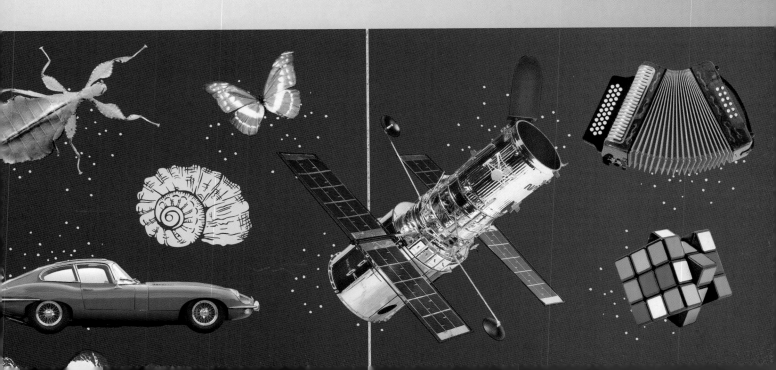

Senior editor Jenny Sich
US Senior editor Jennette ElNaggar
Senior art editor Rachael Grady
Editorial team Virien Chopra, Upamanyu Das,
Binta Jallow, Tim Harris, Hélène Hilton, Sam Kennedy,
Georgina Palffy, Ed Pearce, Vicky Richards,
Rona Skene, Anna Streiffert Limerick
Design team Revati Anand, Kelly Adams,
Chrissy Checketts, Sheila Collins, Noopur Dalal, Mik Gates,
Jim Green, Beth Johnston, Kit Lane, Govind Mittal,
Lynne Moulding, Stefan Podhorodecki
Illustrators Katy Jakeway, Simon Tegg
Picture researchers Sarah Hopper, Jo Walton
Managing editor Francesca Baines
Managing art editor Philip Letsu
Production editor Gillian Reid
Production controller Poppy David
Jacket designer Stephanie Cheng Hui Tan
DTP designers Usman Ansari, Pawan Kumar
Senior DTP designer Harish Aggarwal
Senior jackets coordinator Priyanka Sharma Saddi
Jackets design development manager Sophia MTT
Publisher Andrew Macintyre
Art director Karen Self
Associate publishing director Liz Wheeler
Publishing director Jonathan Metcalf

Additional text Ed Aves, Ian Fitzgerald,
Andrea Mills, Lizzie Munsey

Consultants Dr. Chris Barker, Professor Mike Benton,
Jack Challoner, Professor Peter Doyle, Bethan Durie,
Dr. Jacob Field, Professor Elizabeth Graham,
Professor Scott Hancock, Cat Hickey, Penny Johnson,
Anthea Lacchia, Dr. Jacqueline Mitton, Martin Redfern,
Dr. Kristina Routh, Professor Bill Sillar, Dr. Mel Thompson,
Timothy K. Topper, Dr. Ogechukwu Williams

First American Edition, 2023
Published in the United States by DK Publishing
1745 Broadway, 20th Floor, New York, NY 10019

Copyright © 2023 Dorling Kindersley Limited
DK, a Division of Penguin Random House LLC

Interview text on page 24 © 2023. California Institute of
Technology. Government sponsorship acknowledged.

Interview text on page 38 © 2023 National Aeronautics
and Space Administration for all jurisdictions outside the
United States. Published by Dorling Kindersley Limited
with permission.

23 24 25 26 27 10 9 8 7 6 5 4 3 2 1
001-333632-Sep/2023

All rights reserved.
Without limiting the rights under the copyright
reserved above, no part of this publication may be
reproduced, stored in or introduced into a retrieval system,
or transmitted, in any form, or by any means (electronic,
mechanical, photocopying, recording or otherwise),
without the prior written permission of
the copyright owner.
Published in Great Britain by Dorling Kindersley Limited

A catalog record for this book
is available from the Library of Congress.
ISBN 978-0-7440-8470-2

Printed and bound in China

www.dk.com
For the curious

This book was made with Forest Stewardship
Council™ certified paper – one small step
in DK's commitment to a sustainable future.
For more information go to
www.dk.com/our-green-pledge

CONTENTS

HUMAN BODY 168

SCIENCE 202

HISTORY 264

CULTURE 336

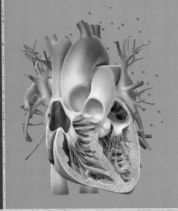

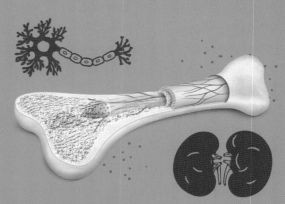

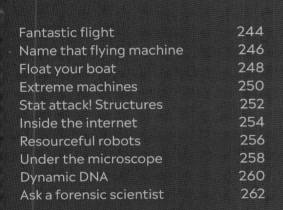

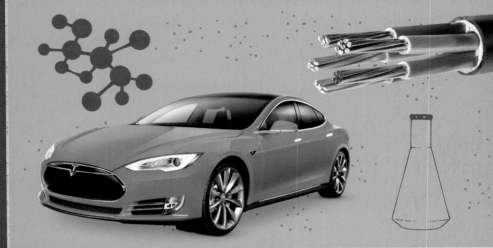

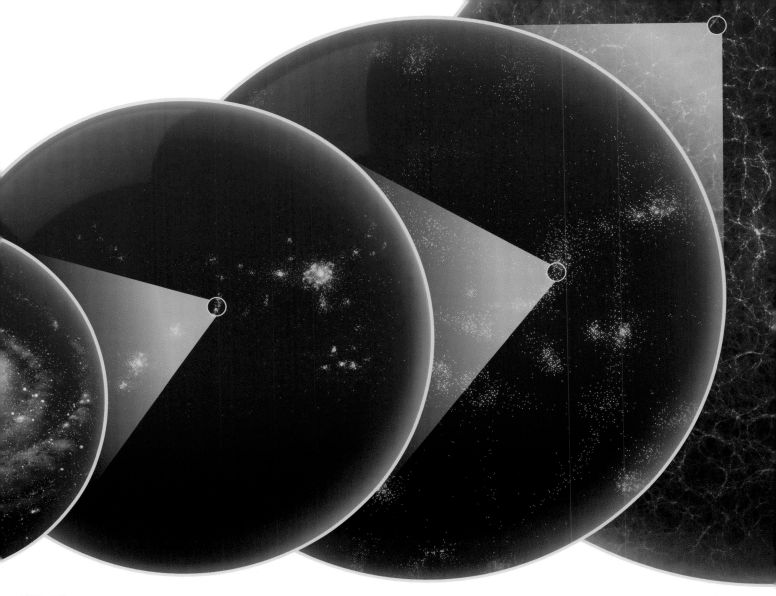

Milky Way
The sun and billions of other stars belong to a galaxy called the Milky Way.

Local Group
The Local Group is a cluster of around 50 galaxies, including ours.

Superclusters
Groups of galaxies can cluster together in turn, as larger "superclusters."

Observable universe
Groups of superclusters form threadlike filaments, separated by empty space.

Binoculars
Using binoculars shows space objects in a little more detail. For example, craters become visible on the moon's surface.

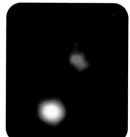

Large Earth-based telescope
These telescopes capture images of very faint objects. The red blob is HD-1 Galaxy, the farthest object seen from Earth.

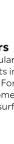

Amateur telescope
Even a small telescope allows us to see sights such as this view of the Andromeda Galaxy. Closer objects, such as planets, also appear sharper.

Space telescope
The best view of space is from space itself. Beyond Earth's atmosphere, telescopes can capture clearer images, such as this of galaxy NGC 346.

THE LARGEST **TELESCOPES** COLLECT **100 MILLION TIMES** MORE LIGHT THAN A **HUMAN EYE!**

The bright galaxies colored white like this one belong to a galaxy cluster.

The telescope creates "spikes" around images of stars in the foreground.

Background galaxies appear distorted into arcs by the gravity of the nearer galaxy cluster.

LOOKING AT **THE PAST**

This picture of a patch of the night sky was taken by the James Webb Space Telescope. Almost every object visible is a galaxy. Because they are so far away, their light has taken billions of years to reach us. The most distant galaxies it shows are 13 billion light-years away. We are seeing them as they looked less than one billion years after the Big Bang.

The universe

THE SECTION OF NIGHT SKY SHOWN IN THE IMAGE ABOVE IS SO TINY IT COULD BE COVERED BY A GRAIN OF SAND HELD AT ARM'S LENGTH!

The universe is everything, everywhere. It includes all the things we can see, from the tiniest atoms to vast galaxies. It also includes things we can't see, such as energy and time, and things we have not yet discovered. Formed more than 13 billion years ago in a fraction of a second, the universe continues to expand and is so vast that its scale is almost impossible for us to comprehend.

ASTRONOMERS PREDICT THAT **THE UNIVERSE** WILL HAVE **DOUBLED IN SIZE** IN **10 BILLION YEARS'** TIME!

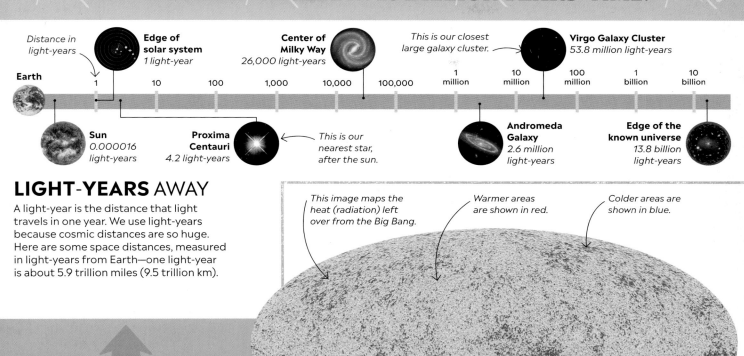

Distance in light-years

Earth

Edge of solar system
1 light-year

Center of Milky Way
26,000 light-years

This is our closest large galaxy cluster.

Virgo Galaxy Cluster
53.8 million light-years

1 · 10 · 100 · 1,000 · 10,000 · 100,000 · 1 million · 10 million · 100 million · 1 billion · 10 billion

Sun
0.000016 light-years

Proxima Centauri
4.2 light-years

This is our nearest star, after the sun.

Andromeda Galaxy
2.6 million light-years

Edge of the known universe
13.8 billion light-years

LIGHT-YEARS AWAY

A light-year is the distance that light travels in one year. We use light-years because cosmic distances are so huge. Here are some space distances, measured in light-years from Earth—one light-year is about 5.9 trillion miles (9.5 trillion km).

This image maps the heat (radiation) left over from the Big Bang.

Warmer areas are shown in red.

Colder areas are shown in blue.

MOST **SCIENTISTS** AGREE THAT THE **UNIVERSE** WON'T END BUT WILL CARRY ON **EXPANDING** FOREVER!

BIG BANG AFTERGLOW

How do we know so much about the Big Bang? One set of clues is given by the energy it released. Our entire night sky emits constant, low-level radiation energy, known as Cosmic Microwave Background (CMB) radiation. This is thought to be the glow of radiation left over from the birth of the universe.

HOW THE **UNIVERSE BEGAN**

Our universe came into existence in a massive explosion known as the Big Bang. Energy streamed outward from one incredibly tiny, dense point, becoming particles that became atoms, which in turn formed stars, planets, moons, and all existing matter.

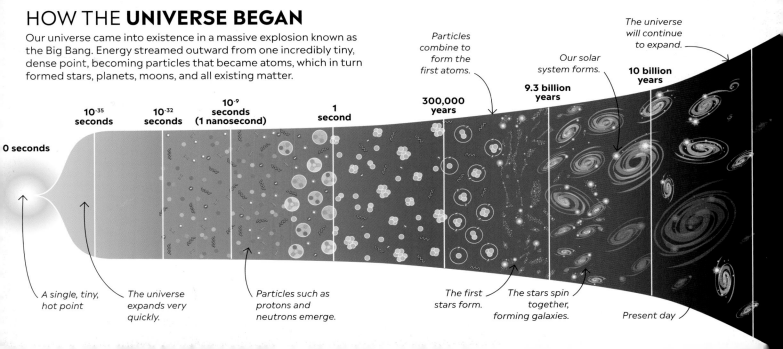

Particles combine to form the first atoms.

Our solar system forms.

The universe will continue to expand.

10^{-35} seconds

10^{-32} seconds

10^{-9} seconds (1 nanosecond)

1 second

300,000 years

9.3 billion years

10 billion years

0 seconds

A single, tiny, hot point

The universe expands very quickly.

Particles such as protons and neutrons emerge.

The first stars form.

The stars spin together, forming galaxies.

Present day

Galaxies galore

A galaxy is an enormous group of stars, planets, dust, and gas, held together by the force of gravity. There are at least 100 billion galaxies in the visible universe and probably billions more beyond that.

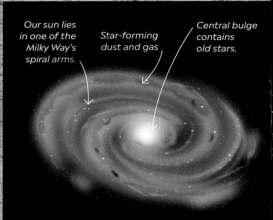

Our sun lies in one of the Milky Way's spiral arms.

Star-forming dust and gas

Central bulge contains old stars.

THE **MILKY WAY**

Our own galaxy is called the Milky Way. Compared to others, it is a medium-sized galaxy, about 100,00 light-years wide with up to 400 billion stars. All large galaxies are thought to have a supermassive black hole in the middle, where gravity is so strong that nothing can escape it. The one in the Milky Way is called Sagittarius A*.

COSMIC **COLLISIONS**

When galaxies are near to each other, their gravity can pull them ever closer until they smash into each other. Around 200 million years ago, the Cartwheel Galaxy was hit by a smaller one that passed right through its center, changing its spiral shape and leaving it with a dense core that looks like a bull's-eye.

Gas and dust ripple out from the impact site, creating "spokes."

Outer ring of intense star-forming activity

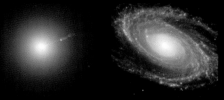

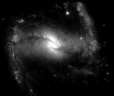

Elliptical
A simple "squashed" sphere, with more stars clustered at the center.

Spiral
A central bulge of stars, surrounded by arms that spiral outward.

Barred spiral
Arms spiral out from each end of the bar-shaped bulge.

Irregular
A collection of stars, gas, and dust, with no clear shape.

GALAXY **SHAPES**

Galaxies are thought to begin as swirling clouds of stars and dust. As other clouds come close, gravity makes these objects collide and knits them into larger spinning packs. There are four main galaxy shapes: elliptical, spiral, barred spiral, and irregular.

THE **MILKY WAY** AND NEIGHBOR GALAXY **ANDROMEDA** ARE ON COURSE TO **COLLIDE** IN **4 BILLION YEARS' TIME!**

EARTH VIEW

All the stars in our night sky are part of the Milky Way. From our position along one of its spiral arms, our galaxy appears to us as a glowing, hazy band, stretching across the sky.

In the darker areas, light from the stars is blocked by thick dust clouds.

Bright white glow of dense clouds of stars

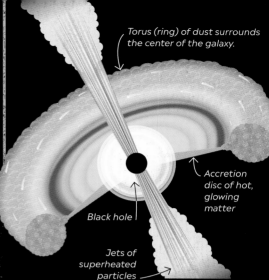

Torus (ring) of dust surrounds the center of the galaxy.

Accretion disc of hot, glowing matter

Black hole

Jets of superheated particles

ACTIVE GALAXIES

Galaxies that produce massive amounts of energy from their central black holes are known as active galaxies. The black hole's super-strong gravity sucks in matter and rips it apart, causing huge jets of superheated particles to shoot out. These jets can stretch out for thousands of light-years.

THE **TRIANGULUM GALAXY** IS ONE OF THE **MOST DISTANT** OBJECTS **VISIBLE FROM EARTH** WITH THE NAKED EYE!

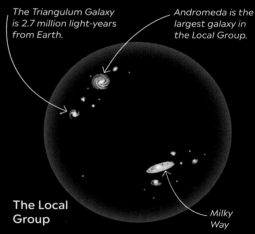

The Triangulum Galaxy is 2.7 million light-years from Earth.

Andromeda is the largest galaxy in the Local Group.

The Local Group

Milky Way

GALAXY GROUPS

Like stars, galaxies tend to group together in clusters. In turn, these sometimes group together as superclusters. Our Milky Way is part of a cluster known as the Local Group. It contains only three large galaxies; the rest are smaller dwarf galaxies. The Local Group is part of the Virgo Supercluster.

RECORD RINGS

Saturn's rings are the biggest in the solar system. At 168,000 miles (270,000 km), 21 Earths lined up in a row would fit inside the four main rings!

BIGGEST MOONS

There are at least 255 moons in the solar system. The biggest are larger than the smallest planets. Here are the five largest moons by diameter.

Ganymede and **Titan** are both **bigger** than the planet **Mercury!**

1 GANYMEDE (JUPITER)
3,270 miles (5,270 km)

STAT ATTACK!
SPACE

Although it contains countless galaxies, stars, and other worlds, the universe is so unimaginably huge that most of space is still empty! Here are some facts and figures about the biggest, brightest, most incredible wonders of our amazing universe.

GOING SUPERNOVA

When a massive star dies in a supernova explosion, it can briefly outshine whole galaxies. This glowing shell of gas and dust is a supernova remnant called Cassiopeia A.

SPACE TIME

A day is the amount of time it takes a planet to spin once on its axis. A year is the length of time it takes to orbit once around the sun.

← Axis

MERCURY
Length of a day: 1,408 hours
Length of a year: 88 Earth days

VENUS
Length of a day: 5,832 hours
Length of a year: 225 Earth days

EARTH
Length of a day: 24 hours
Length of a year: 365 Earth days

MARS
Length of a day: 25 hours
Length of a year: 687 Earth days

JUPITER
Length of a day: 10 hours
Length of a year: 4,333 Earth days

SATURN
Length of a day: 11 hours
Length of a year: 10,759 Earth days

URANUS
Length of a day: 17 hours
Length of a year: 30,687 Earth days

NEPTUNE
Length of a day: 16 hours
Length of a year: 60,190 Earth days

Heavily cratered surface

Hundreds of volcanoes cover Io's surface.

2 TITAN (SATURN)
3,200 miles (5,150 km)

3 CALLISTO (JUPITER)
3,000 miles (4,820 km)

4 IO (JUPITER)
2,260 miles (3,640 km)

5 MOON (EARTH)
2,160 miles (3,480 km)

NEAREST STARS

These are the closest stars to Earth. The distance is given in light-years, and how long it would take to get there in a car traveling at 70 mph (110km/h).

1 THE SUN
Distance: 0.000016 light-years
Driving time: 160 years

2 PROXIMA CENTAURI
Distance: 4.2 light-years
Driving time: 42 million years

3 ALPHA CENTAURI A, B
Distance: 4.3 light-years
Driving time: 43 million years

4 BARNARD'S STAR
Distance: 6 light-years
Driving time: 60 million years

5 WOLF 359
Distance: 7.9 light-years
Driving time: 79 million years

CLOSE ENCOUNTER

In 2019, an asteroid dubbed 2019 OK came within 44,300 miles (71,300 km) of Earth—one-fifth the distance between Earth and the moon. It was the largest object ever to come so close, and nobody had spotted it coming!

Asteroid 2019 OK is about the size of a football field.

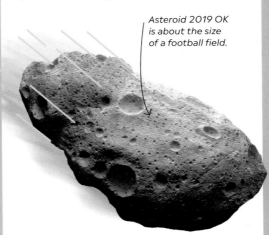

There are more than **30,000 asteroids** classed as **Near Earth Objects!**

GIANT JUPITER

The planet Jupiter is the biggest in the solar system. It has more than twice the mass of all the other planets put together.

COMET MCNAUGHT

BRIGHTEST COMETS

Astronomers think there are billions of comets in the solar system but only a few come close enough to Earth to be seen with the naked eye. These are the most spectacular comets of recent years.

NEOWISE 2020
The brightest comet of the century so far will not be seen again for 6,800 years.

MCNAUGHT 2007
This comet was so bright, it was even visible during the day time.

HALE-BOPP 1997
Visible for more than 18 months, and witnessed by millions of people worldwide.

HYAKUTAKE 1996
This comet's 360-million-mile (570 million km) tail was the longest ever measured.

WEST 1976
This amazingly bright comet won't be back for another half a million years.

Star light

SUPERGIANT **UY SCUTI** IS ONE OF THE **BIGGEST** KNOWN STARS. **FIVE BILLION** OF OUR **SUNS** COULD FIT INSIDE IT!

Stars in our night sky look like tiny, sparkling points of light. Up close, they are colossal balls of superheated gas. Nuclear reactions in their cores smash elements together, throwing heat and light out into the universe. There are up to 400 billion stars in our galaxy alone.

Much of the dust was once part of older stars.

COMPANY IN SPACE

Many stars spend their lives alone, like our sun. Others are bound together by their gravity in pairs or groups. The stars orbit each other, and are sometime orbited by groups of planets in turn.

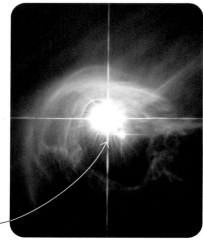

This pair of stars is part of a young star system called DI Cha.

This comet-like object is actually a protostellar jet—a stream of gas spewing out of an unseen new star.

STAR **JETS**

This yellow area shows where a high-speed jet, fired out of a newborn star, has plowed into the surrounding gas, making it glow. The star itself is shrouded in dust and not visible.

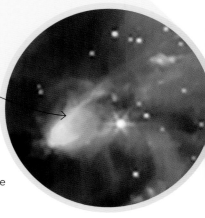

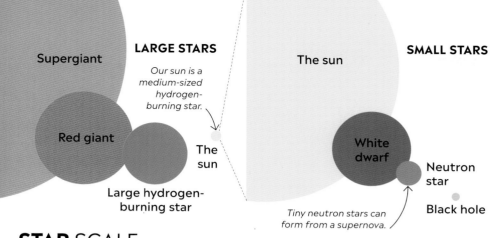

Supergiant

LARGE STARS

Our sun is a medium-sized hydrogen-burning star.

Red giant

The sun

Large hydrogen-burning star

SMALL STARS

The sun

White dwarf

Neutron star

Black hole

Tiny neutron stars can form from a supernova.

STAR SCALE

Compared to Planet Earth, the sun is enormous. However, compared to other stars, it is only average—some supergiants are around 1,500 times bigger. Some stars smaller than our sun are the remains of larger stars that have died.

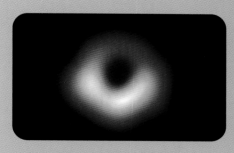

DARK AND DENSE

This image is the first photo ever taken of a black hole. It shows the supermassive black hole in the middle of the M87 Galaxy. Black holes at the center of galaxies are thousands of times bigger than those that form from dying stars.

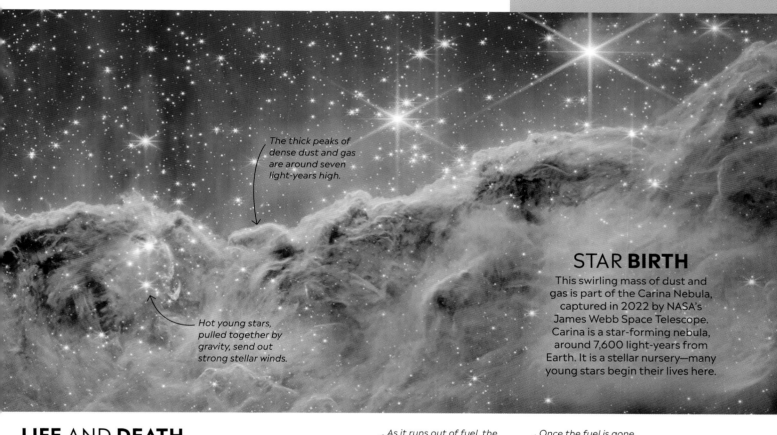

The thick peaks of dense dust and gas are around seven light-years high.

Hot young stars, pulled together by gravity, send out strong stellar winds.

STAR BIRTH

This swirling mass of dust and gas is part of the Carina Nebula, captured in 2022 by NASA's James Webb Space Telescope. Carina is a star-forming nebula, around 7,600 light-years from Earth. It is a stellar nursery—many young stars begin their lives here.

LIFE AND DEATH

All stars undergo a life cycle—over billions of years they form, change, and eventually die. The type of life cycle a star follows depends on its mass. Here are three examples of the stages of life a star might travel through.

Massive star

As it runs out of fuel, the star swells, becoming a supergiant.

Once the fuel is gone, the star explodes in a supernova.

Dense, spinning neutron star

Part of a nebula starts to collapse, forming the core of a new star.

Average-sized star, like our sun

As fuel runs out, the star swells and becomes a red giant.

Without fuel, the star becomes a white dwarf.

Eventually it becomes a cold, dead black dwarf.

The most massive stars become black holes.

The **sun**

Our star is a giant ball of electrically charged gas, called plasma. It is so big you could fit a million Earths inside it. The sun's gravity holds the solar system in place, and its energy powers all life on Earth. It will shine for another 5 billion years before running out of fuel.

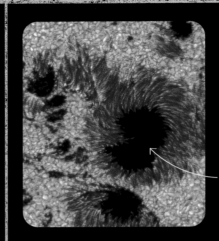

SUN**SPOTS**

Dark sunspots are slightly cooler patches of the sun's surface. They are areas where high magnetic activity stops hot gases from reaching the surface. The number of sunspots rises and falls on an 11-year cycle.

Though cooler than the surrounding surface, sunspots are still around 6,500°F (3,600°C).

The surface has an orange-peel like texture, known as "granulation."

The outermost part of the sun's atmosphere is called the corona.

SURFACE **STORMS**

The sun's atmosphere is a turbulent place. Superheated jets of plasma are blasted out from within and then fall back down as coronal rain. The blast waves from these solar storms can interfere with technology on Earth, even causing power outages.

Jets of gas called prominences shoot up from the sun's surface. They can be hundreds of thousands of miles high.

Prominences are caused by the sun's magnetism and can last for days or months.

The sun is made of electrically charged hydrogen and helium.

EACH SECOND, THE SUN RELEASES **HALF A MILLION TIMES** MORE ENERGY THAN EVERYONE ON EARTH **USES IN A YEAR**!

WHAT'S **INSIDE?**

The sun is a giant ball of hydrogen and helium gas. Inside its dense core, nuclear reactions produce huge amounts of energy and generate temperatures of up to 27 million °F (15 million °C).

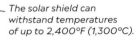

Core

Layers of gas

The visible surface is called the photosphere.

Above the photosphere are layers of atmosphere that are invisible.

The Aurora Australis around Antarctica, as seen from the ISS (International Space Station)

SOLAR WIND

A continuous stream of plasma, known as the solar wind, blasts away from the sun. Earth's magnetic field traps some of the particles, which can then funnel down into the atmosphere to make glowing auroras in the skies around Earth's North and South poles.

The solar shield can withstand temperatures of up to 2,400°F (1,300°C).

CLOSE ENCOUNTERS

Launched in 2018, the Parker Solar Probe's mission is to fly through the sun's atmosphere to study it up close. It is the fastest human-made object ever built, traveling at more than 330,000 mph (532,000 km/h).

Solar panels power the probe.

IT TAKES **100,000 YEARS** FOR ENERGY FROM THE SUN'S CORE TO REACH ITS SURFACE—AND THEN JUST **8 MINUTES** FOR IT TO REACH EARTH!

COSMIC COINCIDENCE!

A total solar eclipse happens when the moon passes between Earth and the sun. We get this unique view from Earth because the sun is 400 times larger than the moon but also happens to be 400 times farther away.

THE SUN'S INFLUENCE

The sun's gravity not only holds the planets in orbit but also countless other objects beyond them. The Kuiper Belt is made up of asteroids, dwarf planets, and comets. The distant Oort Cloud extends halfway to the next nearest star.

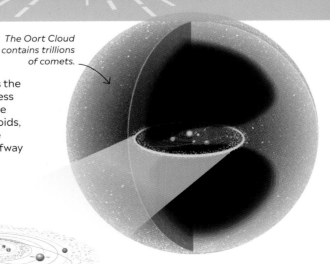

The Oort Cloud contains trillions of comets.

The Kuiper Belt lies beyond Neptune.

OUR **SOLAR SYSTEM**

Our sun is orbited by eight planets, as well as the millions of asteroids, comets, and other bodies that make up our solar system. This image shows the planets in order from the sun, but not their relative sizes or distances from each other.

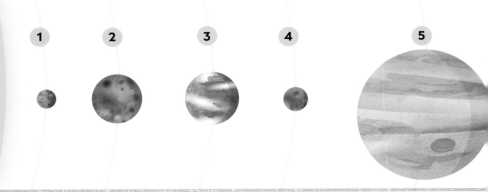

1 2 3 4 5

Perfect **planets**

Planets are spheres of rock or liquefied gas, which orbit (make circuits) around a star. Each planet follows its own path, spinning like a top as it travels. Our planet, Earth, is the third-closest planet to the sun. So far, Earth is the only planet we know of that can support life.

JUPITER THE GIANT

The gas giant Jupiter is the largest planet in the solar system—Earth would fit inside it more than 1,000 times. Its stripy bands of clouds are shaped by strong winds.

Jupiter's Great Red Spot, a huge spinning storm, appears blue in this infrared image.

URANUS IS THE ONLY PLANET THAT SPINS ON ITS SIDE, LIKE A ROLLING BALL!

DISTANT **EXOPLANETS**

Planets outside our solar system are known as exoplanets. More than 5,000 have been discovered so far. This image is the first-ever photo of an exoplanet, which lies about 170 light-years from Earth.

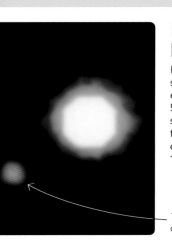

This red exoplanet's catchy name is 2M1207b!

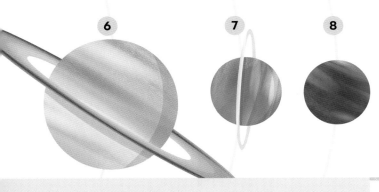

1. Mercury is the smallest planet and orbits closest to the sun.

2. Venus is the hottest planet, with layers of thick clouds.

3. Earth is the only planet known to have water in its liquid form.

4. Mars is cold and dry with a thin atmosphere.

5. Jupiter is orbited by more than 90 moons.

6. Saturn is surrounded by rings made of chunks of ice.

7. Uranus is the coldest planet in the solar system.

8. Neptune's fierce winds are the fastest in the solar system.

ON **MERCURY**, THE **SURFACE TEMPERATURE** SOARS TO **800°F (430°C)** IN THE DAY, THEN PLUMMETS TO **−290°F (−180°C)** AT NIGHT!

The clouds near Jupiter's equator move at speeds of more than 300 mph (500 km/h).

TYPES OF **PLANETS**

The solar system's planets are divided into two main types. The four rocky planets orbit closest to the sun. The gas giants are farthest from the sun.

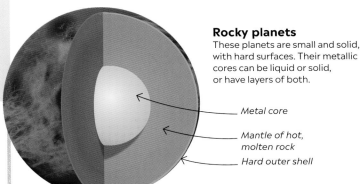

Rocky planets
These planets are small and solid, with hard surfaces. Their metallic cores can be liquid or solid, or have layers of both.

Metal core

Mantle of hot, molten rock

Hard outer shell

Giant planets
These enormous planets do not have solid surfaces. They are mostly made of liquefied gas but also contain some rocky material.

Rocky inner core

Layers of liquefied gas

Atmosphere of gas

RED PLANET

Like Earth, Mars has a rocky surface, clouds, and seasons. However it has a far more extreme environment—its huge dust storms, called dust devils, can last for weeks.

Mars is nicknamed the Red Planet for its rust-coloured, iron-rich soil.

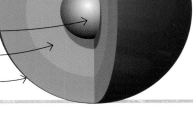

Dr. Katie Stack Morgan is a geologist who works at NASA's Jet Propulsion Laboratory. She is the Deputy Project Scientist of the Mars 2020 Rover Mission.

Ask a... MARS SCIENTIST

Q How do you control the rover from so far away?

A Sometimes people think we control the rover with a joystick in real time. In reality, we build a daily plan that tells the rover what to do, where to drive, and what observations to collect. We work on this plan while the rover is recharging overnight on Mars and send it via the Deep Space Network (a network of Earth-based radio antennas) in time for the rover to "wake up" for a busy day of science and engineering activities on Mars.

Q How can the rover keep going for such a long time? Does it have a big battery?

A Many previous Mars rovers and landers have been solar-powered, but Perseverance is powered by a Radioisotope Thermoelectric Generator (RTG). This system converts heat from the natural decay of nuclear fuel (mostly plutonium-238) into electricity. RTGs are very reliable, long-lived, and are not affected by Martian dust or dust storms.

Q What is the most difficult part of the mission?

A Launch and landing are definitely the most nerve-wracking times. These events pose the greatest risk and if something goes wrong the result can be catastrophic. Everyone on the team breathed a big sigh of relief when the rover arrived safely on Mars.

Q Do you think that you will find signs of life?

A Perseverance has already investigated some promising samples, but we would need to return them to Earth for analysis before confirming whether life is present. NASA is planning a mission to collect the samples and return them to Earth in the 2030s.

Q How do you know where to look?

A We use our experience of looking for ancient life in rocks on Earth. We look for signs that water and a source of energy were once present, and we also look for the types of rocks that we know are good at preserving signs of life.

Q What is special about Jezero crater?

A One of the reasons NASA selected Jezero Crater as the landing site was because it contains so many rock types and potentially habitable environments. Exploring this area is giving us a more complete picture of what Mars was like in the distant past, and the rover is likely to explore some of the oldest and most mysterious rocks in the solar system in the future!

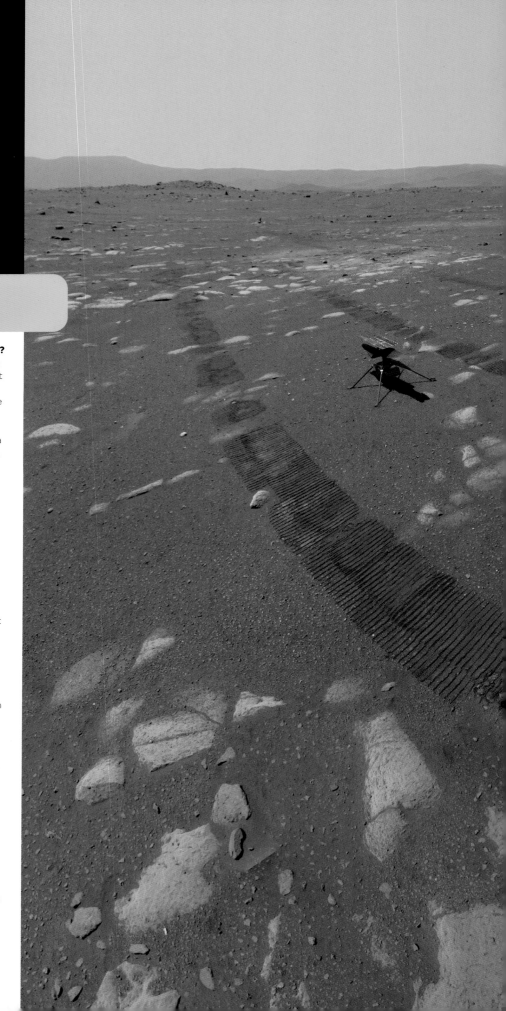

LIFE ON MARS?

NASA's Perseverance rover touched down on the surface of Mars in February 2021. The car-size rover is exploring Jezero Crater, believed to be an ancient river delta, looking for signs that life once existed there. A small helicopter named Ingenuity, pictured left in this image, has proved that powered flight is possible in the planet's thin atmosphere.

Asteroid strike!

As well as planets, there are millions of other bodies orbiting the sun—chunks of rock, metal, and ice left over from the birth of the solar system. Occasionally, a space rock hurtles through our atmosphere and crash-lands on Earth.

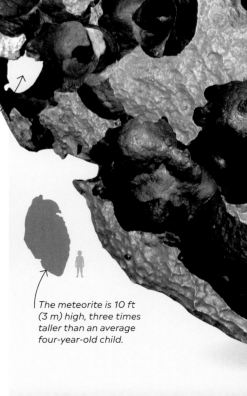

MEGA **METEORITE**

Most of the meteorites that land on Earth are tiny, rocky fragments, but a few are large enough to make a significant impact. This vast iron lump is known as the Willamette meteorite. It is the biggest meteorite ever found in the US and weighs in at 15.5 tons (14 metric tons). Metal meteorites like this are quite rare.

> THE **UTOPIA IMPACT CRATER** ON MARS IS 2,070 MILES (3,330 KM) WIDE—THAT'S ALMOST AS **BIG AS AUSTRALIA!**

SMALL **WORLDS**

The solar system has countless minor members—space objects that are smaller than planets. To date, just over 1.1 million asteroids have been detected, but new bodies are constantly being discovered.

Pits (holes) formed when the metal reacted with rainwater on Earth.

Dwarf planets
Similar to planets but smaller, dwarf planets share their orbits with other objects.

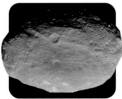

Asteroids
Rocky, metallic, or icy objects that orbit stars, asteroids can be round or uneven in shape.

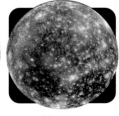

Moons
These are small, rocky, or icy bodies that orbit around a planet or asteroid.

Comets
Made from a mix of rock, dust, and frozen gases, comets have tails of dust and gas.

The meteorite is 10 ft (3 m) high, three times taller than an average four-year-old child.

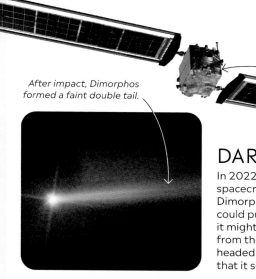

DART spacecraft

After impact, Dimorphos formed a faint double tail.

The surface melted as the object sped through Earth's atmosphere.

The meteorite is made of metal, mostly iron.

DART **MISSION**

In 2022, NASA flew the DART spacecraft into an asteroid called Dimorphos, to see if the impact could push it off course. If so, then it might be possible to protect Earth from the threat of large asteroids headed our way. Early results show that it seems to have worked!

EVERY DAY, **48.5 TONS (44 METRIC TONS)** OF **SPACE ROCK** FALLS TO EARTH, BUT **MOST OF IT VAPORIZES** BEFORE IT HITS THE GROUND!

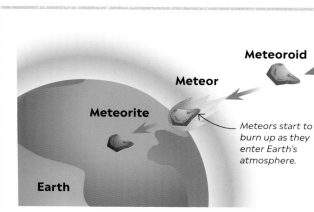

Meteoroid

Meteor

Meteorite

Earth

An asteroid is a large rock that orbits the Sun.

Asteroid

Meteors start to burn up as they enter Earth's atmosphere.

CHANGING **NAMES**

We use different names to describe a space rock that approaches Earth. A rock that breaks off an asteroid or comet is called a meteoroid. If it enters Earth's atmosphere, it becomes a meteor. If a meteor hits the Earth's surface, it is called a meteorite.

HIGH-ENERGY **IMPACT**

Asteroids can hit Earth at speeds of about 44 miles (70 km) per second, releasing a huge amount of energy. This energy vaporizes the meteorite, as well as much of the ground it lands on.

Impact pushes surface up into a rim.

Smaller craters formed by ejecta (debris)

Rings of ridges form in the crater.

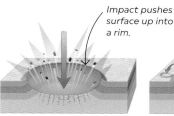

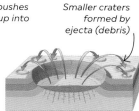

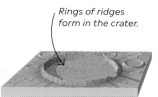

Initial impact
The asteroid hits at immense speed, creating a burst of explosive energy.

Seconds later
Debris from the crater is thrown outward, creating secondary craters.

Much later
Eventually, the floor of the crater levels out. Ejected material surrounds the site.

COLOSSAL **CRATER**

The Barringer Crater in Arizona was formed 50,000 years ago when a 164 ft (50 m) meteorite hit with the force of a 10-megaton nuclear bomb. This created a cloud of ash and dust thick enough to block the sun and affect the local climate.

The crater has a diameter of 0.8 miles (1.3 km).

The bowl-shaped crater is 570 ft (174 m) deep.

Magnificent moon

Earth is orbited by its own natural satellite—our moon. Of more than 250 known moons in the solar system, this dry, dusty sphere is one of the biggest. So far, only 12 humans have walked on the moon's surface, but there are plans to return this decade.

YOU COULD FIT 30 EARTHS INTO THE DISTANCE BETWEEN THE MOON AND EARTH!

LUNAR LANDSCAPE

The moon's surface ripples with mountains and valleys, and huge chunks of rock dot its surface. This panoramic image taken in 1972 shows the valley of Taurus-Littrow, the landing site of Apollo 17.

Highlands make up 83 percent of the moon's surface.

Boulders are the remnants of past meteorite impacts.

BIRTH OF THE MOON

Our moon formed around 4.5 billion years ago, when two planets, Gaia and Theia, collided. The colossal impact created a brand-new planet, Earth, and a cloud of rock and dust, which eventually came together to form the moon.

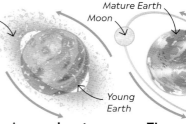

Theia *Gaia*

Leftover rocks formed a ring.

Mature Earth
Moon

Young Earth

Coming together
Gaia's gravity pulled the smaller planet closer, until the two collided.

Crash debris
Metal and rock fragments were created by the planets' impact.

A new planet
As the debris merged, a new planet, Earth, began to form.

The moon
The rocks orbiting Earth are pulled together by gravity to form the moon.

THE FAR SIDE

The moon spins slowly as it travels around the Earth. One full rotation takes the same time as one complete orbit, so we always see the same, "near" side of the moon. This image, taken by a satellite orbiting 1 million miles (1.6 million km) from Earth, shows us the moon's "far" side.

THE MOON'S LOW GRAVITY MEANS YOU CAN JUMP 6 TIMES HIGHER THAN ON EARTH!

SURFACE FEATURES

This is the moon's "face," which we always see from Earth. It has dark areas of flat, low ground called maria, and lighter colored highlands. At night, the moon "shines" with reflected sunlight.

Hundreds of craters pockmark the moon's surface.

The moon's maria were once seas of molten lava.

Some craters are ringed with "rays," formed when rocks blasted away from the crater during an impact.

The lighter areas are highlands—mountainous areas dotted with craters.

The Apollo 17 mission used a moon buggy to explore the moon's surface.

Apollo 17 pilot Harrison Schmitt is one of the last humans to have walked on the moon.

PERMANENT PRINT!

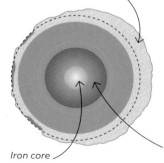

Unlike our Earth, the moon has no wind, water, or weather. This means that every footprint made by an astronaut on the moon is still there, exactly as they left it.

CHANGING VIEW

Our view of the moon changes over a month from a full circle to a thin crescent, as different sections of its face are lit by the sun. During a lunar eclipse (shown here), its shape also seems to change. As Earth moves between the moon and sun, it casts a shadow over the moon. A little sunlight still reaches the moon by refracting (bending) around Earth, making the moon appear red in color.

LOPSIDED CRUST

Thicker crust on the side farthest from Earth

The moon is made from rock, surrounding an iron core. When the moon first formed, all the rock was molten. The side away from the nearby hot Earth cooled more quickly. More crust solidified there, making the crust lopsided.

Iron core

Rocks nearer to the core are partly molten.

THE **MOON** IS DRIFTING **FARTHER FROM EARTH** AT A RATE OF **1.5 IN** (3.8 CM) **EVERY YEAR!**

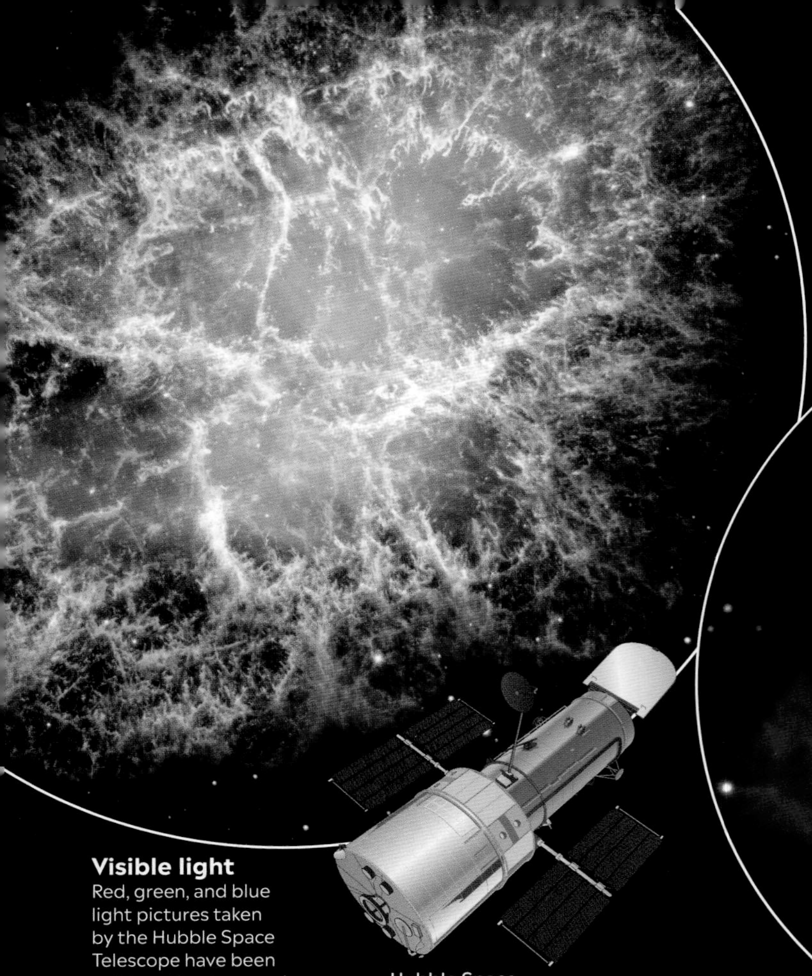

VARIED **VIEWS**

Some telescopes collect visible light, but others detect energy at other wavelengths. This can give a very different view of the universe. All the images in the sequence below show the Crab Nebula, the glowing remnant of a supernova explosion, but each image was taken by a different telescope.

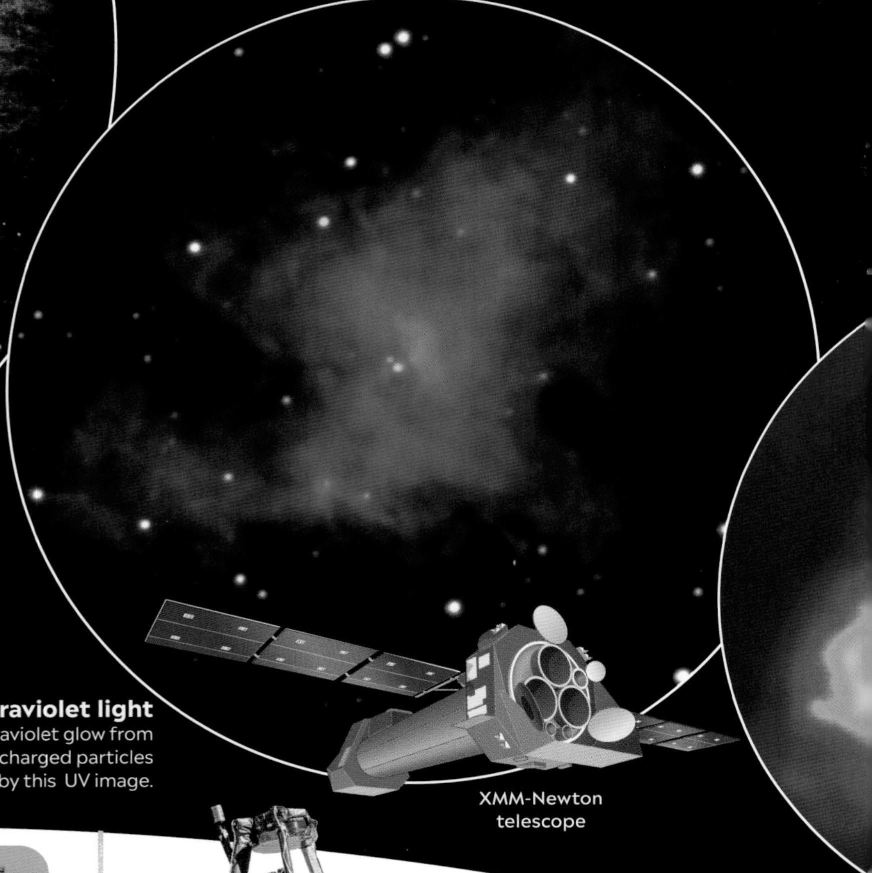

Visible light
Red, green, and blue light pictures taken by the Hubble Space Telescope have been put together to reveal a great tangle of gas blown off by the supernova explosion.

Hubble Space Telescope

Ultraviolet light
The ultraviolet glow from high-speed charged particles is revealed by this UV image.

XMM-Newton telescope

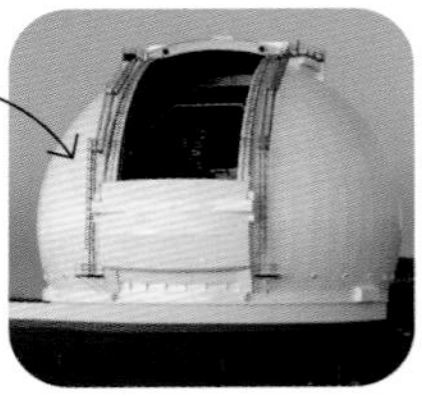

A dome-shaped building houses the telescope.

Light enters the telescope.

A cover can slide over the opening to close it.

Keck 2 Observatory, Hawaii

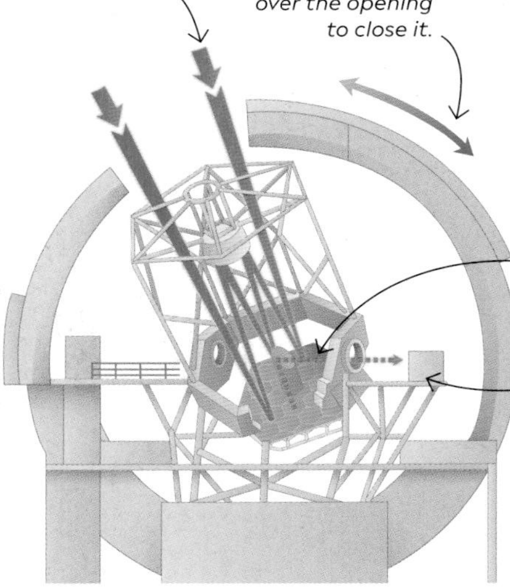

Mirrors reflect the light.

The light is directed into cameras.

INSIDE A **TELESCOPE**

Telescopes that view visible light use huge mirrors to reflect light. The bigger the telescope, the more light it is able to collect, and the sharper the image it will be able to create. Large telescopes are built on remote mountains where the air is dry and the sky is very dark.

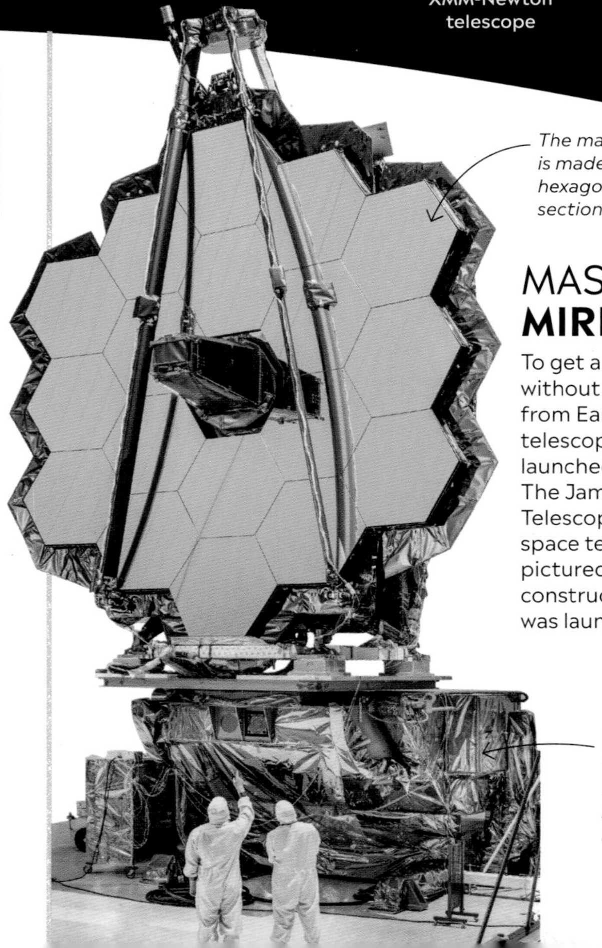

The main mirror is made up of 18 hexagon-shaped sections.

MASSIVE **MIRROR**

To get a truly clear view, without any interference from Earth's atmosphere, telescopes must be launched into space. The James Webb Space Telescope is the biggest space telescope yet. It is pictured here still under construction, before it was launched in 2021.

The huge mirror was tested in a lab before launch, to make sure each section aligned perfectly.

Seeing space

THE DISH OF THE **FAST RADIO TELESCOPE** IN CHINA HAS AN AREA AS BIG AS **750 TENNIS COURTS!**

To see into space in detail, astronomers use powerful, high-tech telescopes. Some of these are based on the ground while others are in orbit around Earth. Many telescopes reveal views that our eyes cannot see.

Radio waves
This colored map shows how radio emissions from the hot gas vary in strength across the nebula.

Very Large Array, US

Infrared
Pictured in the infrared, strands of gas show up in pink against the background white glow of charged particles.

Spitzer Space Telescope

THE **MIRRORS** OF THE **JAMES WEBB** SPACE TELESCOPE ARE **COATED** WITH A THIN LAYER OF **PURE, 24-CARAT GOLD!**

X-rays
X-rays show the pulsar in the center of the nebula. This rapidly spinning neutron star is firing out powerful jets of particles.

Chandra X-ray Observatory

Gamma rays
This huge flare-up of gamma rays shows the immense power of the pulsar in the middle of the nebula.

Artificial star

Laser beam

FINDING FOCUS

Some telescopes use lasers to help them overcome the interference of Earth's shifting atmosphere. Laser beams are aimed at the sky to create an "artificial star." Computers can then track minute changes in the fake star's position. This allows the telescope to focus more accurately.

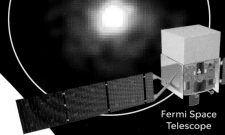

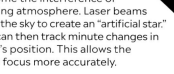

Fermi Space Telescope

Exploring space

People have long been fascinated by the challenge of exploring space. For scientists, observing space from Earth is not enough—to understand it better, we need to get out there! So far, the only place beyond Earth that humans have visited is the moon.

LUNAR **BASE CAMP**

Humans last visited the moon in the 1970s, but that is set to change. NASA's Artemis program is aiming to land humans on the moon in 2024, and then build a permanent camp as a base for missions to Mars or beyond.

ITEMS **LEFT ON THE MOON** BY NASA ASTRONAUTS INCLUDE **SIX US FLAGS, TWO GOLF BALLS,** AND A **FAMILY PHOTO!**

Vehicle for exploring the moon's surface

Glass dome for growing food plants

Solar panels will provide energy to power the lunar base.

WHERE WE HAVE BEEN

Space science has progressed hugely since the first space missions. Here are some of the major breakthroughs in the history of space exploration.

1957 Sputnik 1
The first artificial satellite was launched by the USSR. It stayed in orbit around Earth for three months.

1961 Vostok 1
The first human in space was Yuri Gagarin, who orbited Earth in the USSR's Vostok 1 craft.

1965 Venera 3
Venera crash-landed onto the surface of Venus, becoming the first craft to reach the surface of another planet.

1969 Apollo 11
Americans Buzz Aldrin and Neil Armstrong became the first humans to land on the moon, while Mike Collins orbited above in the command module.

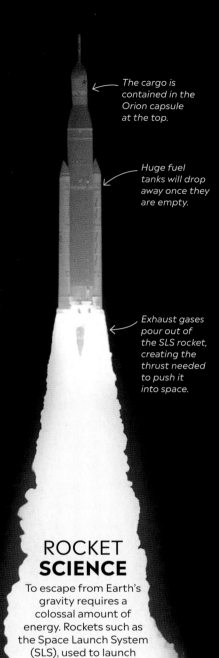

The cargo is contained in the Orion capsule at the top.

Huge fuel tanks will drop away once they are empty.

Exhaust gases pour out of the SLS rocket, creating the thrust needed to push it into space.

ROCKET SCIENCE

To escape from Earth's gravity requires a colossal amount of energy. Rockets such as the Space Launch System (SLS), used to launch Artemis 1 in 2022, achieve this by burning huge amounts of fuel. As the fuel burns, hot gas surges out of the rocket, blasting it upward.

HOW WE EXPLORE SPACE

Type	Function
Launch vehicles	These super-powerful machines are used to launch spacecraft. Once they release their craft, they fall back to Earth.
Uncrewed craft	These fly past or orbit space bodies. They collect data and images then send them back to Earth.
Landers and rovers	Some craft carry and release robotic vehicles. These explore on the ground, while taking photos and samples.
Crewed craft	So far, spacecraft have transported people to and from space stations, and to the moon.
Space stations 	These research stations orbit Earth. Scientists live and work onboard for weeks or months at a time.

NASA's ion-powered DAWN craft has clocked up 4.3 billion miles (6.9 billion km) since 2007.

ELECTRIC POWER

Ion propulsion is a new way of powering craft once they reach space. It works by ionizing (charging) atoms, then forcing them out, enabling the craft to achieve incredibly high speeds.

THE ASTEROID ARROKOTH IS THE MOST DISTANT SPACE OBJECT YET EXPLORED!

Arrokoth is 4 billion miles (6.4 billion km) from Earth.

Ex-NASA pilot Wally Funk finally flew in space at the age of 82!

SPACE TOURISTS

Some companies offer "amateur" astronauts the chance to travel into space. A 90-minute trip costs around half a million dollars. A week on the International Space Station would set you back $55 million!

1971 Salyut 1
The first space station to orbit Earth was launched by the USSR. The cylinder-shaped craft stayed in orbit for 175 days.

1973 Pioneer 10
This spacecraft reached Jupiter, making it the first craft to cross our solar system's asteroid belt.

1997 Mars Pathfinder
Landing on Mars, this craft became the first to successfully carry a rover, Sojourner, to another planet.

2015 New Horizons
This far-flying craft reached the dwarf planet Pluto, then went on to explore the Kuiper Belt.

2022 Artemis 1
The launch of this uncrewed moon orbiter marked the restart of human missions to the moon.

ANIMAL ASTRONAUTS

A surprising variety of animals have been sent into space. The first creatures ever to travel into space were some fruit flies, in 1948. In the early days of space exploration, animals were used for test missions and didn't come back.

SPIDERS
In 1973, Anita and Arabella were sent to the Skylab space station and showed they could spin webs in space.

FROGS
Since the 1970s, frogs have been used to study the effects of weightlessness.

PRIMATES
32 monkeys and apes have been into space. The first was a chimp named Ham.

DOGS
A dog named Laika was the first animal to orbit the Earth, in 1957.

TORTOISES
Two Russian steppe tortoises became the first animals to orbit the moon in 1968.

SPACE STATION

The International Space Station (ISS) orbits Earth at 17,500 mph (28,000 km/h). It completes one orbit every 90 minutes, and astronauts aboard see the sun rise and set 16 times a day.

RECORD BREAKERS

OLDEST IN SPACE
US actor William Shatner traveled into space in 2021 aged 90.

YOUNGEST IN SPACE
Dutch student Oliver Daemen was 18 when he went to space as a tourist.

FIRST SPACE TOURIST
US businessman Dennis Tito paid $20 million to become the first space tourist in 2004. He visited the ISS.

MOST SPACE WALKS
Russian cosmonaut Anatoly Solovyev holds the record for most space walks. He did 16, totaling more than 82 hours.

TRAVELED FARTHEST FROM EARTH
In 1970, the crew of Apollo 13 traveled all the way around the moon when their spacecraft was damaged and they had to slingshot back to Earth.

APOLLO 13 CREW'S RETURN TO EARTH

STAT ATTACK!
BLAST OFF

Since the middle of the last century, humans have been making the dream of space travel a reality. Meet some of space exploration's pioneers and encounter the biggest rockets of all time.

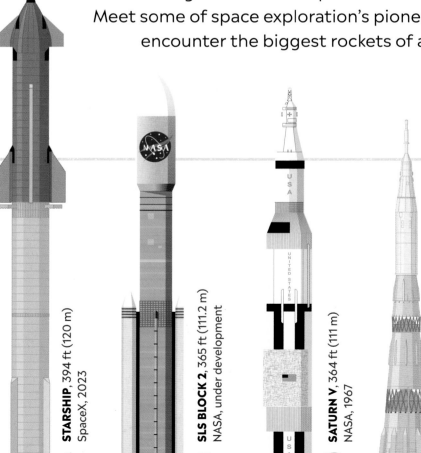

STARSHIP, 394 ft (120 m)
SpaceX, 2023
1

SLS BLOCK 2, 365 ft (111.2 m)
NASA, under development
2

SATURN V, 364 ft (111 m)
NASA, 1967
3

N1, 344 ft (105 m)
Soviet Union, 1969
4

MOON MISSIONS

We've been exploring the moon for decades. NASA's Artemis mission plans to return humans there in the 2020s.

1959 FIRST FLYBY
Launched by the Soviet Union, Luna 1 was the first spacecraft to reach the moon.

1966 FIRST ORBITER
Soviet craft Luna 10 was the first craft to orbit the moon (or any space body besides Earth).

1969 FIRST HUMAN
Neil Armstrong of Apollo 11 was the first person to walk on the moon, in July 1969.

1970 FIRST ROVER
Soviet mission Luna 17 landed a remotely controlled moon rover called Lunokhod 1.

NEIL ARMSTRONG ON THE MOON

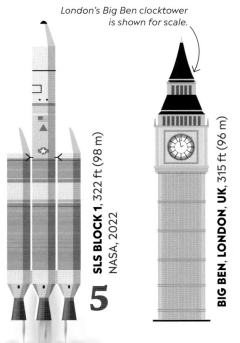

IN ORBIT

There are about 5,000 active satellites orbiting Earth right now. They are used for communication, Earth observation, and satellite navigations systems. But there is a much greater quantity of junk also orbiting Earth—an estimated 1 million pieces of debris bigger than a marble.

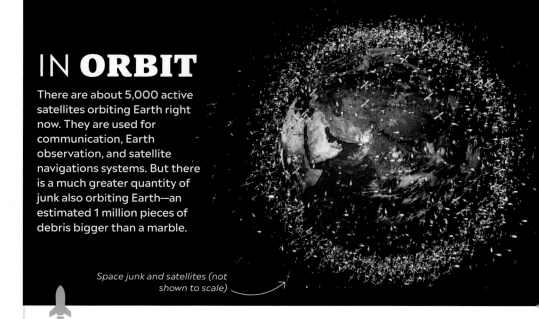

Space junk and satellites (not shown to scale)

SPACE AGENCIES

Many countries have a national space program. Only six agencies currently have the ability to launch missions and successfully land them. This chart shows what each of these agencies spent in 2018 in billions of US dollars.

- **NASA (US)**, $19.5 billion
- **CNSA (CHINA)**, $11 billion
- **ESA (EUROPE)**, $6.3 billion
- **ROSCOSMOS (RUSSIA)**, $3.3 billion
- **JAXA (JAPAN)**, $2 billion
- **ISRO (INDIA)**, $1.5 billion

BIGGEST ROCKETS

The rockets that carry spacecraft into space are called launch vehicles. These are the biggest ever built (with Big Ben shown for comparison).

London's Big Ben clocktower is shown for scale.

SLS BLOCK 1, 322 ft (98 m) NASA, 2022

5

BIG BEN, LONDON, UK, 315 ft (96 m)

In 2022, an **SLS Block 1** rocket launched NASA's Artemis 1 with **8.8 million lb (4,000 meganewtons)** of thrust— **more power** than any rocket ever!

DINOS IN SPACE!

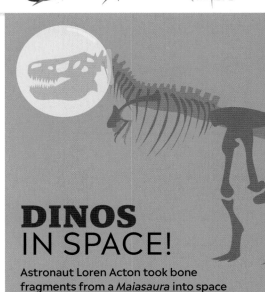

Astronaut Loren Acton took bone fragments from a *Maiasaura* into space in 1985. Then in 1998 the skull of a *Coelophysis* was sent to the Mir space station and returned safely to Earth.

Living in space

The International Space Station (ISS) provides a permanent base in space, with all the facilities people need to live and work. For missions outside the craft, space suits provide astronauts with mobile life-support systems.

SPACE SURVIVOR!

Astronauts undertake experiments to help them find out more about space. In 2007, they learned that micro-animals called tardigrades could survive outside a spacecraft for 10 days!

Tiny tardigrades are less than 0.04 in (1 mm) long.

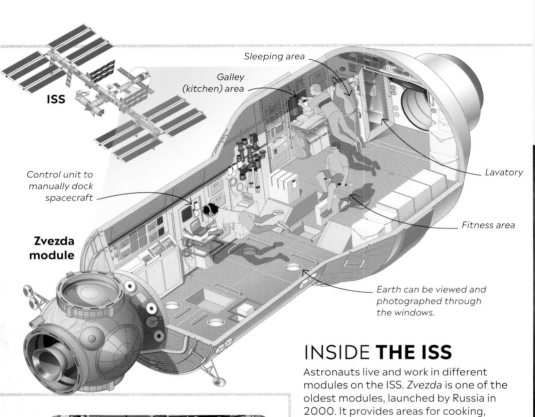

ISS

Sleeping area

Galley (kitchen) area

Control unit to manually dock spacecraft

Zvezda module

Lavatory

Fitness area

Earth can be viewed and photographed through the windows.

The sun

Cameras and flashlights can be attached to the helmet.

Colorful patches are designed for each space mission.

INSIDE **THE ISS**

Astronauts live and work in different modules on the ISS. *Zvezda* is one of the oldest modules, launched by Russia in 2000. It provides areas for cooking, exercising, and sleeping.

KEEPING FIT

Living in micro-gravity conditions can cause long-term damage to the body. To avoid this, astronauts must keep fit. They use exercise machines for around two hours every day, while wearing tethers to prevent themselves from floating away!

ASTRONAUTS ON THE ISS DRINK WATER THAT IS PARTLY RECYCLED FROM THEIR OWN SWEAT AND URINE!

MICRO-GRAVITY
BAKES

In 2021 ISS astronauts crossed a new frontier: space baking. It took two hours for their cookies to bake—much longer than on Earth. Sadly, no one was allowed to sample the cookies, in case they were unsafe to eat.

Gold coating protects the wearer from the sun's rays.

Control unit for life-support backpack

The gloves contain heating elements to keep hands warm.

The legs and feet are well padded for protection.

Backpack contains air filters and a water tank.

HOW A **SPACE SUIT** WORKS

Space suits are designed to keep the wearer alive when outside the spacecraft. They keep the body at the right temperature and a life-support system supplies vital oxygen.

Rigid outer shell

The colored stripe enables crewmates to identify the astronaut.

An underlayer is lined with water tubes, to keep the astronaut cool.

UK ASTRONAUT **TIM PEAKE** RAN A **MARATHON** ON THE ISS TREADMILL IN ONLY **3 HOURS 35 MINUTES!**

SPACEWALK SELFIE

Like any structure, the ISS has to be maintained and repaired. Astronauts must sometimes put on a space suit and head out to inspect the exterior. This selfie was taken by engineer Aki Hoshide.

The ISS, and Earth beyond it, are reflected in Hoshide's visor.

Dr. Megan McArthur is a NASA astronaut, pictured here on the International Space Station in 2021. She spent six months there as part of NASA's SpaceX Crew-2 mission.

ASTRONAUT

Q How does it feel to be blasted into space?
A It feels like you are moving faster than you ever have in your life (because you are!).

Q What does it feel like when you are in space?
A Kind of like floating in water, but kicking your legs won't get you anywhere.

Q What is the best part of your job?
A I love that I get to learn so many different things for my job—for example, how to operate a robotic arm, do science experiments in space, and fix broken equipment.

Q What is the most amazing thing you have seen?
The most amazing thing I've seen is the aurora or Polar Lights. This is a beautiful natural light show caused by particles from the sun interacting with gases in our atmosphere. I felt very lucky to see it from above!

Q How do you become an astronaut?
A You start by going to school and studying science, math, or engineering. It helps if you like to work with tools and you enjoy working as part of a team. After you are hired as an astronaut, you usually spend a couple more years learning about the spacecraft you will fly and the mission you will conduct.

Q What do you do for work on the ISS?
A The International Space Station is a science laboratory in space! We work on experiments for scientists around the world, including experiments in biology, physics, and chemistry. The results from these experiments can help us create new medicines and cleaner-burning car engines for people on Earth.

Q What do you do for fun? Do astronauts play video games or have cell phones?
A For fun, I liked to look out of the windows and take pictures of the Earth, read books, and watch movies. We even created a Space Olympics, with sports you can do only in space, such as synchronized floating. We don't have cell phones, but we can use software on our laptops to make phone calls.

Q Is space food tasty?
A Yes! My favorite was the mango fruit salad.

Q Will I get to visit space in my lifetime?
A I believe more people will get to travel in space in the near future. Soon we will have humans living for longer periods of time on the moon, and eventually on Mars. I hope to see someone reach Mars in my lifetime. Maybe it will be you!

IN **ORBIT**

SpaceX's Crew Dragon Endeavour craft approaches the International Space Station in April 2021, nose open and ready to dock. The spacecraft was carrying four Crew-2 astronauts, including Megan McArthur who was the pilot. The team spent 6 months on board the ISS, traveling more than 84 million miles (136 million km) during 3,194 orbits of Earth, before safely traveling back down to Earth.

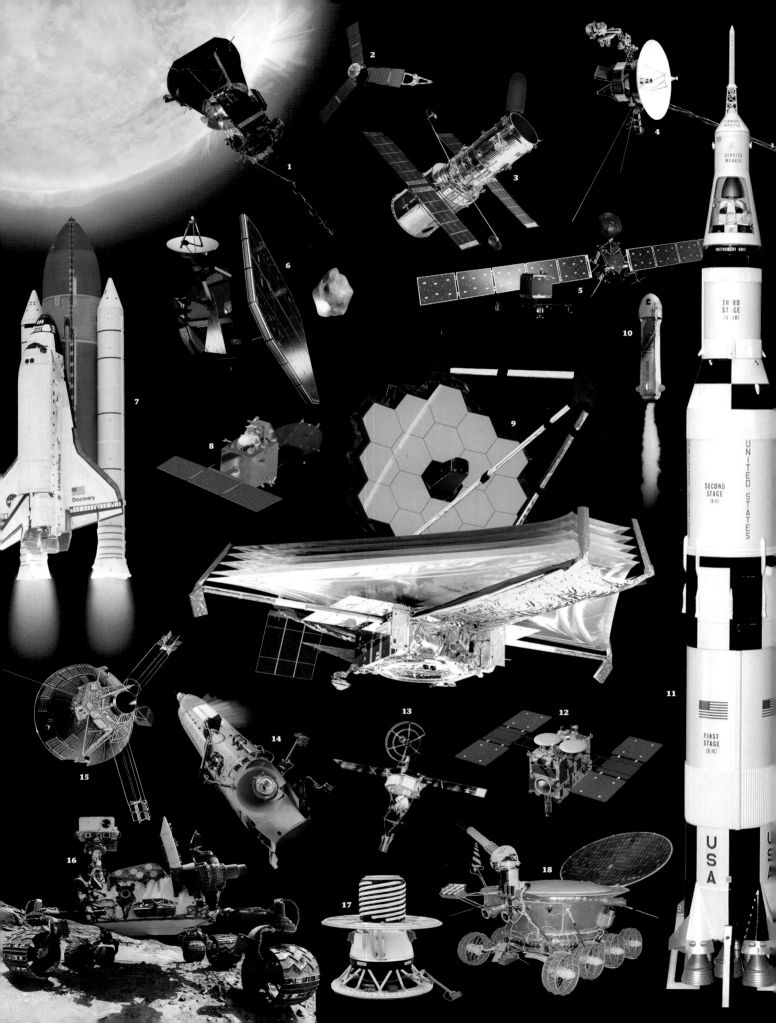

NAME THAT... SPACECRAFT

Can you tell a lunar lander from a Mars rover? Cover up the answers to test your knowledge of some of the most famous spacecraft ever launched—and see if you can spot the odd one out!

Launch dates are given in parentheses.

1. Parker Solar Probe: mission to the sun (2018)
2. Juno: mission to Jupiter (2011)
3. Hubble Space Telescope (1990)
4. Voyager 2: exploring outer planets (1977)
5. Rosetta and Philae: orbited and landed on comet 67P/Churyumov–Gerasimenko (2004)
6. Deep Impact: mission to comet Tempel 1 (2005)
7. Discovery Space Shuttle (1984)
8. Mangalyaan: Mars Orbiter Mission (2013)
9. James Webb Space Telescope (2021)
10. New Shepard: Space tourist craft (2015)
11. Saturn V: launched Apollo missions (1967–1973)
12. Hayabusa 2: explored asteroid Ryugu (2014)
13. Mariner 2: explored Venus (1962)
14. Deepsea Challenger: explored Challenger Deep (2012)
15. Pioneer 11: explored outer planets (1973)
16. Curiosity: Mars rover (2011)
17. Venera 9: landed on Venus (1975)
18. Lunokhod 1: Lunar rover (1970)
19. Cassini-Huygens: explored Saturn (1997)
20. SpaceX Dragon 2: carries crew to International Space Station (2020)
21. Tiangong space station (2021)
22. International Space Station (ISS) (1998)
23. SpaceX Falcon 9: reusable rocket launcher (2010)
24. New Horizons: explored Pluto (2006)
25. Dawn: studied dwarf planet Ceres and asteroid Vesta (2007)
26. Galileo: studied Jupiter and its moons (1989)
27. Space Launch System (SLS): rocket launcher for Artemis program (2022)
28. Telstar: world's first communications satellite (1962)
29. Sputnik 1: world's first artificial satellite (1957)
30. Eagle: landed Apollo 11 astronauts on the moon (1969)

The odd one out is Deepsea Challenger (14). It is a deep-sea submersible that explored the deepest part of the ocean.

EARTH

Planet **Earth**

Our home planet is 4.5 billion years old. It is a ball of rock and metal with a thin, brittle crust. With its atmosphere and oceans of water, it is the only place we know of in the universe that can support life.

HOW EARTH **FORMED**

Our solar system began as a giant cloud of gas and dust. The center of the cloud slowly clumped together to form the sun. Rocks orbiting the sun smashed together, forming bigger and bigger objects. As a young planet, Earth was hot and molten from the energy of these collisions.

The crust is between 6 miles (10 km) and 40 miles (70 km) thick.

The continental crust, which forms the land, is lighter and thicker than crust beneath the oceans.

The mantle transfers heat from Earth's core to the lithosphere.

1. The inner core

At the center of the Earth is a ball of hot, dense iron. The pressure of all the weight above it keeps the metal solid, despite the intense heat.

The center is nearly 4,000 miles (6,370 km) below the crust.

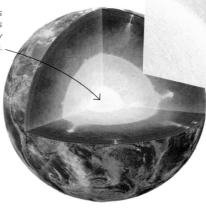

THE EARTH IS TRAVELING AROUND THE SUN AT A SPEED OF 67,000 MPH (108,000 KM/H)!

The outer core is mostly made of iron but also contains nickel, cobalt, carbon, and sulfur.

INSIDE EARTH

The deepest hole ever drilled was only 7.5 miles (12.2 km) deep. That's barely a scratch on a planet with a diameter of 7,926 miles (12,756 km). Scientists know about the layers that lie beneath the surface by studying seismic waves created by earthquakes and how they travel through our planet.

2. The outer core

Here, the metal is molten and flows freely. Electrical currents generated by the metal's movements create Earth's magnetic field.

The atmosphere

A thin blanket of gases surrounds the planet. It traps heat from the sun, keeping Earth at a comfortable temperature, and filters out harmful ultraviolet rays.

The atmosphere is a mixture of gases—mostly nitrogen and oxygen.

The crust beneath the oceans is thin and made from dense rock.

Some parts of the mantle become especially hot and rise toward the surface.

The uppermost layer of the mantle is fused to the crust, forming the lithosphere.

3. The mantle

This thick rocky layer makes up 84 percent of Earth's volume. It is mostly solid rock, but in places the rock flows very slowly.

4. The lithosphere

The outer part of the planet is called the lithosphere. It is made up of the crust and the upper part of the mantle fused together.

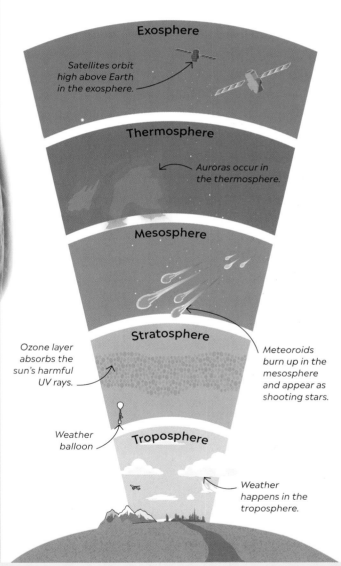

THE EARTH IS **NOT A TRUE SPHERE.** IT IS 25 MILES (40 KM) **WIDER AROUND THE EQUATOR** THAN POLE TO POLE!

EARTH'S **ATMOSPHERE**

About 80 percent of all the gas in the atmosphere is in the lowest layer, the troposphere. The layers get less and less dense as they get higher up. The uppermost layer, the exosphere, eventually merges into space.

Exosphere

Satellites orbit high above Earth in the exosphere.

Thermosphere

Auroras occur in the thermosphere.

Mesosphere

Stratosphere

Ozone layer absorbs the sun's harmful UV rays.

Meteoroids burn up in the mesosphere and appear as shooting stars.

Weather balloon

Troposphere

Weather happens in the troposphere.

EARTH'S **INNER CORE** IS A SCORCHING 9,400°F (5,200°C)!

9,400°F

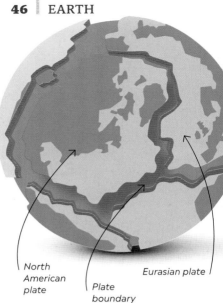

North American plate

Plate boundary

Eurasian plate

JIGSAW EARTH

Tectonic plates fit together like pieces of a giant jigsaw, floating on top of Earth's mantle. As the plates move, they carry Earth's landmasses with them, so over millions of years, the shape of the continents gradually changes.

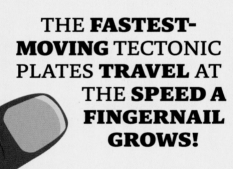

THE **FASTEST-MOVING** TECTONIC PLATES **TRAVEL** AT THE **SPEED A FINGERNAIL GROWS!**

RISING **UP**

The Alps are a mountain range in Europe formed over millions of years as the African and Eurasian tectonic plates pushed together, forcing the ground up. Part of the range is still growing by about 31 in (80 cm) every 1,000 years.

RIFT VALLEY

The Silfra Fissure in Iceland is at the boundary between the North American and the Eurasian plates. These plates are divergent—they are pulling apart, creating a rift that cuts through Iceland. At Silfra, the rift has filled with meltwater from a glacier and divers can swim in the crystal clear water between the two continental plates.

DIVERS IN THE **SILFRA FISSURE** CAN TOUCH THE **NORTH AMERICAN** AND **EURASIAN PLATES** AT THE SAME TIME!

Powerful
plates

Earth's crust is made up of huge rocky fragments called tectonic plates. The plates move slowly, but at their boundaries, tremendous forces are unleashed. Some plates rip apart, creating new ocean floor. Others smash together, forcing up mountain ranges.

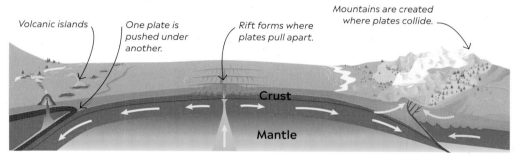

Volcanic islands

One plate is pushed under another.

Rift forms where plates pull apart.

Mountains are created where plates collide.

Crust

Mantle

HOW **TECTONIC PLATES** WORK

Earth's tectonic plates move slowly, powered by currents of heat in the mantle below. Where two plates meet, one can be forced underneath the other. This is called subduction, and it can create mountain ranges and volcanic island chains. Where plates are pulling apart, magma rises from the mantle to create new ocean floor.

IN **250 MILLION YEARS**, MOST OF **THE CONTINENTS** WILL BE **JOINED** IN **ONE SUPER-CONTINENT!**

RING OF **FIRE**

Around 75 percent of all active volcanoes lie along plate boundaries around the edges of the Pacific Ocean. They form a chain of 452 volcanoes known as the "Ring of Fire," which includes this volcano, Tungurahua, on the coast of Ecuador.

Rocky planet

The rocks that form Earth's crust are made from minerals and sometimes from the remains of plants and animals. Earth's rocks are constantly changing in a slow cycle over millions of years.

EARTH'S **BIGGEST SPACE ROCK** IS THE **HOBA METEORITE.** IT LANDED IN NAMIBIA **80,000** YEARS AGO!

TYPES OF **ROCKS**

There are three main types of rocks. Sedimentary rocks form when rock fragments or dead organisms compress over millions of years. Igneous rocks form as magma cools, below or above ground. Both can be changed into metamorphic rocks by high pressure and heat.

Breccia
Large and small fragments mix to form this sedimentary rock.

Pink granite
Granite, an igneous rock, forms as magma cools underground.

Gneiss
High heat and pressure create gneiss, a metamorphic rock.

THE **ROCK CYCLE**

Rocks don't stay the same. Rocks on the surface are worn down into sediments and carried away, while rocks underground are affected by heat and pressure. Over millions of years, the three types of rocks change in a long, slow process called the rock cycle.

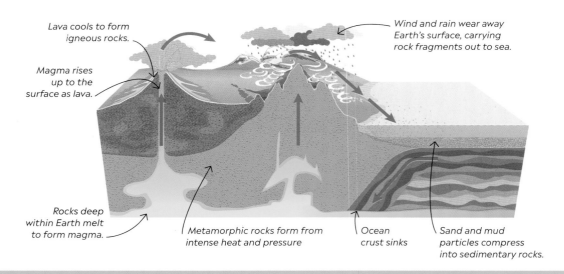

Lava cools to form igneous rocks.

Magma rises up to the surface as lava.

Wind and rain wear away Earth's surface, carrying rock fragments out to sea.

Rocks deep within Earth melt to form magma.

Metamorphic rocks form from intense heat and pressure

Ocean crust sinks

Sand and mud particles compress into sedimentary rocks.

In sedimentary rocks, the layers below are usually older than the layers deposited on top, unless they have been overturned.

THE **OLDEST KNOWN ROCKS** ON EARTH ARE **4.28 BILLION YEARS** OLD— **NEARLY AS OLD AS EARTH ITSELF!**

MARBLE CAVES

The Marble Caves in Chile are made up of metamorphic rock. Over 6,000 years, the icy waters of Lake General Carrera slowly eroded the white marble into caverns, columns, and pillars. Thousands of tourists visit by boat every year.

DEVILS TOWER

Standing at 867 ft (264 m) in Wyoming, Devils Tower is an igneous rock formation that is a sacred place to local Indigenous people. It formed 50 million years ago when magma underground pushed up into sedimentary rock and cooled. Gradually, the sedimentary rock eroded away, revealing the tower.

Summit is about the size of a football field

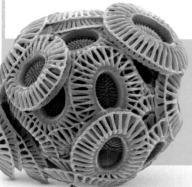

Single coccolithophore surrounded by plates.

CHALK CREATURES!

Chalk is a sedimentary rock made from the remains of microscopic ancient sea creatures called coccolithophores. These single-celled algae are surrounded by hard plates called coccoliths. They are still found in Earth's oceans today.

Sandstone is mainly made up from the minerals quartz and feldspar.

Plants and trees can grow in sandstone because it is porous (contains tiny holes).

SANDSTONE LAYERS

Sedimentary rocks such as sandstone build up in layers. Movements within the Earth's interior can tilt, squeeze, and fold the layers. This sandstone rock formation near Nares Point in northwest Australia is an example of dramatic folding.

AT **$30 MILLION**, THE **SUNRISE RUBY** IS THE **MOST EXPENSIVE RUBY** IN THE WORLD!

EVERYDAY CRYSTALS

The salt that we use to season food is a type of crystal. Seen in close-up, each piece is a perfect cube. Sugar is also made of crystals and snowflakes are frozen water crystals.

Each needle is a single crystal.

Crystals look like the blade of a knife.

Acicular
These scolecite crystals have an acicular habit—spiky needles growing out from the center.

Botryoidal crystals look like bunches of grapes.

Botryoidal
Crystals that grow in round clusters, like this malachite, are called "botryoidal."

Bladed
This bladed kyanite formed in long, thin, and flat crystals.

Colorful crystals

A crystal is a solid with a symmetrical, repeating internal structure. Any mineral can be a crystal, but some can be cut and polished into gems and made into jewelry. The rarest and most beautiful gems are highly prized.

CRYSTAL SYSTEMS

Crystals grow in one of six geometric shapes, called "systems." A crystal's system is determined by the pattern of its atoms.

Cubic
This simple system has six square faces.

Tetragonal
This is a cuboid with some rectangular faces.

Orthorhombic
This blocky crystal has rectangular faces at each end.

Monoclinic
This system is a parallelogram prism shape.

Triclinic
This has the least symmetry of all crystal systems.

Hexagonal
This system's cross section is a hexagon.

REPEATING PATTERN

The atoms in a crystal are organized in a repeating 3-D pattern. This diagram shows how a molecule of galena forms a cube shape, which is repeated in all directions to form a cubic crystal.

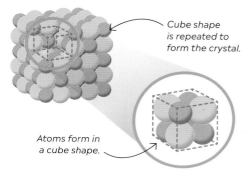

Cube shape is repeated to form the crystal.

Atoms form in a cube shape.

QUARTZ WATCHES USE A TINY, VIBRATING QUARTZ CRYSTAL TO ACCURATELY KEEP THE TIME!

Tabular crystals can look like playing cards or books.

The crystal faces naturally form smooth squares.

Prismatic crystals have six parallel faces.

Cubic
These pyrite crystals have a cubic habit, each with six square, symmetrical faces.

Prismatic
These amethysts formed in a prismatic habit, with pyramid-shaped points.

FORMING HABITS

The final form that a crystal, or a group of crystals, grows into is called its "habit." Crystal habit is determined by the crystal's system, but also by the environment in which it forms, such as the space it has to grow. This means that no two crystals are exactly the same—each one is unique.

Tabular
Tabular crystals, such as these red vanadinite crystals, are longer and wider than they are thick.

This square-cut emerald is mounted as a brooch with 129 clear diamonds.

THE CULLINAN DIAMOND WAS THE BIGGEST ROUGH DIAMOND EVER FOUND!

It was roughly the size of a mango!

ENORMOUS EMERALD

Emeralds are a form of the mineral beryl treasured for their rich green and clarity. Cutting smooth faces into the stone enhances its beauty.

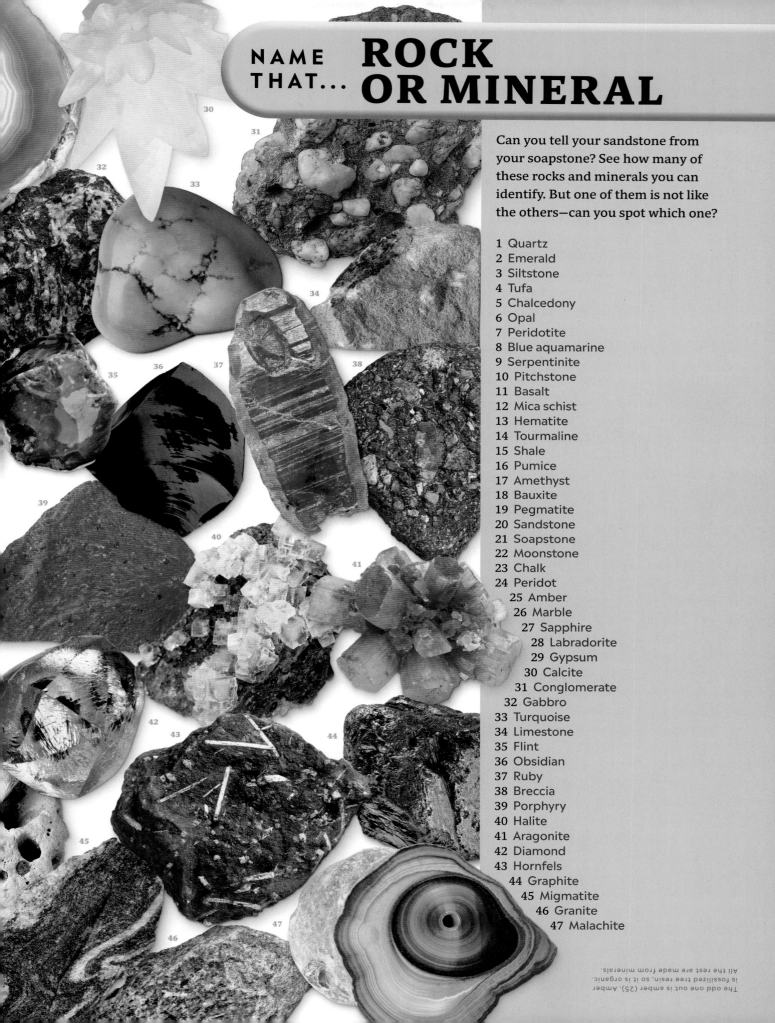

Can you tell your sandstone from your soapstone? See how many of these rocks and minerals you can identify. But one of them is not like the others—can you spot which one?

1 Quartz
2 Emerald
3 Siltstone
4 Tufa
5 Chalcedony
6 Opal
7 Peridotite
8 Blue aquamarine
9 Serpentinite
10 Pitchstone
11 Basalt
12 Mica schist
13 Hematite
14 Tourmaline
15 Shale
16 Pumice
17 Amethyst
18 Bauxite
19 Pegmatite
20 Sandstone
21 Soapstone
22 Moonstone
23 Chalk
24 Peridot
25 Amber
26 Marble
27 Sapphire
28 Labradorite
29 Gypsum
30 Calcite
31 Conglomerate
32 Gabbro
33 Turquoise
34 Limestone
35 Flint
36 Obsidian
37 Ruby
38 Breccia
39 Porphyry
40 Halite
41 Aragonite
42 Diamond
43 Hornfels
44 Graphite
45 Migmatite
46 Granite
47 Malachite

The odd one out is amber (25). Amber is fossilized tree resin, so it is organic. All the rest are made from minerals.

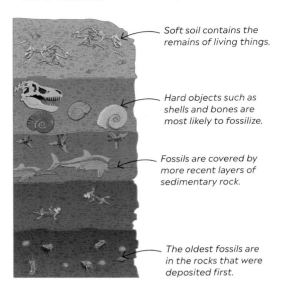

Soft soil contains the remains of living things.

Hard objects such as shells and bones are most likely to fossilize.

Fossils are covered by more recent layers of sedimentary rock.

The oldest fossils are in the rocks that were deposited first.

FOSSIL **LAYERS**

Over millions of years, layers of rock containing fossils form on top of each other. The oldest fossils are in the deepest layers, but these can shift and be exposed with tectonic plate movement and erosion.

Fantastic
fossils

Most of the time, when a living thing dies, it rots away and vanishes forever. But very rarely, it is preserved as a fossil. Fossils give us an amazing glimpse of life that roamed the world long before humans.

SKIN OF **STONE!**

In 2011, the 110-million-year-old fossil of a nodosaur was found in Alberta, Canada. It was so well preserved that its skin and stomach contents were intact!

Heavy, armored skin

This nodosaur was 18 ft (5.5 m) long!

Complex eye, with many lenses

Long horns curved back above the eyes

ANCIENT **ANIMALS**

Trilobites were invertebrates that dominated ancient oceans for 270 million years. There are so many trilobite fossils that scientists use them as "index fossils," to help them date the rocks they are found in. They became extinct 252 million years ago.

Jointed body for crawling over the sea bed

Spines may have been used for defense.

SCIENTISTS HAVE FOUND MORE THAN 20,000 DIFFERENT TRILOBITE SPECIES!

COLOSSAL FOSSIL

This huge femur fossil is the thigh bone of a long-necked sauropod, which lived in the Early Cretaceous period. Sauropods were the largest of all dinosaurs and the biggest animals to have ever lived on land.

The femur is 6.6 ft (2 m) long!

SPIRAL SHELLS

Ammonites were sea-living mollusks with curled shells and octopus-like tentacles. Their hard shells are very common fossils. This ammonite fossil has been cut open to show its chambers and the minerals that formed inside.

Ammonites added new chambers to their shell as they grew.

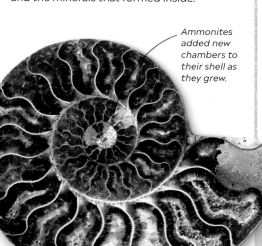

FOSSILIZED FOOTSTEPS

Sometimes the traces of animal activity are preserved as fossils. More than a thousand dinosaur tracks were found along this 98-million-year-old coastal plain in Colorado.

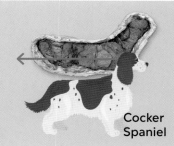

Cretaceous ant

Wispy feathers

TRAPPED IN AMBER

Amber is fossilized tree resin. Animals can get stuck and preserved in the resin as it dries. This amber contains the feathery tail of a 99-million-year-old dinosaur.

THE LARGEST POOP FOSSIL FROM A CARNIVORE IS A 2.2 FT (67.5 CM) LONG T-REX POOP!

Cocker Spaniel

HOW FOSSILS FORM

To become fossilized, a living thing has to die in very specific conditions. Layers of sediment such as mud and sand must quickly cover the body. Then, over millions of years, the weight of these layers turns the soft sediment into rock and the body into a fossil.

Death
The animal dies in a place where its body is quickly covered in mud or sand.

Buried
The soft parts of the animal's body rot away. Sediment builds up on the parts that remain.

Replacement
The layers turn to rock and minerals seep into the bones, turning them into rock too.

Discovery
Eventually, the layers of rock may be worn away and the fossil can be discovered.

WAVE **POWER**

Waves are created as wind pushes against the ocean. They begin as ripples, but these grow bigger and gain energy as more wind blows across the surface. Approaching a coastline, the waves become higher and closer together until they crash on the shore.

This giant wave is in Portugal, where surfers ride waves that reach up to 86 ft (26 m).

As a wave reaches the shore, the crest becomes unstable and topples forwards, forming a breaker.

The Pacific Ocean covers nearly a third of the planet.

WATER COVERS MORE THAN 70% OF THE EARTH'S SURFACE. LESS THAN 30% IS DRY LAND!

Water world

We call it "Earth," but seen from space our planet is mostly blue. Water is all around us—in the oceans and seas, rivers and lakes, underground, and even in the air. Without water, life on Earth would not exist. Humans can survive for around three weeks without food but only three days without water!

Dew forms when moisture in warm air hits cool leaves.

All living things—from ants and whales to plants and bacteria—need water to survive.

SUSTAINING **LIFE**

Water is the key to all life on Earth. No life forms that we know of can survive without it. So far, no other planet is known to have liquid water on its surface—and no other life has been found in the universe.

MORE PEOPLE HAVE BEEN INTO **OUTER SPACE** THAN HAVE **EXPLORED** THE **DEEPEST PARTS OF THE OCEAN!**

WATER **CYCLE**

The amount of water on planet Earth never changes. In fact, we drink the same water that dinosaurs drank millions of years ago! But the water is constantly moving between the land, sea, and sky in an endless cycle powered by the sun.

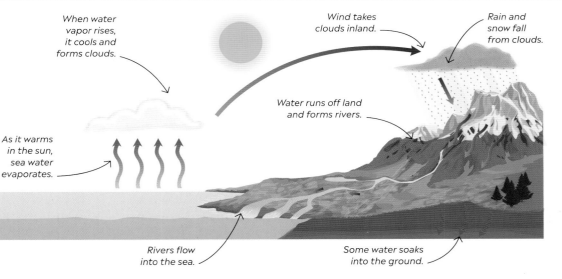

When water vapor rises, it cools and forms clouds.

As it warms in the sun, sea water evaporates.

Wind takes clouds inland.

Rain and snow fall from clouds.

Water runs off land and forms rivers.

Rivers flow into the sea.

Some water soaks into the ground.

BENEATH OUR FEET

Much of Earth's water is hidden underground. In volcanic areas, pockets of underground water can get very hot. The water then erupts as a geyser—a spurt of superheated water that shoots up into the air.

WHERE IS THE WATER?

Most of the water on Earth is salty sea water. Of the fresh water, most is locked up as ice or hidden beneath the ground.

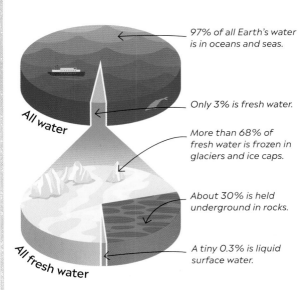

97% of all Earth's water is in oceans and seas.

All water

Only 3% is fresh water.

More than 68% of fresh water is frozen in glaciers and ice caps.

About 30% is held underground in rocks.

A tiny 0.3% is liquid surface water.

All fresh water

MASSIVE **MIRROR!**

High on a Bolivian plateau is Salar de Uyuni, a vast, flat salt plain. In the monsoon season, the plain is covered in a shallow layer of rainwater. It reflects the rolling clouds like an enormous mirror!

ANGEL FALLS IN VENEZUELA IS THE **TALLEST WATERFALL** IN THE WORLD AT **3,212 FT (979 M)!**

WETLANDS WILDLIFE

When water cannot drain, it builds up to form wetlands, such as swamps and marshes. The largest is the Pantanal in South America, which supports water-loving animal and plant species, including these giant water lilies.

Yacare caiman live in the Pantanal.

RED LAKE

Bolivia's Laguna Colorada gets its color from the red algae that grow in it. The algae attract rare flamingos, which flock to the lake to feed. They are born with white feathers, but the algae they eat gradually turns them pink!

Rivers and lakes

Rivers are powerful forces; over time they can cut through rock and create new landscapes. Along with lakes, they are vital resources, providing the fresh water humans, animals, and plants need to survive.

LARGEST DELTA

A delta is a wide area of mud and sand where a river reaches the sea. This satellite view shows the delta of the Ganges River, which covers parts of India and most of Bangladesh. The light blue is sediment that the river is washing into the sea.

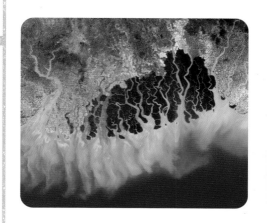

HOW RIVERS **WORK**

A river starts its life as a stream, high up in the mountains, formed by melting ice, rainwater, and groundwater flowing above or below the land. As it flows downhill, it slows down and forms bends, eroding the land as it goes.

Tiny mountain stream flows rapidly downhill.

Young river carves out a valley.

On lower ground, the flow slows and forms meanders.

An oxbow lake is a cutoff meander.

The mouth is where a river meets the sea.

THERE ARE ABOUT **117 MILLION LAKES** ON EARTH!

ACID LAKE

The crater lake of the Ijen volcano in Indonesia may look like an inviting place to swim, but its vivid turquoise color comes from dissolved metals that make its water highly acidic. Other types of lakes are created by glaciers and river erosion, tectonic plate movement, landslides, or even by beavers building dams out of tree branches.

SNAKING RIVERS

As rivers reach flatter land, they develop snakelike bends called "meanders." These form when fast-flowing water erodes the outer bend of a river and deposits the debris on the inside of the next bend. Over time, this creates exaggerated curves such as in Phang Nga Bay, Thailand.

THE **AMAZON RIVER** CARRIES **20 PERCENT** OF **ALL THE FRESH WATER** ON EARTH!

Incredible ice

Some 10 percent of Earth's surface is covered with ice, in the form of glaciers, ice sheets, and frozen seas. While glaciers flow down mountain valleys around the world, most ice is found in polar regions: home to icy oceans and giant icebergs.

IF THE **CLIMATE** CONTINUES TO HEAT, THERE WILL BE **NO SUMMER SEA ICE** IN THE ARCTIC BY **2035**.

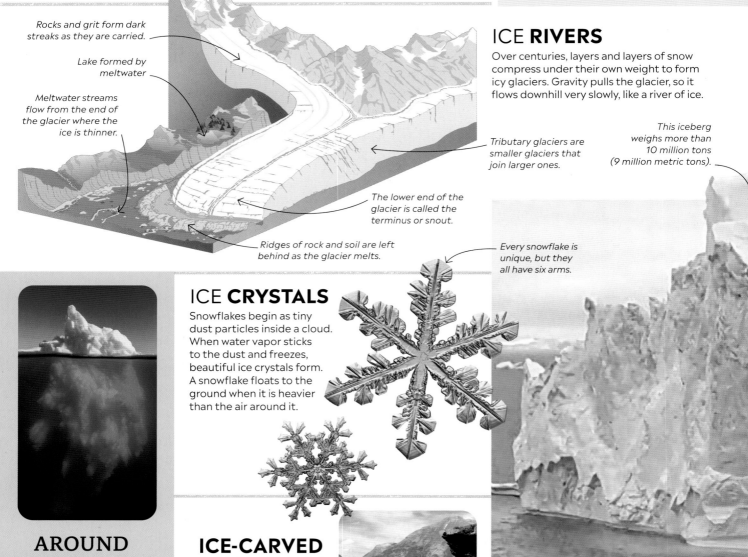

Rocks and grit form dark streaks as they are carried.

Lake formed by meltwater

Meltwater streams flow from the end of the glacier where the ice is thinner.

ICE **RIVERS**

Over centuries, layers and layers of snow compress under their own weight to form icy glaciers. Gravity pulls the glacier, so it flows downhill very slowly, like a river of ice.

Tributary glaciers are smaller glaciers that join larger ones.

The lower end of the glacier is called the terminus or snout.

Ridges of rock and soil are left behind as the glacier melts.

This iceberg weighs more than 10 million tons (9 million metric tons).

Every snowflake is unique, but they all have six arms.

ICE **CRYSTALS**

Snowflakes begin as tiny dust particles inside a cloud. When water vapor sticks to the dust and freezes, beautiful ice crystals form. A snowflake floats to the ground when it is heavier than the air around it.

AROUND **90%** OF AN ICEBERG IS **BELOW THE WATER!**

ICE-CARVED LANDSCAPE

As they flow downhill, glaciers slowly gouge out deep fjords. After the last ice age, many glaciers melted, leaving U-shaped valleys, like Geiranger Fjord in Norway.

DRIFTING **ICEBERGS**

Icebergs are huge chunks of ice that break away from glaciers and ice sheets and float out to sea. This enormous iceberg drifted close to the tiny village of Innaarsuit in North Greenland in 2018. Local residents had to be evacuated in case the iceberg broke apart.

SHRINKING **ICECAP**

In summer, some of the Arctic ice melts but then refreezes in fall. However, since 1979, more ice is melting than refreezing. The map below shows how the amount of ice cover in summer is rapidly shrinking.

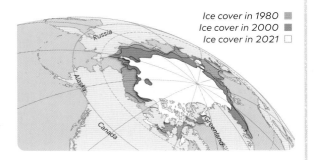

Ice cover in 1980
Ice cover in 2000
Ice cover in 2021

ICE **BREAKER**

Specially designed ships with reinforced hulls known as icebreakers are used to carve passageways through frozen polar seas. The pointed hull glides over ice packs, crushing the ice and clearing a route for other vessels to use.

Powerful icebreakers can smash through ice floes up to 10 ft (3 m) thick.

ICE **SHELF**

Antarctica is home to huge floating ice shelves, which form when sheets of thick ice joined to land spill out over the sea. The largest is the Ross Ice Shelf, covering 182,000 sq miles (472,000 sq km)—almost the size of France.

TWO-THIRDS OF ALL THE WORLD'S **FRESH WATER** IS LOCKED UP IN **GLACIERS!**

Icebergs rise at least 16 ft (5 m) above the water. Smaller chunks of ice are called bergy bits.

Some icebergs have peaks called pinnacles.

This house is dwarfed by the size and scale of the icebergs.

WETTEST PLACE

The town of Mawsynram, India, is the rainiest place on Earth. The town had a record-breaking 39.5 in (1 m) of rain in just 24 hours on June 17, 2022!

STAT ATTACK!
WATER

From rivers to rain, oceans to clouds, water really is found everywhere on our planet—and around it! Here are some incredible facts and stats that show how vital water is and how much of it is on our blue planet.

OCEANS BY AREA

Earth has five oceans, but they are all connected to each other. These vast expanses of saltwalter are listed here from biggest to smallest.

1 PACIFIC
62,500,000 miles²
(161,760,000 km²)

2 ATLANTIC
32,870,000 miles²
(85,133,000 km²)

3 INDIAN
27,243,000 miles²
(70,560,000 km²)

4 SOUTHERN
8,479,000 miles²
(21,960,000 km²)

5 ARCTIC
5,440,000 miles²
(14,090,000 km²)

SPECTACULAR WATERFALL

The Iguazu Falls, on the border between Argentina and Brazil, is one of the world's most spectacular waterfalls. Measuring an incredible 1.7 miles (2.7 km) wide, it is 262 ft (80 m) tall and sprays the surrounding forest with a constant mist. Its name comes from indigenous words meaning "great water."

IGUAZU FALLS

ALL THE WATER

The amount of water on Earth always stays the same: around 332,500,000 miles³ (1,386,000,000 km³). That's enough water to fill 550 trillion Olympic swimming pools!

WATER IN THE AIR

There is water in the atmosphere in the form of clouds, precipitation, and water vapor. If all the atmospheric water fell at once, ocean levels would rise by about 1.5 in (3.8 cm).

The atmosphere holds only about 0.001 percent of Earth's water.

LARGEST LAKES

These are the four biggest fresh water lakes by volume. Some cover a large area but others are very deep.

1 LAKE BAIKAL
Russia
5,660 miles³
(23,600 km³)

2 LAKE TANGANYIKA
East and Central Africa
4,530 miles³ (18,880 km³)

3 LAKE SUPERIOR
North America
2,900 miles³ (12,100 km³)

4 LAKE MALAWI
East Africa
2,015 miles³ (8,400 km³)

Lake Baikal contains about **20 percent** of all the **world's surface fresh water!**

LONGEST RIVERS

1 **NILE**, Africa
4,258 miles (6,853 km)

2 **AMAZON**, South America
At least 4,000 miles (6,400 km)

3 **YANGTZE**, Asia
3,915 miles (6,300 km)

4 **MISSISSIPPI-MISSOURI**,
North America
3,710 miles (5,970 km)

BIGGEST RIVERS

The longest rivers aren't necessarily the biggest. Rivers can also be measured by how much water they carry—how much they discharge into the ocean every second. These are the five biggest rivers by volume.

CONGO, AFRICA
9 million gallons
(41 million liters)

AMAZON, SOUTH AMERICA
45 million gallons
(209 million litres)

GANGES-BRAHMAPUTRA-MEGHNA, ASIA
8.3 million gallons
(38 million liters)

ORINOCO, SOUTH AMERICA
8.1 million gallons
(37 million liters)

MADEIRA, SOUTH AMERICA
6.8 million gallons
(31 million liters)

DEEPEST TRENCHES

The deepest parts of the ocean are known as trenches. All the deepest trenches are in the Pacific Ocean. The Mariana Trench is so deep that Mount Everest could stand in its depths and not reach the surface.

1 CHALLENGER DEEP, MARIANA TRENCH
35,876 ft (10,935 m)

2 TONGA TRENCH
35,702 ft (10,882 m)

3 GALATHEA DEPTH
34,578 ft (10,539 m)

Mount Everest

Mariana Trench

CHALLENGER DEEP IS THE DEEPEST PART OF THE MARIANA TRENCH.

BREAKING IT DOWN

Weathering is the process by which rocks very gradually break down— a tiny fraction at a time. There are four types of weathering.

Physical
Water seeps into cracks in rock. If it then freezes, the water expands and cracks the rock apart.

Chemical
Rainwater is mildly acidic. When this acid hits rocks, it creates a chemical reaction that eats away at the edges of the rock.

Thermal
As rocks warm up, they expand slightly. Then they contract again as they cool. This movement weakens and breaks up the rock.

Biological
Digging animals can cause rocks to break apart. Plant roots can also grow into cracks in rocks, pushing them apart.

STUCK FAST

This big boulder is completely wedged in a crevasse on the Kjerag mountain in Norway. The boulder was carried there by a glacier in the last ice age, around 50,000 years ago. The glacier carved the crevasse, then melted, leaving the boulder stuck, where it will remain for several thousand more years.

A daring hiker stops at the Kjerag boulder for a photo opportunity. The drop below is 3,228 ft (984 m)!

A **SINKHOLE 655 FT (200 M) WIDE** OPENED UP OVERNIGHT ON A FARM IN **NEW ZEALAND** IN 2018!

SAND BLASTED

In deserts, sand picked up by the wind blasts the landscape. The heavy particles travel close to the ground, so carve the lower parts of the rocks, creating top-heavy shapes.

Limestone formations in the Sahara Desert, Egypt

Extreme **erosion**

The Earth's rocky surface might seem unchanging, but it is constantly being worn down by wind, water, and ice. Very slowly, over millions of years, the land is reshaped by erosion.

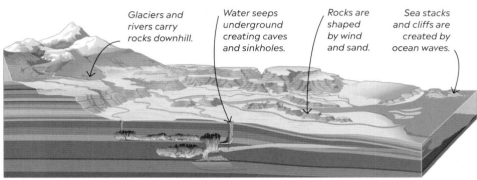

Glaciers and rivers carry rocks downhill.

Water seeps underground creating caves and sinkholes.

Rocks are shaped by wind and sand.

Sea stacks and cliffs are created by ocean waves.

HOW **EROSION WORKS**

Erosion is when ice, water, and wind break off and carry away fragments of rock. Glaciers and rivers carve a path through the landscape, carrying rocks as they go. Wind blows sand, shaping rocks and forming dunes. Waves and wind break up and shape the coastline, carrying debris out to sea.

WAVE POWER

Waves pounding against the coastline wear away at rocky cliffs and carry off material from beaches. Coastal erosion can shape rocks into pillars, called sea stacks, and arches, such as the Azure Window in Malta. This 92 ft (28 m) tall arch finally collapsed after a storm in 2017.

RIVER **CARVING**

Rivers shape the land as they flow through it. Water gently rubs away at the ground and carries rocks downstream, slowly creating deep gorges and valleys. The Grand Canyon is carved by the Colorado River. This tight meander (curve), called Horseshoe Bend, has been cut away over 5 million years.

THE WORLD'S TALLEST SEA STACK IS BALL'S PYRAMID IN THE PACIFIC OCEAN. IT IS 1,843 FT (561 M) HIGH!

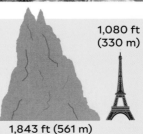

1,080 ft (330 m)

1,843 ft (561 m)

Into the **deep**

Beneath the ground is a hidden world of caves and tunnels. These dark places often contain strange and beautiful rocks that formed over millennia.

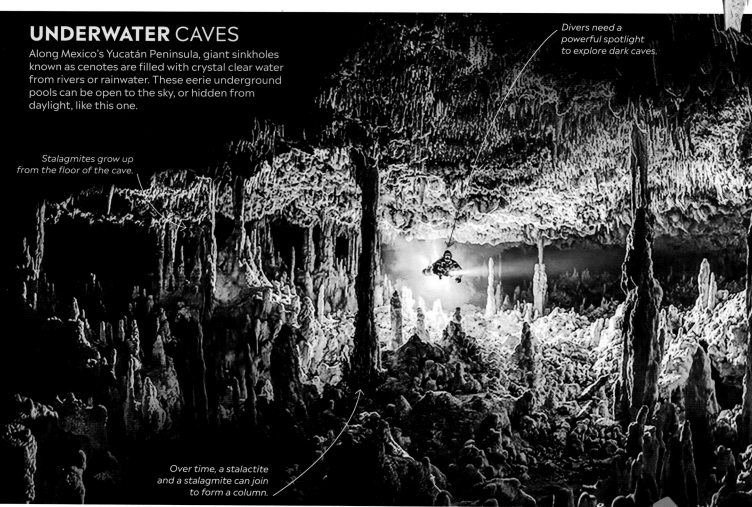

UNDERWATER CAVES

Along Mexico's Yucatán Peninsula, giant sinkholes known as cenotes are filled with crystal clear water from rivers or rainwater. These eerie underground pools can be open to the sky, or hidden from daylight, like this one.

Divers need a powerful spotlight to explore dark caves.

Stalagmites grow up from the floor of the cave.

Over time, a stalactite and a stalagmite can join to form a column.

HOW CAVES **FORM**

Most underground caves form in rock made of limestone. Rainwater seeps into cracks and slowly dissolves the soft rock over millions of years. Water from streams or rivers can penetrate the cracks, widening them and creating vast cave complexes.

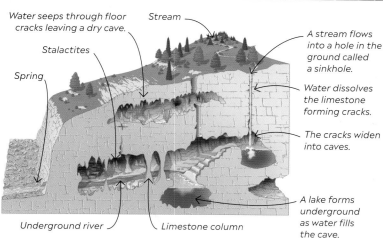

Water seeps through floor cracks leaving a dry cave.

Stream

Stalactites

Spring

A stream flows into a hole in the ground called a sinkhole.

Water dissolves the limestone forming cracks.

The cracks widen into caves.

A lake forms underground as water fills the cave.

Underground river

Limestone column

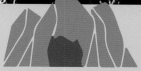

THE **BIGGEST CAVE** IS **HANG SON DOONG** IN VIETNAM. IT IS **5.8 MILES (9.4 KM) LONG!**

GROWING **ROCKS**

Caves are often covered in spiky rock formations. These are created when water drips through the ceiling, leaving minerals behind. Stalactites grow down like icicles while stalagmites build from the ground up.

Minerals build up over thousands of years.

Thousands of stalactites hang in downward-pointing spikes from the ceiling.

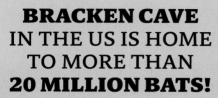

BRACKEN CAVE IN THE US IS HOME TO MORE THAN **20 MILLION BATS!**

ICE CAVES

When meltwater from a glacier forms a stream, it can flow beneath the glacier and carve through the ice, creating an ice cave, like this one in Iceland. Glacial ice reflects blue light, giving the cave its spectacular blue color inside.

The crystals can be up to 39 ft (12 m) long and 3 ft (1 m) wide.

CRYSTAL CAVE

Deep underground in the Naica Cave, Mexico, are enormous milky-white crystals made of a mineral called gypsum. They formed when calcium and sulfur dissolved in the hot water that filled the cave millions of years ago.

CAVE CREATURES!

Blind salamanders called olms live in caves beneath the Dinaric Alps of southern Europe. In the pitch-black conditions, they have no need for sight but can track down prey with their incredible sense of smell.

Violent volcanoes

When volcanoes erupt, they can unleash some of the most destructive forces on Earth. Rocks, ash, and gases are released and red-hot lava can burst or seep out.

BURIED IN **ASH**

When the Cumbre Vieja volcano on the Spanish island of La Palma erupted in 2021, it propelled huge quantities of ash into the atmosphere. As the ash settled, it engulfed thousands of homes.

THE ERUPTION OF **MOUNT TAMBORA**, INDONESIA, IN 1815 CAUSED A DEADLY FAMINE THAT KILLED **80,000** PEOPLE.

Explosive eruptions blast lava up into the sky.

River of molten lava

WHICH IS **WHICH?**

Different types of lava and different kinds of eruption create volcanoes of different shapes. These are the three most common.

Hardened ash and lava form tall flanks.

Cauldron-shaped crater

Thin, runny lava produces gentle slopes.

Stratovolcano
A steep, cone-shaped volcano built from layers of thick, sticky lava that doesn't flow easily.

Caldera
Violent eruptions can destroy the top of a volcano and leave a vast bowl with steep walls.

Shield
The most active type of volcano doesn't grow tall but can be very wide.

MOST **ACTIVE**

Kilauea in Hawaii has been erupting almost continuously since 1983, making it the most active volcanic mass on Earth. Lava flows from the volcano to the ocean, 10 miles (16 km) away.

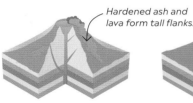

Maleo chicks hatch underground then dig to the surface.

VOLCANO **BIRD**

Most birds sit on their eggs to incubate them, but maleo birds in Sulawesi, Indonesia, let hot volcanic ash do the job for them. They dig a burrow in which to lay an egg, then wander off, leaving the ash to incubate the egg instead.

TURNED TO **STONE!**

When Mount Vesuvius, Italy, erupted in 79 CE, people and animals were trapped in the ash. Their bodies left voids that archaeologists filled with plaster to make casts.

This guard dog died at his post.

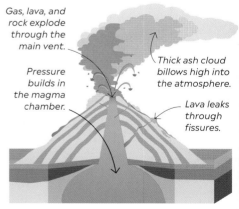

Gas, lava, and rock explode through the main vent.

Pressure builds in the magma chamber.

Thick ash cloud billows high into the atmosphere.

Lava leaks through fissures.

READY TO **BLOW**

Volcanoes occur when molten rock (magma) deep below ground bursts through an opening on the Earth's surface. Most volcanoes lie along the edges of tectonic plates or over hot spots in the Earth's crust.

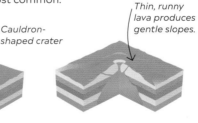

In 2021, people were able to approach and watch the Fagradalsfjall volcano in Iceland without being burned because the sticky lava flowed so slowly.

LAVA FLOW

Lava can reach a scorching 2,192°F (1,200°C), 12 times hotter than boiling water. It glows bright red when it first erupts and the hotter it is, the quicker it moves. As lava cools, it forms a thick black skin and slows down, eventually turning into solid rock.

INTO THE **FIRE!**

In 2014, explorer Sam Cossman went inside a volcano. He got within 50 ft (15 m) of a lava lake. A special suit protected him against the intense heat and poisonous gases.

Dr. Janine Krippner is a volcanologist, studying what happens when a volcano erupts. She is currently working on Ngauruhoe volcano in New Zealand.

Ask a...
VOLCANOLOGIST

Q What is it like being a volcanologist?

A It is exciting being on volcanoes, but it can be challenging at times, too. It's like being a detective. We look for clues to figure out the past, present, and even future activity of volcanoes around the world.

Q Do you get to visit volcanoes?

A Yes! Field trips are my favorite part and are very important for understanding each volcano's personality. I collect samples and make observations, for example, about lava flows, in order to investigate an eruption.

Q Can you predict eruptions?

A There are signs, if we are watching with the right monitoring tools. A volcano that is about to erupt releases gases and causes small earthquakes (usually too small to feel). It might make the surface ground rise slightly, change the chemistry of springwater around the volcano, or make the surface hotter.

Q How do you know a volcano is extinct?

A In the lab, we can figure out how long it has been since a volcano last erupted. After a million years or so, it is unlikely to erupt again. We can also look at the area. Volcanoes can move away from a magma source, such as a hot spot below the crust.

Q What is the most interesting thing you have learned?

A That eruptions produce lightning! This is common even with small explosions, but big eruptions can produce thousands of lightning strikes in the ash plume.

Q How close to an eruption have you been? What is it like?

A I was on Sakurajima volcano in Japan while it was producing small eruptions, and it was so exciting seeing the gray ash plumes rising above! It was beautiful and amazing to experience the forces of our very active planet at work.

MOUNT ETNA

Italy's Mount Etna is one of the world's most active volcanoes. It has been erupting almost nonstop for thousands of years. Every so often, it goes off with a huge bang. This spectacular explosive eruption happened in 2015. A huge column of smoke and ash reached 5 miles (8 km) high.

DESTROYED LIVES

In 1995, the city of Kōbe in Japan was hit by a deadly earthquake—6,400 people died and 40,000 were injured. Much of the city was destroyed, including thousands of homes and part of the Hanshin Expressway.

TYPES OF FAULTS

The border between tectonic plates is called a fault line. Most earthquakes occur at fault lines, when the plates move in different directions.

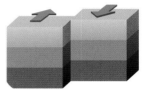

Strike-skip fault
Here the plates slide past each other horizontally in opposite directions.

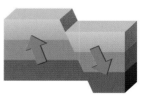

Normal fault
Where plates move apart and one slips down.

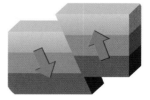

Reverse fault
Where plates squash together and one is pushed up.

90% OF ALL EARTHQUAKES OCCUR ON THE RING OF FIRE, AROUND THE PACIFIC OCEAN!

Unstable earth

EACH YEAR, AROUND **100 EARTHQUAKES** ARE **STRONG** ENOUGH TO CAUSE **MAJOR DAMAGE.**

Where the tectonic plates in Earth's crust meet, pressure builds up causing sudden movements called earthquakes. Every day, there are thousands of earthquakes too small to feel, but powerful earthquakes can be disastrous.

TSUNAMI WARNING

This giant wave is a tsunami that occurred in 2011 on the coast of Japan. Tsunamis are caused by earthquakes under the ocean. The waves can travel huge distances from the earthquake site and crash inland at speeds of up to 500 mph (805 km/h).

On the 126th floor, this suspended weight swings to offset the building's movements during earthquakes and high winds.

RESILIENT **BUILDINGS**

In places close to fault lines, buildings can be engineered to withstand wind and earthquakes. Shanghai Tower in China is one of the tallest buildings in the world. It is made of flexible material so it moves with quakes, rather than shatters. It also contains a shock-absorbing weight on its upper floors.

HOW EARTHQUAKES HAPPEN

As tectonic plates push against each other or slide past each other, pressure builds between them until the plates move. A burst of energy moves in waves from the focus to the epicenter at the surface, where the earthquake is felt at its strongest.

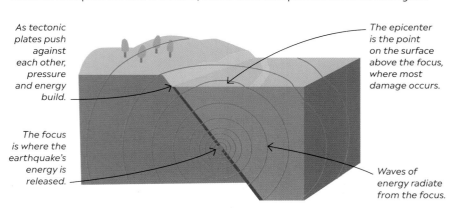

As tectonic plates push against each other, pressure and energy build.

The focus is where the earthquake's energy is released.

The epicenter is the point on the surface above the focus, where most damage occurs.

Waves of energy radiate from the focus.

EARTHQUAKES ALSO HAPPEN **ON THE MOON.** THEY ARE CALLED **MOONQUAKES!**

Wild weather

Weather is the state of the atmosphere at a specific time and place—and it is constantly on the move. It brings us everything from sunshine and rain to dramatic tornadoes, winds whipping around the world, and clouds swirling above its surface.

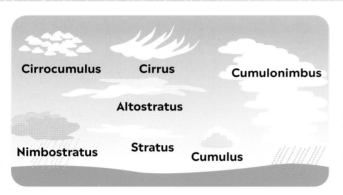

Cirrocumulus

Cirrus

Cumulonimbus

Altostratus

Nimbostratus

Stratus

Cumulus

TYPES OF CLOUDS

Clouds form from tiny droplets of ice or water. They are categorized based on their shape, size, and how high up they are. Cumulonimbus are colossal, towering storm clouds.

SKY SPRITES!

Many storms bring lightning, but some bring something rarer—sprites. Like lightning, sprites are brief flashes of electricity, but these appear red and occur high up in the atmosphere. They are faint so can be seen only at night in places without light pollution.

TORNADO TWIST

Tornadoes are swirling columns of air that form in storm clouds. They are the fastest winds on Earth! Strong tornadoes can uproot trees, rip buildings apart, and lift cars into the air. Tornadoes are most common in North America, in the Midwestern states known as "tornado alley."

MOVING AIR

Earth's weather is caused by the movement of air around the world. The sun heats some areas more than others. Warmer air rises, and cold air rushes in to replace it. This creates winds, which bring different weather conditions.

From space, clouds can be seen moving across the planet's surface.

EXTREME WEATHER

Any type of weather can be dangerous to people and to the environment when it is unusually violent. High winds, such as here in Saltcoat, Scotland, bring violent storms; heavy rains cause flood; and too much sun results in deadly droughts and heat waves.

IN 2001, BLOOD RED RAIN FELL IN KERALA, INDIA. THE COLOR OF THE RAIN WAS CAUSED BY **TINY ALGAE!**

Hailstones are made of layers of frozen water droplets—like an ice onion.

FROZEN **HAIL**

When raindrops get carried upward by the wind into the upper atmosphere, they turn into hailstones. The heaviest hailstone ever recorded fell in Gopalganj, Bangladesh, in 1986. Each stone weighed up to 2.25 lb (1.02 kg)!

A column of swirling air extends from the cloud to the ground.

Tornado winds can destroy everything in their path.

Narrow tornadoes are called "rope tornadoes." They can be even more intense than large tornadoes.

AIR **MASSES**

An air mass is a body of air in the atmosphere that is a consistent temperature and humidity. Masses can be huge, covering entire countries or more. They move with the wind, affecting the weather where they are. Where masses meet, the boundary between them is called a "front."

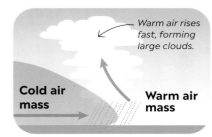

Warm air rises fast, forming large clouds.

Cold air mass

Warm air mass

Cold weather fronts
A cold front occurs when a cold mass pushes into warmer air. The weather gets colder, with huge rain clouds.

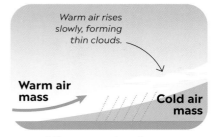

Warm air rises slowly, forming thin clouds.

Warm air mass

Cold air mass

Warm weather fronts
A warm front occurs when a warm mass pushes into colder air. It brings warm weather and often light rain.

WIND SPEEDS INSIDE A **TORNADO** MAY BE MORE THAN **300 MPH (480 KM/H)!**

STRANGE RAIN

Occasionally, things other than water are reported to fall from the sky. Some of these odd items may have been carried by the wind, but no one knows for sure.

SMALL SILVER FISH
Every year in May or June, the city of Yoro, Honduras, experiences a storm that brings heavy rain and small fish.

TINY FROGS
On June 7, 2005, strong winds rained thousands of frogs on the small town of Odžaci, Serbia.

OCTOPUS, STARFISH, AND SHRIMP
A huge storm in Qingdao, China, brought giant hailstones and a variety of sea creatures on June 12, 2018.

GOLF BALLS
On a rainy night in Florida, in 1969, golf balls fell from the sky.

CHUNKS OF MEAT
The "Kentucky Meat Shower" of 1876 saw pieces of meat falling from the sky, possibly dropped by passing vultures.

HOTTEST AND COLDEST

The world record for the hottest air temperature is 130°F (54.4°C) at Furnace Creek, in California's Death Valley, on July 9, 2021. The world record for the lowest-ever recorded temperature was set at Vostok Station, Antarctica, on July 21, 1983. It was a numbing –128.56°F (–89.2°C)!

FURNACE CREEK

VOSTOK STATION

STAT ATTACK!
WEATHER

Planet Earth is home to some incredibly powerful—and sometimes bizarre—weather. From whirling winds to destructive bushfires, here are some of the wildest events that could ever appear on a weather forecast.

FAST AS LIGHTNING

A lightning strike travels at around 270,000 mph (435,000 km/h). With up to 40,000 lightning strikes in one night, Lake Maracaibo in Venezuela receives the most lightning strikes on Earth. Massive thunderstorms occur there on 140–160 nights per year.

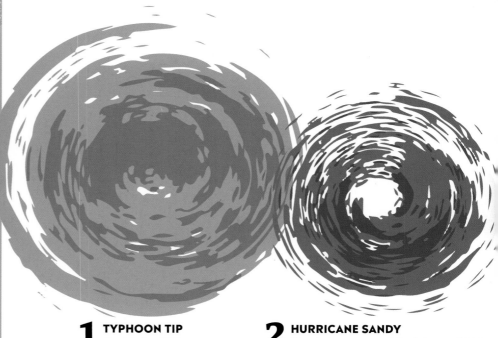

1 TYPHOON TIP
East Asia, 1979
1,380 miles (2,220 km)

2 HURRICANE SANDY
North America and Caribbean, 2012
1,000 miles (1,610 km)

UNUSUAL CLOUDS

Not all clouds are white and fluffy. These strange, sometimes colorful, cloud patterns in the sky are some of the rarest clouds to be spotted.

A typical cumulonimbus cloud weighs about the same as an Airbus A380 airplane!

NACREOUS CLOUDS
Unlike most clouds, these rare clouds form in the stratosphere. They are made of tiny ice particles, which makes them iridescent.

MAMMATUS CLOUDS
These rounded clouds form in unstable cumulonimbus clouds, so they often bring heavy rain, hailstones, and lightning.

KELVIN-HELMHOLTZ CLOUDS
When air above a cloud moves faster than the cloud, it can catch the top of the cloud, creating waves.

FALLSTREAK HOLE
Holes can appear when an airplane flies through a cloud, making water droplets in the cloud suddenly freeze and fall.

WINDIEST PLACE

Antarctica is home to some of the world's fastest winds. The strongest are called katabatic winds. They roll out from the continent toward the coast, traveling downhill as they go. The fastest-ever recorded were at Dumont d'Urville station in 1972 and reached speeds of 203 mph (327 km/h)!

BIGGEST TROPICAL STORMS

Tropical storms are violent, spinning rainstorms. Hurricanes, typhoons, and cyclones are all tropical storms but have these different names in different parts of the world. Here are the largest tropical storms in history, by diameter.

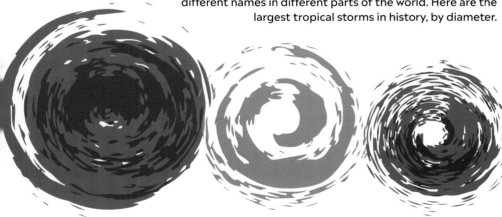

3 HURRICANE IGOR
North America and Caribbean, 2010
920 miles (1,480 km)

4 HURRICANE OLGA
The Bahamas, 2019
865 miles (1,390 km)

5 HURRICANE LILI
North America and Caribbean, 1996
805 miles (1,295 km)

LARGEST BUSHFIRES

Bushfires occur in dry and drought-prone locations and are happening more frequently due to climate change. These are the five that raged over the largest land area.

1 SIBERIAN TAIGA FIRE
Russia, 2003, 85,938 sq miles (222,577 sq km)

2 AUSTRALIAN BUSHFIRES
Australia, 2019/2020, 65,637 sq miles (170,000 sq km)

3 NORTHWEST TERRITORIES FIRES
Canada, 2014, 13,281 sq miles (34,398 sq km)

4 ALASKA FIRE SEASON
US, 2004, 10,311 sq miles (26,707 sq km)

5 BLACK FRIDAY BUSHFIRE
Australia, 1939, 7,812 sq miles (20,234 sq km)

Chris Wright is the Chief Meteorologist for WTTV-4 in Indiana. He broadcasts the weather forecast to a TV audience three times a day.

METEOROLOGIST

Q How accurate are weather forecasts?

A A five-day forecast will be right about 90 percent of the time and a seven-day forecast about 80 percent of the time. But a 10-day forecast is right only about half of the time!

Q What technology do you use?

A We use observations data collected by all sorts of instruments—radar, weather balloons, satellites, and buoys. The data is fed into forecast models that are calculated by supercomputers. The models use equations, along with new and past weather data, to guide our forecasts.

Q What do you do in your job when you are not on TV?

A First, I meet with newsroom staff to talk about the upcoming newscast. Then, I carefully analyze weather data to create the forecasts. After that, I use computer programs to build weather graphics. Once I've got those, I'm ready to go on TV!

Q Have you ever been in an extreme weather event?

A I once covered a tropical storm making landfall. The winds were so strong that the rain felt like rocks as it hit me!

Q What is the scariest weather event you've ever covered?

A In 2004, a tornado outbreak spawned 24 tornadoes across Indiana. One of the twisters touched down within 10 miles (16 km) of the Indianapolis Motor Speedway where 250,000 people were attending a race. It could have been a catastrophic tragedy.

Q Has anything changed since the start of your career?

A Technological advances mean forecasts are much more detailed and accurate. When I started forecasting, almost 40 years ago, we could look ahead only three days with accuracy. Meteorologists are now much better able to forecast weather trends.

SUPERCELL
STORM CLOUD

This enormous, rotating storm cloud is called a supercell. The biggest, most powerful kind of storm, supercells can unleash the most violent weather—torrential rain, giant hailstones, and even destructive tornadoes. They occur across the central areas of North America, where warm, humid air from the equator collides with cold dry air rolling off the Rocky Mountains.

Mighty mountains

Most of the world's highest points formed as tectonic plates smashed against each other millions of years ago. Some mountain ranges are still growing, while others are slowly wearing away. Today, about 20 percent of Earth's land surface is mountainous.

DIZZY HEIGHTS

At 4,406 ft (1,343 m), Ben Nevis in Scotland is the tallest mountain in the UK. It was once an active volcano that collapsed inward on itself around 410 million years ago. Today, more than 150,000 people attempt to reach the summit every year.

A mountaineer dangles under an overhang on one of the most challenging routes to the summit.

A safety rope is anchored to the rock face for climbers to clip onto.

A coating of ice and snow makes the climb especially challenging.

HOW MOUNTAINS FORM

Mountain ranges form when two tectonic plates push together, or when magma pushes up into Earth's crust. Volcanoes (see pages 68-69) can also form mountains.

Fold mountains
This is the most common type of mountain, created when tectonic plates collide. The crust is pushed upwards and crumples.

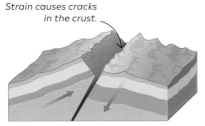

Strain causes cracks in the crust.

Fault block mountains
Stresses within and between tectonic plates can crack Earth's surface, forcing blocks of rock up and down.

Surface rocks forced up by magma below

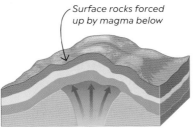

Dome mountains
Magma rises from the Earth's mantle and pushes the rocky crust upward to form dome mountains.

IN 1951, A HUGE 12-IN (33-CM) FOOTPRINT WAS FOUND ON MOUNT EVEREST, SAID TO BELONG TO THE MYTHICAL YETI!

FROM SEABED TO PEAK, MAUNA KEA ON HAWAII IS 33,500 FT (10,211 M) TALL—THAT'S TALLER THAN EVEREST!

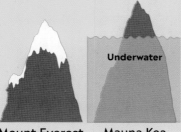

Underwater

Mount Everest   Mauna Kea

AVALANCHE WARNING

Some mountain peaks are so high that they are cold and covered in snow. When a giant mass of snow and ice becomes loose, it tumbles down the mountainside gathering speed and more snow—taking down almost everything in its path.

Avalanches can reach speeds of 200 mph (320 km/h).

TALLEST PEAKS

The top five tallest mountains are located in Asia where the Indian and Eurasian tectonic plates collided 40 to 50 million years ago.

1 Mount Everest 29,029 ft (8,848 m)

2 Godwin Austen (K2) 28,251 ft (8,611 m)

3 Kangchenjunga 28,169 ft (8,586 m)

4 Lhotse 27,940 ft (8,516 m)

5 Makalu 27,838 ft (8,485 m)

MOUNT EVEREST IS GROWING. IT GETS AROUND 0.25 IN (5 MM) TALLER EVERY YEAR!

White fur provides camouflage in the snowy mountains.

HIGH LIFE

Mountain animals have adapted to survive tough conditions. Mountain goats have thick, shaggy fur to keep warm and strong cloven hooves to climb the craggy rocks and steep inclines.

LONGEST RANGE

Earth's longest mountain range lies deep under the sea. The Mid-Ocean Ridge system (shown in red above) is 40,000 miles (65,000 km) long. That's nine times longer than the Andes, the longest range on land.

Dramatic
deserts

Deserts make up one-fifth of Earth's land area. Although we often think of them as sandy, these regions can also be rocky, earthy, mountainous, or icy cold. Deserts are defined as any area with less than 10 in (25 cm) of rainfall per year.

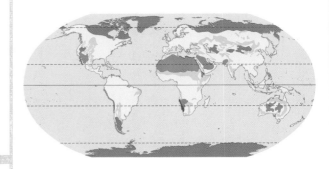

■ Hot desert
■ Coastal desert
■ Cold desert
■ Semiarid desert

WHERE IN THE WORLD?

This map shows where deserts are found. Hot, dry deserts such as the Sahara are found close to the tropics, while cold deserts are located in polar regions and in Central and East Asia.

THE **HOTTEST PLACE** ON EARTH IS **DEATH VALLEY** IN THE US'S **MOJAVE DESERT!**

TYPES OF DESERTS

Only about 20 percent of the world's deserts are covered in sand. They often experience extreme temperatures of scorching hot or freezing cold.

Cold desert
Antarctic and Arctic deserts have very cold climates where most water is frozen solid.

Hot desert
In tropical regions, deserts are hot all year round, but at night temperatures plummet.

Semiarid desert
These are cooler than hot deserts, with long, dry summers and rainy winters.

Coastal desert
Deserts near the ocean can be almost totally rainless yet damp with fog.

Dunes found in the Namib Desert are the tallest in the world, reaching up to 984 ft (300 m).

Gemsbok are nomadic antelopes. They graze at dawn and dusk when condensation on the grasses offers some moisture.

DESERT LIFE

At 55 million years old, the Namib Desert in Namibia is the oldest desert in the world. It is made up of over 1,250 miles (2,000 km) of giant dunes shaped by the wind. It may appear a lifeless habitat, but some highly adapted plants and animals are able to survive in this extreme environment.

WINDS CARRY **100 MILLION TONS** (90 MILLION METRIC TONS) OF **DUST** AWAY FROM THE **SAHARA EVERY YEAR!**

DUST STORM

In desert regions, strong winds can send sand and dust swirling into the air, creating sandstorms that reach up to 60 mph (97 km/h). Sandstorms can carry tons of tiny particles over vast distances and smother everything in their path.

WATER CARRIER

In the Sonoran Desert in North America, the saguaro cactus has adapted to survive without water for long periods of time. It stores water in its sturdy stem and can expand to make more room. Sharp spines line the outside to protect the water inside.

Gila woodpeckers dig out nest holes inside the saguaro cactus to raise their chicks.

ANTARCTICA IS THE **WORLD'S LARGEST DESERT.** IT IS ABOUT **TWICE** THE **SIZE** OF **AUSTRALIA!**

RAIN SHADOW DESERTS

When a mountain range lies close to the coast, a rain shadow desert may form. Ocean water evaporates to create clouds. Rain falls on the ocean side of the mountain leaving cool, dry air to blow across the other side where a desert forms.

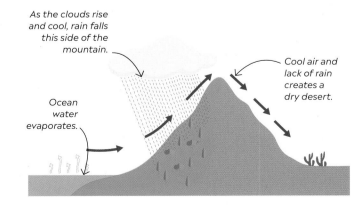

As the clouds rise and cool, rain falls this side of the mountain.

Ocean water evaporates.

Cool air and lack of rain creates a dry desert.

Brown-toed sloths hang from branches high in the rainforest canopy.

THE **AMAZON RAINFOREST**

Spanning eight countries of South America, the Amazon rainforest is by far the world's biggest rainforest. It is home to at least 10 percent of known plant and animal species. Amazingly, a new species is discovered on average every other day!

Fabulous **forests**

THERE ARE AROUND 3 TRILLION TREES ON EARTH!

Trees are the biggest plants on Earth. They are home to over three-quarters of the world's life on land and play a vital part in the fight against climate change by absorbing carbon dioxide from the atmosphere. Gradually, forests are disappearing, with millions of trees cut down every year.

TYPES OF FORESTS

There are three main types of forests. Dense, wildlife-rich rainforests are found close to the equator, while boreal forests grow in cold regions near the Arctic. Temperate forests exist in areas where the climate is mild, with four distinct seasons.

The tallest trees form the emergent layer.

Tropical rainforest
These warm, wet forests have four distinct layers with differing levels of water and sunlight.

Boreal forest
Conifer trees with hard needle-like leaves, such as spruce, pine, and fir, grow in these cold and dry forests.

Temperate forest
Most of these trees have broad, flat leaves that are shed in fall and regrow in spring.

IT TAKES **10 MINUTES** FOR A RAINDROP TO TRAVEL FROM THE **RAINFOREST CANOPY** TO THE **FOREST FLOOR!**

FREEZING FOREST

Almost a quarter of the world's trees are found in boreal forests—mostly made up of conifers such as pine trees, which are well adapted to survive frigid temperatures all year round. Their conical, narrow shape helps them shake off heavy snow that risks breaking branches and to catch and absorb as much sunlight as possible.

FOREST **GUARDIANS**

Many Indigenous communities depend on rainforests for their survival and have long helped protect these areas from deforestation. This young boy is one of Brazil's Paiter-Surui people, who preserve and monitor 958 sq miles (248,147 hectares) of forest in the Amazon.

Tree planting is one of the ways the Paiter-Surui people help preserve the forest.

THE **WOOD WIDE WEB**

Beneath the forest floor lies a network of fungi, known as the "Wood Wide Web," believed to be nearly 500 million years old. Many scientists believe that trees use the network to share resources, such as water and nutrients. The trees may even use it to communicate, warning of insect attacks, for example.

EVERY MINUTE, THE EQUIVALENT OF **27 FOOTBALL FIELDS** OF FOREST IS **DESTROYED.**

NAME THAT... TREE

Are you a budding botanist? Can you tell an oak from an elm or a maple from a beech? Try to identify the trees pictured here without looking at the answers below. Can you unearth the odd one out?

1 Jacaranda
2 Rubber
3 Dragon's blood
4 Moringa
5 Oak
6 Sal
7 Joshua
8 Tamarack
9 Olive
10 Laburnum
11 Banana
12 Chinese Judas
13 Baobab
14 Apple
15 Tree fern
16 Giant sequoia
17 Juniper
18 Maple
19 Rowan
20 Mahogany
21 Tree of heaven
22 Durian
23 Pine
24 Date palm
25 Willow
26 Red mangrove
27 Fir
28 Cherry blossom
29 Monkey puzzle
30 Beech

The odd one out is the banana (11). The trunk of this giant plant is not made of wood, so it is classed as a herbaceous plant, not a tree.

CAUSES OF CHANGE

Burning fossil fuels (coal, oil, and gas) for energy increases levels of the greenhouse gas carbon dioxide in the atmosphere. This has been the main cause of climate change since industrialization. Renewable energy sources, such as wind and solar power, can help reduce emissions.

Climate emergency

Human activity is causing dramatic changes to Earth's climate. Rising temperatures cause more extreme weather, from storms to heat waves, and rising sea levels. To halt climate change, we must reduce emissions of greenhouse gases.

CLIMATE IMPACTS

Earth's average temperature has increased by 1.9°F (1.1°C) in the last 150 years. Rising temperatures create knock-on effects all around the world.

Ice melt
The ice sheets are melting, causing sea levels to rise. White ice reflects the sun's rays, but as it melts, less heat is reflected and the sea warms more.

Habitat destruction
As the Earth warms up, animal habitats are changing and being destroyed. Many species are at risk of extinction.

Extreme weather
Rising global temperatures lead to more extreme and unpredictable weather, from heat waves and droughts to hurricanes and floods.

Ocean damage
Excess carbon dioxide dissolves into oceans, making them more acidic, with a devastating effect on marine species.

Lives destroyed
Extreme weather events and the threats to food and water supplies push people into poverty and can force them from their homes.

THE NUMBER OF CLIMATE-RELATED DISASTERS HAS MORE THAN TRIPLED SINCE 1980.

WORSENING WILDFIRES

Record-breaking heat and extreme droughts are leading to widespread wildfires. In 2019–2020, bushfires in Australia destroyed almost 3,000 homes and killed or displaced nearly 3 billion animals. Plumes of smoke could be seen from space, rising 15 miles (25 km) into the atmosphere.

Firefighters battle intense, fast-spreading, blazes with water.

GREENHOUSE EFFECT

Certain gases in Earth's atmosphere help trap the sun's warmth. Without this greenhouse effect, the planet would be too cold for life to exist. But human activity is causing the levels of these gases to rise, trapping more heat and causing the average global temperature to rise.

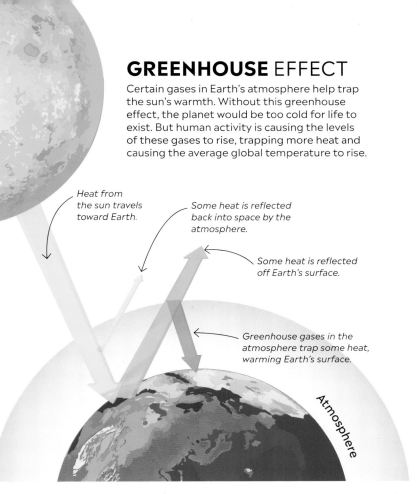

Heat from the sun travels toward Earth.

Some heat is reflected back into space by the atmosphere.

Some heat is reflected off Earth's surface.

Greenhouse gases in the atmosphere trap some heat, warming Earth's surface.

Atmosphere

TREES **ABSORB** AND STORE **CARBON DIOXIDE**. **FOREST LOSS** CAUSES **10%** OF **WARMING**.

SAVING THE PLANET

We can all make a difference by buying less and by reusing and recycling more. However, to reverse climate change, governments and businesses must switch to clean energy and end deforestation.

Eucalyptus trees are highly flammable.

Protecting our planet

Over the centuries, people have used Earth's natural resources, destroyed habitats, and made heaps of waste. But we can protect the planet and reverse this damage, by working together and with the help of new technology.

WALL OF **TREES!**

A Great Green Wall of trees is being planted across Africa to prevent the desert from spreading and increase the amount of farmland. It will stretch for thousands of miles.

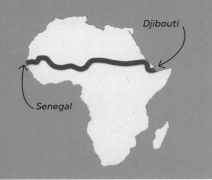

Djibouti

Senegal

LITTER PICKING

Much of our trash, in particular plastic waste, ends up in the oceans and is then washed up on shore. Plastics are now found at every level of the marine food chain. Picking up litter is one way we can all help.

REWILDING HABITATS

Rewilding means letting places return to the way they were before humans changed them. This might mean leaving nature to regenerate in farmed areas or allowing rivers to flood. Over time, this can encourage wildlife to return. In North America, rewilding has led to the reintroduction of species such as wolves.

THE OCEAN **CLEANUP**

Every year, millions of tons of plastic enter the oceans from rivers or as fishing waste. The Ocean Cleanup is a project that has developed a way to capture and recycle it.

Capture
Two boats tow a long, U-shaped barrier through the ocean, gathering up floating plastic.

Extraction
When the barrier's net is full, the plastic is sealed up and lifted on board the boats to be sorted.

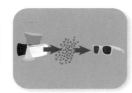

Recycling
Plastic is taken ashore and processed into pellets to make products such as sunglasses.

RESTORING **REEFS**

Living coral reefs are under threat from ocean warming and acidification, overfishing, and pollution. To reverse the decline, scientists are restoring reefs in the waters off the Indonesian island of Bali by creating artificial structures for coral to grow on. These are formed of Biorock™. This is created from minerals in seawater by running an electrical current through a metal frame, such as these bicycles.

Conservationists attach fragments of living corals that have broken off existing reefs to the new reef.

INSECTS SUCH AS LADYBUGS CAN BE USED INSTEAD OF PESTICIDES TO PROTECT CROPS!

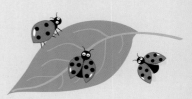

Corals start to grow into new, living reefs, which will create a vibrant ecosystem.

Barnacles grow on the bicycles too.

Discarded steel bicycles provide a framework for corals to grow on.

The structure will become a habitat for tropical fish.

SUSTAINABLE ENERGY

Wind, solar, wave, and tidal power are cleaner alternatives to burning fossil fuels for energy. These wind trees use wind to produce green electricity in public spaces, for street lighting and for charging phones and even cars.

ECO **ALTERNATIVES**

New materials are being developed to replace those that are harmful to the environment. For example, biodegradable plant plastics are slowly replacing plastics made from fossil fuels. We can also reuse more and consume less.

Hemp bag can be used many times.

Bamboo and paper can be recycled.

ONLY 9% OF PLASTIC WASTE IS RECYCLED GLOBALLY!

LIFE

What is life?

Since life first appeared on Earth, it has evolved into an astonishing variety of life-forms. Today, living things range from bacteria too tiny to see with the naked eye to massive blue whales and lush ecosystems teeming with plant and animal life.

KINGDOMS OF LIFE

Scientists group all life on Earth into seven kingdoms. Three of these—archaea, bacteria, and protozoa—are microscopic, but other forms of life could not exist without them. The other four, which vary in size, are chromista, plants, fungi, and animals.

ARCHAEA
These simple, single-celled organisms live in harsh habitats, such as hot, acidic pools or icy oceans.

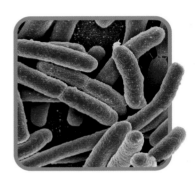

BACTERIA
Single-celled bacteria are found in all habitats. Many live on plants or animals, but few cause disease.

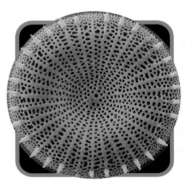

PROTOZOA
More complex cells than bacteria, most protozoa move around and feed like microscopic animals.

TEEMING WITH LIFE

All living things share seven characteristics that set them apart from nonliving things. These are movement, respiration, excretion, nutrition, sensitivity, reproduction, and growth. All life in this coral reef displays these traits.

SCIENTISTS ESTIMATE THERE ARE 8.7 MILLION LIVING SPECIES ON EARTH!

Movement
All life-forms move. Most plants and fungi move on the spot, but animals, such as this feather star, are mobile.

Respiration
Cells release energy from food in a process called respiration. Fish extract oxygen from water to do this.

Excretion
All living things produce waste chemicals in their cells. Getting rid of them is called excretion. Fish excrete them in urine.

Trees and grass use the sun's energy to make food.

Lions are predators that hunt plant-eating zebras and antelopes.

Zebras eat plants to gain nutrition and energy.

ECOSYSTEMS

No life exists on its own. Plants, fungi, animals, and other life-forms live together in ecosystems—areas that are also shaped by landscape and weather. One example is the African savanna.

Hyenas are scavengers. They feed on dead animal carcasses.

CHROMISTA
From microscopic diatoms to giant kelps, most chromista are aquatic and, like plants, make food from the sun's energy.

PLANTS
Made up of many cells, most plants are land-based and all make their own food using the sun's energy.

FUNGI
Single- or multicelled, fungi typically obtain energy by feeding on dead plant and animal matter.

ANIMALS
Virtually all animals are multicelled and have senses and nerves that help them move to find food.

Nutrition
All life-forms need food to stay alive. Nutrition is the process by which they make or get food. Sea goldies eat tiny plankton.

Sensitivity
All living things sense and respond to changes in the environment. Fish can see, smell, taste, and hear and are sensitive to touch.

Reproduction
All life reproduces to ensure its survival. Female fish lay eggs, which are fertilized by males and grow into fish.

Growth
All living things start small and then grow bigger and develop. Feather stars regenerate lost limbs and can grow up to 150 arms.

A **QUARTER** OF **SPECIES LIVE** IN THE **OCEANS!**

NOT LIVING

Viruses are tiny organisms, some of which cause diseases. They are not regarded as living things, because they do not share many of the traits of life. They can only reproduce by invading living cells.

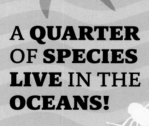

Measles virus

99.9% OF **LIFE** THAT HAS EVER **EXISTED** ON EARTH IS NOW **EXTINCT!**

IN THE **BEGINNING**

Rocklike living fossils, stromatolites are evidence of life that appeared 3.5 billion years ago. They formed when silt trapped layers of cyanobacteria (blue-green algae). The first life-form to photosynthesize, they added oxygen to Earth's atmosphere, creating the conditions for life to evolve.

LIFE **EVOLVES**

Evolution is the theory that species change over many generations. It is driven by natural selection, when the life-forms that are best able to survive pass on their genes to the next generation.

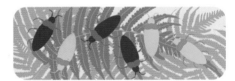

Beetles vary in color
A species of beetle living on the leaves of a tree fern comes in a variety of different colors.

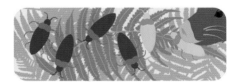

Predator eats colorful beetles
An insect-eating predator picks out the orange beetles, which are easiest to spot on the fern.

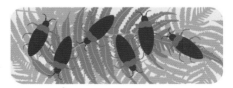

Camouflaged beetles survive
The camouflaged green beetles survive to pass on their genes, and the orange beetles die out.

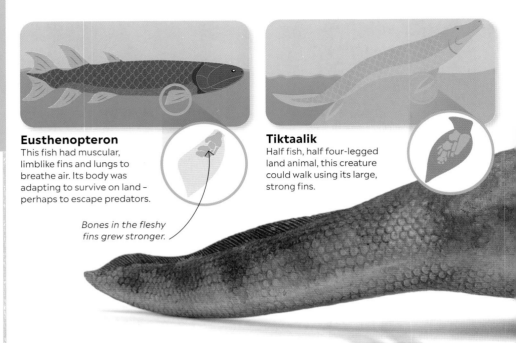

Eusthenopteron
This fish had muscular, limblike fins and lungs to breathe air. Its body was adapting to survive on land – perhaps to escape predators.

Bones in the fleshy fins grew stronger.

Tiktaalik
Half fish, half four-legged land animal, this creature could walk using its large, strong fins.

THE **BIGGEST INSECT** EVER WAS A **GIANT DRAGONFLY** CALLED *MEGANEUROPSIS* THAT LIVED **250 MYA!**

Shown on a soccer ball for scale

Its wingspan was 28 in (71 cm).

Early life

Life first appeared on Earth 3.7 billion years ago. For hundreds of millions of years, microscopic, single-celled life forms were the only living things on the planet. Then, around 542 million years ago (mya), an extraordinary explosion of life took place.

SWAMPY FORESTS

The first, simple plants floated in water, moving onto land around 500 mya. Tiny, mosslike plants evolved into tree ferns, horsetails, and cycads, and towering, lush forests grew.

Lepidonderon, or scale trees, grew up to 164 ft (50 m) tall.

Fossil shows scaly pattern of tree bark.

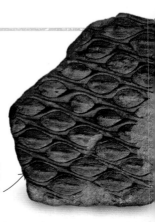

ONTO THE **LAND**

Life first evolved in the water and stayed there for hundreds of millions of years. Around 390 mya, some fishlike creatures began to live partly on land. Eventually, these evolved into the first four-legged animals—the ancestors of many land animals today.

Ichthyostega
One of the first backboned animals with limbs, *Ichthyostega* lived in shallow swamps. Toes and legs may have raised the body off the ground for walking.

Scientists are not sure how many toes Ichthyostega had.

EXPLOSION OF LIFE

Around 542 mya, the variety of life on Earth increased dramatically – an event known as the Cambrian explosion. Oceans teemed with strange-looking creatures, crawling, swimming, catching floating particles of food, and eating each other.

Pikaia, the first known ancestor of vertebrates

Predatory arthropod Anomalocaris

Swimming arthropod Marrella

Spiny, wormlike Hallucigenia

Burrowing, soft-bodied Aysheaia

HORSESHOE CRABS FIRST EVOLVED 480 MYA AND THEY STILL EXIST TODAY!

TIMELINE OF **LIFE**

It is hard to imagine the vast timescale of life's evolution on Earth. To help understand it, this clock represents Earth's existence as 12 hours. For the first hour, the planet was a burning ball of gas and rock, until life slowly started to evolve. Modern humans appear only in the last second!

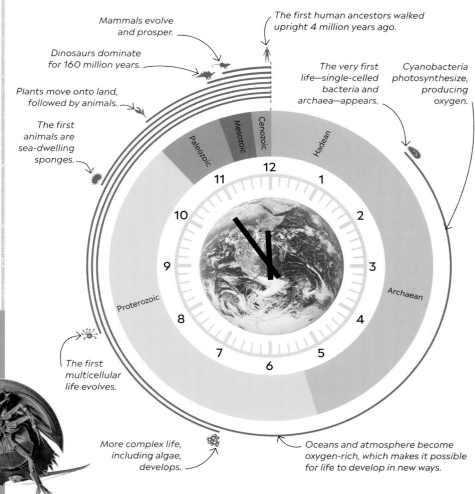

Mammals evolve and prosper.

The first human ancestors walked upright 4 million years ago.

Dinosaurs dominate for 160 million years.

The very first life—single-celled bacteria and archaea—appears.

Cyanobacteria photosynthesize, producing oxygen.

Plants move onto land, followed by animals.

The first animals are sea-dwelling sponges.

Paleozoic

Mesozoic

Cenozoic

Hadean

Proterozoic

Archaean

The first multicellular life evolves.

More complex life, including algae, develops.

Oceans and atmosphere become oxygen-rich, which makes it possible for life to develop in new ways.

Mesozoic monsters

Dinosaurs are the best known of the creatures that roamed the Earth in the Mesozoic Era, but they were not alone. Gigantic reptiles swam in the oceans and flew in the skies around them. The first mammals also appeared, in many shapes and sizes.

SUPER **SWIMMER**

This fossil skeleton of a *Plesiosaurus* gives us an idea of how the mighty marine predator swam through Jurassic waters. Powered by four massive flippers, it cruised through the oceans, extending its long neck to grab swimming prey with its jaws.

Rear flipper

Paddle-like flippers flapped up and down like a penguin's to "fly" underwater.

Long, toothed beak

Donut-shaped eye bone held a huge eyeball in shape.

FISH **LIZARDS**

Ichthyosaurs were marine reptiles with flexible, fishlike bodies that enabled them to swim fast. They were up to 85 ft (26 m) long—this specimen's skull is 6.6 ft (2 m) long.

Around 40 neck bones made up the slender neck.

Jaws in narrow skull could open wide.

THE **LARGEST FLYING CREATURE** EVER, PTEROSAUR *QUETZALCOATLUS* HAD A **WINGSPAN** ALMOST AS WIDE AS A **SPITFIRE PLANE!**

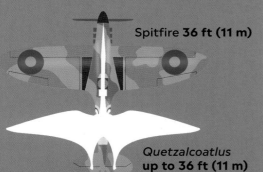

Spitfire **36 ft (11 m)**

Quetzalcoatlus **up to 36 ft (11 m)**

Long, conical teeth enabled the plesiosaur to snatch slippery prey.

AGE OF THE **REPTILES**

The Mesozoic Era lasted from 252 to 66 million years ago (mya). It is divided into the Triassic, Jurassic, and Cretaceous periods. Reptiles ruled the land, sea, and sky throughout this era.

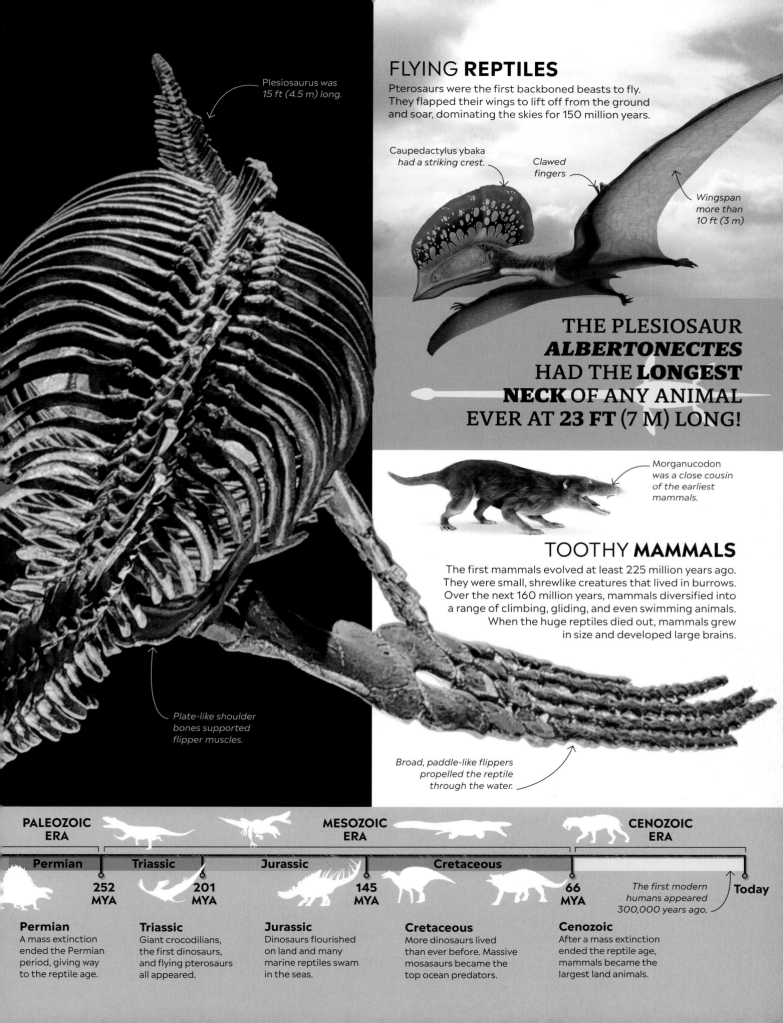

Plesiosaurus *was 15 ft (4.5 m) long.*

FLYING **REPTILES**

Pterosaurs were the first backboned beasts to fly. They flapped their wings to lift off from the ground and soar, dominating the skies for 150 million years.

Caupedactylus ybaka *had a striking crest.*

Clawed fingers

Wingspan more than 10 ft (3 m)

THE PLESIOSAUR **ALBERTONECTES** HAD THE **LONGEST NECK** OF ANY ANIMAL EVER AT **23 FT (7 M) LONG!**

Morganucodon was a close cousin of the earliest mammals.

TOOTHY **MAMMALS**

The first mammals evolved at least 225 million years ago. They were small, shrewlike creatures that lived in burrows. Over the next 160 million years, mammals diversified into a range of climbing, gliding, and even swimming animals. When the huge reptiles died out, mammals grew in size and developed large brains.

Plate-like shoulder bones supported flipper muscles.

Broad, paddle-like flippers propelled the reptile through the water.

PALEOZOIC ERA		MESOZOIC ERA			CENOZOIC ERA
Permian	**Triassic**	**Jurassic**	**Cretaceous**		
	252 MYA	201 MYA	145 MYA	66 MYA	Today

The first modern humans appeared 300,000 years ago.

Permian
A mass extinction ended the Permian period, giving way to the reptile age.

Triassic
Giant crocodilians, the first dinosaurs, and flying pterosaurs all appeared.

Jurassic
Dinosaurs flourished on land and many marine reptiles swam in the seas.

Cretaceous
More dinosaurs lived than ever before. Massive mosasaurs became the top ocean predators.

Cenozoic
After a mass extinction ended the reptile age, mammals became the largest land animals.

Dinosaurs dominate

Dinosaurs ruled the Earth for over 160 million years. From lumbering, scaly titans and ferocious hunters to tiny, feathered creatures, all but a few were wiped out 66 million years ago.

SMALL VS TALL!

Many dinosaurs were giants: the biggest known was *Argentinosaurus*, a titanic sauropod. Others were tiny: the tracks of one dromaeosaur, maybe a chick, are 0.4 in (1 cm) long, suggesting it was the size of a sparrow.

Argentinosaurus

Dromaeosaur
May have been
6 in (15 cm) long

Around 110 ft (33.5 m) long

TYPES OF DINOSAURS

There were five main dinosaur groups. Some researchers suggest that around 2,000 different species existed, but there may be many more undiscovered.

Theropods
Mainly meat-eaters, with sharp teeth, theropods walked on two legs. *Archaeopteryx*, the first bird, and *Velociraptor* are in this group.

Sauropods
Long-necked plant-eaters, sauropods were the largest beasts to stomp the Earth. They included *Diplodocus*.

Thyreophorans
Distinctive thyreophorans had thick, bony armor and spiky or clubbed tails. *Stegosaurus* was among their number.

Ornithopods
Known for their odd-shaped heads and broad snouts, many ornithopods, like *Edmontosaurus*, had complex teeth.

Marginocephalians
Pachycephalosaurus and others in this group used their hard skulls and horns for display and fighting but ate plants.

WHAT IS A DINOSAUR?

Open hip socket

Bony lumps on neck bones for muscle attachment

Two prongs at the back of the cheek bone

Large crest on upper arm bone for muscle attachment

Hand with small, stublike fourth and fifth fingers

Dinosaurs came in all shapes and sizes, but paleontologists identify them by the features they shared. These are shown on this *Herrerasaurus*, one of the earliest dinosaurs.

STRUTHIOMIMUS MAY HAVE RUN AT UP TO **37 MPH** (60 KM/H)—ALMOST THE **SPEED** OF A RACING **GREYHOUND!**

DINOSAUR HERDS

Some dinosaurs really did move in herds! Giraffe-like sauropods roamed in large groups, browsing on the high-up leaves of conifers, ginkgos, and cycads.

Many large plant-eaters were sociable animals that stuck together for defense against fierce predators.

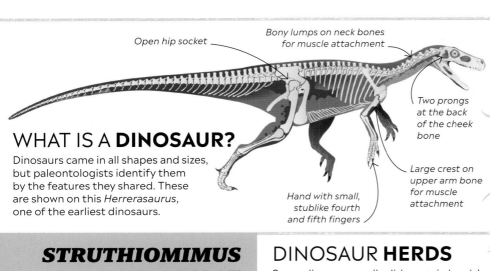

TERRIFYING **T-REX**

Tyrannosaurus rex was one of the largest meat-eaters ever to roam the Earth, preying on plant-eaters such as the frill-necked *Triceratops*. These reconstructed fossil skeletons show the pair locked in a display of bone-crushing ferocity.

Long tail helped T-rex to balance.

Broad skull gave strength to T-rex's mighty bite—the most powerful of any land animal ever.

Claw-like hands

Strong back legs supported T-rex's weight.

Frilled neck of Triceratops shows T-rex tooth marks.

Massive skull has a beak and rows of plant-slicing teeth.

Long horn with a sharp tip, used by Triceratops to attract and fight over mates.

EMBRYO **EGG**

All dinosaurs laid eggs. This fossil embryo of a toothless theropod in its egg was found intact in southern China. It is known as Baby Yingliang.

The embryo is in a "tucked" posture like modern birds.

Caihong juji had iridescent head and tail feathers.

COLORFUL **FEATHERS**

In recent years, fossil finds have revealed that many dinosaurs had feathers. Now, scientists have found traces of pigment-bearing cells that suggest these birdlike dinosaurs had colored plumage.

MASS **EXTINCTION**

An asteroid strike 66 million years ago brought the dinosaurs' rule to an abrupt end. The devastating impact destroyed ecosystems and most of the dinosaurs died out. One branch of theropods survived, however, and are still present today: birds.

NAME THAT... DINOSAUR

Calling all dinosaur experts! Can you tell a *Tyrannosaurus* from a *Triceratops*, and a *Stegosaurus* from a *Scelidosaurus*? See how many of these dinosaurs you can name. Watch out for the odd one out!

1 *Stegosaurus*
2 *Dryosaurus*
3 *Quetzalcoatlus*
4 *Coelophysis*
5 *Archaeopteryx*
6 *Muttaburrasaurus*
7 *Suchomimus*
8 *Isanosaurus*
9 *Dubreuillosaurus*
10 *Corythosaurus*
11 *Carcharodontosaurus*
12 *Triceratops*
13 *Iguanodon*
14 *Parasaurolophus*
15 *Diplodocus*
16 *Velociraptor*
17 *Hypsilophodon*
18 *Struthiomimus*
19 *Baryonyx*
20 *Kentrosaurus*
21 *Euoplocephalus*
22 *Cryolophosaurus*
23 *Allosaurus*
24 *Edmontosaurus*
25 *Anchiornis*
26 *Tyrannosaurus*
27 *Pachycephalosaurus*
28 *Heterodontosaurus*
29 *Eoraptor*
30 *Shunosaurus*
31 *Argentinosaurus*
32 *Scelidosaurus*
33 *Saltasaurus*
34 *Psittacosaurus*
35 *Sinosauropteryx*
36 *Irritator*
37 *Albertosaurus*
38 *Plateosaurus*
39 *Spinosaurus*
40 *Sauropelta*
41 *Monolophosaurus*

The odd one out is *Quetzalcoatlus* (3). It is a pterosaur, a type of prehistoric flying reptile, which is not a dinosaur.

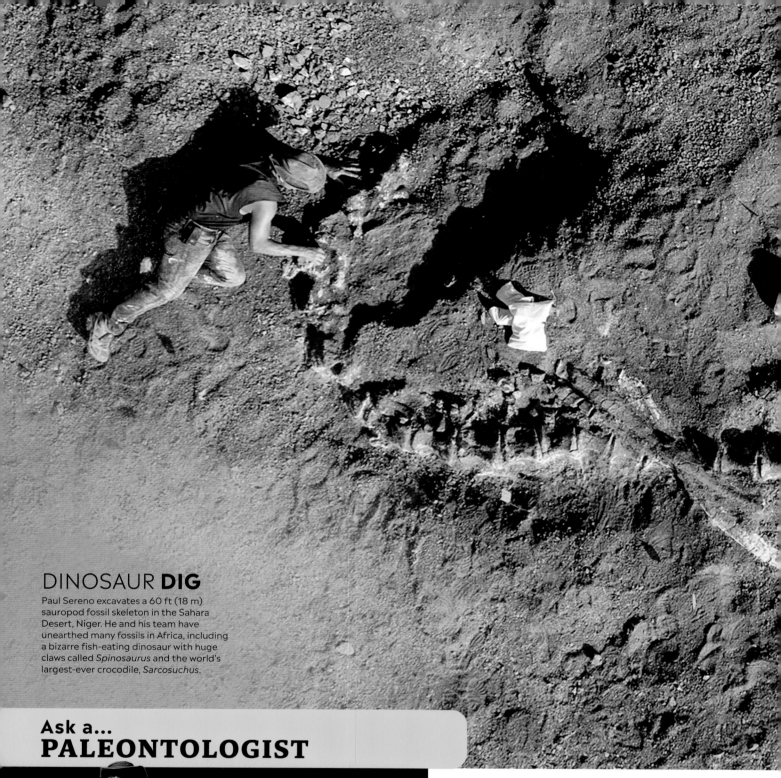

DINOSAUR **DIG**

Paul Sereno excavates a 60 ft (18 m) sauropod fossil skeleton in the Sahara Desert, Niger. He and his team have unearthed many fossils in Africa, including a bizarre fish-eating dinosaur with huge claws called *Spinosaurus* and the world's largest-ever crocodile, *Sarcosuchus*.

Ask a...
PALEONTOLOGIST

Professor Paul Sereno is an American paleontologist, who founded the Fossil Lab at the University of Chicago. He has discovered dinosaurs from the Andes to the Gobi Desert. In recent years, he has excavated a whole menagerie of new species in Africa's Sahara Desert.

Q Are paleontologists still discovering new dinosaurs?

A Once upon a time, new dinosaur discoveries were rare. Now, the rate of new dinosaur finds has skyrocketed to around 50 a year, given all of the eyes looking and folks digging. It's a dinosaur renaissance!

Q Where can I hunt for fossils?

A Fossils can be found in all kinds of rock, from layers of marine limestone to sandstone layers on land. Look for a fossil-lovers' guidebook to find a map of hunting grounds near you.

Q What's your most exciting find?

A The one I am working on right now, which happens to be a bizarre digging raptor from Africa. No one in the world could have imagined it once existed, if it weren't for the single fossil skeleton we chanced upon in the Sahara.

Q How do you figure out how dinosaur bones fit together to make a skeleton?

A The puzzle isn't too hard to put together, as all dinosaur skeletons are made from the same set of bones—a few more than 300 if you were to count every single one in a complete skeleton. All the bones have the same names, connect to some of the same muscles, and even bear some similarity to the set of bones in a human skeleton.

Q What can you tell about a dinosaur by looking at fossils?

A Lots. Even a single jawbone with teeth can tell you what the dinosaur ate, to which group it belongs, and sometimes whether it is a new species or not. If you have most of the skeleton, you can tell how it walked and ran and if it hunted or ate plants.

Q Do we know how dinosaurs looked?

A Sometimes a dinosaur dies and dries out under the sun, its skin turning into hard leather. Rapid burial of these dinosaur "mummies" can preserve a cast of the scaly skin in sediment. The color of its skin, however, remains a mystery.

Q Could Jurassic Park become real?

A No. Dinosaur fossils do not preserve ancient DNA, the oldest record of which is around 2 million years old—from a mastodon that lived more than 60 million years after the dinosaurs.

Plant life

There are more than 390,000 known species of plants, which have adapted to survive almost everywhere in the world. Unlike animals, plants make their own food from the sun's energy, in turn providing food for animals.

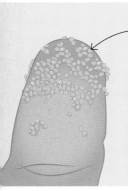

Each plant is the size of a candy sprinkle.

THE **SMALLEST PLANT** ON EARTH IS **WATERMEAL**, A ROOTLESS AQUATIC DUCKWEED!

TYPES OF PLANTS

Plants come in many shapes and sizes. All plants fall into one of these six groups. Flowering plants are the most common.

Liverworts
Among the first plants to grow on Earth, these do not have leaves, roots, or stems.

Mosses and hornworts
These live in damp places, growing in carpets or cushions.

Club mosses
These tiny plants have tubes to move water and food, and hard, scaly leaves.

Ferns and horsetails
These lush plants reproduce using spores, not seeds.

Conifers
These form seeds in cones. Many have needle-like leaves.

Flowering plants
To reproduce, these plants grow flowers to attract pollinators.

HOW PLANTS WORK

Most plants have stems that support them, roots that suck up water and nutrients, and leaves that capture the sun's energy. Tubes in the stem transport water, nutrients, and energy in the form of sugars around the plant.

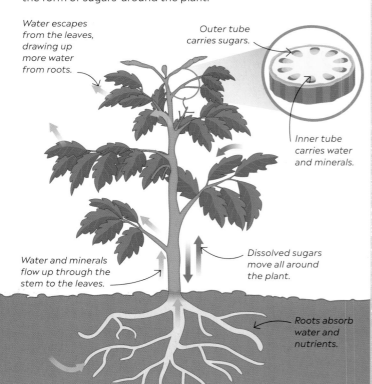

Water escapes from the leaves, drawing up more water from roots.

Outer tube carries sugars.

Inner tube carries water and minerals.

Water and minerals flow up through the stem to the leaves.

Dissolved sugars move all around the plant.

Roots absorb water and nutrients.

GIANT PUMPKIN

Around 200 plant species are grown for food. Some people grow gargantuan vegetables to enter into competitions. This prize-winning pumpkin weighs as much as a small car. It took 79 gallons (300 liters) of water a day to reach its 2,656 lb (1,205 kg) size.

The pumpkin has a thick skin that holds water in and protects its flesh.

Pumpkins grow on sprawling vines.

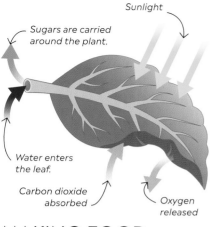

Sugars are carried around the plant.

Sunlight

Water enters the leaf.

Carbon dioxide absorbed

Oxygen released

MAKING **FOOD**

Plants use the energy from sunlight to convert water and carbon dioxide into oxygen and sugars. This process, called photosynthesis, takes place in leaves, with the help of the green pigment chlorophyll.

FLESH-EATING PLANTS

The Venus flytrap snaps shut to catch insects, such as this unfortunate wasp. When prey lands on the leaf, it triggers sensitive hairs, causing the leaf to close. This flytrap is one of 630 known species of meat-eating plants.

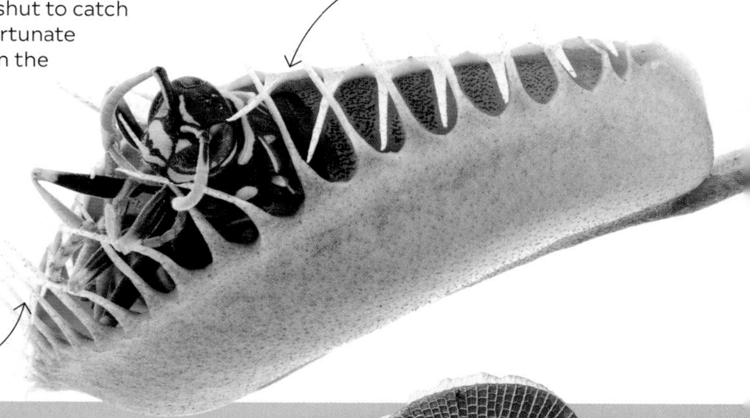

Long, finger-like cilia hold the wasp.

The flytrap digests the wasp for nutrients.

THE **FLOATING LEAVES** OF THE **GIANT WATERLILY** *VICTORIA BOLIVIANA* CAN REACH **10.5 FT** (3.2 M) **WIDE!**

One-year-old twins are dwarfed by the monstrous pumpkin.

Coiling tendrils search for support.

CLIMBING PLANTS

Climbing plants, such as this passion flower, grow by twining up and around a support to reach the light. Most plants are rooted to one spot, but many move toward light, water, or nutrients to increase their odds of survival.

Passion flower

PLANTS OUTWEIGH ALL OTHER **FORMS OF LIFE** ON EARTH!

FLOWER **SHAPES**

Flowers come in many shapes, sizes, and colors to attract bees, butterflies, and other insects. Here are some examples of the different types.

Cone-shaped
Bright yellow daffodils have six petals around a frilled trumpet.

Star-shaped
A ring of petals radiates from the center of colorful gerberas.

Bell-shaped
Purple campanulas are cup-shaped with five petals splaying out.

Dome-shaped
Hydrangeas have big flower heads made up of lots of little flowers.

Rosette-shaped
Roses have several rows of petals, arranged in whorls or circles.

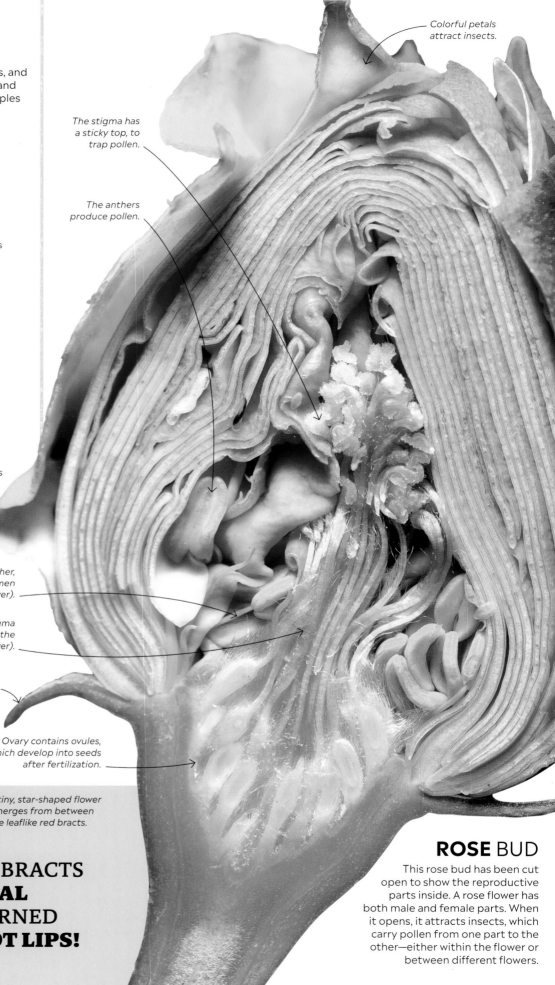

Colorful petals attract insects.

The stigma has a sticky top, to trap pollen.

The anthers produce pollen.

Filament supports the anther, together forming the stamen (male part of the flower).

Tubelike style connects the stigma to the ovary, together forming the pistil (female part of the flower).

Sepal protects the flower.

Ovary contains ovules, which develop into seeds after fertilization.

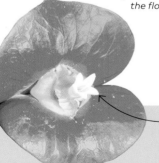

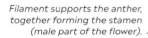

A tiny, star-shaped flower emerges from between the leaflike red bracts.

THE **SHINY RED** BRACTS OF THIS **TROPICAL PLANT** HAVE EARNED IT THE NAME **HOT LIPS!**

ROSE BUD

This rose bud has been cut open to show the reproductive parts inside. A rose flower has both male and female parts. When it opens, it attracts insects, which carry pollen from one part to the other—either within the flower or between different flowers.

Fabulous flowers

Flowering plants make up 90 percent of all plants on Earth. They produce a huge variety of stunning flowers to reproduce. When flowers are pollinated, seeds form that in turn grow into new plants.

The lemur spreads banana pollen on its fur.

THE **SEED** OF THE **COCO-DE-MER** PALM IS THE **HEAVIEST** IN THE WORLD, **WEIGHING** UP TO **55 LB** (25 KG)!

BEASTLY POLLINATION

The most common pollinators are insects, which transfer pollen as they feed. But other animals, including bats, hummingbirds, and this red-ruffed lemur, can also be pollinators.

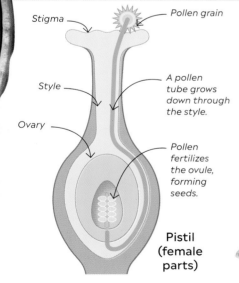

Stigma — Pollen grain

Style — A pollen tube grows down through the style.

Ovary — Pollen fertilizes the ovule, forming seeds.

Pistil (female parts)

BEE ORCHID

Some flowering plants have evolved unusual methods to attract insect pollinators. This bee orchid has parts that look like bees, luring real bees in.

HORNED MELON

Many flowering plants disperse their seeds by producing delicious fruit, such as this horned melon. Animals eat the fruit and poop out the seeds in a different location.

FLOWER FERTILIZATION

When pollen lands on a flower's stigma, it grows a tiny tube through the style, carrying male pollen to the female ovary, where fertilization happens. The seeds develop and the ovary becomes a fruit.

THE **CORPSE FLOWER** IS THE WORLD'S **LARGEST FLOWER**, AT UP TO **3 FT** (1 M) **ACROSS!**

Corpse flower has no leaves, stems, or roots and grows on tropical vines.

POISONOUS PLANTS

While many plants provide food for animals and people, some are toxic if swallowed. Never pick or eat leaves, fruits, or berries unless you know what they are.

☠ MANCHINEEL
Known as "apples of death," the fruit of this tree can fatally blister the mouth and throat.

☠ CASTOR BEAN
The beans of this plant contain a deadly poison, ricin. Tiny amounts can kill an adult.

☠ NIGHTSHADE
This plant's berries cause slurred speech, blurred vision, and hallucinations.

☠ LARKSPUR
These pretty flowers burn the mouth, cause vomiting, and can kill by suffocation.

☠ NARCISSUS
The onion-like bulbs of these cheerful spring flowers can cause convulsions if eaten.

FLESH-EATERS

This meat-eating sundew plant has sticky tendrils to trap insects. The leaf then curls around the insect to digest it. A sundew can kill an insect in minutes but takes weeks to finish it off.

SUNDEW

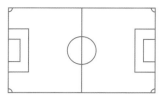

BIGGEST PLANT

The biggest plant in the world is a seagrass off Australia's Shark Bay. It extends nearly 77 sq miles (200 sq km)—an area the size of 30,000 football fields.

PLANTS IN SPACE

NASA scientists have been growing plants in a garden on the International Space Station (ISS). They have grown three types of lettuce, to ward off scurvy in astronauts by boosting the vitamin C in their diet, and zinnias to see how flowering plants grow in space.

STAT ATTACK!
PLANTS

From lethal leaves to healing herbs and foul smells, many plants have astonishing properties. They are among the largest living organisms on Earth and some of the oldest too.

TALLEST TREES

This lineup includes the tallest tree on every continent—some of them taller than the Statue of Liberty. The exact location of the world's tallest-known tree is kept secret to protect it. The tree stands in Redwood National Park in Northern California.

KARRI Karri, Portugal
239.2 ft (72.9 m)

MUYOVU Muyovu, Tanzania
267.4 ft (81.5 m)

GENERAL SHERMAN
Giant redwood, US
274.9 ft (83.8 m)

ANGEL'S HEART
Red angelim, Brazil
290.35 ft (88.5 m)

STATUE OF LIBERTY
New York, US
305 ft (93 m)

PRICEY PLANTS

Bonsai trees are living works of art. A centuries-old white pine bonsai sold for ¥100 million ($13,000) at a bonsai convention in Japan in 2011.

¥100 million

Bamboos are the **fastest growing** of all plants. Some species can grow up to **35 in (91 cm)** per **day,** or around **1.2 in (3 cm)** per **hour!**

MEDICINAL PLANTS

For thousands of years, people have used plants to treat ailments from colds and flu to anxiety. Today, plant extracts are used in conventional medicine too.

WATER HYSSOP
May help protect the brain from aging.

WILLOW BARK
The active ingredient in aspirin, used to treat pain and fever.

SNOWDROPS
Can slow memory loss caused by Alzheimer's disease.

OLDEST TREES

Some trees have lived for thousands of years, since the time of the ancient Egyptian civilization.

1 BRISTLECONE PINE
Over 4,850 years old; California, US

2 ALERCE
Over 3,625 years old; Los Ríos, Chile

3 BALD CYPRESS
Over 2,625 years old; North Carolina, US

4 QILIAN JUNIPER
Over 2,235 years old; Qinghai, China

5 BODHI TREE
Over 2,220 years old; Anuradhapura, Sri Lanka

BRISTLECONE PINE

FOUL FLOWERS

Some flowers smell like rotting flesh to attract carrion flies, which help pollinate them.

TITAN ARUM
This large flower is known as the corpse flower for its carrion stench.

RAFFLESIA ARNOLDII
Also called a corpse flower, this large tropical flower gives off a rotten stink.

DEHERAINIA SMARAGDINA
The putrid smell of this green flower has also been compared to that of smelly feet.

DRAGON LILY
This tall purplish lily is also known as a stink lily for its dead-meat smell.

CENTURION
Mountain ash, Australia
327.5 ft (99.8 m)

MENARA
Yellow meranti, Malaysia
330.7 ft (100.8 m)

HYPERION
Coastal redwood, US
380.8 ft (116.1 m)

Tall flower spike gives off heat to spread the smell of rotting flesh.

Petal-like collar is flesh-colored on the inside.

TITAN ARUM

The fungus's mycelium network extends 3.7 sq miles (9.65 sq km).

A **HONEY FUNGUS** IN OREGON IS ONE OF THE **BIGGEST LIVING THINGS** ON EARTH!

WHAT IS A **FUNGUS?**

The bulk of a fungus lies underground, as a vast network of thread-like hyphae that form a web called the mycelium. The mushrooms we see above ground are the fruit bodies of some fungi, which grow from spores.

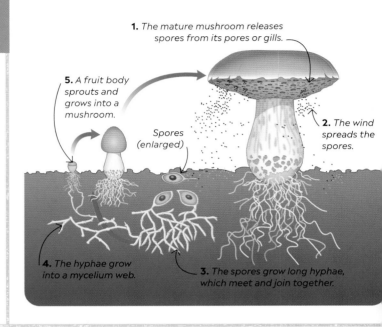

1. *The mature mushroom releases spores from its pores or gills.*

5. *A fruit body sprouts and grows into a mushroom.*

Spores (enlarged)

2. *The wind spreads the spores.*

4. *The hyphae grow into a mycelium web.*

3. *The spores grow long hyphae, which meet and join together.*

EXPLOSIVE **PUFFBALL**

Puffballs store their spores in a ball-shaped sac, which releases the spores like puffs of smoke if squeezed. This stalked puffball-in-aspic grows in a protective layer of jelly. The more common giant puffball releases up to 7 trillion spores.

Jellylike layer

MIGHTY **MUSHROOMS**

Mushrooms come in many shapes, sizes, and colors. Different mushrooms have different ways of spreading their spores. This selection of strange-looking specimens gives a glimpse of the huge variety.

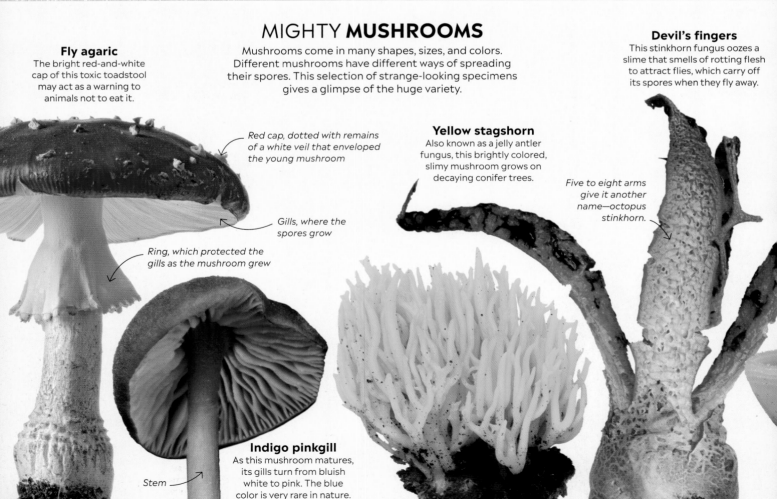

Fly agaric
The bright red-and-white cap of this toxic toadstool may act as a warning to animals not to eat it.

Red cap, dotted with remains of a white veil that enveloped the young mushroom

Gills, where the spores grow

Ring, which protected the gills as the mushroom grew

Yellow stagshorn
Also known as a jelly antler fungus, this brightly colored, slimy mushroom grows on decaying conifer trees.

Devil's fingers
This stinkhorn fungus oozes a slime that smells of rotting flesh to attract flies, which carry off its spores when they fly away.

Five to eight arms give it another name—octopus stinkhorn.

Indigo pinkgill
As this mushroom matures, its gills turn from bluish white to pink. The blue color is very rare in nature.

Stem

Fantastic **fungi**

Fungi may look like plants, but they are in fact more closely related to animals. They play a vital role in life on Earth, breaking down matter to release energy and nutrients. Some form edible mushrooms—but beware of toxic toadstools.

GHOST FUNGUS

This is one of more than 100 species of fungus that glow in the dark. Scientists think they do this to attract insects, which help spread the fungi's spores.

TYPES OF **FUNGUS**

Scientists have identified 144,000 fungus species, but there may be as many as 4 million. They range from microscopic molds to massive mushrooms. These are the four main groups.

FUNGI AND **TREES** FORM AN **UNDERGROUND NETWORK** CALLED THE **WOOD WIDE WEB**. THEY USE IT TO **COMMUNICATE** AND **SHARE FOOD!**

Mushrooms
These are the fruit bodies of one group of fungi. They make spores, which grow into new fungi.

Sac fungi
This is the largest group of fungi. They produce their spores in tiny containers or sacs.

Mold
These fuzzy-looking fungi consist of hyphae, which rot plant and animal matter.

Yeast
These single-celled fungi feed on sugar and produce carbon dioxide. Some are used to make bread rise.

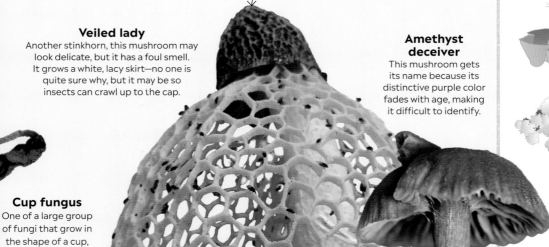

Slimy cap attracts insects, which spread spores on their feet.

Veiled lady
Another stinkhorn, this mushroom may look delicate, but it has a foul smell. It grows a white, lacy skirt—no one is quite sure why, but it may be so insects can crawl up to the cap.

Amethyst deceiver
This mushroom gets its name because its distinctive purple color fades with age, making it difficult to identify.

Cup fungus
One of a large group of fungi that grow in the shape of a cup, these colorful mushrooms carry spores on their inner surface.

Cup, where spores grow

FAST FUNGUS!

The hat-throwing fungus squirts off its spores at up to 55 mph (90 km/h). They reach their top speed faster than a bullet!

Invertebrates

Invertebrates are creatures that do not have a backbone or skeleton inside them. They make up 97 percent of animals and range from tiny insects to giant squids with tentacles more than 35 ft (10 m) long.

UP TO **90,000 ROUNDWORMS** CAN LIVE ON ONE ROTTEN APPLE!

Microscopic worms feed on bacteria in the fruit.

TYPES OF **INVERTEBRATE**

Invertebrates are incredibly varied. There are more than 30 main groups. Here are six of the most common.

Mollusks
Most mollusks, such as snails and oysters, have shells, but some, such as slugs and squids, do not.

Cnidarians
Jellyfish, anemones, and corals (left) are aquatic animals armed with stinging tentacles.

Annelids
Worms with segmented bodies, these include earthworms, leeches, and marine bristle worms.

Echinoderms
These sea-dwellers have spiny bodies. They include sea stars (left), sea urchins, and sea cucumbers.

Sponges
Very simple animals, sponges are fixed to the seabed and filter food from water.

Arthropods
The largest group, this includes crustaceans and insects, with tough external skeletons and jointed legs.

GIANT **CLAM**

These massive mollusks have shells that can grow 4.5 ft (1.4 m) long. They feed off sugars made by tiny algae that live in their soft tissues.

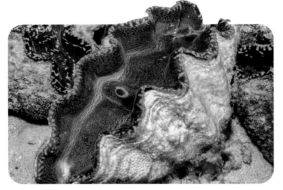

SEA **STINGERS**

Often mistaken for plants, sea anemones are predatory animals that grip onto the sea floor. Their stinging tentacles paralyze prey such as tiny fish or plankton and then guide it into their mouth.

FIGHTING **CRABS**

Male Sally Lightfoot crabs battle for females by trying to break off each other's claws. The victorious crustacean chases away his rival and claims the female as his mate.

Young crabs have dark shells for camouflage.

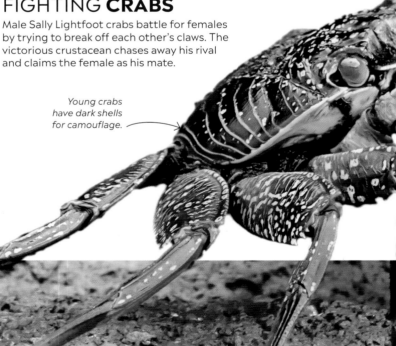

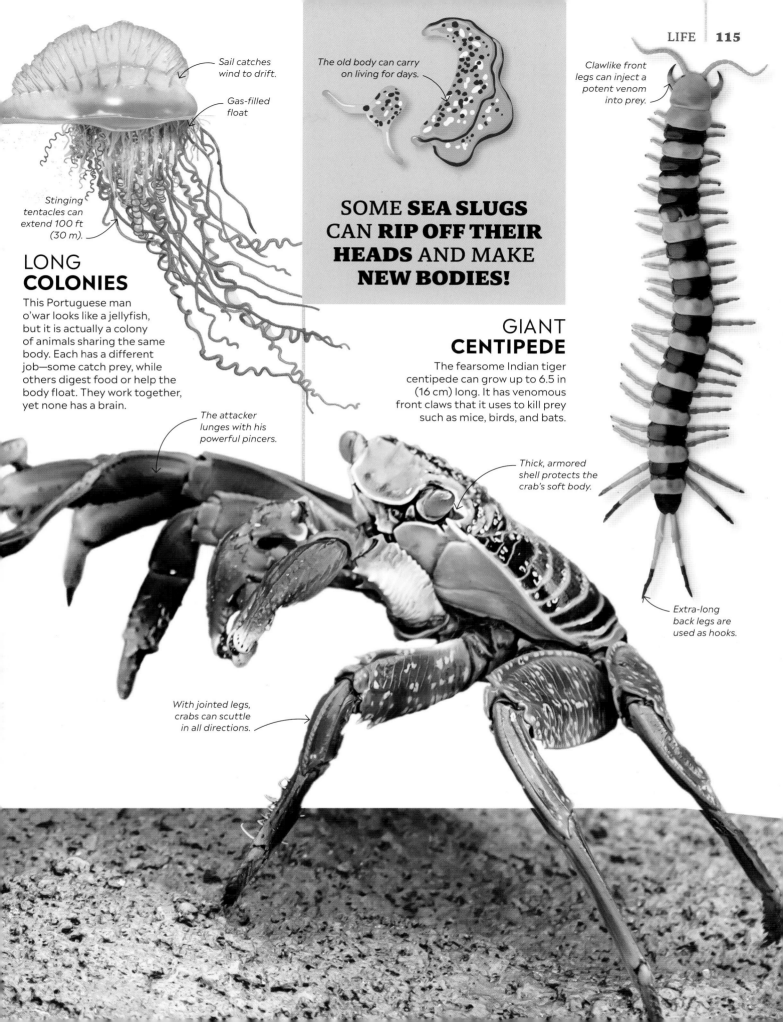

Sail catches wind to drift.

Gas-filled float

Stinging tentacles can extend 100 ft (30 m).

LONG COLONIES

This Portuguese man o'war looks like a jellyfish, but it is actually a colony of animals sharing the same body. Each has a different job—some catch prey, while others digest food or help the body float. They work together, yet none has a brain.

The old body can carry on living for days.

SOME **SEA SLUGS** CAN **RIP OFF THEIR HEADS** AND MAKE **NEW BODIES!**

Clawlike front legs can inject a potent venom into prey.

GIANT CENTIPEDE

The fearsome Indian tiger centipede can grow up to 6.5 in (16 cm) long. It has venomous front claws that it uses to kill prey such as mice, birds, and bats.

The attacker lunges with his powerful pincers.

Thick, armored shell protects the crab's soft body.

Extra-long back legs are used as hooks.

With jointed legs, crabs can scuttle in all directions.

Clever creatures

Cephalopods—octopuses, squids, and their relatives—are agile, sharp-eyed hunters with highly developed brains and clever strategies to avoid predators.

SHELL SUIT

This veined octopus hides in an old clam shell to avoid predators and waits to ambush prey. Other species of these intelligent animals can change color for camouflage or squirt ink to deter attackers.

DUMBO OCTOPUS

So called because their fins look like elephant ears, these unusual octopuses live at incredible depths of up to 4 miles (7 km).

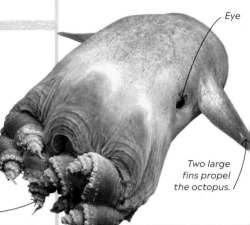

Eye

Two large fins propel the octopus.

Eight short arms help the octopus to steer.

1. Mobile shelter
The octopus finds a shell and, using its long arms as legs, walks it along the sea floor to a good spot for hunting.

The octopus grasps the shell with its arms.

GIANT SQUID EYES ARE THE LARGEST OF ANY ANIMAL!

Human eye

Whale eye

Squid eye

TYPES OF CEPHALOPODS

All cephalopods have arms or tentacles and some have both. Most move fast through water using jet propulsion—shooting out water at speed to push themselves forward. There are four main groups.

Cuttlefish
Cuttlefish have a buoyant internal shell and a big brain relative to their size.

Squid
Tube-shaped squids have two long tentacles, as well as arms like those of an octopus.

FLYING **SQUIDS**

To escape predators, Japanese flying squids can jet-propel themselves 100 ft (30 m) through the air. Once airborne, they glide by flattening their tail fins and spreading out their arms.

Suckers on the arms help catch prey.

THIS **DEADLY,** SUPER-VENOMOUS OCTOPUS **WARNS** OFF **PREDATORS** WITH FLASHING **BLUE RINGS!**

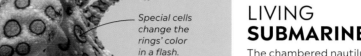

Special cells change the rings' color in a flash.

LIVING **SUBMARINE**

The chambered nautilus is the closest thing the natural world has to a submarine. It rises and sinks by letting gas and water out of chambers in its shell.

2. Hiding place
It holds onto the inside of the shell with its suckers and folds its long arms in.

The octopus keeps a watchful eye on its surroundings.

3. Lying in ambush
It is safe and ready to spring into action when prey, such as crabs or shrimp, approaches.

Nautilus
These tropical creatures are the only cephalopods with an external shell.

Octopus
With blue blood, three hearts, eight arms, and nine brains, octopuses are truly amazing!

TWO-TONE **SQUID!**

Male Caribbean reef squids turn red to attract females and white to scare off rivals. They can even turn two-tone: red on one side and white on the other! Here, two males are competing for a female (not seen).

Insect world

Insects are the largest group of animals on Earth. More than a million species of insects have been identified—and scientists estimate there could be 10 times as many.

SUPER **SIGHT**

This iridescent tiger beetle has "compound" eyes, which enable it to spot rapid movement. It also has almost 360-degree vision. This super sight helps it to avoid attack.

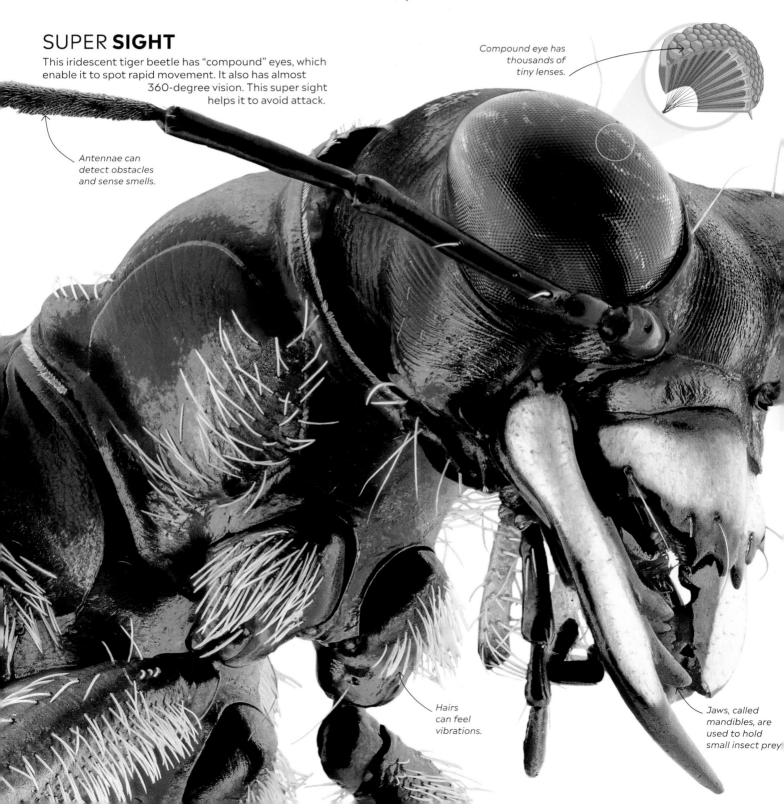

Compound eye has thousands of tiny lenses.

Antennae can detect obstacles and sense smells.

Hairs can feel vibrations.

Jaws, called mandibles, are used to hold small insect prey

Four wings move independently to control flight.

Bristly legs for grip

AERIAL ATTACKER

Many insects have wings, but dragonflies are the most aerodynamic of all, making them lethal hunters. They can control the speed and angle of each wing to change direction, hover, or catch prey midair.

TYPES OF INSECTS

There are around 30 main insect groups. Most species belong to one of the seven shown here.

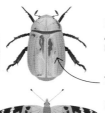

Beetles
Around 350,000 known species

Tough forewings

Butterflies and moths
Around 160,000 known species

Ants, bees, and wasps
Around 150,000 known species

Dragonflies and damselflies
Around 5,600 known species

Crickets and grasshoppers
Around 24,000 known species

Two wings

Flies
Around 152,000 known species

True bugs
Around 100,000 known species

BIG BUG

One of the heaviest insects in the world is the giant weta, a colossal cricket found in New Zealand. They can weigh up to 2.5 oz (71 g), which is about the same as three mice.

A QUARTER OF ALL **KNOWN ANIMAL** SPECIES ARE **BEETLES!**

Checkered beetles are found all over the world.

BUTTERFLY **SWARM**

Every year, millions of monarch butterflies undertake one of the most epic migrations of any animal, 3,000 miles (5,000 km) from Canada to Mexico, and back. It takes up to five generations to complete the round trip.

WHAT IS AN **INSECT?**

Insects are a diverse group, but most share some key features. All have an exoskeleton (outer skeleton) and a body divided into three parts—the head, thorax, and abdomen.

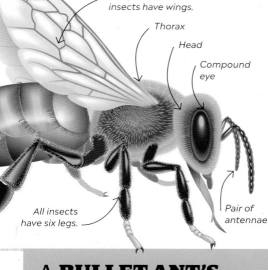

Many but not all insects have wings.

Thorax

Head

Compound eye

Abdomen

Stinger

All insects have six legs.

Pair of antennae

Beetle rolls dung with its back legs

DUNG **BEETLE**

Some insects eat plants, nectar, or other insects, but dung beetles feed on poop. Many roll balls of it into their underground tunnels, while others live in the dung!

A **BULLET ANT'S STING** CAUSES A **SEARING PAIN** THAT LASTS **25 HOURS!**

NAME THAT... INSECT

Put your bug-hunting skills to the test and see how many insects you can recognize. Can you spot the odd one out?

1 Tiger butterfly
2 Swallowtail butterfly caterpillar
3 Red admiral butterfly
4 Potter bee
5 Blue morpho butterfly
6 Goliath birdwing butterfly
7 Himalayan cicada
8 Madagascan moon moth
9 Banana eater butterfly
10 Leaf insect
11 Dampwood termite
12 Red ants
13 Scarlet tiger moth caterpillar
14 Brimstone moth
15 Emperor dragonfly
16 Red wood ants
17 Owl moth
18 Emerald damselfly
19 Lantern bug
20 Leafhopper
21 Glowworm
22 Bed bug
23 Giant water bug
24 Crane fly
25 Neon cuckoo bee
26 Rainbow locust
27 Woodlouse
28 Giraffe weevil
29 Oak bush cricket
30 Hornet moth
31 Hover fly
32 Jewel wasp
33 Yellowjacket wasp
34 Robber fly
35 Bumblebee
36 Hissing cockroach
37 Honey bee
38 Cinnabar moth
39 Stink bug
40 Goliath beetle
41 Mosquito
42 Desert locust
43 Ladybugs
44 Rhinoceros beetle
45 Jewel scarab beetle
46 Atlas moth caterpillar
47 Assassin bug
48 Stag beetle
49 Pond skater
50 Leaf katydid

The woodlouse (27) is the odd one out. It is a crustacean, related to crabs and shrimp, and not an insect.

THE **BITE** OF A **SYDNEY FUNNEL-WEB SPIDER** CAN **KILL** A HUMAN!

Baby spiders

BABY **BOOM**

When baby wolf spiders hatch, their mother carries them around on her back to keep them safe. She can carry more than a hundred spiderlings at a time.

Super spiders

There are more than 45,000 known species of spiders. They are clever hunters that either spin complex webs to catch prey or ambush their victims before killing them with venomous fangs. Most are harmless to humans.

JUMPING SPIDER

Tiny jumping spiders are only about 0.2 in (5 mm) long. They may not look like much to the naked eye, but seen up close, the males are brightly colored to attract females.

Two primary eyes see detail and, unusually for a spider, color.

Secondary eyes give 360-degree vision.

Legs can straighten at explosive speeds to make the spider spring through the air.

Hairy, arm-like structures are used to hold prey.

Hairs on the legs allow the spider to hear sounds from a long way away.

SPINNING A **WEB**

Different spiders spin different webs to catch insect prey. Surprisingly, more than half of all spider species do not make webs but hunt food in other ways.

Orb web
These flat, round webs with a circular pattern spiraling out from the center are the most familiar type of web.

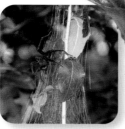

Zigzag web
Zigzag patterns may help camouflage the spider or stop birds from flying into the web.

Tangled web
Some webs are blankets of randomly placed threads. They look messy but are hard to escape from.

CATCHING A **MEAL**

Once this lobed argiope spider has caught its prey, it wraps it tightly in silk and injects it with digestive juices, turning its meal liquid. Then the spider drinks its dinner.

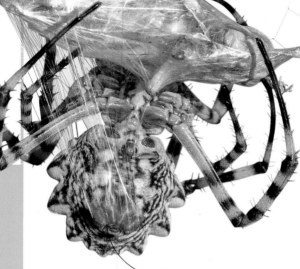

Silk is stored in the spider's body as a liquid but becomes solid and incredibly strong in contact with air.

TARANTULAS FLING TINY, **IRRITATING HAIRS** THAT **STING** THE **SKIN** AND **EYES** OF **PREDATORS!**

INSIDE A **SPIDER**

Spiders' bodies are divided into two parts. The smaller, front part of the body anchors the spider's eight legs. The larger, back body part contains the silk gland, or spinneret. A hard exoskeleton encases the vital organs.

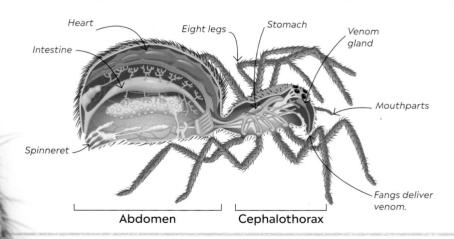

Heart

Intestine

Eight legs

Stomach

Venom gland

Mouthparts

Spinneret

Fangs deliver venom.

Abdomen | Cephalothorax

POWERFUL **JAWS!**

Camel spiders are arachnids with powerful jaws. They hunt bugs, using their jaws to saw their prey up before they swallow, unlike spiders, which digest before swallowing.

Jaws grasp crustacean.

OTHER ARACHNIDS

Spiders belong to a group of animals known as arachnids. They all have two body parts, usually eight jointed legs, and a tough external skeleton.

Scorpions
These fearsome arachnids have pincers to grab hold of their prey and a flexible tail with a venomous sting.

Ticks and mites
Ticks are blood-sucking parasites. Mites are so tiny they cannot be seen with the naked eye.

Whip scorpions
Hunting at night, these arachnids walk on their back six legs and use the first pair as antennae.

Daddy long legs
This arachnid has extremely long legs. Females carry their eggs around in their mouths.

Fish tales

There are around 32,000 species of fish swimming in Earth's waters, with staggering diversity among them. From tiny minnows in tropical swamps to massive whale sharks cruising in sunlit seas, they survive in some surprising ways.

Tail fin propels fish forward.

Lateral line senses movement.

Dorsal fin helps fish swim straight.

Water flows into mouth.

Anal fin stabilizes fish.

Swim bladder acts as a float.

Gills extract oxygen from water

Pelvic fins and pectoral fins help fish steer.

INSIDE A **FISH**

There are three main groups of fish: bony fish, cartilaginous fish such as sharks and rays (see pages 126–129), and jawless fish like the sea lamprey. The illustration above shows the anatomy of a typical bony fish, by far the most common kind.

SWIMMING **SCHOOL**

Many kinds of fish swim together in groups, called shoals. Shoaling can increase the fishes' chance of spotting danger and evading predators. If a shoal is made up of one species, such as these reef-dwelling oriental sweetlips, it is known as a school.

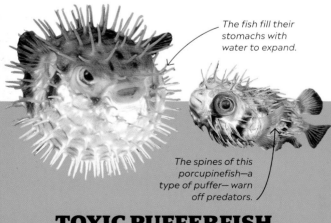

The fish fill their stomachs with water to expand.

The spines of this porcupinefish—a type of puffer—warn off predators.

TOXIC PUFFERFISH CAN INFLATE INTO A SPINY BALL TO SCARE PREDATORS!

Colorful dorsal fin is raised to attract a mate.

Muscular pectoral fins can be used for jumping, walking, and climbing.

Anal fin helps the male fish leap up to 2 ft (60 cm) in the air.

MALE YELLOWHEAD JAWFISH BROOD EGGS IN THEIR MOUTH!

Male fish spread their tail fins to look bigger and attract females.

FRILLY FIGHTERS

Many tropical fish are brilliantly colored to attract mates, repel rivals, and hide from predators. Siamese fighting fish like this one have been selectively bred for their fabulous colors and frilly fins for at least a thousand years.

WHAT IS A **FISH?**

There are more species of fish than all the other backboned animals—mammals, birds, reptiles, and amphibians—put together. But although they are many and varied, all fish have certain features in common.

Vertebrate
All fish have a backbone and most have a bony skeleton.

Cold-blooded
The vast majority of fish are cold-blooded. An exception is the moonfish.

Gills
Fish absorb oxygen into their blood from water flowing through their gills.

Live in water
All but a few fish live in water. A handful of amphibious fish can survive out of water.

Scaly skin
Tough scales protect fish's delicate skin, overlapping to allow movement.

FISH **OUT OF WATER**

While most fish swim and cannot survive out of water, a few can "walk" and breathe on land. These blue-spotted mudskippers crawl across mudflats, using their fins as legs. They can stay on land for hours, absorbing oxygen through their skin.

Female fish have elongated spines on their dorsal fins.

VAMPIRE OF THE SEA!

The jawless sea lamprey is a parasite. It latches on to bony fish, using its rough tongues to rasp away the flesh of its host to feed on its body fluids and blood.

Shark attack

Skillful predators, some sharks are at the top of the ocean food chain. They hunt fish and other sea life, including birds and turtles. In spite of a chilling reputation, sharks include gentle giants and smaller species that rely on their senses for defense as much as attack.

INSIDE A **SHARK**

Sharks are fish with skeletons made not of bone but of cartilage—a tough, bendy tissue like that in human ears. Keen senses help them hunt. A powerful tail and fins propel and steer them in water.

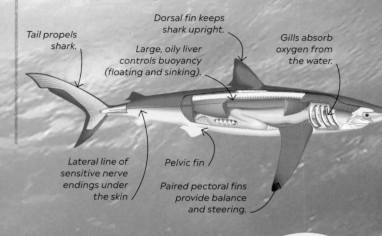

Tail propels shark.

Dorsal fin keeps shark upright.

Large, oily liver controls buoyancy (floating and sinking).

Gills absorb oxygen from the water.

Lateral line of sensitive nerve endings under the skin

Pelvic fin

Paired pectoral fins provide balance and steering.

SUPER **SENSES**

This hammerhead shark is hunting for prey such as smaller fish, squid, and crustaceans. Sharks have the amazing ability to detect electrical signals given off by living things, through a set of pores in their snout. Their lateral line picks up vibrations in the water.

Shark skin is made up of tiny toothlike scales covered with enamel.

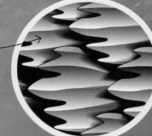

Hammerhead sharks' eyes are set on the sides of their heads, giving them a wide field of vision.

A lateral line of nerves along the side of the body picks up vibrations made by prey.

A pale underside makes the shark hard to see from below.

MONSTER MANTA RAY

The giant oceanic manta ray is a relative of the shark. The largest have a wingspan (the distance between the tips of its two fins) that can reach 23 ft (7 m) across.

Huge, triangular fin

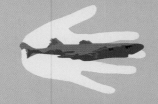

THE **DWARF LANTERN SHARK** IS THE **SMALLEST SHARK**, AT JUST **8 IN** (20 CM) LONG!

BIRTH OF A SHARK

Sharks reproduce in three different ways. Some lay eggs that hatch outside the mother's body, while others lay eggs, but the eggs hatch inside the mother's body. Others give birth to live young.

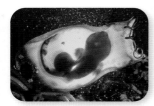

Swell shark
These sharks lay eggs in pouches. The embryo develops inside this "mermaid's purse."

Spiny dogfish
These sharks develop inside eggs inside the mother. This newborn still has its yolk sac.

Lemon shark
In these sharks, the young grow inside the mother and are fully developed at birth.

SHARK RELATIVES

Sharks are not the only cartilaginous fish. There are two other groups: chimaeras, and skates and rays. Sharks are the biggest group, containing hundreds of species.

Chimaeras
These fish mainly live in the deep sea. Big eyes help them find their way around in the dark.

Ratfish

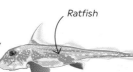

Common stingray

Skates and rays
These fish have wide, flat bodies. Many have long thin tails.

Sharks
Most sharks have sharp teeth, strong senses, and powerful jaws.

Leopard shark

GHOST SHARKS FIRST SWAM THE SEAS 420 MILLION YEARS AGO— LONG **BEFORE** THE DINOSAURS EVOLVED!

Snout used to search for prey in the sand

SHARK TEETH

This sand tiger shark's teeth grow in three ragged rows. When they fall out, there are more rows ready to replace them. Some sharks get through 30,000 teeth in their lifetime.

Small pores on the snout called ampullae of Lorenzini detect electrical currents given off by fish.

The teeth are pointed, with sharp tips and serrated edges.

Pointy head and cone-shaped snout

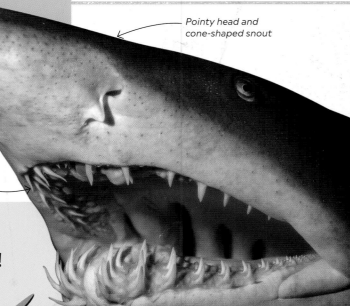

BLACKTIP REEF SHARKS CAN **SENSE PREY** 0.6 MILES (1 KM) AWAY!

Dr. Brad Norman is the founder of ECOCEAN, which is a citizen science program to monitor whale sharks. He is a Research Fellow at Murdoch University in Western Australia.

OPEN WIDE

The biggest fish in the world, whale sharks can be up to 40 ft (12 m) long, but they are gentle giants that eat tiny plankton. Small fish often swim alongside them for protection. Every whale shark has a unique pattern of spots and lines that can be used to identify it, just like a fingerprint.

Ask a...
MARINE BIOLOGIST

Q What is your work with whale sharks?

A I set up the ECOCEAN library in 1995 to monitor whale sharks. This has now become the Sharkbook and has input from citizen scientists in more than 50 countries. Anyone with a waterproof camera can help research whale sharks, by taking a photo if they spot one when diving and uploading it to Sharkbook.

Q What is the most interesting thing you have learned?

A We've identified thousands of individuals so far and we've been able to identify "hot spots" for whale sharks—places that are important habitats for them—but, surprisingly, we still don't know where they breed. It is also very rare to see very small or very large whale sharks.

Q Do whale sharks travel far?

A They can travel thousands of miles, but some whale sharks return to the same place every year, like Stumpy (the first whale shark I ever swam with, back in 1995)—he's been coming back to Ningaloo Reef in Western Australia for more than 25 years.

Q What is it like to dive with whale sharks?

A It's a truly amazing experience! Life-changing for me. I've been swimming with the big fish for nearly 30 years—and I'm not stopping anytime soon. Sometimes a shark is a little curious (which is fun, not scary), but mostly they swim along ignoring you.

Q Does swimming with whale sharks disturb them?

A If you're swimming with whale sharks, swim alongside them but give them plenty of room— don't crowd them or swim in front of them. Always stay a minimum of 10 ft (3 m) away from the shark—and don't try to touch them. This is for your safety as well as theirs.

Q How can we protect whale sharks?

A Keeping the oceans healthy is the best way to protect whale sharks. Everyone can make a difference by reducing waste and respecting the planet as a whole.

Q What advice would you give to an aspiring marine biologist?

A Go with your passion. If you love oceans, make it your goal to help however you can.

WHAT IS AN AMPHIBIAN?

All amphibians are air-breathing, cold-blooded vertebrates with thin, smooth skins. Most lay eggs and spend part of their lives in water.

Vertebrate
All amphibians have a backbone and internal skeleton made of bone.

Cold-blooded
The body temperature of amphibians is the same as their surroundings.

Lay eggs
Most amphibians lay soft eggs in damp places where they cannot dry out.

Aquatic young
Amphibians begin life in water, growing into adults that can also live on land.

Moist skin
All amphibians can breathe underwater through their thin, moist skins.

FROG **SONG**

Some frog species, like this marsh frog, have vocal sacs—pouches of skin that fill with air to amplify sounds. Frog calls can be heard as far as 1 mile (1.6 km) away!

Dragonfly is a tempting meal for insect-eating frogs.

Frog

Tadpole

PARADOXICAL FROG!

Most frog species develop from an egg to a small tadpole to a large adult frog. Paradoxical frog tadpoles grow supersize, then shrink into an adult frog one-third of their size.

Blue-green back provides camouflage if seen from above.

Bulging eyes give frogs a wide field of view.

Bright colors on underside warn off predators.

Sticky toe pads help frogs cling to branch.

Toes are used to grip.

Long, powerful back legs

AMERICAN **BULLFROGS** CAN LEAP **20 TIMES** THEIR OWN **BODY LENGTH!**

The biggest frogs, bullfrogs grow up to 6 in (15 cm) long.

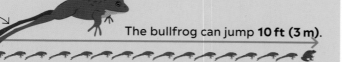

The bullfrog can jump **10 ft (3 m)**.

GIANT **CAECILIAN**

There are nearly 200 known species of caecilians. This 5 ft (1.5 m) long giant is the biggest. Like most caecilians, it is a powerful digger.

Hard, pointed head to burrow through earth

Needle-sharp teeth help capture prey.

Amphibian antics

Amphibians evolved from fish millions of years ago and have an amazing ability—when adult, most can live both on land and in water.

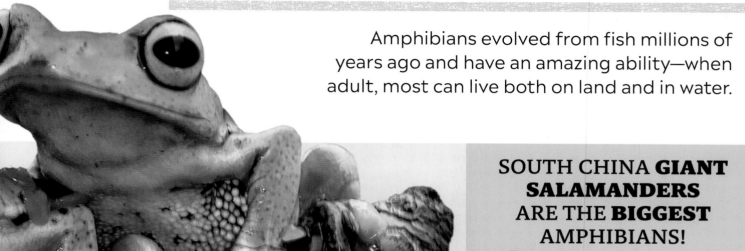

Partially webbed feet

SOUTH CHINA **GIANT SALAMANDERS** ARE THE **BIGGEST** AMPHIBIANS!

The giant salamander is **6 ft (1.8 m) long.**

CRESTED **NEWT**

Young amphibians, like this great crested newt, live underwater, breathing through their gills. Later, the gills shrink and they breathe through their lungs, so they can leave the water.

Long, feathery gills →

TREE FROGS

These Reinwardt's frogs live high in the moist rainforest canopy. They grasp onto trees with wide feet and can also glide from tree to tree, using their webbed feet like parachutes. The frogs lay eggs on leaves over water, so the tadpoles drop in when they emerge.

TYPES OF AMPHIBIANS

There are only three groups of amphibians, but they look very different from one another. Altogether, there are about 8,100 amphibian species.

Caecilians
Wormlike, limbless caecilians live underground or in water. They are rarely seen.

Salamanders and newts
These lizardlike creatures have long tails and four limbs.

Frogs and toads
The largest group, frogs and toads have long back legs and shorter front legs.

Reptiles rule

TYPES OF REPTILES

There are four main groups of reptiles, but one of these contains just two living species—the tuataras.

Lizards and snakes
This is the largest group. It contains a variety of leathery lizards and limbless snakes.

Tortoises and turtles
Easy to recognize with their domed shells, turtles live in water and tortoises on land.

Crocodilians
Crocodiles, alligators, and caimans are some of the most formidable reptiles. They live mainly in water.

Tuataras
These lizard-like reptiles are the only survivors of a group that lived alongside the dinosaurs.

These scaly survivors include some of the world's most fearsome creatures, from giant Komodo dragons to super-sized snakes and fierce crocodiles.

THE **GREEN CRESTED BASILISK** CAN **WALK ON WATER. IT DASHES ACROSS THE SURFACE** ON ITS **BACK FEET!**

FIERY **LIZARDS**

The largest of the lizards, Komodo dragons battle for supremacy, wrestling and spitting venom at each other to compete for mates.

The skin is covered in a protective layer of tough, bony scales.

Each eye has a scaly lid, which is shaped like a cone.

GIANT TORTOISES

Galápagos tortoises are the world's largest tortoises. Some weigh more than 500 lb (225 kg) and measure up to 5 ft (1.5 m) from head to tail. They are also among the longest-lived land animals, surviving for over 100 years.

The scales on the shell are made of keratin, the same substance as human fingernails.

A hard shell protects the soft body.

This panther chameleon's tail can wrap around tree branches, for support while climbing.

CHANGING **COLOR**

Chameleons are best known for their ability to change color, which they do depending on their mood and temperature. These lizards also have eyes that move separately, giving them 360-degree vision.

WHAT IS A REPTILE?

All reptiles are cold-blooded vertebrates with tough, waterproof skins that allow them to survive in dry places.

Cold-blooded
Reptiles rely on heat in the environment to keep their bodies warm.

Vertebrate
A reptile's body is supported by a bony spine and skeleton.

Scaly skin
Scales protect the skin, restrict water loss, and allow heat to escape.

Most lay eggs
Reptiles usually lay eggs, with waterproof shells.

Live young
Some snakes and lizards bear fully formed young.

THE **NANO-CHAMELEON** IS EARTH'S **SMALLEST REPTILE,** AT **0.5 IN** (13.5 MM)!

REPTILE WRANGLE

Golden tree snakes glide from tree to tree, searching for prey. This one has pounced on a red-spotted tokay gecko and is squeezing it to death. Here, the snake has won, but often these geckos outwit the snakes.

The snake coils itself around the gecko.

The snake's long, muscular body is strong and flexible.

The gecko's eyes bulge as it struggles to breathe.

The snake uses its fangs to grip its prey.

Amazing climbers, geckos have tiny hairs on their toe pads to help them grip, so they can run up walls and across ceilings.

SCALY SKIN

All reptiles have an outer layer of protective armor. Lizards and snakes are covered in scales, while tortoises, turtles, and crocodilians have horny plates.

Snake skin
The patterned scales of a boa constrictor help it to hide while hunting.

Lizard skin
The scales of an ocellated lizard change color as it grows, forming mazelike patterns.

Crocodile skin
The horny plates of a crocodilian are known as scutes. They are thickest on its back.

Top crocs

The largest of the reptiles, crocodilians are fierce hunters. These fast swimmers lurk below the surface in tropical rivers and swamps, waiting for the perfect moment to attack their prey.

ENDANGERED GHARIAL

Gharials are native to rivers with sandy banks in northern India and Nepal, but dam building has destroyed much of their habitat. They are also threatened by fishing—caught in nets and hunted.

Adults can reach 21 ft (6.5 m) long.

Flattened, muscular tail helps propel the gharial in water.

STRONGEST **BITE!**

Crocodiles have the most powerful bite of all living land creatures—it is strong enough to crush a victim's skull. The only land animal to top it was the terrifying *Tyrannosaurus rex*, whose bite was more than three times stronger.

WHO'S **WHO?**

There are 24 species of crocodilians, which belong to three families: alligators and caimans, crocodiles, and gharials. Here's how to tell which is which.

A transparent third eyelid protects the eye underwater.

American crocodile has a gray back.

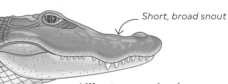

Short, broad snout

Alligators and caimans
When these reptiles have their mouth shut, you won't see their bottom teeth. They live in fresh water in the Americas.

Pointed snout

Crocodiles
Found in both fresh and salt water in the tropics, crocodiles have long, V-shaped noses. Their sharp teeth are visible when the mouth is closed.

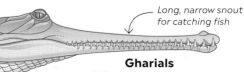

Long, narrow snout for catching fish

Gharials
You'll find 110 teeth in a gharial's thin snout. Males have a distinctive knob on the end. They live in fresh water.

BIGGEST AND SMALLEST!

The biggest crocodilian is the mighty saltwater crocodile, or saltie, which is the largest of all living reptiles. The smallest is Cuvier's dwarf caiman.

Dwarf caiman 4.5 ft (1.4 m)

Saltie
23 ft (7 m)

SURPRISE ATTACK

Crocodiles are stealthy hunters that lurk in the water before ambushing their prey. Launching itself out of the water, a croc grips its victim and drags it underwater to drown it. A crocodile will swallow small animals whole but tear bigger ones apart.

Lying in wait
The crocodile approaches its victim.

Deadly grip
It snares the animal with its jaws.

Death roll
The croc then drags its prey underwater.

SALTWATER HATCHLING

Egg tooth on the end of the snout

When they are ready to hatch, baby crocodiles smash out of their shells using a special "egg tooth." The tiny creatures begin to chirp and their mothers carry them safely down to the water in their mouths.

Bony scutes cover the body.

Feet are webbed, for swimming.

WHAT IS A CROCODILIAN?

Crocodilians are large, meat-eating reptiles that live in water. They have tough, armored skin and powerful jaws with sharp teeth. Their eyes, ears, and nostrils are positioned on the top of their heads, so they can see, hear, and smell while almost completely submerged in the water, waiting to ambush their prey.

Pointed teeth for holding prey

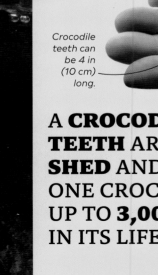

Crocodile teeth can be 4 in (10 cm) long.

A CROCODILE'S TEETH ARE OFTEN SHED AND REPLACED. ONE CROC CAN GROW UP TO 3,000 TEETH IN ITS LIFETIME!

Slithering snakes

These slinky reptiles are found in almost every country in the world, and there are 3,000 different species. Although they are feared, most snakes are harmless to humans. They can be deadly—but usually only to small animals, such as rats and frogs.

SNAKE **BITE**

This emerald tree boa spends its days coiled in a tree, gripping on with its powerful tail. At night, it springs into action, lunging at birds, which it snatches with its mobile jaws. The snake hooks its prey with its fangs, then coils its body around it and constricts until it dies.

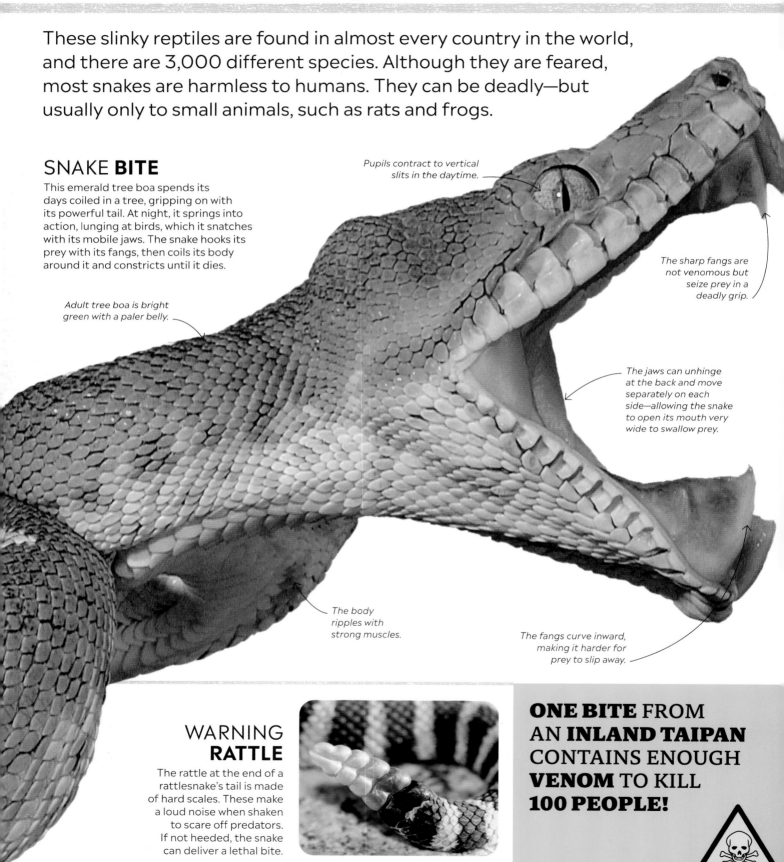

Pupils contract to vertical slits in the daytime.

The sharp fangs are not venomous but seize prey in a deadly grip.

Adult tree boa is bright green with a paler belly.

The jaws can unhinge at the back and move separately on each side—allowing the snake to open its mouth very wide to swallow prey.

The body ripples with strong muscles.

The fangs curve inward, making it harder for prey to slip away.

WARNING **RATTLE**

The rattle at the end of a rattlesnake's tail is made of hard scales. These make a loud noise when shaken to scare off predators. If not heeded, the snake can deliver a lethal bite.

ONE BITE FROM AN **INLAND TAIPAN** CONTAINS ENOUGH **VENOM** TO KILL **100 PEOPLE!**

THE **RETICULATED PYTHON** CAN REACH **33 FT** (10 M) IN **LENGTH!**

The baby snake uses an "egg tooth" to make a hole in its egg.

The baby then wriggles out through the hole.

HATCHING OUT

Most snakes reproduce by laying eggs. A female snake may lay up to 100 eggs, in warm sand or soil. The eggs have leathery shells that keep moisture in. Generally, the mother abandons the eggs to hatch alone.

VENOMOUS VIPERS

Vipers, such as this rare blue pit viper, have hinged fangs to inject venom into their prey. When not in use, the fangs fold up into the roof of the snake's mouth.

Overlapping scales allow viper to bend and twist.

SMILEY ASSASSIN!

Don't let the smiley face on the back of its hood fool you—the spectacled cobra is one of India's most venomous snakes. It rears up and flares its hood to scare off potential threats.

SNAKE **SENSES**

Snakes use their tongues to "taste" the air, searching for the smell of a potential meal. This is possible thanks to a taste organ called the Jacobson's organ.

Nerves carry signals to the brain.

The tongue collects scent particles.

The tongue retracts into the Jacobson's organ.

SNAKE **SNACKS**

This python is trying to swallow a deer whole after squeezing it to death. Almost all snakes, venomous or not, swallow their food without chewing. They use their gaping jaws to push the prey into their stomach.

COLOR **MIMIC**

Some harmless snakes use disguise to defend themselves. To make them less tempting to predators, their colors mimic other, more dangerous snakes.

Bold colors of venomous coral snake warn off predators.

Milk snake is not venomous, but its colors may trick predators into staying away.

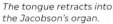

BIG **EATERS**

The American pygmy shrew is one of the smallest mammals in the world but has a huge appetite for its size. It needs to consume around three times its body weight every day just to stay alive.

An adult shrew weighs around 0.1 oz (3 g).

VENOMOUS ANIMALS

Many animals use venom to immobilize prey or when defending themselves from attack.

1 BOX JELLYFISH
These jellies produce toxins to stun prey. The poison is so powerful it can kill a swimmer.

2 STONEFISH
Camouflaged as rocks on the sea floor, these fish can deliver a lethal sting if trodden on.

3 GILA MONSTER
This lizard's venomous bite causes agonizing pain when it grips onto prey with its jaws.

4 SLOW LORIS
These primates secrete an oil that is toxic when mixed with their saliva. They use it to bite rivals.

5 CONE SNAIL
These pretty mollusks hunt by sending out a venom-filled "harpoon" to immobilize prey.

6 PLATYPUS
Male platypuses use venom-filled spurs on their hind legs to fight off rivals.

STAT ATTACK! **SURVIVAL** STRATEGIES

Life in the wild is a constant fight for survival. Animals have developed some truly terrifying strategies to make sure they get to eat and do not get eaten.

FASTEST ANIMALS

Some animals are known for the speeds they can reach when hunting prey. Here are the fastest animals on land, under the sea, and in the air.

FASTEST BIRD Peregrine falcon, 186 mph (300 km/h)

FASTEST FISH Black marlin, 80 mph (129 km/h)

FASTEST LAND ANIMAL Cheetah, 75 mph (120 km/h)

FASTEST INSECT Australian dragonfly, 36 mph (58 km/h)

STRENGTH IN **NUMBERS**

If animals are not powerful enough to see off predators alone, they may mass together for strength. This massive shoal of mackerel will protect at least some of its number from the predatory striped marlin circling below.

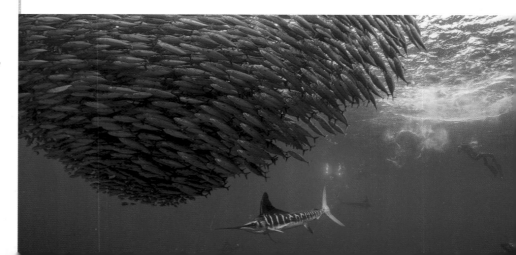

LONGEST CLAWS

The giant armadillo has the longest claws of any animal. It uses them to rip open termite mounds in search of food. By comparison, a harpy eagle's talons and a tiger's curved claws are tiny!

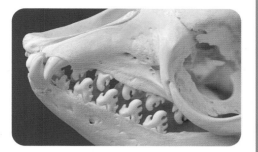

8 in (20 cm)
GIANT ARMADILLO

7 in (18 cm)
GIANT ANTEATER

5 in (12.5 cm)
SOUTHERN CASSOWARY

5 in (12.5 cm)
GRIZZLY BEAR

4 in (10 cm)
THREE-TOED SLOTH

4 in (10 cm)
HARPY EAGLE

4 in (10 cm)
TIGER

TERRIBLE TEETH

SHARPEST Blood-sucking vampire bats have razor-sharp teeth, which they sink into their victims to feed at night. They rarely bite humans.

LONGEST Male narwhals have a long tooth that grows through their upper lip into a swordlike tusk. It can reach 10 ft (3 m) in length.

MOST Wide-mouthed whale sharks have about 3,000 tiny teeth arranged in 300 rows—but have evolved as filter feeders and no longer use their teeth.

WEIRDEST Crabeater seals have interlocking teeth (pictured above) that act like sieves to filter krill (tiny crustaceans) from seawater.

FASTEST-GROWING Pacific lingcod have more than 500 ragged teeth in their mobile jaws. The deep-sea fish lose and grow 20 teeth a day.

SMALL BUT DEADLY

Mosquitoes kill more people than any other animal. These small, biting insects cause around 1 million human deaths a year. Their bites spread deadly diseases, such as malaria.

FASTEST FISTS

The peacock mantis shrimp packs the most powerful punch of the animal kingdom. It can whip out its clublike front legs at speeds of up to 50 mph (80 km/h).

DRAMATIC DEFENSE

Animals use a range of astonishing weapons to defend themselves. Some even sacrifice themselves for the good of the community.

Texas horned lizards can puff up their bodies into spiky balloons!

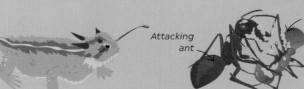

Exploding ant

Attacking ant

TEXAS HORNED LIZARD
Horned lizards squirt noxious blood from their eyes to confuse predators.

EXPLODING ANT
This ant explodes, releasing a sticky yellow goo that kills attackers.

SPANISH RIBBED NEWT
If threatened, this newt pushes its ribs through its skin to make spines.

Brilliant birds

Not all birds fly, but some perform astonishing airborne acrobatics. Soaring through the sky with their powerful wings, these birds are found on every continent and in many different habitats, from wetlands to deserts.

KING **DIVER**

When a kingfisher dives down to snap up a fish, the attack is over in seconds. The bird moves at such speed that, to the naked eye, it appears as a blur of blue and red.

4. Returning to its perch, the kingfisher can enjoy its catch.

1. The bird spots its prey in the water and begins to dive.

3. Just a few flaps of the wings lift the bird easily back into the sky.

2. The pointed bill hits the water first, ready to snatch up a fish.

EGG SHELL

A bird's egg contains everything an embryo needs to develop. The shell protects the embryo, while letting air in and out, and the yolk nourishes it.

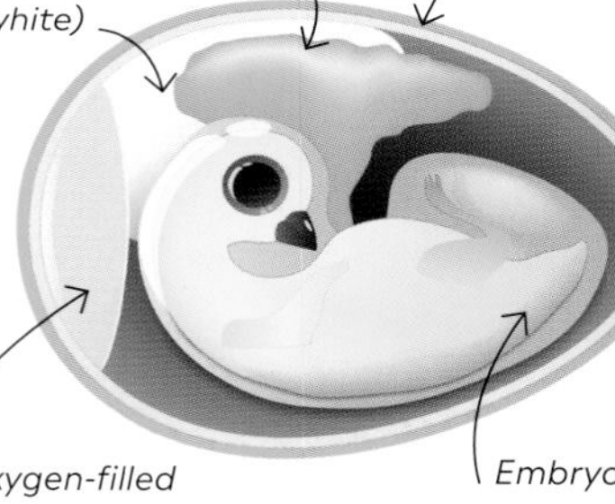

Albumen (egg white)

Yolk

Hard shell

Oxygen-filled air sac

Embryo

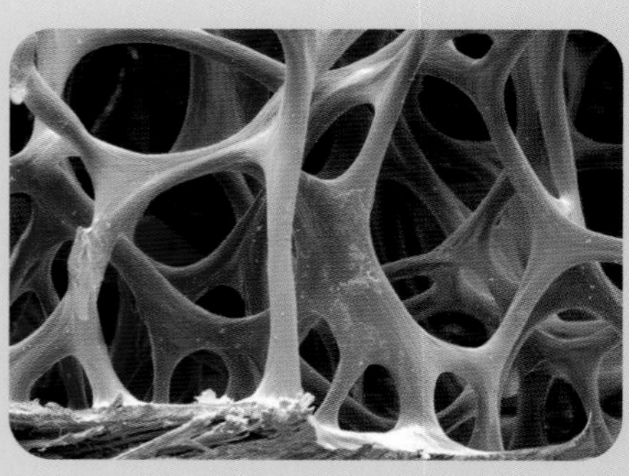

STRONG **STRUTS!**

As this magnified view shows, birds' bones are not solid but made up of a network of bony struts. This structure makes them super strong!

WHAT IS A **BIRD?**

There are around 10,000 species of birds—from small, brown sparrows to colorful birds of paradise. All of them share some key characteristics.

Warm-blooded
Like mammals, birds are able to regulate their own body temperature—they are "warm-blooded."

Vertebrate
All birds have a hard, bony skeleton inside their bodies, to which their muscles are attached.

Feathered
Soft, downy feathers keep birds warm, while stiff feathers for flight provide lift.

Lay eggs
Birds lay hard-shelled eggs and brood them in nests until the young hatch and fly the nest.

Most fly
Although there are exceptions, such as the ostrich, most birds are able to fly.

LITTLE AND LARGE!

Bee hummingbird

Ostrich

The ostrich is the world's biggest bird, at 9 ft (2.8 m) tall. The tiny bee hummingbird is the smallest—it is only 2.2 in (5.5 cm) long and could perch on the top of a pencil.

LONGEST WINGSPAN

Wandering albatross

The wandering albatross has the longest wings in the world, with a wingspan of up to 11 ft (3.5 m). It spends its life gliding through the air over the Southern Ocean.

A DIVING **PEREGRINE FALCON** TRAVELS AT MORE THAN **186 MPH (300 KM/H)!**

Wings are folded close to the body to make a streamlined shape.

FEATHER LIGHT

Fluffy bird feathers do not just look pretty. They are made of a lightweight material called keratin and have a streamlined shape for smooth flight.

Strong central shaft

Barbs

Barbules

Barbicels

Close-up
Each feather is made of lots of tiny branches.

WHAT'S **INSIDE?**

Eye socket

Beak

Keel bone anchors strong wing muscles.

Air sacs

Strong, stiff flight feathers on wings generate lift.

Tail

Four-toed foot can grip perches.

Birds have strong bones and powerful flight muscles. Their bodies contain sacs that pump air into the lungs to maintain a constant supply of oxygen, providing the energy for flight.

NEST BUILDER

Many birds lay their eggs in nests, but the village weaver bird's nest is more elaborate than most. It is made of woven grass and suspended from a tree.

Cool characters

Penguins cannot fly—but they are super swimmers. These birds are more at home in water than they are on land. Their streamlined bodies zip through the ocean, pushed along by flipper power.

PENGUIN DIVERSITY

There are 18 species of penguins. These represent four of the main groups.

Chinstrap
This brush-tailed penguin is common in Antarctica.

Fairy
The smallest species is also known as the little blue penguin.

Macaroni
A crested penguin, it is named for its yellow plumes.

African
This banded penguin is the only African species.

Galápagos penguins

Equator

Antarctic penguins

Subantarctic penguins

SOUTHERN HOME

Penguins (red on map) live in the southern hemisphere, in Antarctica, and on subantarctic islands and continents. Only Galápagos penguins sometimes stray north of the equator.

PENGUINS **CHAT UNDERWATER,** CHANGING THEIR **CALLS** TO ECHO THEIR **FRIENDS!**

TRAPPING **TONGUE**

Penguins hunt small, slippery sea creatures, such as fish and squid. To stop prey from escaping before it can be swallowed, their tongues are covered in spikes, called barbs.

PRECIOUS **EGG**

The male emperor penguin spends the whole winter guarding his mate's egg. He keeps it on top of his feet so that it does not touch the ice below.

The barbs point down this Rockhopper's throat.

MEGA PENGUIN!

Emperor penguins are the largest penguins alive. However, 40 million years ago a now-extinct penguin measured a whopping 6.6 ft (2 m) from beak to toe.

4.5 ft (1.36 m)

5.4 ft (1.65 m)

6.6 ft (2 m)

Emperor penguin

Average adult

Colossus penguin

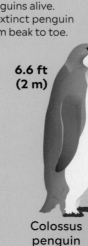

PENGUIN **HUDDLE**

To survive the freezing Antarctic winter, groups of emperor penguins huddle together. They rotate positions so that each bird gets a chance to spend some time being warm, in the center of the huddle.

AN **ADÉLIE PENGUIN** EATS **A FIFTH OF ITS BODY WEIGHT** EVERY DAY. THAT'S LIKE YOU EATING **30 BURGERS!**

MAKING A **SPLASH**

Penguins' flippers are perfectly adapted for propelling them through the water. If danger threatens, they can "porpoise," leaping out of the water and into the air.

Diving
A penguin dives into the water in search of food, such as fish.

Swimming
The penguin uses its flippers for power and steers with its tail.

Leaping
Swimming quickly, the penguin can launch itself back onto land.

Penguins live in large groups, which are known as colonies.

Stiff, narrow flippers work like paddles in the water.

LEAPING **EMPERORS**

This emperor penguin is rocketing up out of the water and onto the ice—perhaps to avoid a predator. Emperor penguins can swim at up to 15 mph (24 km/h), and hold their breath for 20 minutes at a time!

NAME THAT... BIRD

Are you a bird-spotting brainbox?
Can you tell a robin from a roadrunner?
Don't forget to look for the odd one out!

1 Lappet-faced vulture
2 Yellow-chevroned parakeet
3 European robin
4 Blue-crowned motmot
5 Great tit
6 Mallard
7 Black-browed albatross
8 Ultramarine flycatcher
9 Eurasian jay
10 Swallow-tailed hummingbird
11 Common kingfisher
12 Gouldian finch
13 Nicobar pigeon
14 Emu
15 Scarlet ibis
16 Toco toucan
17 White-tailed eagle
18 Lanner falcon
19 Ringed turtle-dove
20 European starling
21 Eurasian blue tit
22 Temminck's tragopan
23 Blue-footed booby
24 Red junglefowl
25 Common ostrich
26 Lesser flamingo
27 Indian peafowl
28 Southern brown kiwi
29 Wattled jacana
30 Scarlet macaw
31 Atlantic puffin
32 Rock pigeon
33 Southern flying squirrel
34 Great white pelican
35 Barn owl
36 Magnificent frigatebird
37 Western tanager
38 Arctic tern
39 Trumpeter swan
40 Barn swallow
41 Jackal buzzard
42 Southern cassowary
43 Eurasian bullfinch
44 Great blue heron
45 Zebra finch
46 Emperor penguin
47 Sulphur-crested cockatoo
48 Grey-crowned crane
49 Wild turkey
50 Greater roadrunner

The odd one out is the flying squirrel (33). This rodent
can glide through the air by spreading out its furry limbs,
but it is not a bird.

WHAT IS A MAMMAL?

The defining features of mammals are that most have fur and they drink their mother's milk. They also share other traits.

Warm-blooded
Mammals can regulate their body temperature, turning food into heat.

Vertebrate
All mammals have internal skeletons made of bone.

Fur or hair
Almost all have some fur. It traps air to retain body heat.

Live birth
Most mammals give birth to live young; monotremes lay eggs.

Produce milk
Mothers feed young with milk containing vital nutrients.

Huge, tusklike teeth

HIPPOS ARE THE **DEADLIEST** LAND **MAMMALS, KILLING** UP TO **500 PEOPLE** A YEAR!

GIANT ANTEATER

Anteaters belong to a group of mammals that eats insects. They have no teeth, instead using their long, sticky tongues to scoop up ants and termites. They can eat up to 35,000 insects in one day.

The long snout is perfect for probing termite mounds and anthills.

The tongue can be 2 ft (61 cm) long.

Fur is water-repellent to keep the pup warm and dry.

OTTERLY CUTE!

Sea otters spend most of their lives in the water. Mothers even give birth in water. They float on their backs to look after their young, holding pups on their chest for nursing.

HOODED SEAL MILK IS 60% FAT—RICHER THAN ICE CREAM!

FLYING FOX

There are a surprising number of mammals that can fly or glide, including more than 1,100 species of bats. Lyle's flying foxes are the largest bats in the world. Some have a wingspan of up to 6.6 ft (2 m).

A flying fox pup clings to its mother and feeds as she flies.

Furry
mammals

Mammals are the animals most familiar to us, because we too are mammals. There are around 5,500 known mammal species, ranging from our closest relative, chimpanzees, to spiny porcupines, star-nosed moles, and deep-sea whales.

TYPES OF MAMMALS

There are many types of mammals, but they can all be placed in one of three groups, depending on how they reproduce.

A moose cow nursing its calf

Placental mammals

Most mammals give birth to live young. The mothers care for their offspring for varying periods of time.

Marsupials

Marsupial mothers give birth to premature young (joeys) that they nurture in pouches. Koalas and opossums are marsupials.

A western gray kangaroo with its joey

A platypus hunts underwater.

Monotremes

These rare mammals lay eggs. There are only five species of monotreme— the platypus and four species of spiny echidna.

Sea otters have the thickest fur of any mammals. An adult may be covered in 800 million hairs per sq in (124 million hairs per sq cm).

40% OF ALL MAMMAL SPECIES ARE RODENTS!

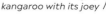

Whopping whales

Massive whales live in the oceans, where their bulk is supported by water. They are mammals and must visit the water's surface to breathe in oxygen through their blowholes.

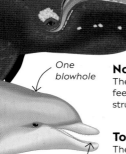

Two blowholes

Baleen

One blowhole

Nontoothed
These cetaceans filter feed using a comb-like structure called baleen.

Toothed
These cetaceans use their teeth to grab hold of their prey.

Teeth

WHAT IS A **WHALE?**

Whales are part of a group of marine mammals called cetaceans, which includes dolphins and porpoises. Cetaceans are divided into two groups: toothed and nontoothed, or baleen.

ORCA PODS

Orcas are the largest of the dolphins. They live in family groups, known as pods, of up to 40 animals. These smart and playful pods hunt in a variety of ways, using whistles and clicks to communicate.

DOLPHIN TWIST!

Only a few dolphins live in fresh water. One is the pink Amazon River dolphin. These intelligent animals have super bendy spines and can turn their heads at right angles to their bodies.

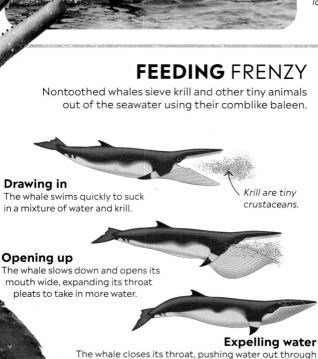

UNICORNS OF THE SEA

Narwhals are toothed whales. Each male has a single spiral tusk, which is actually one of his teeth, protruding from the upper jaw. The tusks are thought to be used for showing off to females and rivals.

Tusks can be up to 10 ft (3 m) long.

FEEDING FRENZY

Nontoothed whales sieve krill and other tiny animals out of the seawater using their comblike baleen.

Drawing in
The whale swims quickly to suck in a mixture of water and krill.

Krill are tiny crustaceans.

Opening up
The whale slows down and opens its mouth wide, expanding its throat pleats to take in more water.

Expelling water
The whale closes its throat, pushing water out through the baleen while keeping the krill in its mouth.

A CUVIER'S BEAKED WHALE CAN DIVE ALMOST **2 MILES** (3 KM) **DOWN** AND **HOLD ITS BREATH** FOR MORE THAN **2 HOURS!**

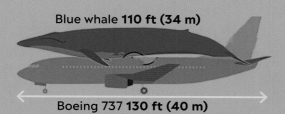

Blue whale **110 ft (34 m)**

Boeing 737 **130 ft (40 m)**

BLUE WHALES ARE THE LARGEST ANIMALS KNOWN TO HAVE LIVED ON EARTH!

SNOTBOTS ON THE GO!

How healthy is that whale? One way to find out is by sending in a SnotBot®. These drones capture samples of the water that is sent out through a whale's blowhole, then carry it back to scientists to be tested.

A whale-watching boat is tiny compared to the whale below.

The whale's rostrum, or snout, pokes out of the water before it surfaces.

SCALE OF A WHALE

Whales can be absolutely huge. Humpbacks are the second-largest species after the blue whale. They can reach lengths of up to 56 ft (17 m). This humpback is about to breach, propelling itself out of the water to see above the surface.

The pleats in the underside of the throat allow it to expand when the whale is filter feeding.

Barnacles have attached themselves along the edge of the whale's flipper.

CAT CLANS

There are two main groups in the cat family—big and small cats. Cheetahs and clouded leopards do not belong to either group.

Big cats
These include the snow leopard (above), lion, tiger, jaguar, and leopard, all of which roar.

Small cats
This group includes the ocelot (above), puma, and domestic cats, which purr but cannot roar.

Cheetahs
The cheetah is known as a running cat because of its unique hunting style (see page 152).

Clouded leopards
The clouded leopard does not roar like a big cat or purr like a small cat.

Powerful paw can knock prey over with one blow.

Deadly cats

Cats are predatory meat-eaters, with well-developed senses, the ability to leap or run fast, and razor-sharp teeth for hunting. There are 38 species of wild and domestic cats, all belonging to the same family.

CHEETAHS **ACCELERATE** FAST—FROM **0 TO 60 MPH** (0 TO 95 KM/H) IN **3 SECONDS!**

STRONG **TIGER**

The biggest and most powerful of all cats, tigers can weigh up to 660 lb (300 kg). Fearsome hunters, they are striped for camouflage in long grass. They are native to parts of Asia, including India and Siberia.

Strong shoulder muscles, flexed to pounce

THE **ANCIENT EGYPTIANS** WORSHIPPED A **CAT GODDESS** WITH A **LION'S HEAD!**

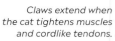

Claws extend when the cat tightens muscles and cordlike tendons.

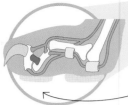

Relaxing tendons pulls in toe bones, with claws on, to retract claws.

RETRACTABLE **CLAWS**

Most cats extend their claws for climbing and hunting, but keep them retracted (pulled in) for walking and when resting.

LION PRIDE

Lions live and hunt in groups known as prides. This makes it possible to catch prey larger than themselves. Females outnumber males in a pride and are the main hunters.

Tail helps jaguar to balance.

Jaguar is at full stretch in midleap.

Front leg bones are strong to support the large muscles needed to hunt prey.

LEAPING **JAGUAR**

All cats are extremely agile and can leap with great power. A cat can judge its landing position with great accuracy. This is essential for jaguars, such as the one above, which hunt fast-moving prey.

STRAY CATS OUTNUMBER HUMANS **TEN** TO **ONE** ON JAPAN'S **CAT ISLAND** AOSHIMA!

CLIMBING **LEOPARD**

Leopards are unusual among the big cats because they climb trees for safety. Most leopards are golden brown with spots, but some have dark coats like this one.

Spots are still visible on rare black leopards.

CHEETAH CHASE

Cheetahs are the fastest land animals in the world, but catching prey, such as this impala, is still a challenge. The cheetah starts out hunting low to the ground, accelerating to 60 mph (95 km/h) when it gets close. The impala zigzags quickly across the savanna. The cheetah has only just caught it here.

Ask a...
ZOOLOGIST

Professor Sarah Durant is a conservation scientist and practitioner at the Institute of Zoology, Zoological Society of London. She has led the Serengeti Cheetah Project in Tanzania since 1991. She also heads the Africa Range-wide Cheetah Conservation Initiative.

Q How many cheetahs are there in the world?
A There are an estimated 6,500 adult cheetahs living in the wild, with the main populations found in eastern and southern Africa. Numbers are declining and the species is threatened.

Q Where is your cheetah project?
A My longest-running project is in the Serengeti ecosystem in Tanzania, which borders with the Maasai Mara in Kenya. It supports a major part of one of the largest remaining cheetah populations, which inhabits the landscape from the Serengeti to Tsavo. Cheetahs here are

threatened by habitat loss and fragmentation; loss of prey, because much wild antelope habitat is now dominated by livestock; and conflict with people. Climate change intensifies these threats.

Q   Are cheetahs dangerous to people?
A   Cheetahs do sometimes take livestock (mainly goats and sheep), in particular, if there are few wild prey available. This can lead to conflict with livestock keepers. It is very rare for a cheetah to attack a person. One thing conservationists do is help local communities live with cheetahs.

Q   What can I do to protect animals?
A   To save threatened species, people must learn to live with wildlife. This might mean eliminating pesticides to allow insects to thrive or living alongside larger wildlife species such as bears.

Q   What is a day in your life like?
A   There is no typical day. As I write this, I am heading out to the Serengeti to fit satellite collars to cheetahs living on the borders of the park. I will be working with my team to locate, dart, and fit the collars. The cheetahs will be monitored to check

that they are okay. We will then be able to download two-hourly locations from satellite, to understand how cheetahs move across the ecosystem.

Q   How can we save big cats?
A   Don't forget the people! Understanding big cat ecology and behavior is important for conservation, but the key lies with people. People are the cause of the problems, as they encroach ever more on the big cats. However, they are also key to solving these problems, for example, by changing their own behavior.

SUN BEARS HAVE **STICKY TONGUES** 10 IN (25 CM) LONG, WHICH THEY USE TO **EXTRACT HONEY** FROM BEES' NESTS!

The belly fur is softer than the back fur.

Fur is "grizzled"—it is brown with silver or golden tips.

BACK **SCRATCHING**

Many species of bears can be seen using tree trunks to scratch their backs. They stand up on their back legs, lean against the tree, and wriggle from side to side. This grizzly bear is showing her cub just what to do.

Paws help bear to climb and swim.

Front paws have long claws for digging.

AMERICAN AND ASIAN BLACK BEARS ARE AGILE **TREE CLIMBERS!**

Bear necessities

Large, furry mammals found in the Americas, Europe, and Asia, bears are fiercely intelligent. These oversize animals are highly resourceful in hunting out food, from roots, shoots, and berries to fish and meat.

Sloth bears use their claws to hook termites out from their nests.

BEAR **CLAWS**

All bears have powerful claws, which they put to use in various ways, from digging dens and climbing trees to swiping salmon.

GIANT PANDAS EAT NOTHING BUT **TOUGH BAMBOO**. THEY SPEND UP TO **16 HOURS** A DAY **EATING!**

Kodiak bear

TYPES OF **BEARS**

There are only eight species of bears. However, some species include several subspecies—for example, Kodiak and grizzly bears are both brown bears.

| Brown bear | Polar bear | Spectacled bear | Giant panda | Human (for scale) | Sloth bear | American and Asian black bears | Sun bear |

WINTER **DENS**

Female polar bears dig dens where they give birth to their cubs in winter. The cubs stay sheltered beneath the snow until spring.

The mother sleeps in the main chamber.

The cubs have their own, smaller chamber.

GONE **FISHING**

Every summer, brown bears head to rivers to catch salmon that are trying to swim upstream. The salmon leap out of the water and the bears catch them in midair. These fish make up half of a bear's yearly food, sustaining it through winter hibernation.

This bear has caught a female sockeye salmon full of eggs.

SEAL **HUNT**

Polar bears are the only purely meat-eating bears. To catch seals, a bear waits next to a hole in the ice. When a seal comes up onto the ice to breathe, the bear gives chase.

THERE ARE MORE THAN 350 DOMESTIC **DOG BREEDS!**

WOLF **HOWL**

Wolves are social animals that live in family groups and hunt in packs. A wolf's howl may be a call to hunt or simply a way of telling other wolves where it is.

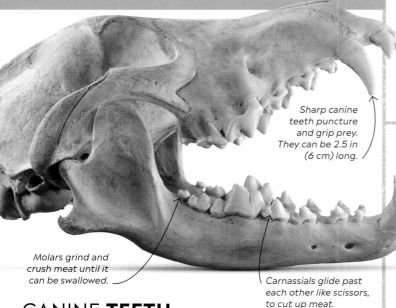

Sharp canine teeth puncture and grip prey. They can be 2.5 in (6 cm) long.

Molars grind and crush meat until it can be swallowed.

Carnassials glide past each other like scissors, to cut up meat.

CANINE **TEETH**

Canines have an impressive set of teeth, designed for hunting live prey and eating meat. This gray wolf skull shows the different types of teeth in a wolf's powerful jaws—its bite is three times as strong as a human's.

ARCTIC FOX

The Arctic fox changes its fur with the seasons so that it is always camouflaged in the changing landscape. In summer, its coat is gray to blend in with the rocky ground and in winter it is white to match the snow.

Summer coat   Winter coat

WOLVES CAN **SPRINT** AT **38 MPH** (60 KM/H)!

Canine
capers

The pet dogs we keep in our homes are the tame descendants of the wild gray wolf. Both dogs and wolves are members of a larger, varied group of animals known as canines.

A strong sense of smell helps identify pack members and detect prey.

DOG
FAMILY

The dog family contains 34 different species, including foxes, jackals, and coyotes. These six represent some of the main groups as they have evolved. They all share features, such as a good nose for hunting.

Red fox
These foxes have pointed ears and noses and long, bushy tails.

Ethiopian wolf
These wolves live in packs, but only the alpha female gives birth to pups.

Golden jackal
Jackals live in pairs, which stay and hunt together for their whole lives.

Coyote
These wolf relatives live in packs and communicate using growls and yelps.

Gray wolf
Gray wolves are the largest wild canines. Their fur can vary in color.

Dog
Domestic dogs descended from gray wolves around 40,000 years ago.

THE **LARGEST** EVER **LITTER** OF **PUPPIES** IS **24**, BORN TO A **NEAPOLITAN MASTIFF!**

URBAN FOX

All over the world, red foxes have adapted to live in cities, close to people. They build dens in suburban yards, hunt rats and pigeons, and scavenge from trash cans.

WILD DOGS

These fierce hunters often face off against other predators as they track antelopes in the African savanna. Hunting in packs of 10 or more, African wild dogs can reach speeds of 44 mph (70 km/h) in the chase.

Large ears aid hearing and help dogs stay cool by radiating heat.

Each dog has a unique pattern on its coat, giving them the nickname "painted dogs."

SWINGING APE

Tropical rainforests are home to all of the world's apes and most of its monkeys. Some apes, such as gibbons, are able to swing hand-to-hand through the branches. This is called brachiation.

Twisty wrists
Ball-and-socket joints allow the gibbon to swivel its wrists.

Rotate and swing
The wrists allow the gibbon to rotate as it swings.

Long reach
The gibbon can move 7.5 ft (2.25 m) between handholds.

Side-to-side
It swings its body from side to side as it moves its hands.

USING TOOLS

Chimpanzees are skilled at making and using tools for all sorts of different tasks. This chimp is using a stick to find insects inside a log. They also use stones to crack open nuts and bundles of leaves to wipe dirt away. They have even been spotted using twigs to pick their teeth.

SAUCER EYES!

Tarsiers have huge eyes, which allow them to see at night. If our eyes were as big in relation to our body, they would be the size of grapefruits.

Primate party

Primates—the group of mammals that includes humans—have big brains, nimble fingers, and live in complex social groups. Although they have these characteristics in common, they are a diverse bunch.

Male mandrills, from central Africa, have brightly colored red and blue faces.

Opposable thumbs for gripping and swinging

Tail is prehensile—it can bend and grip onto branches.

Black-and-white striped tail, which cannot grip branches.

Four-fingered hands with tiny thumbs

Ring-tailed lemur
Lemurs are prosimians found only in Madagascar. Other prosimians include lorises and bushbabies.

Spectral tarsier
Tarsiers are in a group all of their own. They live in Southeast Asia and hunt at night.

Spider monkey
Long-haired spider monkeys are a New World monkey. These live in South America.

Mandrill
The biggest monkeys, mandrills are an Old World monkey. These live in Africa and Asia.

Pileated gibbon
Lesser apes include these Southeast Asian gibbons. Females are white and males black.

SOCIABLE MONKEYS

Primates usually live in family groups and have close social relationships. Female Japanese macaques stay in the same group their whole lives. They live in cold areas and spend time bathing and grooming in the local hot springs!

Opposable thumb moves independently.

Bonobo has fingerprints like a human.

HANDS LIKE OURS

Apes such as the bonobo have hands with four fingers and an opposable thumb. This gives them the power to grasp large branches for climbing and the precise control to grip small twigs as tools.

THE SMALLEST MONKEY, A PYGMY MARMOSET GROWS TO JUST 5.4 IN (13.5 CM) LONG!

TYPES OF PRIMATES

There are hundreds of primate species. This lineup reflects some of the main groups. Humans belong to a group called the great apes, which also includes orangutans, gorillas, and chimpanzees.

Hairless face and broad chest and shoulders

Chimpanzees are able to walk upright.

Opposable toes allow orangutans to swing by the feet as well as the hands.

Orangutan
These great apes live only in Borneo and Sumatra, Southeast Asia. They care for their young for nine years.

Gorilla
Gentle giants who display emotions such as laughter and sadness, these large apes are omnivores.

Chimpanzee
Chimpanzees do many of the things humans do, such as using tools and grooming.

NAME THAT... MAMMAL

Mammals range from huge whales to tiny shrews. How many can you name? See if you can spot the odd one out!

1 Koala
2 Cape porcupine
3 Giant ground pangolin
4 European mole
5 Bald-headed uakari
6 Sunda flying lemur
7 European bison
8 Round-eared elephant shrew
9 African elephant
10 Fennec fox
11 Gemsbok
12 Eastern gray kangaroo
13 Eurasian red squirrel
14 Lesser hedgehog tenrec
15 White rhinoceros
16 North American beaver
17 Sperm whale
18 Dugong
19 Common warthog
20 Aardvark
21 Giant anteater
22 Rock hyrax
23 Long-nosed armadillo
24 Golden hamster
25 Great white shark
26 Spinner dolphin
27 Walrus
28 Duck-billed platypus
29 Domestic rabbit
30 European hedgehog
31 Vampire bat
32 Bonobo
33 Tasmanian devil
34 Common hippopotamus
35 Plains zebra
36 Spectacled bear
37 Reticulated giraffe
38 Serval
39 Llama
40 Red deer
41 Bactrian camel
42 Red panda
43 Gray wolf
44 Meerkat

The odd one out is the great white shark (25). All the others are mammals, while a shark is a fish.

ZOMBIE **ANTS!**

The cordyceps fungus uses ants to spread its spores. Infected with the fungus, an ant changes its behavior and climbs to the right height for the fungus to thrive. Then the fungus sends a fruiting stalk out of the ant's head to shoot out spores, infecting more ants and restarting the cycle.

A long stalk grows out of the ant's head.

Ant locks its mandibles to a leaf and waits for death.

Living together

Animals, fungi, and plants often rely on each other for survival. This kind of relationship is called symbiosis. Sometimes the arrangement benefits both partners, sometimes just one, but frequently one comes to a very nasty end.

Trevally fish uses its fins to wedge itself inside.

The jellyfish's tentacles contain a venom that the trevally is immune to.

Fish and jellyfish swim together as they move through the currents.

1, Fish
A young trevally fish looks for a hiding spot.

2, Jellyfish
The fish makes its way inside a Thysanostoma jellyfish for safety.

HIDING **SPOT**

At first glance, this trevally may look trapped, but young fish are known to seek cover in jellyfish. It offers the fish shelter and protection from predators, and remains unharmed itself.

TYPES OF **SYMBIOSIS**

Parasitism
A parasite, such as a mosquito, lives off another organism, causing it harm.

Remora rides on shark's back for safety.

Commensalism
Sharks and remora fish have a relationship that benefits one, without harming the other.

Bee feeds on nectar.

Mutualism
Bees pollinating flowers is a relationship that benefits both organisms.

Green fur, where algae grow on the sloth hairs.

THERE IS A **LOUSE** THAT **FEEDS ON** THE BLOOD OF A **FISH'S TONGUE** AND EVENTUALLY **REPLACES IT!**

PROTECTIVE **POISON**

Monarch butterflies feed on nectar in milkweed flowers, carrying pollen from flower to flower. Their caterpillars then feast on the plant, which contains poisonous chemicals. This protects the butterfly by making it toxic to birds.

COZY **HANGOUT**

Woolly bats and tropical pitcher plants have a mutually beneficial relationship. The bat uses the pitcher plant as a small home to rest in and, in turn, the pitcher plant catches the bat's nutrient-rich poop as food.

BROOD **PARASITES**

Cuckoos are brood parasites—a species that relies on other animals to raise their offspring.

Cuckoo egg

1 An extra egg
The female cuckoo sneaks her egg into the host bird's nest.

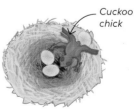
Cuckoo chick

2 Pushed out
The cuckoo chick hatches first and pushes the host eggs over the edge.

Chick is larger than its host.

3 Cuckoo grows
The cuckoo makes a begging call like a brood of chicks to get fed.

CAMOUFLAGE FUR

A sloth's fur is home to an ecosystem of life, including algae. While the algae get the perfect place to thrive, the sloth gains camouflage to avoid predators and feeds on the nutrient-rich algae that grow on its fur.

BIRD **ALARM**

Oxpecker birds feed on parasites such as ticks that live on an impala's body, offering pest control in exchange for a meal. Oxpeckers even help their hosts further by screaming a warning when danger is near.

80% OF ALL **KNOWN SPECIES** ARE **PARASITES!**

Tapeworms are parasites that live in animals' guts.

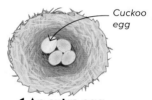

PANGOLIN PROTECTION

Pangolins are the world's most trafficked mammals. They are sold illegally for their scales and meat. Despite a global ban on their trade since 2017, more than a million have been taken from the wild in the last 10 years. The Chinese pangolin is critically endangered but is making a recovery in some regions with the help of rescue programs.

MORE THAN 10,000 SPECIES IN THE AMAZON RAINFOREST ARE UNDER THREAT!

Wildlife conservation

Wildlife is being driven to extinction at an alarming rate, with more than 42,000 species known to be at risk. People are working in sometimes surprising ways to bring natural areas and animal species back from the brink.

TURTLE TAGGING

Scientists learn about sea turtles by satellite tracking. Loggerhead turtles migrate many hundreds of miles from feeding grounds to nesting beaches.

Turtle caught
A diver catches a young loggerhead turtle in the water.

Tracker attached
Scientists attach a satellite tracker to its shell with glue.

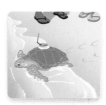

Turtle released
The turtle is released back into the ocean and tracked.

RHINO AIRLIFT

This rare black rhino is being helicoptered to safety away from poachers. Numbers are increasing and there are now more than 6,000 of these rhinos in the wild.

BEE REWILDING

Bees are known as a keystone species because of their role in pollinating plants. This supports ecosystems and is essential for farming. Reducing pesticide use and rewilding land can help increase bee populations.

Honeybees carry pollen and make honey.

A rescued eagle is cared for by its handler.

The 2.8-ton rhino can breathe more easily upside down.

EAGLES DARE

Road-building threatens rainforest that Philippine eagles share with the Indigenous Dumagat people. Only around 500 of the birds survive in the wild. Conservation groups are working with the Dumagat to protect forest and eagles.

THERE ARE 10,000 NATIONAL PARKS AND WILDLIFE RESERVES IN THE WORLD TODAY!

Millions of crabs migrate at the same time each year.

A steel lattice helps crabs grip on.

PEOPLE POWER

Indigenous peoples are the custodians of a fifth of Earth's land, including many wildlife hot spots. Their relationship with nature plays a vital role in its conservation. Here, students from the Pacific island of Tokelau join a climate protest.

CRAB COMMUTE

As roads carve up natural habitats, animals are unable to roam freely in search of food and mates. In some places, wildlife bridges can help them cross safely. Here, Christmas Island red crabs are using a bridge to migrate from forests to the ocean to breed.

STAT ATTACK!
ANIMALS AT RISK

Many naturalists believe that a mass extinction of plants and animals is under way on our planet. This is a result of human activity, as we use ever more resources and encroach on natural habitats. While it is too late for some species, lots of people and organizations are working to ensure the survival of the vast range of life on Earth.

SPIX'S MACAW

BACK FROM THE BRINK

Conservation work has brought a number of species back from the brink of extinction. While numbers are increasing, many of these animals remain endangered.

TIGER These big cats are endangered worldwide, but conservation efforts in India have increased their numbers.

REEF MANTA RAY Manta rays are endangered globally, but ecotourism has boosted reef manta numbers in Indonesia.

SPIX'S MACAW More than 20 years after it vanished from the wild, Spix's macaw has been returned to forests in Brazil.

GIANT PANDA Giant panda numbers in the wild have nearly doubled since their lowest point in the 1970s, when these bears became conservation icons.

DRIVEN TO EXTINCTION

In recent centuries, many species have become extinct as a result of human activities, from hunting to climate change. Here are some of the animals that will never roam, fly, or swim again.

1690

DODO Overhunting drove this flightless bird, from the Indian Ocean island of Mauritius, to extinction.

1768

STELLER'S SEA COW Humans killed off this aquatic mammal, which once swam in the Bering Sea, for its fur and oil.

1870

LABRADOR DUCK Overharvesting of birds, eggs, and feathers led to this North American duck's demise.

1936

TASMANIAN WOLF Competition with dogs brought to Tasmania by colonial settlers brought an end to this wolf.

1989

GOLDEN TOAD Climate change caused the disappearance of this toad, once endemic to Costa Rica's cloud forest.

THREATENED SPECIES

The International Union for Conservation of Nature (IUCN) lists species at risk of extinction on its Red List. Of the 150,000 species assessed, 42,000 are threatened. This graphic shows the percentage of certain groups it considers under threat.

BIRDS 13%
REPTILES 21%
MAMMALS 27%
CRUSTACEANS 28%
LIVING CORAL 36%
SHARKS AND RAYS 37%
AMPHIBIANS 41%

Global **wildlife** populations have **declined** by **69%** since 1970.

MAMMOTH EXTINCTION

For 5 million years, woolly mammoths roamed the Earth, until they went extinct 4,000 years ago. Scientists do not know if humans hunted them to death or if natural climate change led to their disappearance.

BORN TO BE FREE

Some species of animals are extinct in the wild but live on in breeding programs. Zoos run these to increase species numbers and reintroduce animals to their native habitat—but both breeding and release are tricky.

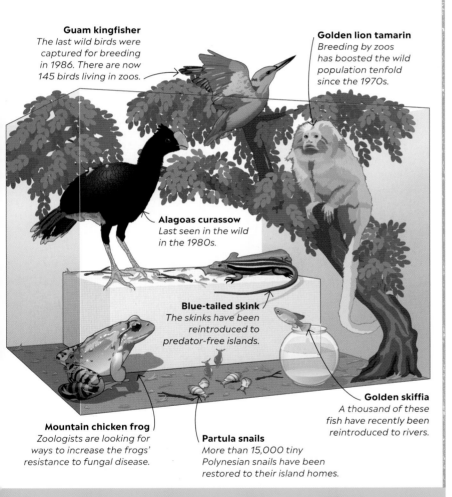

Guam kingfisher
The last wild birds were captured for breeding in 1986. There are now 145 birds living in zoos.

Golden lion tamarin
Breeding by zoos has boosted the wild population tenfold since the 1970s.

Alagoas curassow
Last seen in the wild in the 1980s.

Blue-tailed skink
The skinks have been reintroduced to predator-free islands.

Golden skiffia
A thousand of these fish have recently been reintroduced to rivers.

Mountain chicken frog
Zoologists are looking for ways to increase the frogs' resistance to fungal disease.

Partula snails
More than 15,000 tiny Polynesian snails have been restored to their island homes.

RISEN FROM THE DEAD

The coelacanth is a species of fish that was thought to have gone extinct 66 million years ago, until it was found alive off the coast of South Africa in 1938. The fish are believed to live for more than 100 years.

ENDANGERED ANIMALS

These are some of the most endangered animals on Earth. Human activity has led to the dramatic destruction of their natural habitats.

1 JAVAN RHINO
These rhinos were once found across Southeast Asia, but today only around 75 individuals are left, on the Indonesian island of Java.

2 AMUR LEOPARD
This is one of the rarest big cats in the world. There are only around 100 individuals surviving, in Russia's Amur region and northeast China.

3 SUMATRAN TIGER
The smallest tiger species, this striped cat lives on the Indonesian island of Sumatra. Only around 600 of the tigers are left there.

4 MOUNTAIN GORILLA
These gorillas live in high-altitude forests in the mountains of Central Africa. There are about 1,000 of them living in the wild.

5 TAPANULI ORANGUTAN
All orangutans are threatened, but there are fewer than 800 left of this species, which lives in only one small area of Sumatra, Indonesia.

6 YANGTZE FINLESS PORPOISE
The only freshwater porpoise in the world, this aquatic mammal faces various threats in the Yangtze River in China. Around 1,000 still swim in its waters.

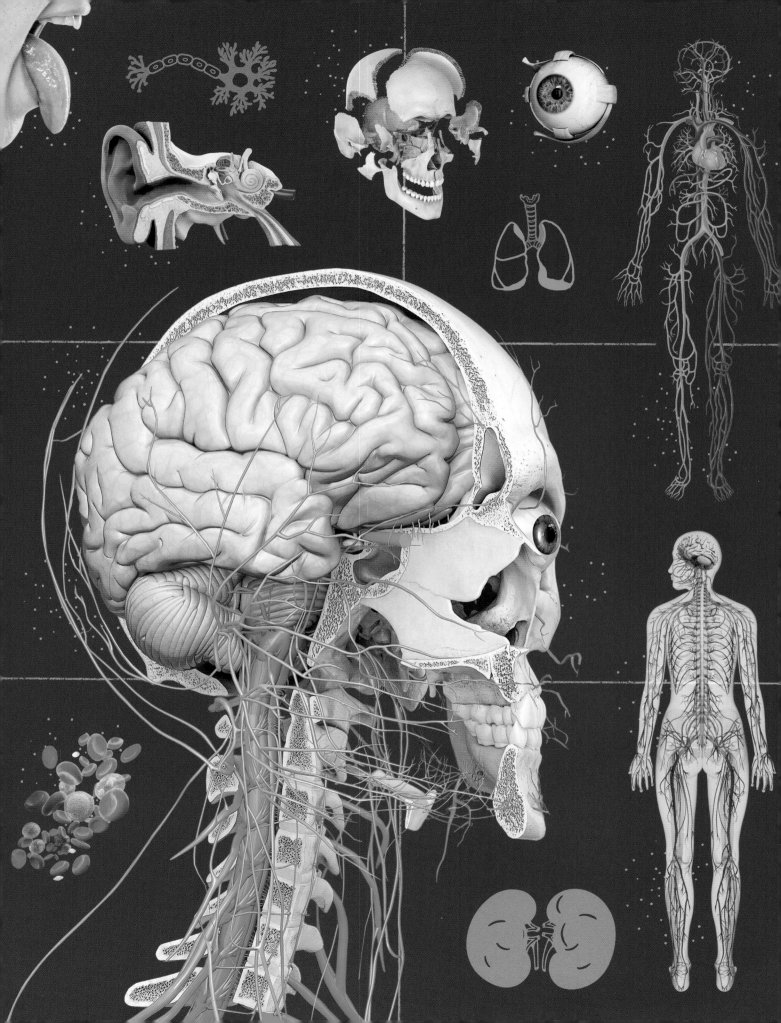

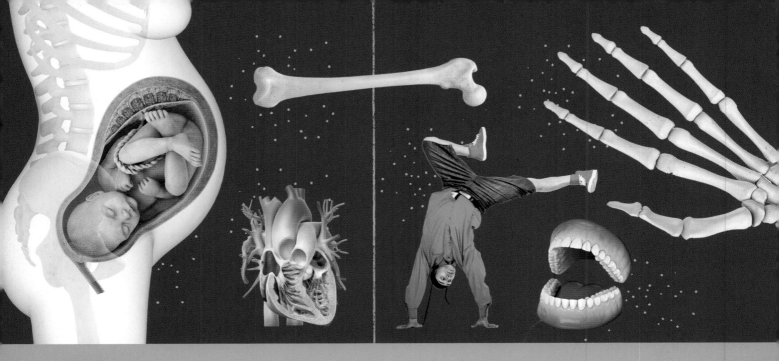

HUMAN BODY

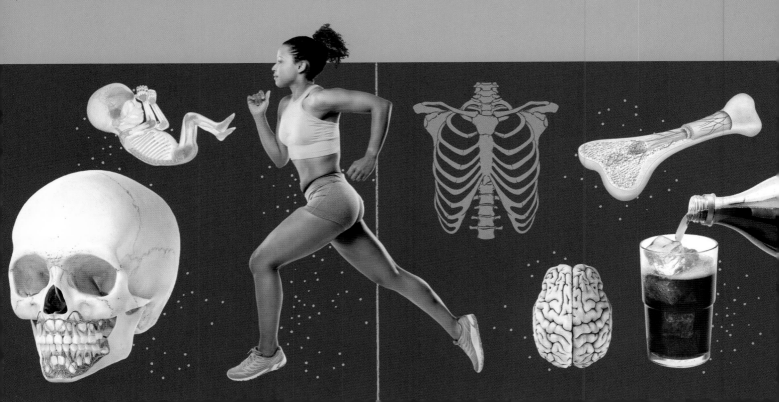

Body basics

The human body is an amazingly complex structure, made up of hundreds of body parts working together to keep us alive and healthy. Although more is known about the body today than ever before, much of how it works still remains a mystery.

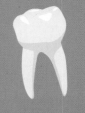

ENAMEL, A TOOTH'S THIN COVER, IS THE HARDEST TISSUE IN THE HUMAN BODY!

BUILDING A BODY

Like all living things, the human body is made up of trillions of tiny cells. In your body, groups of cells create tissues, which in turn form organs. Multiple organs can work together as part of body systems, to perform vital jobs.

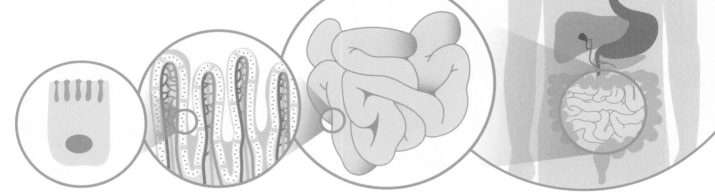

Cell
Cells are the smallest unit of life. Each one has a specialized function. This cell is found in the lining of the intestines.

Tissue
Cells of the same type come together to form tissues. For example, the intestines are lined with a tissue that makes digestive enzymes.

Organ
Different types of tissues join together to form an organ, such as the small intestine.

Body system
Organs work together as a system to do a specific job, such as digestion.

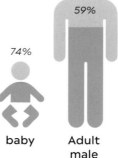

THERE ARE AS MANY BACTERIAL CELLS IN YOUR BODY AS HUMAN CELLS!

MOSTLY WATER

At birth, almost three-quarters of your body consists of water. As you grow older, the makeup of your body changes and the amount of water gradually decreases. For instance, older adults have less water because they lose water-rich muscle tissue.

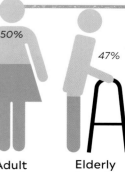

74% baby

59% Adult male

50% Adult female

47% Elderly female

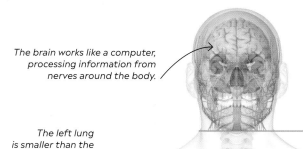

The brain works like a computer, processing information from nerves around the body.

The left lung is smaller than the right lung to allow space for the heart.

Nervous system
The brain and nerves control how you respond to your surroundings and automatic functions like breathing.

Respiratory system
The airways and lungs bring oxygen into the body and remove carbon dioxide.

Circulatory system
The heart pumps blood around the body using blood vessels to deliver oxygen to the body's cells.

Digestive system
The digestive system processes food to release energy and nutrients.

Reproductive system
Differing in men and women, these organs produce human offspring.

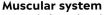

These are male reproductive organs.

BODY SYSTEMS
This diagram shows a selection of the main systems found in the human body. Although each has its own specific job, individual systems work closely together to keep you alive.

Lymphatic vessels transport a fluid called lymph from body tissues into the bloodstream.

Muscular system
Every move you make is produced by muscles attached to the skeleton. Other types of muscles make the heart beat and push food into the intestine.

Lymphatic and immune system
The lymphatic system works alongside the immune system to help protect the body from infection and disease.

Skeletal system
Bones act as a support structure for the body, protect internal organs, and allow movement.

MYSTERIOUS FEATURES
As humans have evolved, some structures in the body have lost their original function. These features are called vestigial, meaning they remain in a form that is small or underdeveloped.

Third molars, also known as wisdom teeth

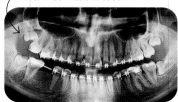

Wisdom teeth
Third molars were vital for our ancestors' rough diets, but as we have evolved, our jaws have shrunk. Today, these teeth can cause complications and are often removed.

Inner fold helps drain tears.

Third eyelid
Humans no longer have a third eyelid to protect the eye, just a tiny fold, but many other animals do.

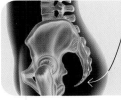

Tailbone is at the base of the spine.

Tail bone
Many scientists believe the coccyx (tailbone) is a remnant of a tail from our ancestors that now just helps support our weight.

THE **HUMAN BODY** CONTAINS **TINY AMOUNTS** OF **GOLD!**

Super cells

The human body is made up of trillions of tiny cells too small for the eye to see. Together, cells form the different tissues of the body. Each type of cell has its own specialized job to do.

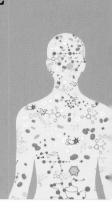

THERE ARE ABOUT 37 TRILLION CELLS IN THE HUMAN BODY!

TYPES OF CELLS

There are about 200 different types of body cells that perform a variety of functions. Some of the main ones are shown here in close up.

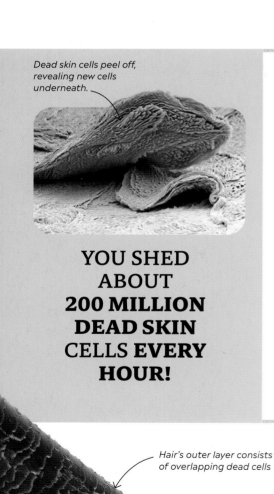

Dead skin cells peel off, revealing new cells underneath.

YOU SHED ABOUT 200 MILLION DEAD SKIN CELLS EVERY HOUR!

INSIDE A CELL

The nucleus is the control center of a cell. It contains DNA, which carries instructions to make the cell work. Most human cells have the same basic structure.

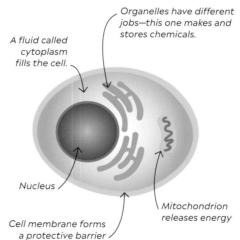

Organelles have different jobs—this one makes and stores chemicals.

A fluid called cytoplasm fills the cell.

Nucleus

Cell membrane forms a protective barrier

Mitochondrion releases energy

Muscle cells
Known as myocytes, muscle cells can contract to move parts of the body.

Bone cells
These cells are responsible for new bone growth and repairing bones.

Red blood cells
Red blood cells absorb oxygen and release it around the body.

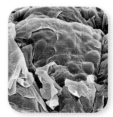

Skin cells
Creating a strong barrier that covers the body, skin cells are vital for protection.

Hair's outer layer consists of overlapping dead cells

DEAD OR ALIVE?

All the hair you see on your head and body is dead. It is made of keratin, a protein also found in nails and skin. When the hair shaft peeks through the skin's surface, the cells are no longer alive. Living cells exist in the hair roots where blood vessels keep the hair growing.

Nerve cells
As part of the nervous system, nerve cells send electrical signals around the body.

Fat cells
These cells store body fat. They are an important source of energy and warmth.

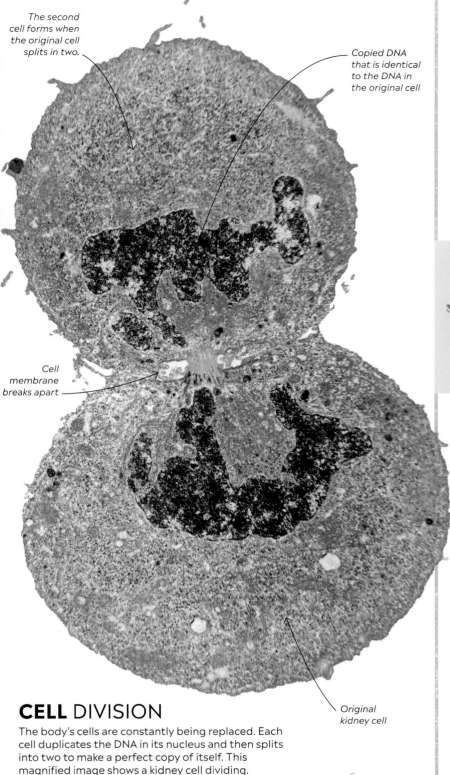

The second cell forms when the original cell splits in two.

Copied DNA that is identical to the DNA in the original cell

Cell membrane breaks apart

Original kidney cell

CELL DIVISION

The body's cells are constantly being replaced. Each cell duplicates the DNA in its nucleus and then splits into two to make a perfect copy of itself. This magnified image shows a kidney cell dividing.

THE LONGEST BODY CELLS ARE NERVE CELLS. SOME ARE 3 FT (1 M) LONG!

Many nerve cells have long tails that relay messages.

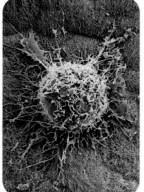

STEM CELLS

Amazing cells called stem cells are the body's building blocks. Stem cells have the unique ability to develop into any other type of cell. This highly magnified image shows a stem cell from adult bone marrow (brown) on cartilage tissue (pink).

THE BIGGEST CELL IN THE ANIMAL KINGDOM IS AN OSTRICH EGG AT 5.9 IN (15 CM) LONG!

BIGGEST AND SMALLEST

Shown on a pin in this magnified image, the female egg cell is the largest human cell. It is just visible to the unaided eye. A male sperm cell, the tiniest cell, is about 10,000 times smaller than an egg cell. Like most cells, it can be seen only with a microscope.

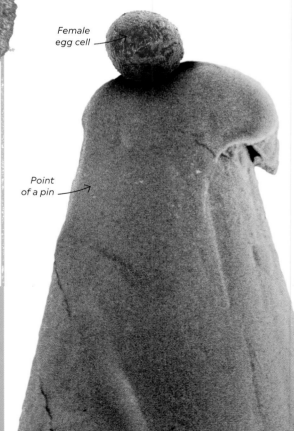

Female egg cell

Point of a pin

Bare bones

Your bony skeleton makes up nearly 15 percent of your body weight. It gives your body shape—so you aren't floppy like a rag doll—protects vital organs, and enables you to move around.

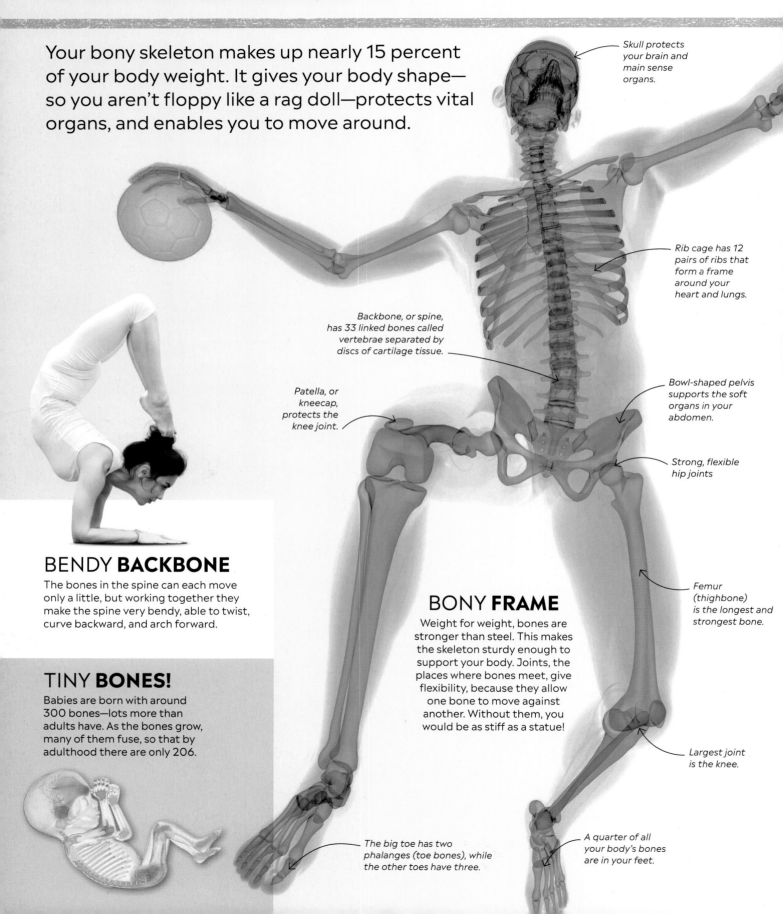

Skull protects your brain and main sense organs.

Rib cage has 12 pairs of ribs that form a frame around your heart and lungs.

Backbone, or spine, has 33 linked bones called vertebrae separated by discs of cartilage tissue.

Patella, or kneecap, protects the knee joint.

Bowl-shaped pelvis supports the soft organs in your abdomen.

Strong, flexible hip joints

Femur (thighbone) is the longest and strongest bone.

Largest joint is the knee.

The big toe has two phalanges (toe bones), while the other toes have three.

A quarter of all your body's bones are in your feet.

BENDY **BACKBONE**

The bones in the spine can each move only a little, but working together they make the spine very bendy, able to twist, curve backward, and arch forward.

TINY **BONES!**

Babies are born with around 300 bones—lots more than adults have. As the bones grow, many of them fuse, so that by adulthood there are only 206.

BONY **FRAME**

Weight for weight, bones are stronger than steel. This makes the skeleton sturdy enough to support your body. Joints, the places where bones meet, give flexibility, because they allow one bone to move against another. Without them, you would be as stiff as a statue!

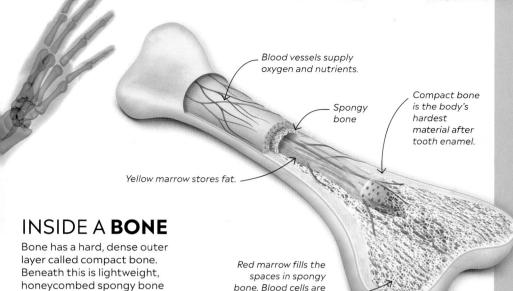

Blood vessels supply oxygen and nutrients.

Spongy bone

Compact bone is the body's hardest material after tooth enamel.

Yellow marrow stores fat.

Red marrow fills the spaces in spongy bone. Blood cells are made in red marrow.

INSIDE A **BONE**

Bone has a hard, dense outer layer called compact bone. Beneath this is lightweight, honeycombed spongy bone and soft tissue called marrow.

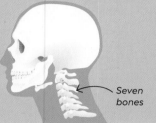

Seven bones

HUMANS HAVE THE **SAME** **NUMBER** OF **NECK BONES** AS **GIRAFFES!**

Seven bones

YOU ARE **A TINY** **BIT TALLER** IN THE **MORNING** THAN BEFORE BED, BECAUSE YOUR **SPINE** **STRETCHES** OUT WHILE YOU **SLEEP!**

STRONG **SKULL**

The skull has 22 bones. The only one that moves is the mandible, or jawbone. The rest are locked together at fixed joints called sutures, forming a strong, protective structure.

There are 14 finger bones, or phalanges.

The five palm bones are the metacarpals.

Eight carpal bones form the wrist.

Eight bones form the dome-shaped cranium.

Temporal bone is the body's densest bone.

Fourteen facial bones

UNIQUE **HANDS**

Multiple joints and thumbs that can touch the fingertips enable human hands to grip strongly and yet make precise and delicate movements. No other mammal has such versatile hands.

FIXING **FRACTURES**

Bone is made of living tissue that can grow, renew itself, and repair any fractures, or breaks, that occur.

Mandible is moved by powerful jaw muscles.

Hammer bone

SMALLEST BONES!

Three tiny bones in the ear, named the hammer, anvil, and stirrup, are the smallest in the body. They help amplify sounds captured by your eardrum.

First hours
A blood clot forms around the fracture to seal the wound.

Days later
Fibers of new bone begin to form in the gap between the bones.

Weeks later
Spongy bone replaces the fibers and blood vessels regrow.

Months later
Compact bone replaces spongy bone, healing the fracture.

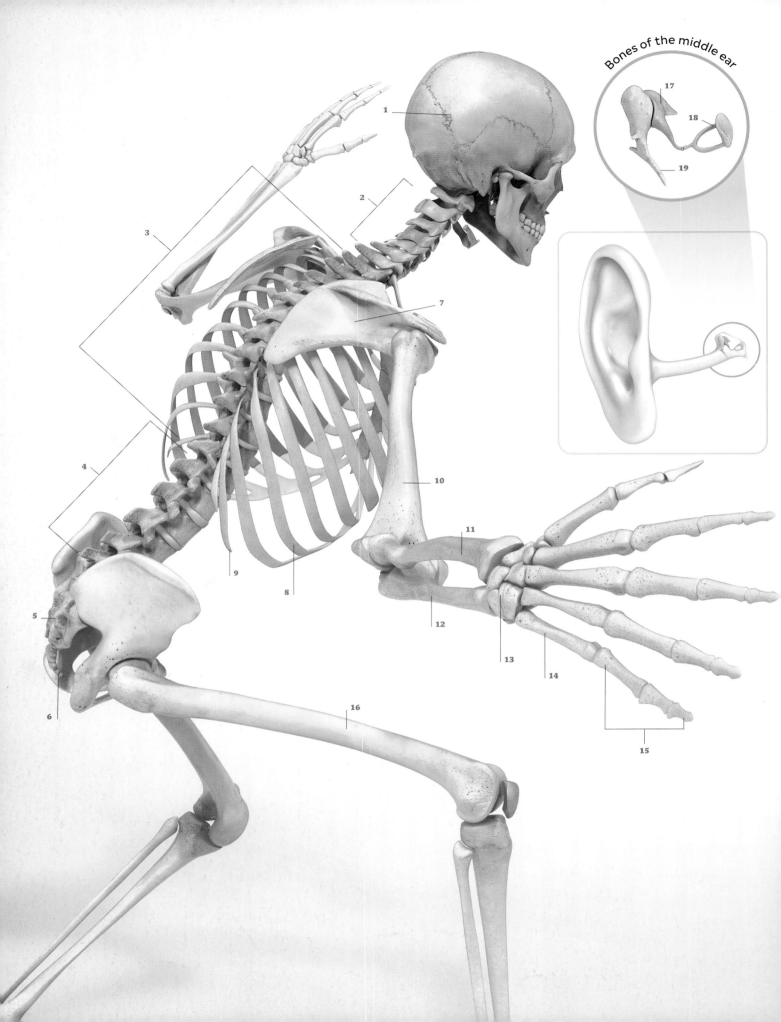

Bones of the middle ear

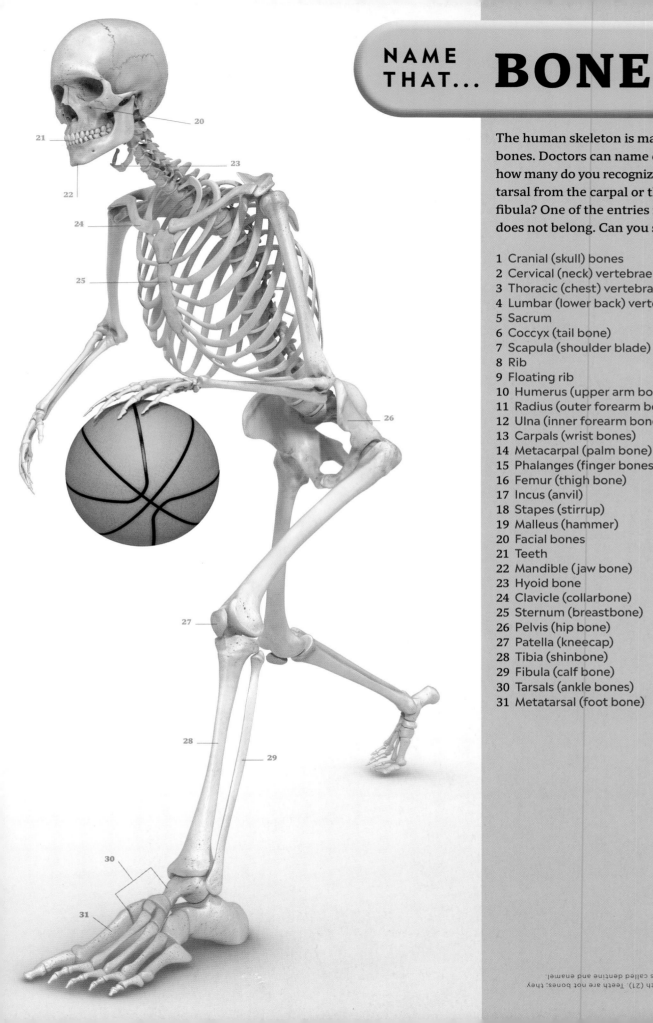

NAME THAT... BONE

The human skeleton is made up of 206 bones. Doctors can name every bone, but how many do you recognize? Can you tell the tarsal from the carpal or the tibia from the fibula? One of the entries in the list below does not belong. Can you spot which one?

1 Cranial (skull) bones
2 Cervical (neck) vertebrae
3 Thoracic (chest) vertebrae
4 Lumbar (lower back) vertebrae
5 Sacrum
6 Coccyx (tail bone)
7 Scapula (shoulder blade)
8 Rib
9 Floating rib
10 Humerus (upper arm bone)
11 Radius (outer forearm bone)
12 Ulna (inner forearm bone)
13 Carpals (wrist bones)
14 Metacarpal (palm bone)
15 Phalanges (finger bones)
16 Femur (thigh bone)
17 Incus (anvil)
18 Stapes (stirrup)
19 Malleus (hammer)
20 Facial bones
21 Teeth
22 Mandible (jaw bone)
23 Hyoid bone
24 Clavicle (collarbone)
25 Sternum (breastbone)
26 Pelvis (hip bone)
27 Patella (kneecap)
28 Tibia (shinbone)
29 Fibula (calf bone)
30 Tarsals (ankle bones)
31 Metatarsal (foot bone)

The odd one out is teeth (21). Teeth are not bones; they are made of substances called dentine and enamel.

Muscle power

Your super strong body is packed with more than 600 muscles attached to your skeleton. They make up 40 percent of your body weight and are involved in every move you make. But muscles also allow you to talk, move food through your digestive system, and send vital blood around your body.

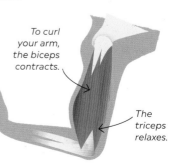

The hottest areas show up on the thermogram in red.

The bicycle, in blue, stays cool.

BODY HEAT

When your muscles are working hard during exercise, such as bike riding, they produce heat. This thermal image shows in red the areas where the body is trying to get rid of excess heat.

Tongue muscles help you speak, eat, and swallow.

TOUGH TONGUE

Your tongue contains eight different muscles. Half of these muscles link the tongue to the head and neck. The rest give your tongue the flexibility to stretch, speak, and move food around your mouth.

THE **STRONGEST MUSCLE** FOR ITS SIZE IS THE **MASSETER**. IT IS CAPABLE OF **EXERTING 200 LB** (90 KG) OF FORCE!

Masseters control your jaw.

HOW MUSCLES WORK

Muscles can pull bones but cannot push them back again. They are usually arranged in opposite pairs to move bones in two different directions. For example, two muscles in your upper arm work together to curl and uncurl your arm.

To uncurl your arm, the biceps relaxes.

The triceps contracts.

To curl your arm, the biceps contracts.

The triceps relaxes.

INSIDE A MUSCLE

Resembling an electric cable, a muscle is made up of hundreds of long cells called muscle fibers crammed together. Each fiber consists of myofibrils, tiny strands that relax and contract. Blood vessels supply oxygen and energy to make the muscles move.

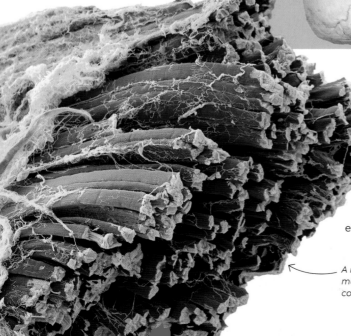

A magnified view of muscle fibers (red) and connective tissue (white)

THE **MUSCLES** THAT CONTROL YOUR **EYES** MOVE MORE THAN **100,000** TIMES A DAY!

Your longest muscle is the sartorius, running from your hip to your knee.

The gluteus maximus in the buttock is your largest muscle.

Stretching ensures muscles stay flexible.

Seven muscles connect the upper arm bone to the shoulder blade.

Toned muscles create definition under the skin.

GOOSEBUMPS!

Each of the five million hairs growing on your body has a muscle, called an arrector pili muscle. When you are cold or scared, these tiny muscles contract, making your hairs stand upright. This traps a layer of air near the skin and warms you up.

MUSCLE BUILDING

The more your skeletal muscles work, the stronger they get. Regular exercise, such as dancing, creates tiny tears in the muscle fibers. The body repairs the torn fibers, creating bigger and bulkier muscles.

Strong arm muscles help the dancer keep his balance.

TYPES OF MUSCLES

Muscles in the body are divided into three types. You consciously control skeletal muscles, but smooth muscle and cardiac muscle work automatically.

smooth muscle tissue

Smooth muscle
This type of muscle is found inside the body's organs and all the blood vessels that transport blood and nutrients from food.

Cardiac muscle tissue

Cardiac muscle
Found only in the heart, cardiac muscle pumps blood around the body 24/7. This is the only muscle that never gets tired!

Skeletal muscle tissue

Skeletal muscle
Attached to the body's bones, these bundles of muscle fibers move the skeleton, including the arms and legs.

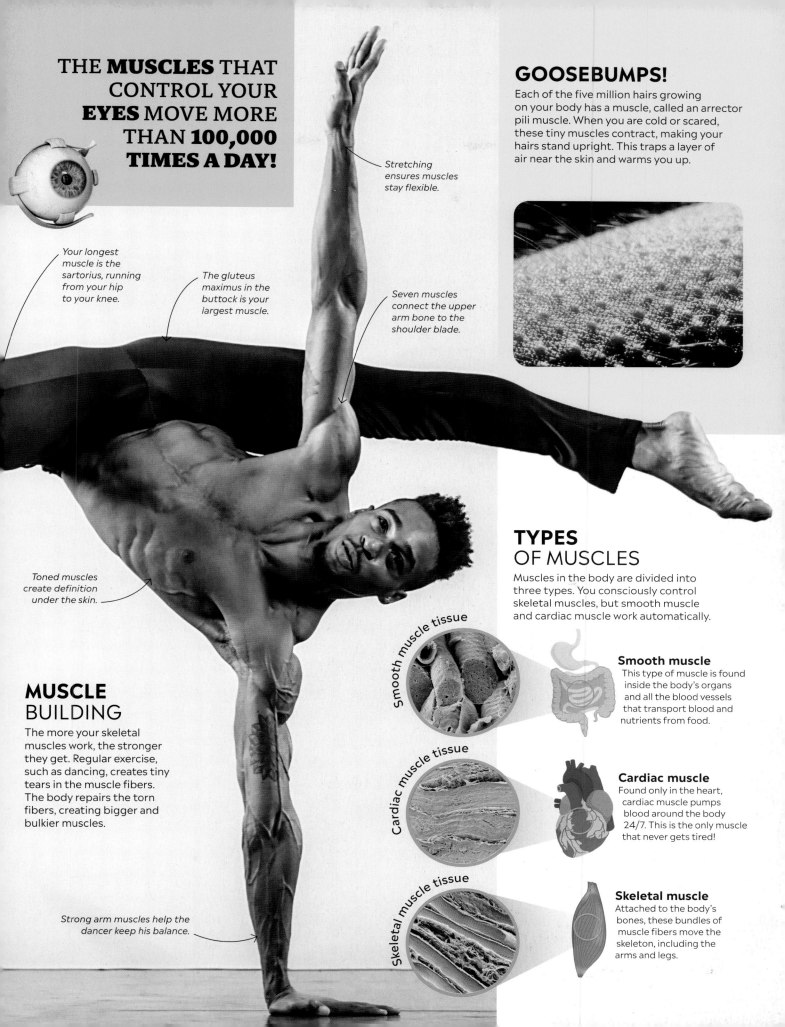

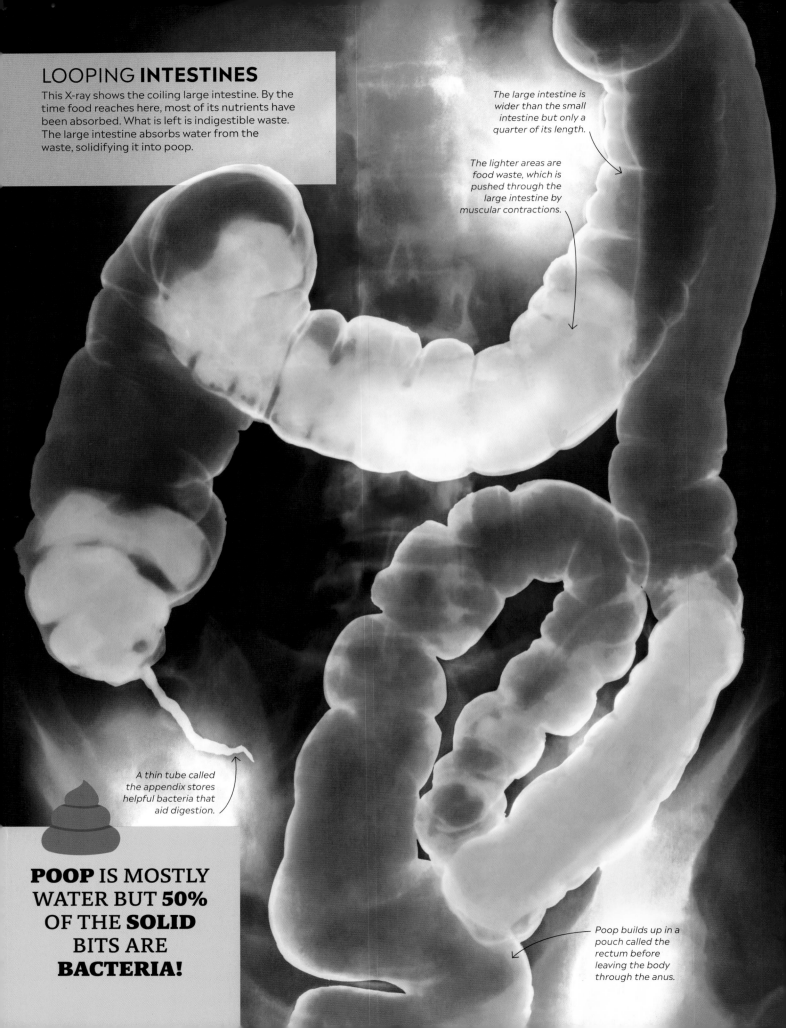

LOOPING **INTESTINES**

This X-ray shows the coiling large intestine. By the time food reaches here, most of its nutrients have been absorbed. What is left is indigestible waste. The large intestine absorbs water from the waste, solidifying it into poop.

The large intestine is wider than the small intestine but only a quarter of its length.

The lighter areas are food waste, which is pushed through the large intestine by muscular contractions.

A thin tube called the appendix stores helpful bacteria that aid digestion.

Poop builds up in a pouch called the rectum before leaving the body through the anus.

POOP IS MOSTLY WATER BUT **50%** OF THE **SOLID** BITS ARE **BACTERIA!**

Food processor

The digestive system breaks down tens of thousands of meals over a lifetime. Each meal is converted into nutrients and energy as it travels through about 30 ft (9 m) of digestive organs.

YOU PRODUCE UP TO **1.6 QUARTS** (1.5 LITERS) OF **SALIVA EVERY DAY!**

One day's worth of saliva could fill a big bottle.

ACID ATTACK

The muscular stomach churns up food and mixes it with digestive juices that help break it down. The juices contain powerful acid that kills any harmful bacteria.

Thick wall has three layers of muscle.

Four quarts (4 liters) of gastric juice are produced every day.

Thick mucus lining stops the stomach from digesting itself!

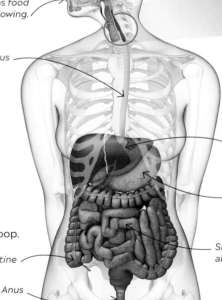

Muscle contracts behind food to push it forward.

In the mouth, food is broken down into smaller pieces by chewing.

Saliva softens food for swallowing.

Esophagus

Pushing through
Muscles found in the throat and intestines contract and relax to move food along. This is called peristalsis.

DIGESTIVE SYSTEM

It takes around 24 to 72 hours for food to travel through the digestive system. As it goes, food is broken down and vital nutrients and water are absorbed. Undigested waste is pushed out as poop.

Liver releases bile, a fluid that breaks down fats.

Stomach turns food into a lumpy liquid called chyme.

Small intestine absorbs nutrients.

Large intestine

Anus

THE AVERAGE PERSON **DEVOURS** ABOUT **1,500 LB** (675 KG) OF **FOOD** IN A **YEAR!**

WHY DO WE **BURP?**

When you drink carbonated drinks, air can get trapped in the esophagus. The body responds by burping, which pushes the excess air out through your mouth. It is normal to burp up to 30 times a day!

Sharp canines help with gripping and tearing.

Premolars and molars crush and grind food.

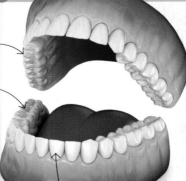

TOUGH TEETH

Teeth start the process of digestion by chomping food into smaller pieces. Saliva produced by glands in the mouth helps soften food.

Incisors are for cutting and biting.

YOU **RELEASE** UP TO **2.3 QUARTS** (2.2 LITERS) OF **GAS EVERY DAY!**

Heart and blood

Your heart is a powerhouse pump that circulates blood around your body nonstop. Each day your heart beats about 100,000 times, sending 8 pints (5 liters) of blood on an epic journey to your organs and muscles.

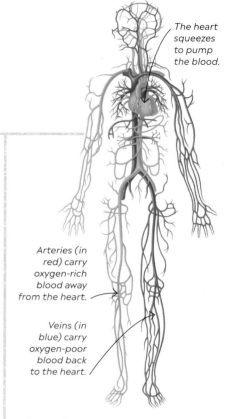

The heart squeezes to pump the blood.

Arteries (in red) carry oxygen-rich blood away from the heart.

Veins (in blue) carry oxygen-poor blood back to the heart.

THE BODY'S BLOOD VESSELS ARE 60,000 MILES (100,000 KM) LONG—ENOUGH TO WRAP TWICE AROUND EARTH!

BLOOD **VESSELS**

There are three types of blood vessels. Arteries take blood away from the heart. Veins return blood back to the heart, while small capillaries connect veins and arteries together.

Arteries
These have thick, muscular walls.

Veins
These vessels have thin walls.

Capillaries
These are the smallest vessels.

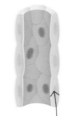

Vein valves stop blood from flowing backward.

Walls are only one cell thick.

CIRCULATION

The cardiovascular system is made up of the heart and an intricate network of blood vessels. Your heart delivers blood carrying oxygen and nutrients to every cell, muscle, and organ in your body.

IN THE **BLOOD**

A watery fluid called plasma makes up 55 percent of your blood, and red blood cells account for 44 percent. The remaining 1 percent consists of white blood cells and platelets.

Platelets help the blood clot and seal cuts to the skin.

White blood cells attack invading germs.

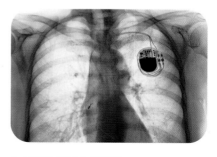

LIFE **SAVER**

Pacemakers are small electronic devices placed under the skin to correct irregular heartbeats. This X-ray shows a pacemaker attached to a wire that is guided through a blood vessel to the heart.

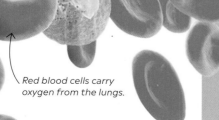

Red blood cells carry oxygen from the lungs.

IRON GIVES OUR BLOOD ITS **RED** COLOR, WHILE **COPPER** MAKES OCTOPUS BLOOD **BLUE!**

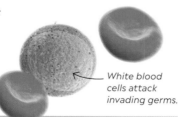

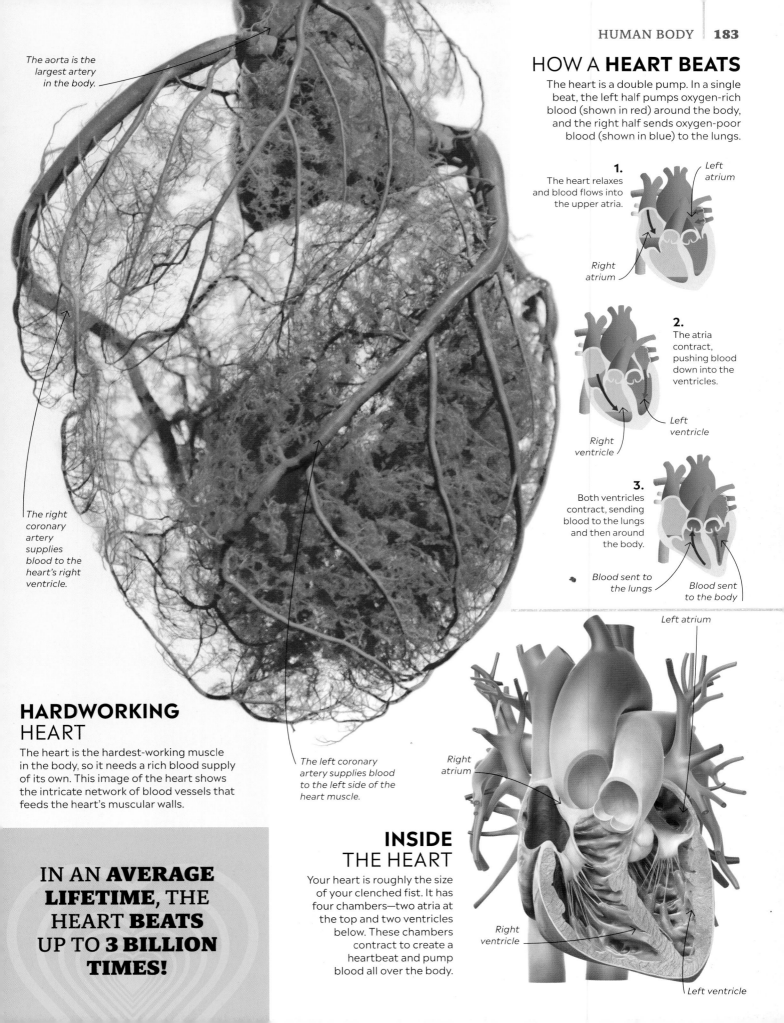

The aorta is the largest artery in the body.

The right coronary artery supplies blood to the heart's right ventricle.

HOW A **HEART BEATS**

The heart is a double pump. In a single beat, the left half pumps oxygen-rich blood (shown in red) around the body, and the right half sends oxygen-poor blood (shown in blue) to the lungs.

1.
The heart relaxes and blood flows into the upper atria.

Left atrium

Right atrium

2.
The atria contract, pushing blood down into the ventricles.

Left ventricle

Right ventricle

3.
Both ventricles contract, sending blood to the lungs and then around the body.

Blood sent to the lungs

Blood sent to the body

HARDWORKING
HEART

The heart is the hardest-working muscle in the body, so it needs a rich blood supply of its own. This image of the heart shows the intricate network of blood vessels that feeds the heart's muscular walls.

The left coronary artery supplies blood to the left side of the heart muscle.

IN AN AVERAGE LIFETIME, THE HEART **BEATS** UP TO **3 BILLION TIMES!**

INSIDE
THE HEART

Your heart is roughly the size of your clenched fist. It has four chambers—two atria at the top and two ventricles below. These chambers contract to create a heartbeat and pump blood all over the body.

Left atrium

Right atrium

Right ventricle

Left ventricle

STAT ATTACK!
BODY

The human body is capable of astonishing things, from continually replenishing its cells to controlling many body functions simultaneously without us realizing. Here are some facts and figures about our brilliant bodies.

RAREST EYES

A tiny 2 percent of the population have green eyes, making it the world's rarest eye color. At about 80 percent, the vast majority of people have brown eyes.

LIFE SPAN OF A CELL

The cells in your body have different life cycles, depending on their function. Skin cells constantly replace themselves and last as little as a day. Others, such as brain cells, can last your entire life.

70+ YEARS
Brain cells

15 YEARS
Skeletal muscle cells

10 YEARS
Fat cells

6-9 MONTHS
Liver cells

3-5 DAYS
Intestinal lining cells

1-3 DAYS
White blood cells

BLINKING
Your eyes will blink around 416 million times.

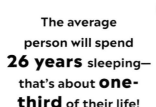

The average person will spend **26 years** sleeping— that's about **one-third** of their life!

BREATHING
You will breathe in about 54 million gallons (250 million liters) of air.

PUMPING BLOOD
Your heart will pump around 43 million gallons (200 million liters) of blood around the body.

TOILET TRIPS
You will spend one whole year sitting on the toilet.

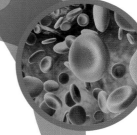

WALKING
You will take approximately 146 million steps.

IN YOUR LIFETIME

A person who lives for 80 years will start a new day around 29,220 times. During that time, the body gets through a truly incredible workload.

RECORD GROWTH

With great care and attention, some people have grown their hair and nails to remarkable lengths. Here are some of the world's greatest growers.

LONGEST NAILS

Diana Armstrong, US, grew the world's longest fingernails, which measured 4ft 6 in (1.38 m).

LONGEST HAIR

In 2004, China's Xie Qiuping's hair measured 18 ft 5 in (5.62 m)— nearly the height of an adult giraffe.

LONGEST MUSTACHE

American Paul Slosar's mustache measured 2 ft 1 in (63.5 cm).

LONGEST EYELASHES

China's You Jianxia's eyelashes measured 8 in (20 cm) and reached her chin.

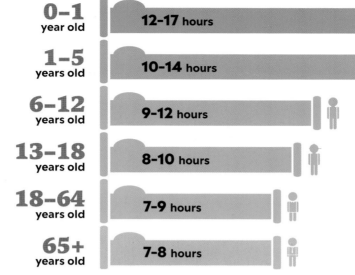

0–1 year old	**12–17** hours
1–5 years old	**10–14** hours
6–12 years old	**9–12** hours
13–18 years old	**8–10** hours
18–64 years old	**7–9** hours
65+ years old	**7–8** hours

SLEEP LEVELS

Humans need different amounts of sleep depending on their age. Babies and young children need more because sleep is essential for their growth and development. This chart shows the different amounts of sleep we need as we age.

LONGEST LIFE

Jeanne Louise Calment from France holds the world record for the oldest-ever person. She was 122 years and 164 days old when she died in 1997.

ELEMENTS IN THE BODY

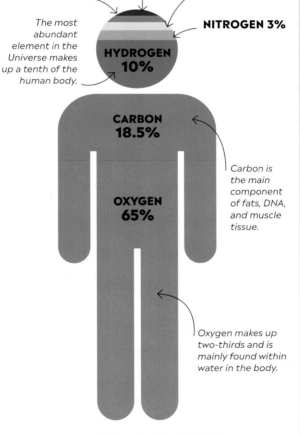

PHOSPHORUS 1%

OTHERS 1%

CALCIUM 1.5%

NITROGEN 3%

The most abundant element in the Universe makes up a tenth of the human body.

HYDROGEN 10%

CARBON 18.5%

Carbon is the main component of fats, DNA, and muscle tissue.

OXYGEN 65%

Oxygen makes up two-thirds and is mainly found within water in the body.

Most of the human body is made of six elements that combine in different ways to form thousands of different compounds. This illustration shows the proportions that make up our bodies.

TONGUE TWISTER

Most of us can roll up the sides of our tongue—one study found that 83 percent of people are tongue-rollers. However, only 14 percent could shape their tongue into folds, making this clover-leaf shape one of the rarest tongue tricks.

SWEATY WORK

The body produces varying amounts of sweat depending on how hard we exercise and how hot it is. A person doing lots of exercise in hot weather can produce up to 2.6 gallons (12 liters) of sweat in a day!

BREATHING **CONTROL**

Breathing happens automatically, but when you exercise, your brain recognizes the need for more oxygen and makes you breathe harder and faster. It is possible to consciously control your breathing. Swimmers train themselves to breathe rhythmically to maintain a steady flow of oxygen to their muscles.

Swimmer breathes out under water, creating a stream of bubbles, then raises his head above the surface to take in more air.

Strong abdominal muscles assist the diaphragm and rib muscles, giving the swimmer good breathing control.

ROUTE TO **THE LUNGS**

Air travels to the lungs through the trachea, or windpipe. This tube spreads out like an upside-down tree, with two big branches, called bronchi, and multiple smaller ones, known as bronchioles. At the end of the bronchioles are microscopic air sacs called alveoli.

Bronchi carry air into your lungs.

Trachea

Bronchioles carry air to the alveoli.

Drawing **breath**

The two spongy lungs in your chest enable you to breathe about 22,000 times a day. With each breath, a vital exchange of gases takes place. Oxygen from the air inhaled passes into your blood. At the same time, waste carbon dioxide from your body's cells passes from the blood to the air in your lungs and is breathed out.

BY LEARNING TO **HOLD THEIR BREATH** FOR LONGER, SOME **FREE DIVERS** CAN DIVE OVER **330 FT** (100 M) WITHOUT **OXYGEN TANKS!**

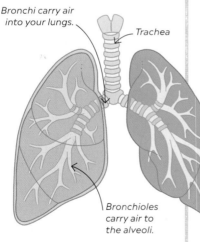

SLIMY MUCUS

Mucus is a sticky liquid that catches inhaled dust and germs and helps fight infections in the body. Every day, your nose, throat, and lungs secrete up to 2.5 pints (1.5 liters) of mucus.

THE **SURFACE AREA** OF YOUR **LUNGS** IS ABOUT **30 TIMES BIGGER** THAN THE **SURFACE AREA** OF YOUR **SKIN!**

GAS **EXCHANGE**

The exchange of gases in the lungs takes place via tiny blood vessels called capillaries that surround about 480 million air-filled sacs called alveoli (singular: alveolus).

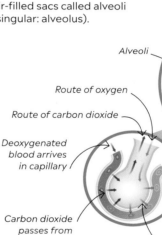

Lungs

Bronchiole

Alveoli

Route of oxygen

Route of carbon dioxide

Deoxygenated blood arrives in capillary

Capillaries surround each alveolus

Carbon dioxide passes from blood to the air

Oxygenated blood flows away

Oxygen from air passes into blood

Muscles need a regular supply of oxygen to keep working hard until the end of a race.

BREATHING IN AND OUT

The diaphragm is a sheet of muscle below the lungs. When you breathe in, your diaphragm contracts and flattens. This increases the volume of your chest cavity, so your lungs can inflate with air. When the diaphragm relaxes, air is pushed out of your lungs.

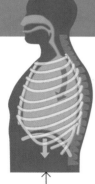

The diaphragm (yellow) flattens and muscles raise the ribs, sucking air into the lungs.

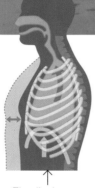

The diaphragm rises and the ribs descend, reducing the chest cavity and expelling air.

EACH ALVEOLUS CAN BE SMALLER THAN A GRAIN OF SAND!

MOUNTAIN AIR

At high altitude, air contains less oxygen so it is harder to breathe. Mountain people, such as these Sherpas from Nepal, produce extra red blood cells to carry more oxygen from the lungs.

LUNG CAPACITY

The lungs can be trained to hold much more air than usual. Musicians who play mouth-blown instruments, like the trumpet, generally have much greater lung function and better control of their breathing.

BRAIN MAP

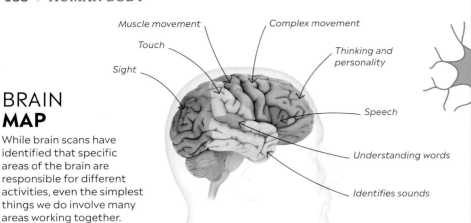

Muscle movement
Complex movement
Touch
Thinking and personality
Sight
Speech
Understanding words
Identifies sounds

While brain scans have identified that specific areas of the brain are responsible for different activities, even the simplest things we do involve many areas working together.

SENDING SIGNALS

Fibers called dendrites connect to other neurons.

Long body or axon carries signals

Fibers here pass signals to dendrites of other neurons.

The nervous system is made of a network of nerve cells called neurons. These messenger cells relay information as electrical signals. The brain alone contains 86 billion neurons.

SOME **NERVE SIGNALS** CAN TRAVEL **AS FAST AS** A **FORMULA 1 RACE CAR!**

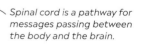

Control center

BUSY BRAIN

Active areas of the brain are shown in red.

Brain scans reveal which parts of the brain are working the hardest. This one shows that during REM (rapid eye movement) sleep, the brain is active and dreaming, and as busy as when you are awake.

Your brain is the most complex organ in your body. It controls your actions, body processes, thoughts, feelings, and memory—all at the same time! With the spinal cord and nerves, it forms your nervous system.

Brain is the largest organ in the nervous system.

THE **BRAIN** IS MOSTLY **MADE OF FAT** AND IS VERY **SOFT AND SQUISHY,** LIKE JELLY!

REFLEX ACTIONS

Not all actions are controlled by the brain. If you touch something sharp, your hand automatically moves away within half a second, quicker than a signal can reach your brain. This is called a reflex action, and it is controlled directly by the spinal cord.

Nerves are large bundles of cells called neurons.

Spinal cord is a pathway for messages passing between the body and the brain.

NERVOUS SYSTEM

The nervous system enables you to sense and respond to the world around you. Nerves carry signals from sense organs to the brain. Then signals from the brain and spinal cord tell your muscles, organs, and glands what to do.

INSIDE **THE SKULL**

Weighing about 2.8 lb (1.3 kg), the brain is one of the body's largest organs and fills up most of the space in the skull. It is directly connected to a network of nerves in the skull that help you taste, smell, hear, and make facial expressions.

In the gap between the skull and the brain is a thin layer of protective fluid.

Grooves increase the surface area of the cortex. Spread out flat, it would be the size of a small tablecloth.

The wrinkly top layer of the brain is called the cerebral cortex. This is where thoughts occur.

Facial nerves control the muscles that help you smile and frown.

The cerebellum, at the base of the brain, is for balance and muscle control.

The brain stem regulates the functions you do not actively control, such as breathing.

Spinal cord relays nerve signals between the brain and every part of the body.

RIGHT AND **LEFT**

The brain is split into two. Both halves, or hemispheres, contain similar structures, so they are mirror images of each other. The left hemisphere controls the right side of the body, while the right hemisphere controls the left side.

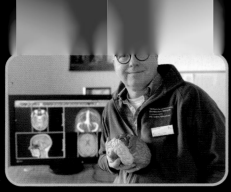

Dr. Jörn Zeller leads the neurology department at Bernkastel/Wittlich Hospital, Germany. He says neurology is the most interesting part of medicine he can imagine.

Ask a...
NEUROLOGIST

Q Does the brain feel pain?

A The brain itself doesn't, even if you poked it with a toothpick. But it collects pain signals from all over the rest of the body on special pain pathways and then relays them to us. When you have a headache, it is not the brain itself that is hurting, but other tissues in your head such as the blood vessels or soft tissue surrounding the brain.

Q What are memories made of?

A There are an unimaginable number of nerve cells connected to each other in our brains. When we want to remember something, the connections that are important for this interconnect particularly closely. The brain then creates proteins to act as a kind of "thought glue" to strengthen these connections.

Q Where do thoughts come from?

A Even the cleverest brain researchers don't know! We have pictures and certain ideas in our heads, but we still don't understand in what way sensible and logical thoughts are formed from them.

Q Can I change my brain?

A Yes! If you use your brain a lot, you make it stronger. Whether it's reading, playing, painting, or playing music—all of these things are good for the brain.

Q What does my brain do when I sleep?

A It continues to work. In dreams and other sleep phases, it organizes all the experiences of the day and provides new processing power for the next day. But the sleep has to be long enough for this.

Q Is it true that larger brains are smarter than smaller ones?

A The clear answers is: no! Size doesn't matter at all. There is the same number of cells in each brain and cleverness comes from exercising the brain.

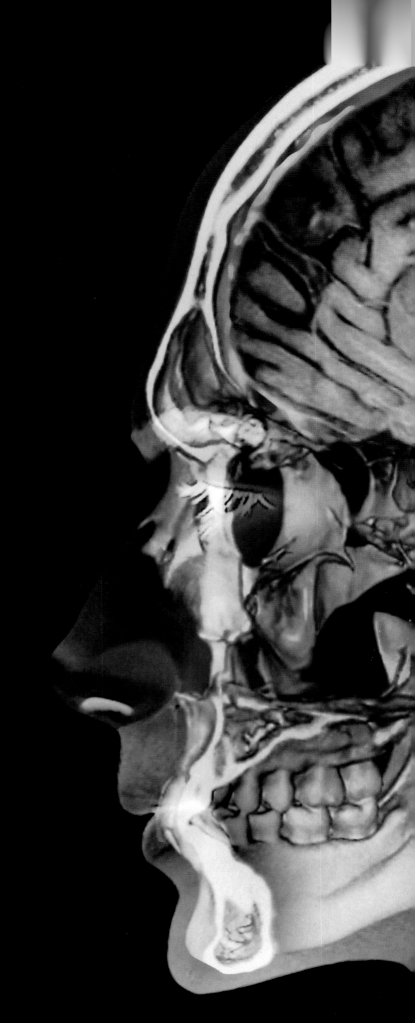

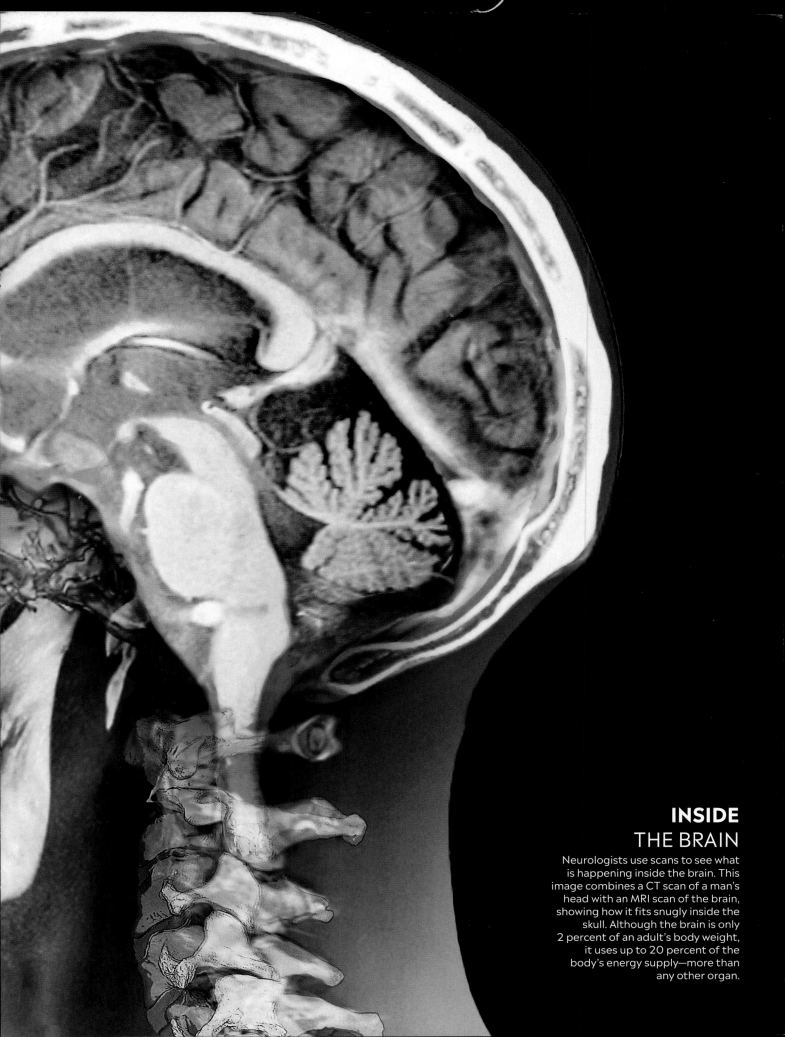

INSIDE
THE BRAIN

Neurologists use scans to see what is happening inside the brain. This image combines a CT scan of a man's head with an MRI scan of the brain, showing how it fits snugly inside the skull. Although the brain is only 2 percent of an adult's body weight, it uses up to 20 percent of the body's energy supply—more than any other organ.

Fingertips feel the raised Braille dots to read words.

READING **BY TOUCH**

If a person has a visual impairment, their sense of touch can be used to read Braille. This system uses patterns of raised dots to represent words and numbers.

Super sense

Your senses tell your brain what is happening in the outside world. The brain processes the information, enabling you to experience the world around you. Without senses, life would be very dull indeed!

ON AVERAGE, A **HUMAN TONGUE** HAS BETWEEN 2,000 AND **4,000** TASTE BUDS!

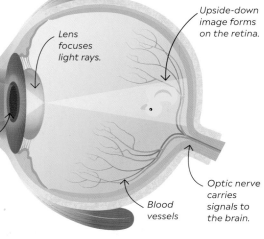

FIVE **SENSES**

Each sense plays a special part in helping you understand and interact with your surroundings.

Touch
Skin sensors can respond to pain, pressure, touch, and temperature.

Sight
Your eyes work together, focusing light to create 3-D images.

Taste
Taste buds identify salty, sweet, sour, bitter, and umami (savory) tastes.

Hearing
The ears capture sounds— waves of vibration that travel through the air.

Smell
Odors—from perfumes to pongs—are detected by your nose.

THE **HUMAN EYE** CAN SEE AT LEAST **1 MILLION** DIFFERENT **COLORS!**

Light reflects off an object into the eye.

Light rays bend when they hit the cornea, the clear front of the eye.

Lens focuses light rays.

Upside-down image forms on the retina.

Pupil

HUMAN **EYE**

Light rays enter the eye through the pupil. They form an upside-down image on the retina at the back of the eye. Around 125 million light-sensitive cells on the retina relay nerve signals to the brain, which flips the image the right way up.

Blood vessels

Optic nerve carries signals to the brain.

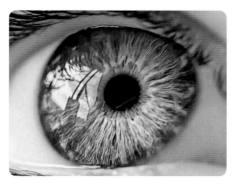

UNIQUE **IRIS**

The iris is the colored ring of muscle that makes your pupil bigger or smaller. Its pattern is so intricate that no two irises are the same. Even identical twins have different iris patterns.

Dancer moves his feet into the correct position without looking.

SIXTH SENSE

Sensors in your muscles and joints are constantly alerting your brain to the position of all your body parts. This awareness is called proprioception. It's why someone can dance without watching what their arms and legs are doing.

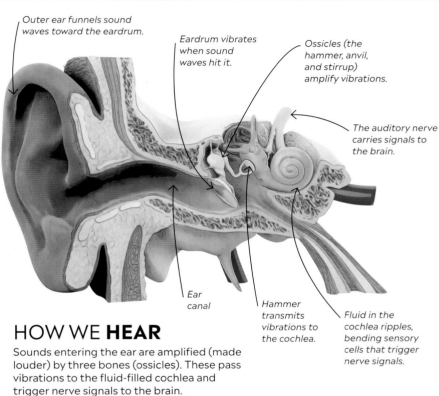

Outer ear funnels sound waves toward the eardrum.

Eardrum vibrates when sound waves hit it.

Ossicles (the hammer, anvil, and stirrup) amplify vibrations.

The auditory nerve carries signals to the brain.

Ear canal

Hammer transmits vibrations to the cochlea.

Fluid in the cochlea ripples, bending sensory cells that trigger nerve signals.

HOW WE **HEAR**

Sounds entering the ear are amplified (made louder) by three bones (ossicles). These pass vibrations to the fluid-filled cochlea and trigger nerve signals to the brain.

SOME PEOPLE HAVE **JOINED SENSES.** THEY DON'T JUST **HEAR MUSIC**—THEY CAN **SMELL, FEEL,** OR **SEE IT IN COLOR!**

OPTICAL **ILLUSIONS**

Your brain has to work quickly, and if it has difficulty making sense of what the eyes see, it takes a guess and fills in the gaps itself. This is the basis of optical illusions, which fool the brain into seeing things that aren't there.

When viewed from an angle, the shading on this hand tricks the brain into seeing a deep hole.

ELEPHANTS HAVE THE LONGEST PREGNANCIES IN THE ANIMAL KINGDOM, AT UP TO 22 MONTHS!

Whiplike tail helps sperm swim at a speed of ⅕ in (5 mm) per minute.

EGG **RACE**

Fertilization occurs when a sperm breaks through the egg's outer coating and its nucleus fuses with the nucleus of the egg. Many sperm compete to fertilize the egg—as seen in this magnified image—but only one can be successful.

When one sperm enters the egg, chemical changes in the egg stop other sperm from getting in.

EVERY DAY MORE THAN 350,000 BABIES ARE BORN WORLDWIDE!

FROM CELL **TO BABY**

The fertilized egg cell contains genetic material (instructions to make a new human) from both parents. At first, the growing baby is called an embryo. From the ninth week of pregnancy until birth, it is known as a fetus.

The head of the sperm carries genetic material.

First division creates two cells

Cluster resembles a raspberry

Outer cells burrow into uterus lining

Yolk sac provides food

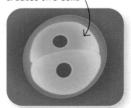

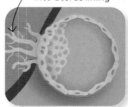

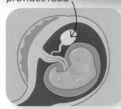

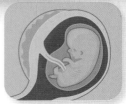

Division
The fertilized egg divides repeatedly, forming new cells with each division.

Cell cluster
As the egg continues to divide, it becomes a berrylike cluster of cells.

Implantation
After a week, the cell cluster, now a hollow ball, attaches to the uterus.

Embryo
By week five, the baby's brain, heart, and spinal cord are developing.

Fetus
By week eight, arms and legs are well formed and the head becomes round.

Thick, protective outer coating

Human reproduction

Every person begins life when two tiny sex cells—a female egg cell and a male sperm cell—fuse in a process called fertilization. Over nine months, the fertilized egg divides and grows to form a complete new human being.

DOUBLE TROUBLE

In about 1 in every 250 pregnancies, the egg splits into two shortly after fertilization, creating identical twins—two babies with the same genes that look alike. Nonidentical twins occur when two eggs are fertilized instead of one.

NONSTOP SPERM!

From puberty onward, sperm are produced in the male reproductive organs, or testes. Sperm are short-lived, so the testes make sperm constantly—1,500 every second, and more than 100 million each day! In contrast, the female reproductive organs, the ovaries, do not make any new eggs once a girl is born.

A BABY GIRL HAS OVER A MILLION EGGS IN HER OVARIES AT BIRTH!

IN THE WOMB

Ultrasound scans make images using sound waves. Doctors look at ultrasound scans to check the health and organs of a baby in the womb (the uterus). Some scans have shown babies appearing to wave or give the thumbs-up sign!

LIFE SUPPORT

During pregnancy, the baby develops inside its mother's uterus for about 40 weeks. An organ called the placenta forms to supply nutrients and oxygen from the mother's blood, and to remove waste. A tubelike umbilical cord links the placenta and baby.

Uterus stretches to the size of a watermelon.

Placenta

Umbilical cord

The baby floats in amniotic fluid, which protects it against sudden jolts.

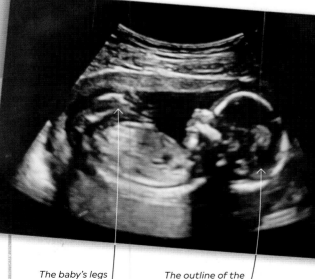

The baby's legs are tightly folded.

The outline of the skull is clearly visible.

BRAIN GROWTH

Babies are born with almost all the neurons (brain cells) they need. But children's brains still grow rapidly in early years, because they are learning new skills that create connections between neurons. By early adolescence, the brain has reached full size, but it continues to develop for many years.

At birth
The brain is about a quarter of its adult size at birth.

Adolescence
Between 11 and 14, the brain reaches full size, but it continues to change.

BONE TISSUE REGENERATES OVER TIME, GIVING YOU A NEW SKELETON EVERY 10 YEARS!

WATER BABIES

Babies have automatic underwater reflexes. They instinctively hold their breath when submerged and wave their arms as though swimming. We lose these reflexes as we grow older.

Growing up

Our bodies undergo dramatic changes during the course of a lifetime. From tiny, helpless babies, we grow throughout childhood and puberty to become adults. In later life, as our bodies age, we continue to gradually change.

Keeping the legs straight while upside down takes a lot of practice!

GOING STRONG

In 2012, German Johanna Quaas became the world's oldest active competitive gymnast at 86 years old. In old age, muscles and bones weaken, but keeping active helps slow this process down.

Strong torso muscles aid balance and stability.

Parallel bar exercises help build and maintain upper body strength.

BETWEEN **BIRTH** AND THEIR **FIRST BIRTHDAY**, A **BABY** GROWS ABOUT **10 IN** (25 CM)!

TINY **TEETH**

Babies are born with 20 small baby teeth that erupt through the gums in the early years of life. As they age, baby teeth are gradually replaced by 32 permanent adult teeth.

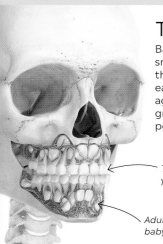

This image shows a seven-year-old with baby teeth.

Adult teeth are hidden beneath baby teeth in a child's jaw.

MAKING **BONES**

When bones form, they are made of flexible cartilage. Gradually, a process called ossification turns this soft cartilage into bone tissue. These X-rays show the difference between the hand bones of a 3-year-old child and an adult.

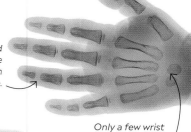

Child's hand has cartilage between each finger bone.

Only a few wrist bones have formed.

Adult's hand has a thin layer of cartilage between bones at the joints.

Wrist bones are all present.

STAYING **HEALTHY**

A varied diet and regular exercise keeps your body healthy. Most doctors recommend a balance of different types of food, especially fruits and vegetables. Exercise helps keep the heart, muscles, and bones strong, and even improves your mood.

GRAY HAIR

Hair seems to turn gray as people age. In fact, the hair doesn't change its color, it merely loses it. With age, the pigment cells that color hair die out and are not replaced. As pigment levels fall, hair becomes gray, silvery, or white.

A YOUNG CHILD'S **BRAIN** MAKES OVER **1 MILLION** NEW **NERVE CONNECTIONS** EVERY **SECOND!**

STAGES **OF LIFE**

Each phase of life sees a change in the body's shape, size, and strength. In later life, as cells get older, the body starts to age.

A teenager can grow 3 in (8 cm) in a year.

Changes in the joints and spine mean we get shorter with age.

Childhood
Babies grow fast, but from age 2 until adolescence growth is steady.

Adolescence
Growth spurts and puberty occur during adolescence.

Adulthood
Bones are strongest in early adulthood, when we are fully grown.

Middle age
Older adults get wrinkles as skin becomes thinner and less elastic.

Old age
Muscles and bones weaken with age, and joints become less mobile.

Allan Williams is a British pole vaulter who has performed at international competitions, including the Commonwealth Games. He now coaches the next generation of athletes.

Ask an...
ATHLETE

Q How did you get into athletics?

A One day, to my surprise, I was asked to represent my school in a pole vaulting competition. When we got there, the other pole vaulter didn't show up, so I won by default. But I was hooked. Four years and a lot of work later, I was a British International.

Q What does an athletics coach do?

A The coach's role is to help their athlete develop as a young person. To build confidence and the physical and technical skills to perform efficiently and effectively. Particularly when it matters most—in competition.

Q What are the most important things other than training?

A Mental strength is essential to deal with the setbacks and disappointments that competitive sports inevitably throw at you. Nutrition is important for any athlete, and rest and sleep are vital too. The physical benefit from training comes not during the session itself but while the athlete is refueling (eating well), resting, and recovering.

Q Do you need to have a certain body shape to pole vault?

A Pole vaulters have many different body types: tall, short, muscular, lean, and more. I would never discourage somebody based on body type. After all, it's possible, based on their body and wing size, to prove that a bumble bee cannot fly. Fortunately, nobody ever told the bees!

Q Why don't pole vaulters just use a very long pole to help them jump higher?

A This is a good question, and one that I am asked frequently. It's not so much the length of the pole, it's how high up the pole the vaulter can grip. If they can't get the pole into a vertical position after takeoff because it's too long for them to maneuver, they won't be able to get over to the safety of the mat.

POLE VAULTING

To propel their bodies up and over the crossbar, pole vaulters need to be a combination of sprinter, jumper, and gymnast. Carrying and controlling the pole during the run-up and the jump requires strong back and shoulder muscles. Vaulters then use their abdominal muscles to swing up into a handstand-like position at the top of the jump.

Fighting germs

Your body is under daily threat from enemy attackers, such as bacteria and viruses. Luckily, your built-in defense system hunts them down and destroys them, keeping you fit and healthy.

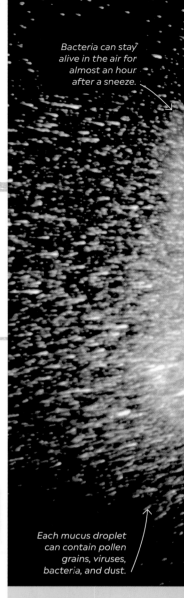

Bacteria can stay alive in the air for almost an hour after a sneeze.

Each mucus droplet can contain pollen grains, viruses, bacteria, and dust.

ABOUT **200** DIFFERENT VIRUSES CAN CAUSE THE COMMON COLD!

HUNGRY **HUNTERS**

Special white blood cells, called macrophages, are key players in your defense team. They hunt down anything harmful, such as bacteria, damaged tissue, or diseased cells, before digesting it.

This macrophage (white) is capturing tuberculosis bacteria (green).

Macrophage engulfs bacteria and digests them with chemicals called enzymes.

BRILLIANT **BARRIERS**

You are protected by a variety of natural barriers that stop germs from invading and making you ill.

Skin
As one of your body's first lines of defense, skin is a tough, waterproof barrier.

Stomach acid
Strong acids in your stomach kill germs in food and drink.

Tears
Salty tears in the eyes help kill bacteria and clean away dirt.

Mucus
Sticky mucus lining in the nose traps germs entering the nostrils.

Saliva
Your mouth produces saliva to wash away bacteria and keep your teeth clean.

Earwax
Thick earwax cleans and protects your ears by trapping dust and dirt.

WONDER **JABS!**

A vaccine is a medicine that trains your body to fight a disease before you encounter it. Vaccines made to combat COVID-19 during the 2020 global pandemic saved around 20 million lives in their first year!

Antibodies (pink) attach to a coronavirus particle to prevent it from entering a human cell.

Sneezes send air, saliva, and mucus flying out of your nose and mouth.

A sneeze produces up to 40,000 tiny droplets of saliva.

ACHOO!

A sneeze is an automatic response to an itchy irritation caused by pollen or dust inside the nose, or by a viral infection. This image of a typical sneeze shows fluid shooting out at speeds of nearly 100 mph (160 km/h).

MAKING **ANTIBODIES**

Some white blood cells make proteins called antibodies that disable germs or mark them for destruction. The cells remember the invaders if they return. The body can make billions of different types of antibodies, each targeting a specific type of germ.

Antibodies are Y-shaped proteins that stick to germs.

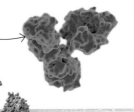

HOW **SCABS** FORM

When a blood vessel is damaged by a cut, blood cells begin to repair the wound immediately. White blood cells attack any germs entering the cut. Other cells plug and seal the wound.

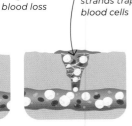

White cells fight germs

Plug halts blood loss

Protein strands trap blood cells

Clot's surface hardens into a scab

Plug
Clotting cells called platelets stick together, plugging the wound.

Clot
Strands of protein bind red blood cells into a lump called a clot.

Scab
A scab (hard crust) forms, and the wound beneath heals.

COVID-19

The respiratory disease COVID-19 is caused by a coronavirus—a virus that spreads through close contact with infected people. Inside the body, the virus particles enter human cells and make copies of themselves.

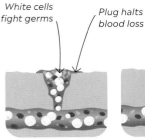

1 BILLION BACTERIA LIVE ON EVERY 1 SQ CM OF YOUR SKIN!

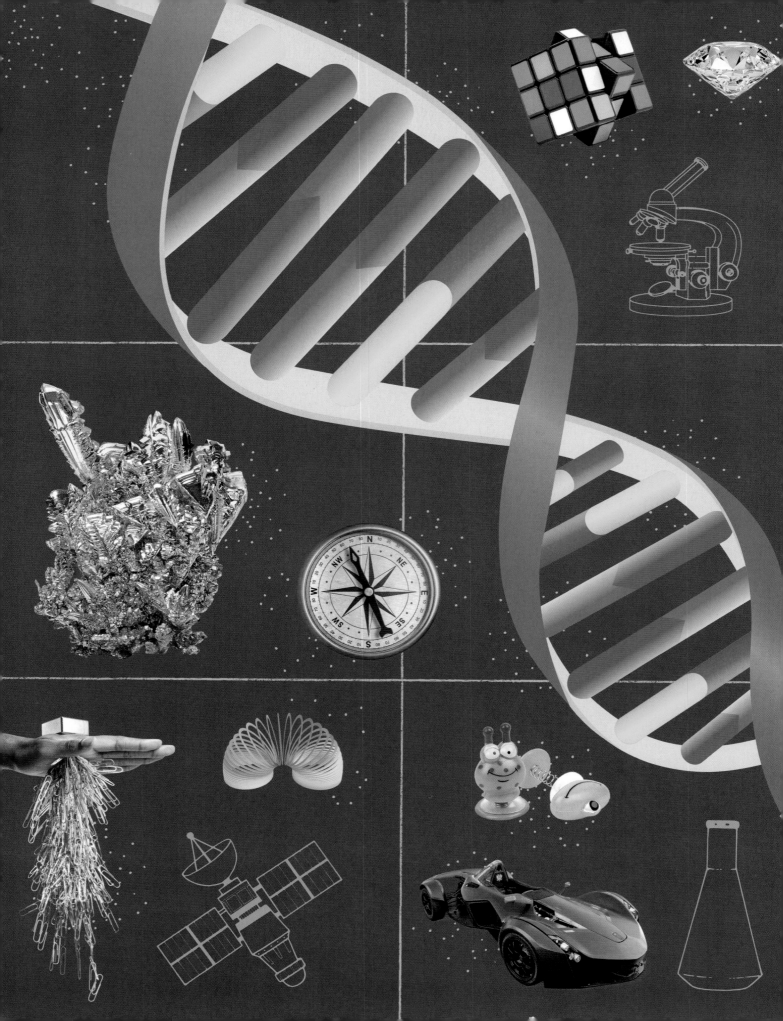

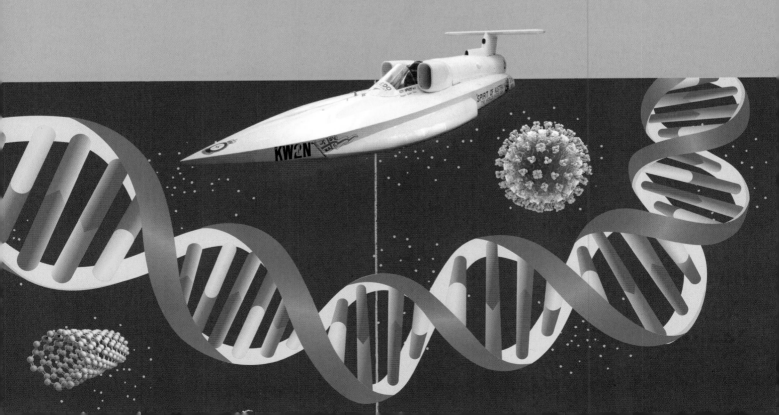

SCIENCE

What is science?

Science is all about asking questions, testing your ideas, and forming conclusions. Scientists investigate how everything works—from the insides of our bodies to the world around us.

FIELDS OF SCIENCE

There are hundreds of different fields of science that focus on very specific research—from studying the very small (microbiology) to the very big (astronomy). Some of the main areas in science include matter and materials, life, and forces, and energy.

Molten glass can be blown into a variety of shapes.

MATERIALS

The field of materials science examines the properties of existing materials, as well as developing new ones.

Heating water changes its matter to a different state.

MATTER

Chemists study how atoms make up elements and how these change when they react with other matter.

CITIZEN SCIENCE

Science projects can be as simple as spotting changes in your local environment, and everyone can get involved. These volunteers are looking for microplastics in Sydney, Australia—helping to map the scale of the plastic pollution problem.

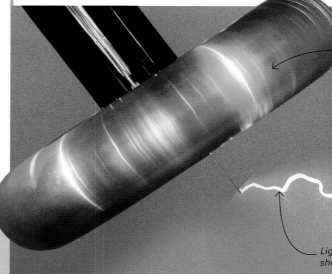

The charge on this top coil builds up until it is high enough to send an electric current through the air in a flash of lightning.

Lightning-like bolts shoot out of the coil.

THERE ARE MORE THAN 8.8 MILLION SCIENTISTS WORKING AROUND THE WORLD!

LIGHTNING GENERATOR

At Phaeno Science Center in Wolfsburg, Germany, a daring demonstrator shows the power of the Tesla coil—an experiment built to investigate powerful high-voltage electricity. The electricity doesn't hurt the demonstrator, as he wears a special suit that is grounded, meaning there is a route for the current to flow down to the ground rather than into his body. The Tesla coil was created by Serbian-American scientist Nikola Tesla in 1891.

SMASHING
SCIENCE!

Opened in 2008, the Large Hadron Collider was designed to smash subatomic particles together and allow scientists to test their theories about particle physics. Located in a circular tunnel, it stretches for 17 miles (27 km).

SCIENTIFIC
METHOD

When beginning research, scientists start out with a hypothesis—an idea they want to test. They test this in a variety of ways, often using lab equipment or computer models. Their results will then be reviewed by other scientists to check for errors.

The tiny microorganism Daphnia is carrying eggs inside its body.

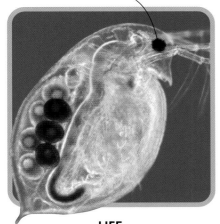

LIFE
The study of life involves looking at the complex systems that keep life-forms alive and allow them to reproduce.

Fireworks release lots of light energy.

ENERGY
Physicists examine all the different ways energy is transferred, whether as heat, light, or the movement of objects.

Many forces act on a spinning Ferris wheel.

FORCES
How objects, people, and planets are pushed or pulled on by forces is another key area studied by physicists.

The demonstrator is dressed in a suit like the armor of medieval knights.

States of **matter**

Everything around us is made of matter—tiny particles not visible to your eyes. Matter exists in three main forms: solids, liquids, and gases.

STRANGE STATE!

Most of the matter in the universe is made of a fourth state of matter called plasma. This electrically charged gas is what stars are made from. On Earth, you can see it in colorful plasma balls like this one.

DEEP **FREEZE**

Severe storms and cold weather have frozen the water falling on this lighthouse—changing this liquid into a solid. Due to the speed of the freezing, the dripping patterns of the liquid water have been captured as spiky icy tendrils.

Beneath the ice
This lighthouse is in Duluth, Minnesota, a port on Lake Superior.

CHANGING **STATES**

Substances can exist in any of the three states of matter, and they can change between one state and another if they are heated up or cooled down. Heating water makes it evaporate into a gas. Cooling it down makes it condense into a liquid, which can then freeze into a solid.

Deposition is where a gas turns straight into a solid without first becoming a liquid.

Solid

Sublimation

Deposition

Freezing

Melting

Gas

A solid will sometimes become a gas without first turning into a liquid.

Evaporation

Condensation

Liquid

Over time, more and more layers of icicles form.

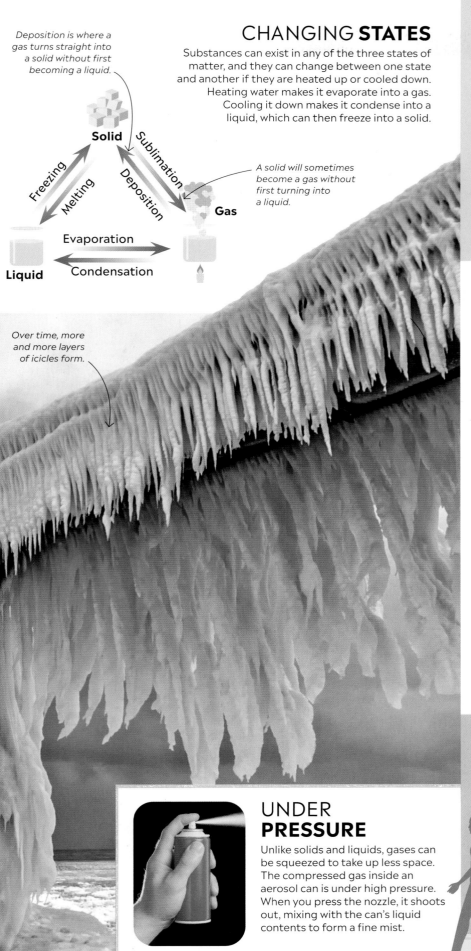

SUBLIME **SLIME!**

If you have ever squeezed sticky slime, you will know it turns more liquid the more you squeeze. That's because it is a non-Newtonian fluid—a substance that becomes either more liquid or more solid when compressed.

Solid
Inside a solid, the particles are held together in a fixed arrangement by strong forces called bonds.

Liquid
The particles in liquids are held together by weaker bonds than in a solid. They can move past each other, so the liquid can be poured.

Gas
The molecules in a gas are not bonded to each other—they are able to move freely and spread out.

MOLECULE MOVEMENT

Most matter on Earth is made up of particles (atoms or molecules). Although the particles in a substance are the same in each of the three states of matter, they behave differently—those in gases and liquids move around more than the particles in a solid.

UNDER **PRESSURE**

Unlike solids and liquids, gases can be squeezed to take up less space. The compressed gas inside an aerosol can is under high pressure. When you press the nozzle, it shoots out, mixing with the can's liquid contents to form a fine mist.

CUSTARD IS A LIQUID THAT GETS **MORE SOLID UNDER PRESSURE,** SO IF YOU FOUND ENOUGH OF IT, **YOU COULD WALK ACROSS IT!**

ATOM **ANATOMY**

Small as it is, an atom is made up of even smaller particles. Its center, or nucleus, is formed of protons and neutrons. Whizzing around the nucleus are electrons. Each element (see pages 210-211) has a different number of protons in its nucleus. This is a carbon atom—it has six protons.

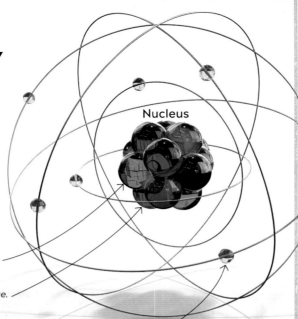

Nucleus

Protons have a positive charge.

Neutrons have no charge.

Electrons have a negative charge. Atoms always have the same amount of protons and electrons so overall they have no charge.

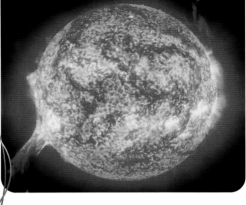

STAR SMASHING

The sun is powered by nuclear fusion. Nuclei in its core smash together, forming new elements and producing light and heat. Every second, the sun converts 600 million tons (544 million metric tons) of hydrogen into helium.

ANCIENT ATOMS!

The idea of atoms goes back to the ancient Greeks. They came up with the theory that everything could be broken down into tiny building blocks. The Greek philosopher Democritus named them atoms in around 430 BCE, from the Greek word *atomos* meaning "indivisible."

Atom power

UNLOCKING ATOMS

Strong forces hold the particles inside an atom's nucleus together. Splitting the nucleus apart, in a process called nuclear fission, releases huge amounts of energy. Nuclear power stations harness this reaction to produce electricity.

Everything in the universe—from the tiniest bug to the biggest galaxy—is made up of atoms. These minuscule particles are the building blocks of our whole world.

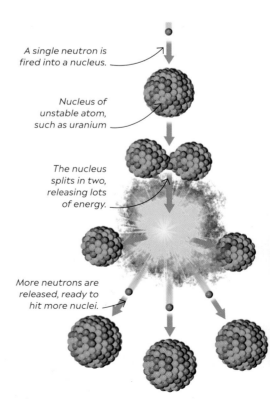

A single neutron is fired into a nucleus.

Nucleus of unstable atom, such as uranium

The nucleus splits in two, releasing lots of energy.

More neutrons are released, ready to hit more nuclei.

AROUND **10 MILLION HYDROGEN ATOMS** FIT ACROSS THE **HEAD OF A PIN!**

Pin head

MAKING **MOLECULES**

Atoms can combine together to make bigger structures called molecules. A water molecule is made from two hydrogen atoms joined to one oxygen atom.

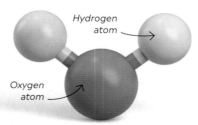

Hydrogen atom

Oxygen atom

Water molecule

THERE ARE MORE THAN **400 NUCLEAR POWER PLANTS** WORLDWIDE THAT MAKE ENERGY FROM ATOMS!

The plume of smoke generated by the explosion forms a mushroom-shaped cloud.

Billowing smoke hides debris and destruction beneath.

ATOMIC **BLAST**

The massive amount of energy released from splitting an atom can be channeled into destructive purposes. During World War II, a team of scientists designed an atomic bomb to use this energy. The bombs were tested at sites around the world, causing explosions like this one in Kazakhstan.

KEY

The major categories of elements are shown in these colors.

Hydrogen

Alkali Metals

Alkaline Earth Metals

Transition Metals

Lanthanides

Actinides

Boron Group

Carbon Group

Nitrogen Group

Oxygen Group

Halogen Group

Noble Gases

This glass sphere contains the colorless gas hydrogen.

1
H
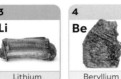
Hydrogen

Elements are pure substances, each made up of just one type of atom. In 1869, Russian chemist Dmitri Mendeleev organized the elements into a grid known as the periodic table.

THE **PERIODIC TABLE**

There are 118 elements in the periodic table. Elements are listed in rows in order of their atomic number, and in groups (columns) that share similar properties, such as how easily they react with other elements.

3 **Li**

Lithium

4 **Be**
Beryllium

11 **Na**
Sodium

12 **Mg**
Magnesium

19 K Potassium	20 Ca Calcium	21 Sc Scandium	22 Ti Titanium	23 V Vanadium	24 Cr Chromium	25 Mn Manganese	26 Fe Iron
37 Rb Rubidium	38 Sr Strontium	39 Y Yttrium	40 Zr Zirconium	41 Nb Niobium	42 Mo Molybdenum	43 Tc Technetium	44 Ru Ruthenium
55 Cs Caesium	56 Ba Barium	57-71 La-Lu Lanthanides	72 Hf Hafnium	73 Ta Tantalum	74 W Tungsten	75 Re Rhenium	76 Os Osmium
87 Fr Francium	88 Ra Radium	89-103 Ac-Lr Actinides	104 Rf Rutherfordium	105 Db Dubnium	106 Sg Seaborgium	107 Bh Bohrium	108 Hs Hassium

Uraninite is a mineral from which radium can be extracted.

57 La Lanthanum	58 Ce Cerium	59 Pr Praseodymium	60 Nd Neodymium	61 Pm Promethium
89 Ac  Actinium	90 Th Thorium	91 Pa Protactinium	92 U Uranium	93 Np Neptunium

Native copper

Elements are not usually found in their pure form, but pure copper sometimes occurs naturally. It was the first metal to be worked into tools and jewelry by early people.

The Lanthanides and Actinides belong next to the Alkaline Earth Metals but are shown pulled out at the bottom to give them more room.

Uranium is used to produce both nuclear fuels and weapons.

ATOMIC **NUMBER**

Each element is made of a unique kind of atom that has different numbers of protons, neutrons, and electrons. Elements are ordered by the number of protons in the nucleus of their atoms—the atomic number.

Artificial elements

Most elements are found on Earth, and can be extracted from natural materials. But some exist only in space or in such small quantities on Earth that they cannot be isolated. Scientists have created these elements artificially, by smashing particles together in a lab.

Artificially made elements are illustrated below with this symbol.

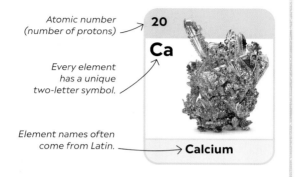

Atomic number (number of protons)

20

Ca

Every element has a unique two-letter symbol.

Element names often come from Latin.

→ **Calcium**

2 **He** Helium					
5 **B** Boron	6 **C** Carbon	7 **N** Nitrogen	8 **O** Oxygen	9 **F** Fluorine	10 **Ne** Neon
13 **Al** Aluminum	14 **Si** Silicon	15 **P** Phosphorus	16 **S** Sulfur	17 **Cl** Chlorine	18 **Ar** Argon

27 **Co** Cobalt	28 **Ni** Nickel	29 **Cu** Copper	30 **Zn** Zinc	31 **Ga** Gallium	32 **Ge** Germanium	33 **As** Arsenic	34 **Se** Selenium	35 **Br** Bromine	36 **Kr** Krypton
45 **Rh** Rhodium	46 **Pd** Palladium	47 **Ag** Silver	48 **Cd** Cadmium	49 **In** Indium	50 **Sn** Tin	51 **Sb** Antimony	52 **Te** Tellurium	53 **I** Iodine	54 **Xe** Xenon
77 **Ir** Iridium	78 **Pt** Platinum	79 **Au** Gold	80 **Hg** Mercury	81 **Tl** Thallium	82 **Pb** Lead	83 **Bi** Bismuth	84 **Po** Polonium	85 **At** Astatine	86 **Rn** Radon
109 **Mt** Meitnerium	110 **Ds** Darmstadtium	111 **Rg** Roentgenium	112 **Cn** Copernicium	113 **Nh** Nihonium	114 **Fl** Flerovium	115 **Mc** Moscovium	116 **Lv** Livermorium	117 **Ts** Tennessine	118 **Og** Oganesson

62 **Sm** Samarium	63 **Eu** Europium	64 **Gd** Gadolinium	65 **Tb** Terbium	66 **Dy** Dysprosium	67 **Ho** Holmium	68 **Er** Erbium	69 **Tm** Thulium	70 **Yb** Ytterbium	71 **Lu** Lutetium
94 **Pu** Plutonium	95 **Am** Americium	96 **Cm** Curium	97 **Bk** Berkelium	98 **Cf** Californium	99 **Es** Einsteinium	100 **Fm** Fermium	101 **Md** Mendelevium	102 **No** Nobelium	103 **Lr** Lawrencium

This element is named after America, because it was first made in the US.

Curium is named after the scientists Pierre and Marie Curie.

15 OF THE **ELEMENTS** ARE NAMED AFTER **FAMOUS SCIENTISTS!**

NAME THAT... **ELEMENT**

How many of these elements can you identify? The chemical symbol for each one is there to help you. See if you can find the odd one out!

1 Hydrogen
2 Iron
3 Arsenic
4 Bronze
5 Copper
6 Gold
7 Chlorine
8 Nickel
9 Magnesium

17 U
18 C
19 Ti
20 N
21 Pb
22 Al
23 Li
24 S
25 W
26 He
27 Ca
28 Pt
29 O
30 Co
31 Na
32 Nd
33 Sn
34 Pu
35 Ne
36 Si
37 Zn
38 P
39 Hg

10 Silver	19 Titanium	28 Platinum	37 Zinc
11 Bromine	20 Nitrogen	29 Oxygen	38 Phosphorus
12 Potassium	21 Lead	30 Cobalt	39 Mercury
13 Iodine	22 Aluminum	31 Sodium	
14 Thallium	23 Lithium	32 Neodymium	
15 Europium	24 Sulfur	33 Tin	
16 Bismuth	25 Tungsten	34 Plutonium	
17 Uranium	26 Helium	35 Neon	
18 Carbon	27 Calcium	36 Silicon	

The odd one out is bronze (4). This is an alloy made of two elements—copper and tin.

THE CARBON **CYCLE**

Carbon moves around in a never-ending cycle between water, air, soil, and living things. Some parts of the cycle happen in moments; others—such as living matter breaking down—take many years.

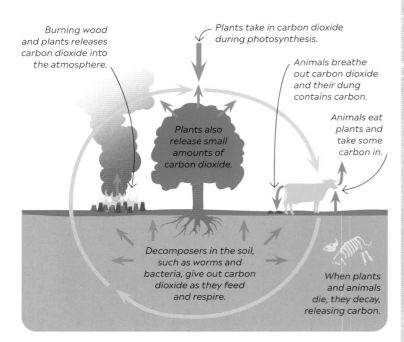

Burning wood and plants releases carbon dioxide into the atmosphere.

Plants take in carbon dioxide during photosynthesis.

Animals breathe out carbon dioxide and their dung contains carbon.

Plants also release small amounts of carbon dioxide.

Animals eat plants and take some carbon in.

Decomposers in the soil, such as worms and bacteria, give out carbon dioxide as they feed and respire.

When plants and animals die, they decay, releasing carbon.

CARBON **CRUSHER**

When plants decay, the carbon within them is usually released into the air. However, in some cases, rotting plants sink into a waterlogged bog and are squeezed together over millions of years. This process makes coal—a carbon-dense fossil fuel that we burn to power our world.

Plant matter

Leaves begin to rot.

Peat

In a swamp, compressed plants eventually form peat.

Lignite (soft coal)

Coal

A harder coal is formed.

Increasing depth and pressure crushes carbon even further.

This form of coal is shiny and clean to the touch.

The hardest coal is more than 90 percent carbon.

Anthracite (hard coal)

ASTRONOMERS HAVE DISCOVERED A DISTANT **STAR MADE OF DIAMOND**—TOTALING 10 BILLION TRILLION TRILLION CARATS!

Graphite
The carbon atoms in graphite are joined together in distinct separate layers that can easily slide over each other.

DRAWING ATTENTION

Graphite is a pure form of carbon, but it is soft and flaky. This means it is easy to carve—as these tiny graphite pencil-tip sculptures demonstrate. The way the atoms are arranged and held together allows this form of carbon to conduct electricity.

Graphite is soft and can be shaped easily.

Graphite is used to make the "lead" of pencils.

Each of the frog's cells are made of carbon compounds.

Plant cells also contain carbon.

TINY **TUBES!**

Scientists have developed new forms of carbon—such as these cylindrical tubes that are so small thousands of them can fit across 1 mm! They have many potential uses both in medicine and in making up strong new materials.

CARBON **LIFE-FORMS**

Carbon compounds are present in all living things—they make up the sugars, fats, and proteins that plants and animals are built from. Animals find the carbon their bodies need in food, while plants take in carbon dioxide from the air.

Cool **carbon**

Carbon is one of the most versatile elements. Pure carbon occurs naturally in two main forms—diamond, one of the hardest natural substances, and graphite, one of the softest.

Diamond
Inside a diamond, each carbon atom is joined to four others, in a rigid 3-D structure.

TOUGH THREADS!

Carbon fibers are long chains of carbon that are tiny and light but five times stronger than steel! When woven into a mesh and combined with resin, they can be formed into very strong sheets—the perfect material for making panels for fast cars.

COSTLY **CARBON**

Diamonds are the hardest natural substance on Earth. They are tough, cold, almost unscratchable, and made entirely of carbon. As well as making valuable jewelry when cut and polished, diamonds are also used in machinery.

BAC Mono sports car

SOFT **SODIUM**

Most metals are hard, but sodium is so soft that it can be easily sliced using just a table knife. This metal is part of a group called the alkali metals that very easily react with other substances, even water and air.

FLOWING **FREE**

The atoms in pure metals form a close-knit lattice structure, where electrons can move around between them. This free movement of electrons is what allows electric currents to flow through metals.

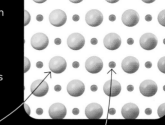

Metal atoms

Electrons are free to move around.

Marvelous **metals**

Metals make up more than three-quarters of all the elements in the periodic table. As well as being shiny and cold to touch, they are often hard and strong and used to create everyday items from wires to weights.

BUILDING **BRIDGES**

Mixing iron with carbon produces a strong alloy called steel. Its tough properties mean it is used to build big, load-bearing structures, such as the Sydney Harbour Bridge, Australia.

The liquid gold is poured into a mold. Once cool, it will take the mold's shape.

OSMIUM IS THE DENSEST METAL. **A PIECE THE SIZE OF A MICROWAVE OVEN** WEIGHS AS MUCH AS A CAR!

PROPERTIES OF **METALS**

Metals are not all the same. However, most of them have a few key physical properties in common.

Shiny
Most metals reflect light well, which means they have a shiny, reflective surface.

Solid
Almost all metals are solid at room temperature. Mercury is the only metal that is liquid at room temperature.

Malleable
Most metals are malleable, which means they can be shaped into wires or sheets.

Conduct electricity
Metals are able to conduct electricity, which means electricity can travel through them.

Conduct heat
Metals are also good at conducting heat, because their free electrons help the energy move through the metal.

The cube would be taller than the White House.

ALL THE **GOLD EVER MINED** WOULD MAKE A **CUBE 72 FT (22 M)** ACROSS!

Gold has a melting point of 1,943°F (1,062°C), when it begins to turn liquid.

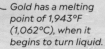
Gold ingot

When cool, the gold forms a solid bar.

LIQUID **GOLD**

Most metals are solid at room temperature. When heated, they turn softer, allowing them to be worked into different shapes. If they are heated further, such as the gold above, they melt and can be poured into molds.

METAL **MERGING**

Metals can be mixed with other metals and nonmetal elements to create substances called alloys. Some alloys are harder than pure metals, and they can also be stronger, lighter, and less likely to wear down.

Many instruments are made of brass, an alloy that contains copper and zinc.

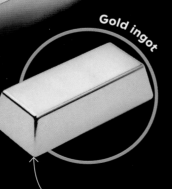

IN THE **MIX**

If substances come together but don't react with one another, a mixture can form. In a mixture, two or more substances are blended together but don't form chemical bonds. They can easily be separated again.

The ink will gradually mix with the water, but the mixture can be separated by evaporation.

INSTANT REACTION!

Cooking or even just chopping food can cause a chemical reaction. When a freshly cut apple's flesh begins to turn brown, that is due to it reacting with elements in the air!

Chemical
reactions

Sometimes slow and silent and other times over in a flash and a bang, chemical reactions occur all around us. They change the substances involved into different ones by making and breaking chemical bonds.

HOW **REACTIONS** WORK

When a chemical reaction takes place, the atoms in each substance involved rearrange themselves. Bonds break down and new bonds form. The product is a completely new substance.

The end result of a chemical reaction is called the product.

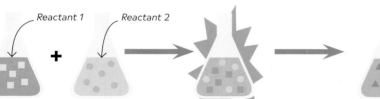

Reactant 1 *Reactant 2*

Reactants
The substances that will react together are called the reactants. This reaction has two.

Reaction
In the reaction, molecules break apart and the atoms rearrange to form new molecules.

Product
The product is a new substance that can have different properties to the individual reactants.

HYDROGEN AND CARBON FORM **MORE COMPOUNDS** THAN ANY OTHER ELEMENTS!

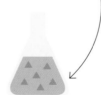

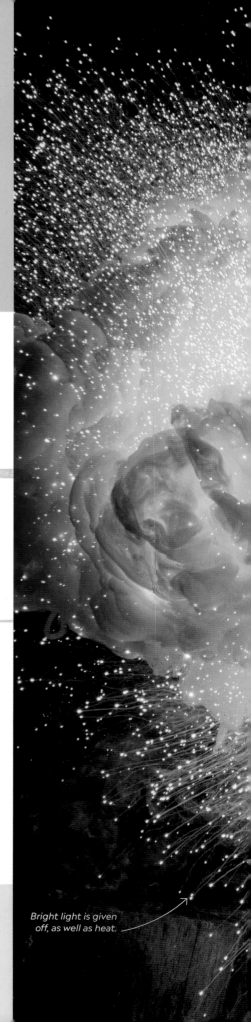

Bright light is given off, as well as heat.

BIG **BANG**

When thermite (a mix of aluminum powder and iron oxide) is ignited, it can go off with a bang! This is an example of an exothermic reaction—one that releases heat. The thermite reaction can reach temperatures of 3,600°F (2,000°C). Other reactions absorb heat and are known as endothermic reactions.

Tiny sparks fly in all directions.

BILLIONS OF CHEMICAL **REACTIONS** TAKE PLACE **EVERY SECOND** IN THE **HUMAN BODY!**

CREATING **COMPOUNDS**

Compounds are substances made up of more than one element and can be very different to the pure elements that form them. When the shiny metal sodium reacts with chlorine gas, the two join to produce white salt (sodium chloride).

Sodium + **Chlorine** = **Salt**

FIERY **FLAMES**

Fire is caused by a chemical reaction called combustion. This takes place when fuel reacts with oxygen in the air, causing lots of heat and light. Fires can be a rapid reaction, spreading quickly.

RUST REACTION

Some reactions happen very slowly. For example, it can take weeks for iron to react with water and oxygen in the air, but eventually a flaky red-brown coating forms on the surface of the metal.

Patches of rust (iron oxide) are the product of the reaction.

Material world

Different materials are all around us. You probably don't think about them much, but that's because they are doing their job so well. Imagine life without soft, warm clothes, or sturdy weatherproof buildings!

A PLASTIC BOTTLE TAKES **450 MILLION YEARS** TO BREAK DOWN!

FROZEN **SMOKE**

Aerogels are human-made materials with amazing properties. Made from silica gel, they have so many tiny holes that they are more than 95 percent air. This makes them incredibly light and very good insulators, as demonstrated in the picture below.

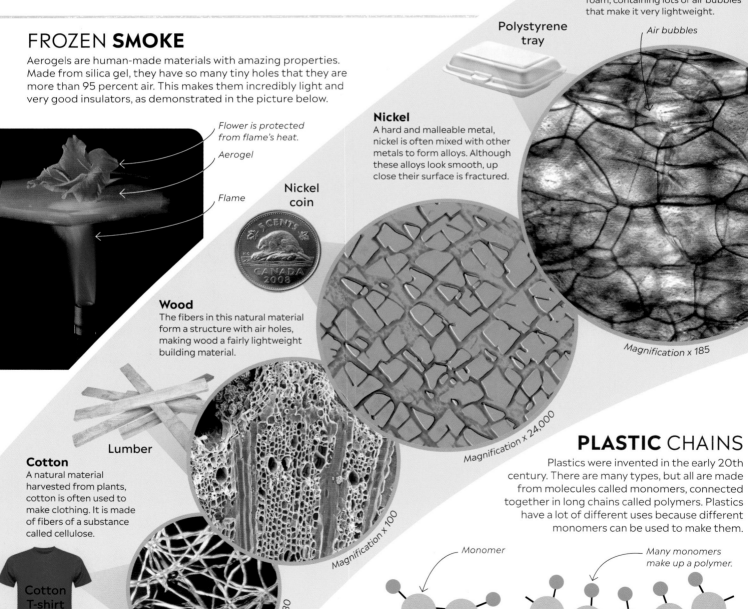

Flower is protected from flame's heat.

Aerogel

Flame

Polystyrene
Polystyrene is a plastic often used in packaging. This is polystyrene foam, containing lots of air bubbles that make it very lightweight.

Polystyrene tray

Air bubbles

Nickel
A hard and malleable metal, nickel is often mixed with other metals to form alloys. Although these alloys look smooth, up close their surface is fractured.

Nickel coin

5 CENTS · CANADA 2008

Magnification x 185

Wood
The fibers in this natural material form a structure with air holes, making wood a fairly lightweight building material.

Lumber

Magnification x 24,000

Cotton
A natural material harvested from plants, cotton is often used to make clothing. It is made of fibers of a substance called cellulose.

Cotton T-shirt

Cellulose fibers

Magnification x 100

Magnification x 80

PLASTIC CHAINS

Plastics were invented in the early 20th century. There are many types, but all are made from molecules called monomers, connected together in long chains called polymers. Plastics have a lot of different uses because different monomers can be used to make them.

Monomer

Many monomers make up a polymer.

MICRO **STRUCTURES**

We use materials for different purposes, based on whether they are hard or soft, stretchy or rigid. But underneath the microscope, they can often look very different!

Nylon pads

Nylon
One of the first synthetic (human-made) fibers, nylon is a plastic often made into clothing. It can be made into long fibers that are strong and lightweight and break down less easily than natural ones.

Concrete block

Concrete
A mixture of cement and small stones and sand, concrete has properties similar to rocks. It can be mixed with a polymer coating to make it smoother, like in the image below.

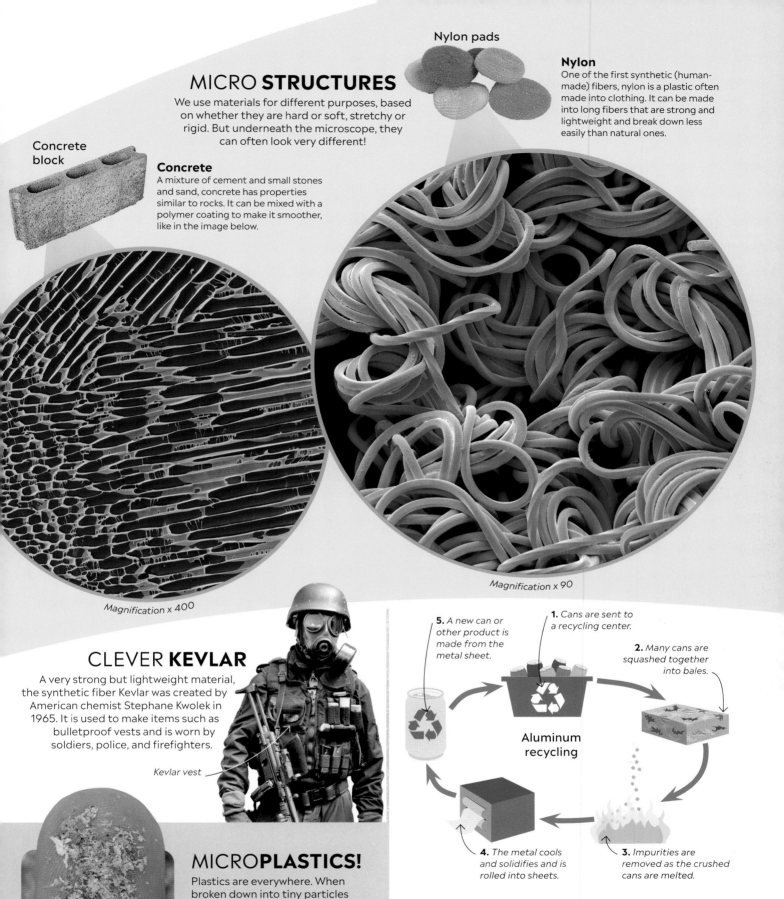

Magnification x 400

Magnification x 90

CLEVER **KEVLAR**

A very strong but lightweight material, the synthetic fiber Kevlar was created by American chemist Stephane Kwolek in 1965. It is used to make items such as bulletproof vests and is worn by soldiers, police, and firefighters.

Kevlar vest

MICRO**PLASTICS!**

Plastics are everywhere. When broken down into tiny particles smaller than 0.2 in (5 mm), they are known as microplastics. Trillions of these float in the oceans and some are even found inside the human body. A person is thought to ingest around 0.2 oz (5 g) a week!

5. *A new can or other product is made from the metal sheet.*

1. *Cans are sent to a recycling center.*

2. *Many cans are squashed together into bales.*

Aluminum recycling

4. *The metal cools and solidifies and is rolled into sheets.*

3. *Impurities are removed as the crushed cans are melted.*

MATERIAL **RECYCLING**

We waste many materials by throwing them away, but some can be recycled instead. For example, aluminum cans can be turned back into aluminum sheets—ready to be made into new cans, or different products entirely.

TEA BAG MADE OUT OF SEAWEED

EDIBLE PACKAGING

Plastic packaging protects much of our food and drink but produces a lot of waste when thrown away. To get around this problem, some companies have designed new packaging that you can eat—made of natural materials.

MILK
Milk can be used to make an edible stretchy film packaging that looks just like plastic.

WHEAT HUSKS
The disposable outer parts of wheat can be turned into edible takeout containers.

POTATOES
Cones for packaging fries can now be made from dried potato peelings.

SEAWEED
A material made from this ocean algae can be used to form a protective bubble to package liquids.

STAT ATTACK! MATERIALS

Many materials are used in our modern lives—some from natural sources and others made in factories and furnaces. Here are some surprising facts about our material world.

SELF-REPAIRING MATERIAL

Even durable materials can break over time, but scientists are developing substances that can overcome this. New groundbreaking plastics can heal themselves if split or cut. Simply pushing the parts back together allows the material to repair itself.

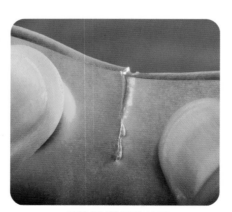
SELF-HEALING PLASTIC

ROTTING AWAY

Lots of materials will end up as waste eventually, but some break down (biodegrade) much faster than others.

 PAPER
Made out of trees, paper can return to nature in 2–5 months.

 NYLON
Clothes made from the artificial fabric nylon take 30–40 years to decompose.

 ALUMINUM CAN
It takes between 80 and 100 years for a metal to fully break down.

 PLASTIC BAG
These thin bags can take anywhere from 500 years onward to fully decompose.

 GLASS BOTTLE
It can take around a million years for hard glass to be broken fully down.

INSPIRED BY NATURE

Animals and plants have amazing natural properties—from their protective skin to the substances they produce. Many scientists have taken inspiration from the natural world to make new materials.

GECKO TOES
Geckos can climb walls due to the tiny hairs on their feet. Scientists have designed a glue that sticks in a similar way.

SHARK SCALES
Speedy swimsuits have been designed based on shark skin. Its overlapping scales are thought to reduce drag.

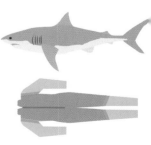

WEIGHING IT UP

In 2020 the weight of all human-made things outweighed all the living things on the planet for the first time. The amount of stuff humans produce every year is currently doubling every 20 years.

STRONG STUFF

While scientists try to make ever tougher substances, many strong materials exist already in nature. The tiny teeth of a creature called a limpet are thought to be one of the strongest biological materials—5 times as strong as spider silk!

A LIMPET PREPARES TO CLING TO A ROCK

ICE HOTEL

Buildings are usually made of materials such as wood and concrete, but some grand designers have been a bit more creative. The Icehotel in Sweden has walls sculpted out of huge blocks of ice! Constructed in winter each year, it then melts in the spring.

A YEAR IN MATERIALS

Every year, massive amounts of materials are produced, shipped around the world, and put to use. Many of the most common are materials used in construction, but we also use plastic and glass to make lots of familiar household items. Here is how much of each one is produced in a year.

33 **BILLION TONS OF CONCRETE**
Used to build houses, roads, and other infrastructure.

2.2 **MILLION TONS OF STEEL**
A strong and sturdy building material.

390 **MILLION TONS OF PLASTIC**
Mainly used for packaging goods.

440 **MILLION TONS OF PAPER**
Used to make books, but also as a packaging material or insulation.

25.8 **MILLION TONS OF GLASS**
Often used in housing, packaging, and to make tableware, such as glasses.

BURRS
The velcro you find on clothing is inspired by burrs—plant seeds that have tiny hooks to attach to things.

LOTUS PLANTS
The leaves of a lotus plant repel water. Some waterproof materials used in raincoats use the same principle.

TYPES OF **ENERGY**

Energy can be stored and transferred in different ways. Light, heat, and sound are examples of how energy is transferred from place to place.

Kinetic
A moving object stores kinetic energy. As it speeds up, it gains more kinetic energy.

Electrical
Particles called electrons transfer energy when they flow as current or can be stored as charge.

Light
Light is a way of transferring energy that our eyes can detect. It travels in waves.

Sound
Sound is energy moving as waves of vibration through materials.

Heat
The energy of the jiggling particles that make up matter is called heat.

Chemical
Energy is locked up in the chemical bonds between atoms and molecules.

Nuclear
The nucleus (center) of an atom stores vast amounts of energy.

Potential
This is the energy an object gains if it is raised, squeezed, or stretched.

BODY-POWERED TECH!

Much of the body's energy ends up transferred to its surroundings by heating. However, tiny wearable gadgets called thermoelectric generators (TGMs) can use this heat from the body to produce electricity. This technology could soon power watches, fitness monitors, and even pacemakers!

01:22

Eternal energy

There is a fixed amount of energy in the universe, which constantly transfers between things. It makes everything happen—from lighting your home to moving your muscles.

SEEING **HEAT**

Heat never stays put—it moves to cooler objects or surroundings. Thermal cameras can detect the heat objects give off. The hottest areas are shown as pink and red, followed by green, blue, and black—the coldest.

WASTED ENERGY

When you use energy, some of it is always wasted because it transfers to the surroundings. A bowling ball hurtling toward the pins loses some of its kinetic energy to the air as sound—and even more when it crashes into the pins!

THE LOUDEST SOUND EVER WAS THE ERUPTION OF KRAKATOA IN 1883. IT WAS HEARD **OVER 3,000 MILES (4,800 KM) AWAY!**

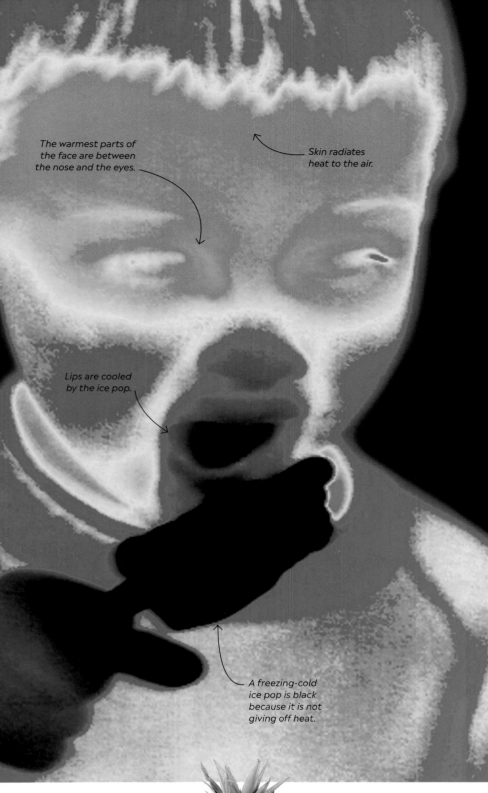

The warmest parts of the face are between the nose and the eyes.

Skin radiates heat to the air.

Lips are cooled by the ice pop.

A freezing-cold ice pop is black because it is not giving off heat.

SPRING **LOADED**

There are several ways energy can be stored—such as chemical energy in batteries. These spring toys store energy as elastic potential energy. However, once their sucker loses its grip, the energy is released and they bounce upward!

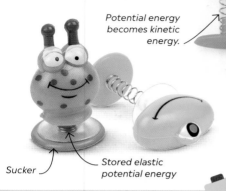

Potential energy becomes kinetic energy.

Sucker

Stored elastic potential energy

IT WOULD TAKE MORE THAN **500 AA BATTERIES** TO **POWER A HUMAN** FOR ONE DAY!

ENERGY **TRANSFER**

Whenever anything happens, there is always the same amount of energy after as there was before. No energy disappears—it just transfers. Here is what happens when a ball bounces.

1. A raised ball has gravitational potential energy.

2. The ball's stored energy becomes kinetic energy as the ball falls.

4. Potential energy turns into kinetic energy as the ball bounces.

3. As it squashes, the ball gains elastic potential energy.

ENERGY **IN FOOD**

The food you eat contains stored chemical energy. During digestion, food is broken down, releasing this stored energy. Much of it becomes heat energy or kinetic energy, keeping your body moving.

Plants and their fruits grow using energy from sunlight.

MORE THAN 90% OF NORWAY'S ELECTRICITY IS PRODUCED BY **HYDROPOWER!**

Powering
our world

We use energy in all parts of our lives—for light, heat, and getting around. But all energy sources have drawbacks. Fossil fuels are harmful to the environment, while renewable sources can be difficult to harness.

FOSSIL **FUELS**

Many of the fuels we burn to release energy are made from the remains of ancient life-forms. Over millions of years, they were crushed under layers of sediment, turning into gas and oil. Fossil fuels are not replaceable and emit harmful gases when burned.

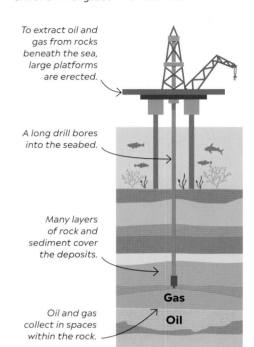

To extract oil and gas from rocks beneath the sea, large platforms are erected.

A long drill bores into the seabed.

Many layers of rock and sediment cover the deposits.

Oil and gas collect in spaces within the rock.

Gas

Oil

The driver must fit into a small space in order to reduce drag.

The car's solar panel contains 232 smaller solar cells that can turn sunlight into electricity.

GEOTHERMAL POWER

Pumping water deep into the ground, where it meets the naturally hot rock beneath Earth's crust, heats the water and produces steam to drive turbines. At the Svartsengi Geothermal power plant in Iceland, this process also created a hot outdoor pool—perfect for soaking in!

SOLAR MIRRORS

Solar panels are not the only way to use the sun's energy. Vast circles of mirrors can direct the sun's heat toward a central structure containing water. This boils into steam, which drives turbines.

TURNING TURBINES

Wind power is a renewable form of energy, as it uses a natural resource that can never run out—the wind. This turns the blades of giant turbines at sea and on hillsides, generating energy.

THE TOTAL AMOUNT OF ENERGY USED ACROSS THE WORLD EACH YEAR HAS INCREASED BY MORE THAN 400% SINCE 1950!

SOLAR SPEED

Traveling at speeds of up to 80 mph (130 km/h), this solar-powered car was one of many to compete in the 2019 Bridgestone World Solar Challenge in Australia. It was able to travel 932 miles (1,500 km) powered entirely by the sun.

CLIMATE CRISIS

Since the 1800s, humans have burned large amounts of fossil fuels, releasing gases such as carbon dioxide into the atmosphere. This is causing Earth's climate to warm up, leading to melting ice and extreme weather events such as wildfires and droughts (see pages 88-89).

ENERGY SOURCES

The world has traditionally relied heavily on fossil fuels (coal, oil, and gas). However, in recent years, the amount generated from renewable and more environmentally friendly sources has increased.

Where does our power come from?

Coal 27%
Oil 31%
Gas 24%
Hydropower 7%
Renewables 7%
Nuclear 4%

Ask a...
CLIMATE SCIENTIST

Sam Hardy is a climate scientist working to help people and businesses adapt to climate change. He previously worked at the University of Leeds, UK, studying tropical cyclones across Southeast Asia.

Q How do we know for sure that climate change is happening?

A There are many forms of reliable measurements that show that Earth's surface temperature has risen by more than 1.8°F since 1850. This warming cannot be explained by natural climate processes such as solar activity. We also know that during the same period, human activity has increased the amount of greenhouse gases in the atmosphere. We can see the effects all around us—oceans warming, sea levels rising, and ice sheets and glaciers melting.

GLACIER RETREAT

Climate change is causing glaciers to melt. These flowing rivers of ice have retreated rapidly over the past decades, as seen in these images of Briksdal Glacier, Norway, from 2002 and 2019. Melting glaciers also contribute to rising sea levels and affect local water supplies and ecosystems.

Q What's your biggest worry about the effects of climate change?

A My greatest concern is that large parts of the world, particularly tropical regions, will become uninhabitable. This could force hundreds of millions of people from their homes.

Q Have you seen any effects firsthand?

A I live in the United Kingdom where we saw record-breaking heatwave temperatures in July 2022, with parts of the country reaching 104°F (40°C) for the first time. Worryingly, such extreme heatwaves are becoming more frequent and severe across the world.

Q What area of the climate do you research?

A My own research focuses on the intensification of tropical cyclones, large storm systems that are responsible for some of the most damaging winds and extreme rainfall on Earth. Scientists think that climate change could make tropical cyclones less frequent, but more violent. Research will help us prepare for the most extreme cyclones.

Q Do you think we can stop climate change? What can I do to help?

A With global action, climate change can definitely be tackled, but we don't have long! One way to help is to make your voice heard—for example, by contacting your elected representatives. You can also cut down on the amount of meat and dairy products you eat, and fly less!

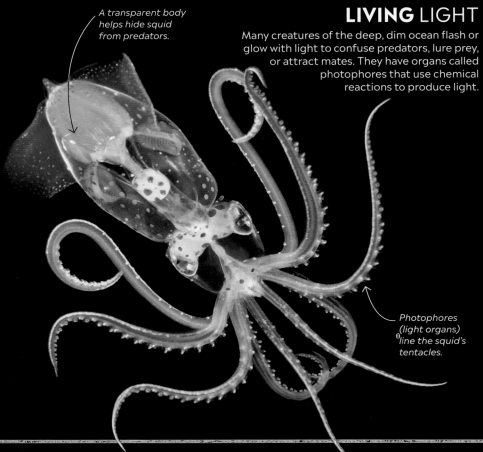

A transparent body helps hide squid from predators.

Photophores (light organs) line the squid's tentacles.

LIVING LIGHT

Many creatures of the deep, dim ocean flash or glow with light to confuse predators, lure prey, or attract mates. They have organs called photophores that use chemical reactions to produce light.

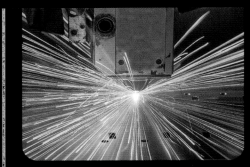

CUTTING POWER

Lasers create narrow, straight beams of concentrated light. Some lasers are so intense they can cut through steel. Doctors use low-powered lasers for eye surgery and other delicate operations.

HIDDEN COLORS

White light is actually a mix of colors, which you can separate by passing light through a glass block called a prism. The prism bends each color by a different amount, fanning them out into a spectrum.

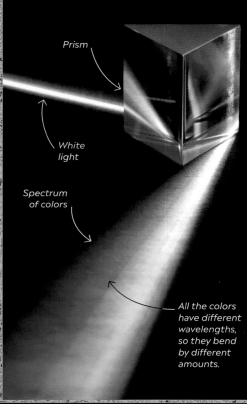

Prism

White light

Spectrum of colors

All the colors have different wavelengths, so they bend by different amounts.

Seeing the light

Whether coming from the sun or a lamp, light is a form of electromagnetic radiation—energy that travels in waves at around 186,000 miles per second (300,000 km per second).

TRAVELING AT THE SPEED OF LIGHT, YOU COULD ZOOM AROUND EARTH 7.5 TIMES IN A SECOND!

BENDING LIGHT

A pencil in a glass of water looks crooked or broken, but it is just an illusion. It occurs because light waves slow down as they travel from air into water or glass. This causes the waves to bend, so the part of the pencil in the water looks shifted. A prism splits up light by bending, or refracting, it.

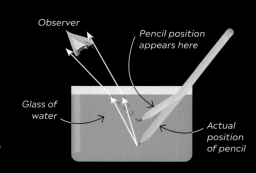

Observer

Pencil position appears here

Glass of water

Actual position of pencil

LIGHT **SHOW**

Even without the sun in the sky, this Norwegian fishing village is a riot of light. A spectacular natural display of shimmering colors called an aurora takes place in the sky against a backdrop of twinkling stars, while electric lights illuminating buildings and streets are reflected in the calm sea.

Starlight is produced by nuclear reactions in the cores (centers) of stars.

Aurorae occur near the poles when streams of charged particles from the sun strike molecules in the air and cause them to emit light.

Electric lights pass current through a thin wire or a tube of gas to make the wire or gas glow.

Light reflects, or bounces, off the surface of the water.

ELECTROMAGNETIC **SPECTRUM**

Our eyes can detect light, but there are other types of radiation that we can't see. Each type has waves of a different length. Radio waves can be feet or miles long, while gamma rays are shorter than the width of an atom.

Radio waves **Microwaves** **Infrared** **Visible light** **Ultra-violet** **X-ray** **Gamma rays**

MANY **ANIMALS** CAN SEE PARTS OF THE **SPECTRUM** HUMANS CAN'T—BEES CAN SEE **ULTRAVIOLET** AND SNAKES CAN DETECT **INFRARED!**

Awesome electricity

Nothing will spark your interest like the force of nature that is electricity. Powering everything from computers to cars, it is carried to our homes by long overhead wires or cables buried underground.

WHAT IS **ELECTRICITY?**

Electricity is the movement of tiny charged particles called electrons. These are part of an atom, but in metals, some are free to move around. When connected to a power supply, they all flow in one direction.

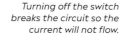

The electrons flow between the postively charged atoms as a current.

Battery

Turning off the switch breaks the circuit so the current will not flow.

Switch

Light

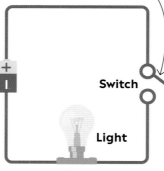

Stream of electrons
Negatively charged electrons flow away from the negative end of the power supply toward the positive.

Circuit
An electric current needs a continuous unbroken loop of wire to flow.

A **BOLT OF LIGHTNING** IS ROUGHLY 53,540°F (29,730°C)— **HOTTER THAN THE SURFACE OF THE SUN!**

HAIR **RAISING**

An electric charge can build up when items are rubbed together and electrons transfer between them. A balloon rubbed on hair gains electrons and a negative charge, causing it to attract positively charged hair. This is known as static electricity.

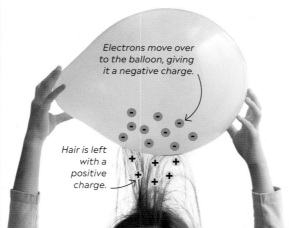

Electrons move over to the balloon, giving it a negative charge.

Hair is left with a positive charge.

BOLTS FROM THE BLUE

Lightning is a powerful form of electrical energy, caused by static electricity building up inside a cloud. An average bolt could power a light bulb for six whole months!

HIGH VOLTAGE HUNTER

Predators in the animal kingdom have a clever use for electricity—to detect their next meal. Creatures such as sharks can sense the tiny electrical currents given out by fish and other prey and use this information to track them down.

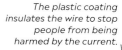

Electro receptors in the shark's head

Hidden prey

CONDUCTORS AND INSULATORS

Only some substances allow electricity to flow through them. Metals are the best conductors, but current can also flow through substances such as water. Materials that do not conduct electricity are called insulators.

The plastic coating insulates the wire to stop people from being harmed by the current.

Electrical wires are often made out of copper, a good conductor.

POWER TO THE PEOPLE

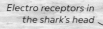

Viewed from space, Earth at night is illuminated by electric lighting that enables us to be active in the dark. The brightest parts of the globe are built-up cities and other large settlements. Almost 20 percent of the world's electricity is used to light up cities.

28% OF THE WORLD'S ELECTRICITY IS GENERATED BY RENEWABLE FORMS OF ENERGY!

NOBEL PRIZE

Established in 1901 by Swedish chemist Alfred Nobel, these annual awards recognize achievements in many fields. Polish scientist Marie Curie was the first person to receive the Nobel prize twice, and is the only person to win prizes in two different sciences!

IG NOBEL PRIZE

Recognizing the sillier side of science, these awards have given prizes to some strange discoveries. Winners include researchers who investigated amount of friction between a banana and a shoe!

WORLD-CHANGING INVENTIONS

From the earliest tools to today's high-tech gadgets, humans have always designed ways to make our lives easier. These landmark inventions brought about big changes in science and wider society.

 1436 **PRINTING PRESS**
Enabled much easier communication of ideas.

 1590 **FIRST MICROSCOPE**
Showed scientists the smallest kinds of life.

 1831 **ELECTRICAL GENERATOR**
Paved the way for greater use of electricity.

 **1860** **INTERNAL COMBUSTION ENGINE**
Many versions of this engine powered transport.

 1942 **NUCLEAR ENERGY**
Released the energy from atoms to generate electricity.

 1946 **COMPUTERS**
Launched the digital revolution.

STAT ATTACK!
BIG IDEAS

Ever since the first scientists started to investigate how the world works, great thinkers and experimenters have come up with bold new theories and designed exciting new inventions. Here are some of the brainiest and most unusual ideas in science!

ARTIST'S CONCEPT OF WHAT ITER COULD LOOK LIKE

FUTURE FUSION

Scientists are currently working on an International Thermonuclear Experimental Reactor (ITER) that can carry out nuclear fusion. The energy that powers stars is released by nuclear fusion. The reactor needs to get very hot to work and, when finished, will be able to reach temperatures of 302 million°F (150 million°C)—10 times as hot as our sun.

SMART SCIENTISTS

Very occasionally, a clever thinker comes up with a brand-new way of looking at the world. These scientific brainboxes produced unique theories that changed science forever!

It was not until the 17th century that scientists realized the Earth orbited the **SUN!**

ALBERT EINSTEIN
1879–1955

German-born Einstein famously showed how time and space are linked together.

ISAAC NEWTON
1643–1727

This English scientist discovered that it is a force (gravity) that makes things fall.

CHARLES DARWIN
1809–1882

English naturalist Darwin came up with the theory of evolution—how life on Earth developed.

DMITRI MENDELEEV
1834–1907

This Russian chemist figured out how to organize the elements in the Periodic Table.

UNEXPECTED TOYS

Designs for inventions do not always work out. Instead, some ideas have turned into popular toys instead!

SUPER SOAKER
The Super Soaker water pistol was created in the 1980s by an engineer at NASA's Jet Propulsion Laboratory, who was trying to use water in a refrigeration system.

PLAY-DOH
Originally invented to be used as wallpaper cleaner, this squishy clay became a brightly colored toy in 1956.

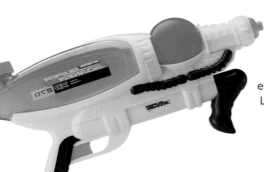

SLINKY
This springy toy was invented in 1943 by a mechanical engineer who wanted to use it to measure a ship's movement.

RUBIK'S CUBE
Designed in 1974 to be a puzzle about geometry, the Rubik's cube became a massively popular plaything.

SILLY STRING,
This squirty substance created in 1972 was at first intended to be a spray that would form a cast for broken limbs.

ACCIDENTAL DISCOVERIES

Many of the greatest discoveries have been made completely by accident, by scientists looking for different things.

1895 — X RAYS

German physicist Wilhelm Roentgen was working with electrons when he accidentally came across X-rays.

1928 — PENICILLIN

When Scottish scientist Alexander Fleming forgot about a dirty petri dish, he discovered a fungus that could treat infections.

1946 — MICROWAVE

After his snack bar melted due to the machine he was designing, US engineer Percy Spencer realized it could be used for cooking.

YOUNG INVENTOR

British child Samuel Thomas Houghton was only three years old when he came up with the idea for a two-headed broom. In 2008, at the age of five, he received a patent for his design—making him one of the youngest inventors in the world!

MANY **ANIMALS,** INCLUDING BIRDS, LOBSTERS, AND DOGS, **NAVIGATE USING EARTH'S MAGNETIC FIELD!**

POWERFUL **PULL**

Most magnets contain one of the magnetic metals (iron, nickel, or cobalt). Iron-containing neodymium magnets are so strong that they can attract metal paper clips even with a nonmagnetic material (your hand) in the way!

Neodymium magnet

Paper clips contain steel, so they are attracted to the magnet.

MAGNETIC **FIELDS**

Around every magnet is a magnetic field—an area in which magnetic materials (metals such as iron and nickel) are affected by the magnet's force. Here, iron filings show the shape of this magnet's magnetic field.

The compass needles line up with the magnetic field.

REPULSION AND **ATTRACTION**

Every magnet has two poles—the north and south poles. When a magnet's pole comes close to that of another, their magnetic fields interact, causing the magnets to either pull together or push apart.

Repulsion
If two magnets are placed with the same poles facing each other, the two poles will push each other away.

Attraction
If two magnets are placed with the opposite poles facing each other, the two poles will pull together.

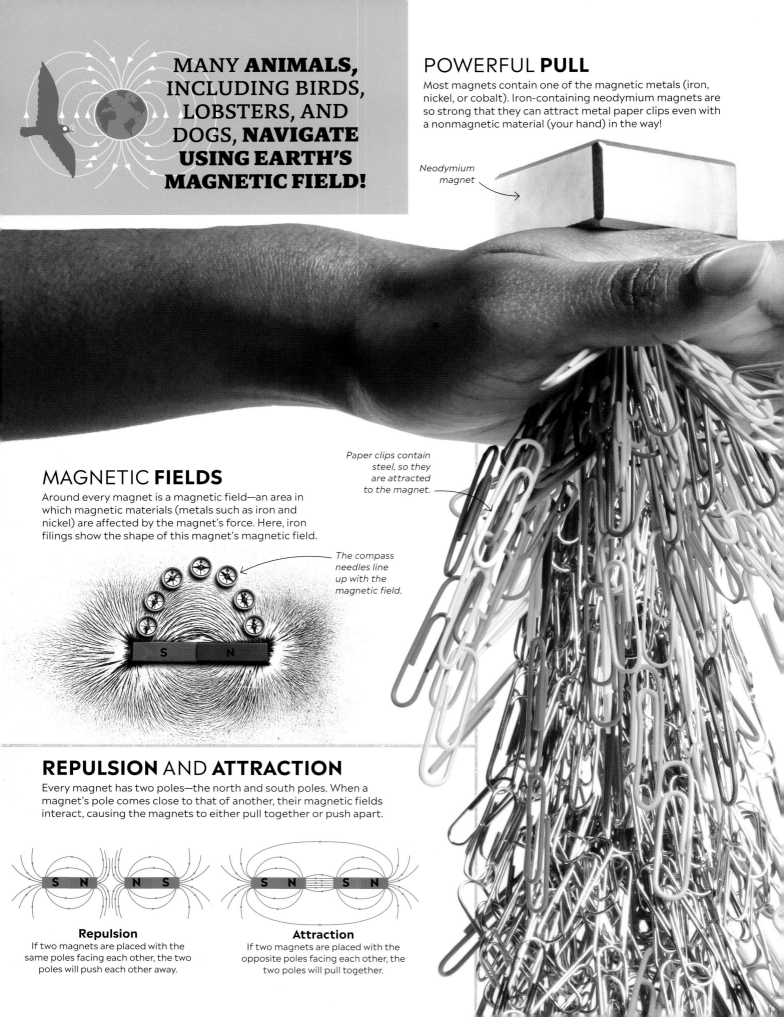

ELECTROMAGNETS

Wrapping a wire around a piece of iron creates a different type of magnet—called an electromagnet. By adding more wire or more current, electromagnets can be made stronger than permanent magnets.

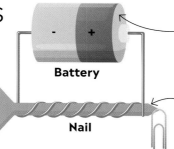

A battery sends electrical current through the wire.

Battery

The nail becomes magnetic when the current is turned on.

Nail

THE **MOST MAGNETIC THINGS** IN THE UNIVERSE ARE DENSE **COLLAPSED STARS** CALLED MAGNETARS!

The points of the compass are marked around the edge.

The needle will always point north. Lining it up with the N allows you to figure out which way the other directions are.

POLE POINTER

Earth is a massive magnet, with its own magnetic field. Compasses are designed to show us the position of Earth's magnetic north pole, helping us find our way around.

The compass needle contains a magnet and can move freely.

Mighty **magnets**

An invisible force, magnetism pushes or pulls on some other objects. Even the tiniest of magnets can attract each other so strongly that they snap violently together!

MAGNETIC **STORM!**

When the charged particles from the sun collide with Earth's magnetic field, they create a shimmering spectacle of colored light in the sky. These displays are called aurora borealis at the North Pole and aurora australis at the South Pole.

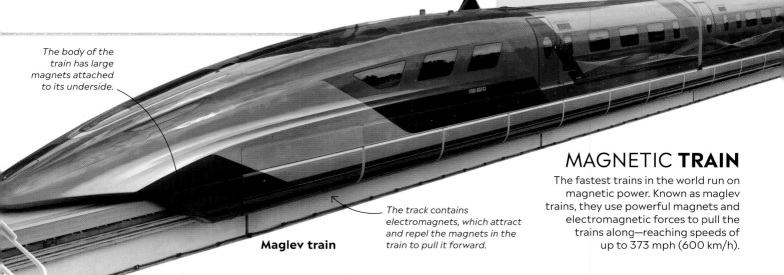

The body of the train has large magnets attached to its underside.

The track contains electromagnets, which attract and repel the magnets in the train to pull it forward.

Maglev train

MAGNETIC **TRAIN**

The fastest trains in the world run on magnetic power. Known as maglev trains, they use powerful magnets and electromagnetic forces to pull the trains along—reaching speeds of up to 373 mph (600 km/h).

THE **WORLD RECORD** FOR THE LONGEST **SKI JUMP** OF **832 FT (253.5 M)** IS HELD BY AUSTRIAN **STEFAN KRAFT!**

DEFORMING FORCES

Forces do not just move an object—they may squeeze, bend, stretch, or twist it so that it deforms (changes shape) or even breaks. Squished between a dog's jaws, this ball has deformed.

Sources of **forces**

Forces seem mysterious; they are invisible, yet you can often see or feel their effects. But forces are really just pushes and pulls. They can make things move, change speed, stop, switch direction, or change shape.

REDUCING **FRICTION**

When one surface moves over another, a force called friction acts to slow it down. Rough surfaces create more friction, which is why it is easier to ski over smooth snow than lumpy gravel!

This team pulls with greater force.

BALANCED OR **UNBALANCED?**

When forces are balanced, things stay the same. When two tug-of-war teams pull in opposite directions with equal force, the forces balance, canceling each other out so nobody moves. But when one team pulls harder, there is an overall force in that direction and the teams begin to move.

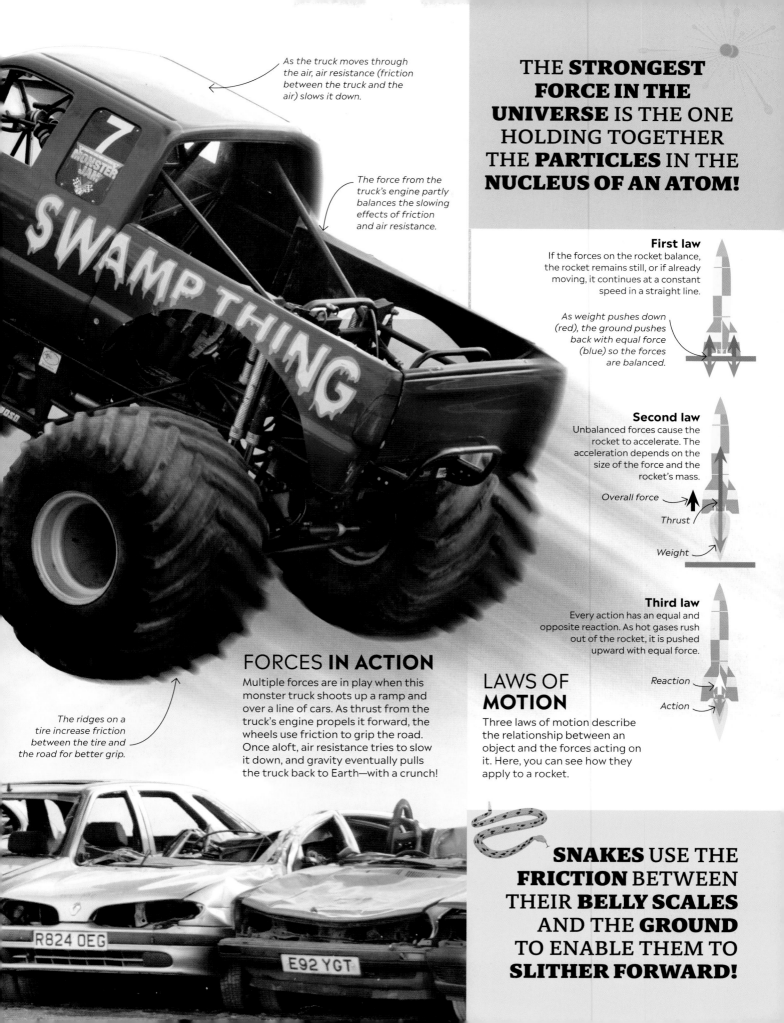

As the truck moves through the air, air resistance (friction between the truck and the air) slows it down.

The force from the truck's engine partly balances the slowing effects of friction and air resistance.

The ridges on a tire increase friction between the tire and the road for better grip.

THE **STRONGEST FORCE IN THE UNIVERSE** IS THE ONE HOLDING TOGETHER THE **PARTICLES** IN THE **NUCLEUS OF AN ATOM!**

First law
If the forces on the rocket balance, the rocket remains still, or if already moving, it continues at a constant speed in a straight line.

As weight pushes down (red), the ground pushes back with equal force (blue) so the forces are balanced.

Second law
Unbalanced forces cause the rocket to accelerate. The acceleration depends on the size of the force and the rocket's mass.

Overall force

Thrust

Weight

Third law
Every action has an equal and opposite reaction. As hot gases rush out of the rocket, it is pushed upward with equal force.

Reaction

Action

FORCES **IN ACTION**
Multiple forces are in play when this monster truck shoots up a ramp and over a line of cars. As thrust from the truck's engine propels it forward, the wheels use friction to grip the road. Once aloft, air resistance tries to slow it down, and gravity eventually pulls the truck back to Earth—with a crunch!

LAWS OF MOTION
Three laws of motion describe the relationship between an object and the forces acting on it. Here, you can see how they apply to a rocket.

SNAKES USE THE **FRICTION** BETWEEN THEIR **BELLY SCALES** AND THE **GROUND** TO ENABLE THEM TO **SLITHER FORWARD!**

NAME THAT... CAR

Are you a motorhead? Shift your mental gears and try to name these speedy vehicles from different eras. Watch out for a speed bump—there's an odd one out!

1 Citroën SM: sleek 1970s French coupé
2 Chevrolet Camaro (2010): sporty American coupé
3 DMC DeLorean: 1980s sports car featured in the *Back to the Future* movies
4 Ferrari F300: 1998 Formula 1 car
5 Chevrolet Bel Air: 1950s American convertible
6 Smart Fortwo: electric, two-seater car
7 Jeep Wrangler: modern four-wheel drive car
8 Pontiac Firebird Trans Am: 1960s American high speed car
9 Benz Patent-Motorwagen: first motor car, invented in 1885
10 Austin Seven Mini: 1960s compact car
11 Reliant Robin (1975): British three-wheel hatchback
12 Hyundai i10: compact hatchback car produced since 2007
13 Soapbox car (1992)
14 Volkswagen Beetle (1968): classic family car
15 Rolls Royce Silver Ghost: 1906 British luxury car
16 Lancia Aprilia: 1930s–1940s family car
17 Bugatti Veyron Super Sport: 2010 supercar
18 Mercedes-Benz 500K: 1930s grand touring vehicle
19 Ford Model T: world's first mass-produced car, released in 1908
20 BMW Isetta: late 1950s bubble car
21 McLaren F1 GTR: 1990s race car
22 Tesla Model S: modern electric car
23 Toyota Prius: hybrid car (with a fuel engine and a separate electric motor)
24 Peugeot 205 GTi: 1980s hatchback
25 Jaguar E-Type: 1960s British sports car
26 Mclaren Senna: 2017 supercar
27 Porsche Boxster: 1998 sports car
28 Nissan Skyline GTR R34: 1990s Japanese sports car
29 Bugatti T39: 1920s race car
30 Range Rover Sport: sports utility vehicle (SUV)

The odd one out is the soapbox car (13). This is the only vehicle here that doesn't have an engine. Soapbox cars are often homemade and compete in downhill races where they rely only on gravity to power them.

The Newton meter shows the force in newtons.

WEIGHING THINGS UP

When we talk about how much something weighs in pounds or kilograms, we are actually referring to its mass—a measure of how much matter is in something. Weight is how much force is acting on an object due to gravity, measured in newtons.

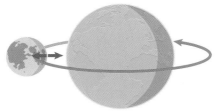

PLANETARY PULL

Gravity is the reason all the planets in our solar system orbit the sun. It is also the force that holds the moon in orbit around us, as the moon and Earth pull on each other.

Cannisters emit smoke to mark the fall.

The force of gravity

One of the most important forces in the universe, gravity is both what keeps our feet on the ground and Earth orbiting around the sun.

HOW GRAVITY WORKS

Gravity is a force that attracts objects together. It works both ways—when the Earth pulls on you, you also pull back on the Earth. How strong gravity is depends on how much mass the objects have and the distance between them.

Double pull
Anything with mass pulls on other matter. The other matter pulls back with the same force.

Bigger and better
The more mass (matter) an object has, the stronger its gravitational pull.

Going the distance
The farther apart two things are, the weaker the gravity that pulls them together.

The jumper will open their packed-away parachute when they get closer to the ground.

DOWN TO EARTH

These daredevils opted to feel the full force of gravity by making the world's highest BASE jump (a leap from a fixed structure). Jumping from the top of the building, they descended 2,717 ft (828 m) to the ground.

The Burj Khalifa in Dubai, United Arab Emirates is the tallest building in the world.

SUCKING YOU IN

When a massive star reaches the end of its life, it can collapse under the force of its own gravity and form a black hole. The pull of a black hole is so great that not even light can escape. Any matter that comes close will be ripped apart.

Artist's impression of debris being sucked into a black hole.

THE HIGHEST-EVER PARACHUTE JUMP WAS MADE BY ALAN EUSTACE IN 2014—FROM **25.7 MILES (41.3 KM)** ABOVE EARTH!

Eustace had to wear a special suit.

FEEL THE **FORCE**

Extreme acceleration can generate higher gravitational forces, or G-forces, than the Earth's gravity (1 g). The forces experienced on a roller coaster can be up to 3 g and some pilots and astronauts are subjected to even higher amounts—putting them at risk of blacking out.

Cameras mounted on a helmet record the record-breaking fall.

ALTHOUGH IT MIGHT SEEM STRONG TO YOU, GRAVITY IS THE UNIVERSE'S WEAKEST MAIN FORCE!

FLIGHT **FORCES**

During flight, four forces act on an airplane: thrust, lift, gravity, and drag. Gravity pulls the plane downward, and drag (air resistance) pulls it backward. Thrust from the engines allows the plane to overcome these—pushing the plane forward and moving air over the wings to create lift.

The cross section of the wing is symmetrical, so this plane can fly just as well upside down as it can the right way up.

Lift
The special shape of the wing creates lift as air is forced over it by the engine's forward thrust.

Thrust
When burning fuel, the engines push hot gases out of the back of the plane to move it forward.

Weight
The lifting force needs to be equal to the plane's weight, which drags it down.

Drag
As the plane moves through the air, the air pushes against the plane, slowing it down.

Fantastic flight

Getting an object to fly through the air is a battle of forces. Aircraft such as gigantic jumbo jets must be equipped with powerful engines to keep them continually flying high.

COMMON SWIFTS CAN STAY FLYING IN THE AIR FOR UP TO **10 MONTHS WITHOUT STOPPING—** EVEN SLEEPING WHILE THEY FLY!

CREATING **LIFT**

This cross section shows how the wing is more curved on top, while the front is angled upward. This causes air flow to speed up as it passes above the wing. Air beneath the wing moves more slowly and so is at a higher pressure, creating lift.

Air flows faster, at lower pressure, over the wing.

Lift

Air flows more slowly, at higher pressure, below the wing.

Two wings provide more lift, so the wings can be shorter. This increases the maneuverability.

DURING A **PLANE FLIGHT,** YOU ARE AROUND **7.5 MILES** (12 KM) OFF THE GROUND!

HIGH **FLIERS**

There can be around 10,000 planes in the air at one time. To avoid each other, they travel in special airways, and a traffic collision avoidance system tells the pilot if anything else draws near.

EXCITING **AEROBATICS**

Stunt pilots go head-to-head in an air show, in a skillful display of tight formation flying. When planes fly this close together, any wrong move can be deadly. A bright red biplane (an aircraft with two sets of wings) soars over several US Navy aircraft—flying so close together that they look like one!

Two other planes fly beside the first.

The plane's pointed nose and shape reduces the drag it experiences.

FASTEST FLIGHT!

In 1976, the military plane Lockheed SR-71 Blackbird reached a speed of 2,193.2 mph (3,529.6 km/h). This was the fastest speed ever achieved by a jet-powered plane—more than three times the speed of sound!

Unlike other drones, those with rotors can hover in place.

DYNAMIC **DRONES**

Aerial vehicles, known as drones, don't need pilots to control them and can be controlled remotely. They often use rotors or propellers to fly and were first used by the military but now are also used to spray crops, deliver supplies, or assist in rescue missions.

Drone cameras can capture a bird's-eye view of events.

Rotors create lift by pushing air downward.

NAME THAT... FLYING MACHINE

Put your plane-spotting skills to the test and identify these aircraft from their name and the date they were introduced. However, one of these can't lift off the ground.

1 *Spirit of St. Louis*: flew nonstop across the Atlantic in 1927
2 LZ 127 Graf Zeppelin airship (1928)
3 Cessna Skyhawk (1955): most produced single engine plane
4 Goodyear Pilgrim blimp (1925): advertising airship
5 Avro Avian 7083 (1926): light aircraft
6 Breitling Orbiter: first hot-air balloon to fly around the world in 1999

7 Supermarine Spitfire (1936): World War II fighter plane

8 Pegasus Quantum (1996): ultralight powered hang glider

9 Yakovlev Yak-9 (1942): World War II fighter plane

10 Sopwith Baby (1915): World War I fighter plane

11 Mitsubishi A6M Zero (1940): World War II fighter plane

12 Eurocopter X³ (2010): high-speed helicopter

13 Heinkel He 177 Greif (1939): World War II bomber

14 MacCready *Gossamer Condor* (1976): human-powered aircraft

15 Lockheed U-2 (1955): spy plane

16 Montgolfier hot-air balloon: made the first hot-air balloon flight in 1783

17 Boeing 747 (1970): jet airliner

18 *Solar Impulse 1* (2009): solar-powered aircraft

19 Concorde (1976): supersonic passenger aircraft

20 Boeing CH-47 Chinook (1961): military transport helicopter

21 SpaceShipOne (2004): experimental space plane launched by White Knight One

22 Airbus A380 (2007): jet airliner

23 DJI MAVIC 3 drone (2021)

24 Leonardo da Vinci's helical aerial screw (1400s)

25 Northrop Grumman RQ-4 Global Hawk (1998): uncrewed aircraft

26 Antonov An-22 (1965): heavy transport aircraft

27 Airbus Beluga (1996): cargo plane

28 Pipistrel Velis Electro (2020): first electric-powered aircraft

29 Messerschmitt Me 262: World War II aircraft

30 Wright Flyer (1903): first successful powered airplane

The odd one out is the helical aerial screw (24), which was a design by Leonardo da Vinci. Nobody knows if it ever flew.

THE LARGEST CONTAINER SHIP IS 1,312 FT (400 M) LONG—FIVE TIMES THE LENGTH OF A JUMBO JET!

WILL IT **FLOAT?**

Objects float if they are less dense than water. If more dense, they sink. Density is the amount of matter packed into a certain volume of an object.

Cork is light and less dense than water, so it floats.

A fish has roughly the same density as the water.

A metal coin is denser than water, so it sinks.

Float your boat

From tiny grass-made coracles to enormous cruise ships with swimming pools on board, all boats float because they are less dense than water.

WATER **RACER**

Racing trimarans like this one can whip through the waves at speeds of 30 mph (48 km/h). Their three-hulled structure cuts through the water and also helps keep each boat upright.

The wind can tilt the boat, so crew need a head for heights!

The trimaran's main hull is in the middle of the boat, supported by two side hulls.

THE WORLD'S **FASTEST BOAT** IS THE **SPIRIT OF AUSTRALIA,** WHICH REACHED A SPEED OF **317.59 MPH (511.11 KM/H)!**

HOW SHIPS **FLOAT**

A steel block sinks in water, but a steel boat of the same weight floats. This is because it contains air, so is less dense. As it floats, a boat pushes water out of the way. The water pushes upward with a force called upthrust that equals the weight of the water displaced.

Weight

A steel block sinks because its weight is greater than the upthrust.

Upthrust

Weight

Upthrust balances weight

Upthrust

FISHING **FLEET**

There are around four million fishing boats around the world. Although there are many big vessels, more than 80 percent of fishing boats are less than 39 ft (12 m) long.

THERE ARE AN ESTIMATED **3 MILLION SHIPWRECKS** AT THE BOTTOM OF THE OCEAN!

All three hulls are narrow and streamlined, allowing the boat to cut through the water.

THE VERY **FIRST** SIMPLE MACHINES WERE HAND AXES USED MORE THAN **ONE MILLION** YEARS AGO!

SIMPLE **MACHINES**

There are six main types of simple machines. Each can be used to alter the force applied to them—to make the force bigger, smaller, or change its direction.

Inclined plane
Also known as a ramp, this makes it easier to lift objects, although the object needs to be pushed farther.

Wedge
A wedge is two inclined planes put together. Wedges such as axes can be used to split objects in two.

Screw
A screw ends in a sharp point. Turning the top of the screw in a circular motion produces a downward action.

Lever
A bar that moves over a fixed point (the fulcrum) is a lever. A simple lever can be used to pry heavy objects off the ground.

Wheel and axle
A wheel spins around a central rod—the axle. Spinning the axle turns the wheel edge further, while using less force.

Pulley
Pulleys change the direction of a force—the load is lifted upward when the rope is pulled downward.

EARTH **EXTRACTOR**

Some machines are built to epic proportions. One of the world's heaviest land vehicles is the Bagger 288 Excavator, a mining machine that weighs 13,000 tons (11,800 metric tons). Its massive arm swings around and burrows into the earthbanks, scooping up more than 8.5 million cubic feet (241,000 cubic meters) of dirt a day.

Long cables move the main arm up and down.

Counterweights prevent the machine from toppling over.

Wide tracks support the weight of the machine.

Single pulley
A pulley with one wheel can change the direction of a force. The load is lifted up by the same force as the effort used to pull the rope.

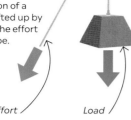

Effort

Load

Double pulley
With a double pulley, the effort needed to lift the load is halved, but the force has to move over twice the distance.

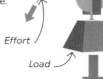

Effort

Load

REDUCING **EFFORT**
Simple machines can be used to enlarge or reduce forces, to make jobs such as lifting easier. Adding more wheels to a pulley system makes the load easier to lift, but the pulling force has to move farther over a longer distance.

COLOSSAL **CRAWLER**
Built to carry rockets to the launchpad, NASA's crawler-transporters are huge vehicles—twice as long as a baseball field. However, they travel only at 1 mph (1.6 km/h).

Earth is carried away on a conveyor belt.

These bucket-shaped indents are used to carve into the ground.

Extreme machines

Machines are tools we create to do jobs or to make jobs easier to do. There are six simple machine types that can be combined to create complex vehicles and gadgets.

THE **BIGGEST TRUCK** CAN CARRY A LOAD **WEIGHING 496 TONS** (450 METRIC TONS)—AROUND **90 ELEPHANTS!**

TERRIFIC TUNNELS

Beneath our feet, the earth is honeycombed with tunnels. Some carry water supplies, while others allow trains and cars to pass beneath mountains and hills and even under the sea.

LONGEST ROAD TUNNEL:
Lærdal Tunnel (Norway)—15.2 miles (24.5 km)

LONGEST UNDERSEA TUNNEL:
Channel Tunnel (England-France)—23.5 miles (37.9 km)

LONGEST AND DEEPEST RAIL TUNNEL:
Gotthard Base Tunnel (Switzerland)—35 miles (57 km)

LONGEST WATER SUPPLY TUNNEL: Delaware Aqueduct (New York, US)—85.1 miles (137 km)

11 boring machines were used to drill the Channel Tunnel. Altogether they weighed **13,200 tons** (12,000 metric tons) - more than the **Eiffel Tower.**

STAT ATTACK!
STRUCTURES

The new wonders of the world are spectacular, human-made structures that reach awesome heights, span incredible distances, and take engineering and technology to new levels.

AMAZING BRIDGES

LONGEST BRIDGE The Danyang-Kunshan Grand Bridge, China is 102.4 miles (164.8 km) long.

HIGHEST BRIDGE The Duge Bridge in China crosses a deep river gorge, a 1,854 ft (565 m) drop from the bridge's deck.

OLDEST BRIDGE The single arch bridge that crosses the Meles River in Izmir, Turkey, was built in 850 BCE and is still in use today.

TALLEST BRIDGE The Milau viaduct in France (below) is 1,125 ft (343 m) tall at its highest point.

MILAU VIADUCT

TALLEST BUILDINGS

The record for the world's tallest building is rarely held for very long. However, the current record holder, Burj Khalifa, has managed to hang on to the title since 2010.

The **Burj Khalifa** contains **6,210 miles** (10,000 km) of **steel** and is **covered** in **26,000 glass panels.**

BURJ KHALIFA, Dubai, UAE, 2,717 ft (828 m)

MERDEKA 118, Kuala Lumpur, Malaysia, 2,227 ft (679 m)

SHANGHAI TOWER, Shanghai, China, 2,073 ft (632 m)

ABRAJ AL BAIT CLOCK TOWER, Mecca, Saudi Arabia, 1,972 ft (601 m)

ARTIFICIAL ISLANDS

These feats of engineering are often created in locations where space is scarce. The islands can be defensive forts, airports, residential communities, or luxury resorts.

KANSAI INTERNATIONAL AIRPORT

1 FLEVOPOLDER
Flevoland, Netherlands
374 sq miles (970 sq km)

2 YAS ISLAND
Abu Dhabi, UAE
9.7 sq miles (25 sq km)

3 KANSAI INTERNATIONAL AIRPORT
Osaka, Japan
4.2 sq miles (10.7 sq km)

4 HONG KONG INTERNATIONAL AIRPORT
Hong Kong, China
3.6 sq miles (9.4 sq km)

5 PORT ISLAND
Chuo-ku, Kobe, Japan
3.2 sq miles (8.3 sq km)

PING AN FINANCE CENTRE, Shenzhen, China, 1,966 ft (599 m)

LOTTE WORLD TOWER, Seoul, South Korea, 1,819 ft (554 m)

HEAVIEST BUILDINGS

The Great Pyramid at Giza is the weightiest ever construction, at an estimated 6.6 million tons (6 million metric tons). The heaviest modern building is the Palace of Parliament in Bucharest, Romania, which weighs in at 4.5 million tons (4.1 million metric tons).

TALLEST STATUES

STATUE OF UNITY 1
Gujarat, India, 597 ft (182 m) Completed in 2018

SPRING TEMPLE BUDDHA 2
Lushan, China, 420 ft (128 m) Completed in 2008

THE USHIKU GREAT BUDDHA 3
Ushiku, Japan, 390 ft (120 m) Completed in 2008

LAYKYUN SETKYAR 4
Monywa, Myanmar, 381 ft (116 m)
Completed in 2008

SENDAI DAIKANNON 5
Sendai, Japan, 328 ft (100 m)
Completed in 1991

STATUE OF UNITY | **SPRING TEMPLE BUDDHA** | **THE USHIKU GREAT BUDDHA** | **LAYKYUN SETKYAR** | **SENDAI DAIKANNON**

LARGEST CASTLE

Malbork Castle in Poland covers the greatest area of any castle in the world. It was built by Teutonic Knights in the 13th century and spreads across 52 acres (21 hectares)—the same as 26 football fields.

Inside the
internet

MORE THAN
4 TRILLION PHOTOS
ARE STORED BY GOOGLE
IN THE CLOUD!

The internet is a vast network that links computers all over the world. Today, billions of devices are connected to it and can access information in just seconds!

Internet service provider (ISP)
These companies provide the infrastructure to allow devices to connect to the internet, either through cables, a dial-up network, or satellites.

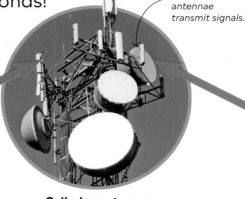

Dishes and antennae transmit signals.

Smartphone
Modern smartphones can connect to the internet through Wi-Fi or through cell towers. Globally, more people now use a phone to access the internet than a computer.

Cell phone tower
Often located in high areas, these towers pick up signals from mobile devices and connect them to an ISP using radio waves.

The router is plugged into a cable, linking it to an ISP.

Wireless router
Routers connect networks of computers to an ISP.

Rows of servers can fill whole rooms and buildings.

Computer
Laptops and desktop computers can connect to a local router through Wi-Fi or through cables directly connecting to the telephone network.

HOW THE **INTERNET** WORKS

There are many devices through which we can access the internet. Connected devices form a local network using a router, which sends and receives information to an Internet Service Provider (ISP). The ISP directs information to and from other local networks around the world.

Data center
The information available on the internet is stored on computers called servers, in vast data centres. These servers can also be referred to as "The Cloud".

UP TO 60% OF INTERNET TRAFFIC
IS THOUGHT TO BE GENERATED
BY BOTS INSTEAD OF HUMANS!

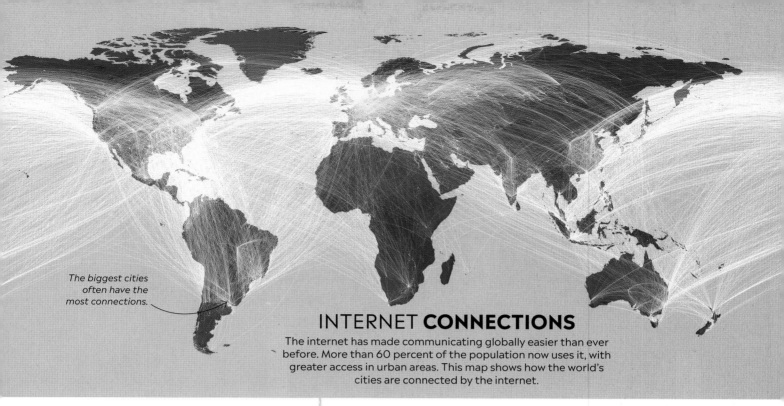

The biggest cities often have the most connections.

INTERNET **CONNECTIONS**

The internet has made communicating globally easier than ever before. More than 60 percent of the population now uses it, with greater access in urban areas. This map shows how the world's cities are connected by the internet.

SATELLITE **SIGNALS**

Although most internet data travels through cables, some is sent via satellites orbiting the Earth. Satellite links can be especially useful for connecting remote areas, where cables don't reach. New companies plan to roll out satellite broadband across whole countries.

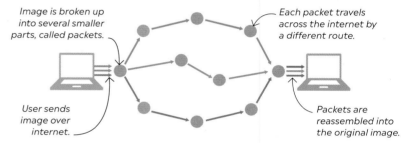

Image is broken up into several smaller parts, called packets.

Each packet travels across the internet by a different route.

User sends image over internet.

Packets are reassembled into the original image.

SENDING **DATA**

A huge amount of information is sent across the internet every day. Connected devices do this by a method called packet switching, in which files are broken up into small chunks, each sent separately by the best available route.

UNDER THE SEA

The majority of internet data is sent across the world through fiber optic cables. Many of these stretch across oceans. Nestled on the sea floor, they can be at risk of damage from ships or even sharks!

An operator slowly unfurls the cable into the sea.

THE **WORLD WIDE WEB**

While the internet is what connects your devices to others, the World Wide Web is all of the web pages you view online. The World Wide Web is just one way of using the internet, as well as email, and file transfer services.

870,000 MILES (1.4 MILLION KM) OF UNDERSEA CABLES CARRY 97% OF ALL INTERNET TRAFFIC!

EARLY INVENTIONS

One of the earliest robots was Shakey, designed in 1966. Using a camera and sensors, it could navigate around rooms and push objects together. Its use of AI paved the way for many of the robots working today.

Electronics were housed in the center.

IN 2021, THERE WERE **3 MILLION INDUSTRIAL ROBOTS** OPERATING IN FACTORIES **AROUND THE WORLD!**

Resourceful robots

In the 21st century, we use robots to do lots of tasks—in factories, hospitals, and even in the military. Some of these intelligent machines can even make decisions for themselves!

ROBOT PARTS

In order to carry out complex tasks, robots need sensors to observe their environment. Information from these can be processed by the robot's internal computers and sometimes a human operator too. Robotic arms or parts called actuators carry out the action. The bomb disposal robot below uses the information it gathers to disable an explosive device.

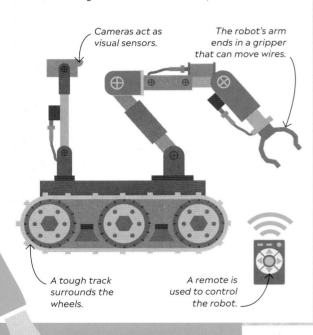

Cameras act as visual sensors.

The robot's arm ends in a gripper that can move wires.

A tough track surrounds the wheels.

A remote is used to control the robot.

SMART SURGERY

The Da Vinci surgery system uses robotic arms for procedures that require more precision than a human is capable of. A human surgeon uses a console to direct the arms and their instruments and cameras. More than 5,000 of these systems operate worldwide.

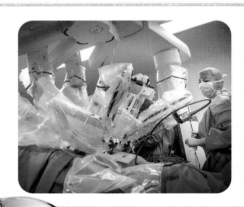

CZECH WRITER KAREL ČAPEK **COINED THE TERM ROBOT**, IN A 1921 PLAY WHERE A ROBOT KILLS A MAN!

The robot's body recognizes when it is being touched and responds.

Aibo's eyes contain cameras.

ARTIFICIAL INTELLIGENCE

Many robots use a form of Artificial Intelligence (AI)—computer programs that can make decisions and learn things from what happens, just like a human would. This dog robot Aibo uses AI to adapt to its environment and develop new ways of interacting with its human owners.

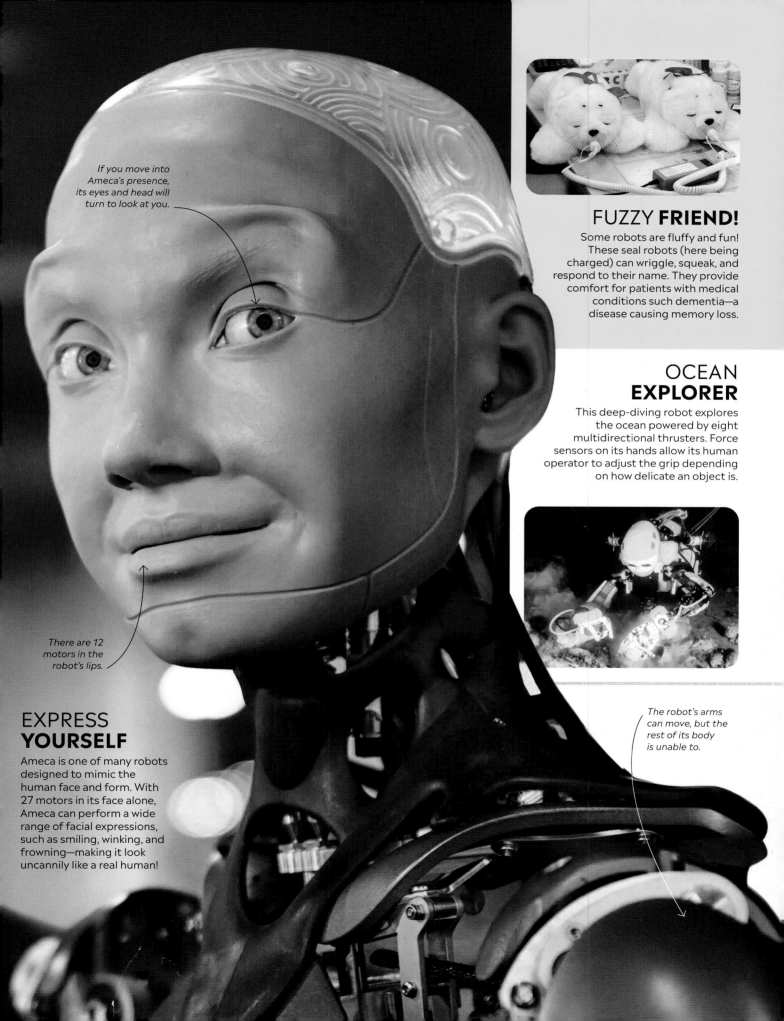

If you move into Ameca's presence, its eyes and head will turn to look at you.

FUZZY **FRIEND!**

Some robots are fluffy and fun! These seal robots (here being charged) can wriggle, squeak, and respond to their name. They provide comfort for patients with medical conditions such dementia—a disease causing memory loss.

OCEAN **EXPLORER**

This deep-diving robot explores the ocean powered by eight multidirectional thrusters. Force sensors on its hands allow its human operator to adjust the grip depending on how delicate an object is.

There are 12 motors in the robot's lips.

EXPRESS **YOURSELF**

Ameca is one of many robots designed to mimic the human face and form. With 27 motors in its face alone, Ameca can perform a wide range of facial expressions, such as smiling, winking, and frowning—making it look uncannily like a real human!

The robot's arms can move, but the rest of its body is unable to.

MICRO ANIMALS

The tiniest life forms are not all simple single cells—some are minuscule animals. These aquatic copepods are less than 0.8 in (2 mm) long. Relations of shrimp and other crustaceans, they are found in oceans and freshwater worldwide.

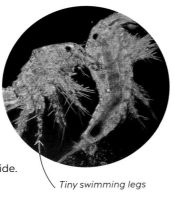

Tiny swimming legs

INSIDE A BACTERIUM

There are more than 30,000 bacteria species, but each individual bacterium is made up of just one simple cell. They come in different shapes, from spherical to corkscrew.

A tail helps propel the bacterium along.

All the bacterium's genetic information is stored in DNA at its center.

Rod-shaped bacterium

Tiny hairs called pili allow bacteria to attach themselves to surfaces.

EXTREME LIVING!

Many microorganisms can survive in places other living things cannot, such as at the bottom of the ocean. Here, chimneys called hydrothermal vents spew boiling water heated by magma in the Earth. Despite the lack of sunlight, microbes still thrive.

The water emitted by the vents is full of minerals that microbes can use to sustain themselves.

Mats of microbes build up around the vents.

Under the microscope

There is a whole world of life that we cannot see with the naked eye. From tiny plantlike algae to colonies of bacteria, legions of microorganisms are all around us, and even inside our bodies.

IT'S A SMALL WORLD

When viewing microscopic images, it can be hard to imagine how tiny they are. The life forms below are so small that it is easiest to measure them in micrometers (one micrometer is 10,000 times smaller than a centimeter)!

Flagella help the alga swim through water.

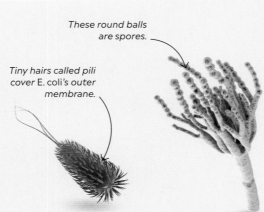

Pointy spikes on the outside of the virus help it to enter the cells of the organisms it infects.

These small blobby bacteria are spherical in shape.

Tiny hairs called pili cover E. coli's outer membrane.

These round balls are spores.

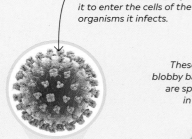

Flu virus
This small but deadly virus is just 0.1 micrometers wide and causes many to get sick in winter.

Staphylococcus
A bacteria commonly found on human skin, *Staphylococcus aureus* can cause an infection.

E. coli bacteria
These bacteria often live in the human gut. Some species are beneficial and some harmful.

Penicillium fungus
This tiny fungus has been turned into a life-saving medicine used to treat bacterial infections.

Microalgae
Little aquatic organisms, algae float in their millions in ponds, rivers, and the oceans.

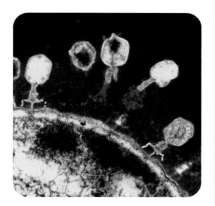

TINY **TERRORS**

Most scientists do not classify viruses as alive, because they cannot reproduce on their own. Instead, they must use other organisms. These bacteriophage viruses inject their DNA into a bacterium, which copies it. The new virus bursts back out!

WORKING WITH **MICROSCOPES**

Light microscopes use glass lenses to focus light and make objects appear bigger to our eyes when viewed through the eyepiece. While these microscopes can magnify items a few thousand times, newer models that use beams of electrons can magnify objects up to 50 million times.

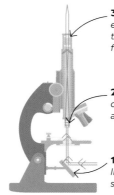

3. *A lens near the eyepiece increases the magnification further.*

2. *Lenses magnify the object between four and 100 times.*

1. *A mirror reflects light toward the specimen on a slide.*

Light microscope

THERE ARE MORE **MICROBIAL SPECIES** ON EARTH THAN **STARS IN THE GALAXY!**

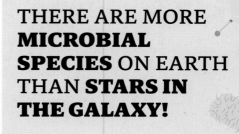

A sperm's long tail propels its body.

Up close, sugar crystals have bumpy sides.

The bulbous part of the organism contains its DNA.

Giardia
Another microorganism that can cause serious harm to humans, giardia is from a kingdom of life called the protozoans.

Sperm cell
Millions of these swimming cells are made everyday in the male body. They are the smallest human cell but are much bigger than many microbes.

Sugar crystal
Many household foods such as sugar, salt, and rice are made up of tiny little particles. Even the smallest sugar crystal is bigger than most microorganisms.

THE **DOUBLE HELIX**

If you uncurl the DNA from inside a cell, it forms a twisting ladderlike structure known as a double helix. An outer backbone surrounds pairings of four different chemicals called bases. The different combinations of these bases is a form of code that holds our genetic information.

Each of the bases can pair with only one other.

The backbone is made of sugars and other chemicals.

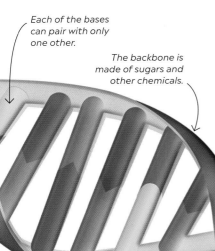

Dynamic **DNA**

Hidden away in each of our cells is a long spiraling molecule that contains all the information that makes us unique—DNA. It is the differences in our DNA that gives each person different physical and mental characteristics.

HUMANS SHARE 40% OF OUR DNA WITH BANANAS!

CLEVER **CHROMOSOMES**

Every person inherits DNA from both their mother and father, packaged up into structures called chromosomes. You have 46 chromosomes—23 from your mother and 23 from your father.

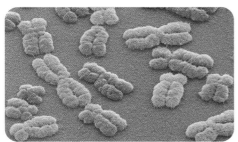

WHAT IS A **GENE?**

A DNA molecule has lots of specific sections called genes. Each gene instructs the body to make a protein—a chemical that can make body parts or carry out tasks. Together, all of these proteins make up your unique characteristics.

Lots of proteins produced by lots of genes can make up a characteristic such as your eye color.

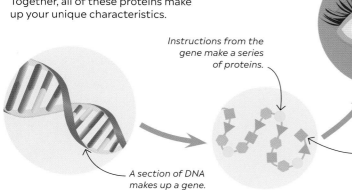

Instructions from the gene make a series of proteins.

A section of DNA makes up a gene.

Proteins join together in long chains called amino acids.

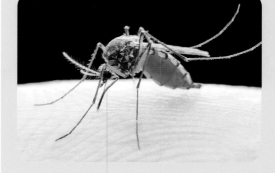

GENE **EDITING!**

Scientists now have the ability to edit DNA. Gene editing has been trialed in mosquitoes, giving them a gene that prevents female mosquitoes (the biting ones) from surviving to adulthood. This means they do not grow up to pass on diseases to humans, such as malaria.

SHARED DNA

Identical twins look the same because they have the exact same DNA. However, your genes do not entirely decide who you grow up to be. Environment and lifestyle have an effect, so twins can end up more different from each other than expected. They even have different fingerprints!

The twins' eye color, skin color, and face shape are all the same.

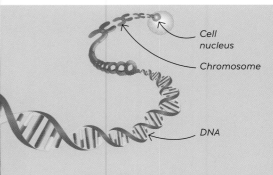

CODE **CHANGES**

Our DNA is copied all the time, causing random changes to occur. Albinism, which reduces the amount of color in skin and eyes, occurs in this way. Offspring get this condition only if they inherit two copies of the changed gene—one from each parent.

Cell nucleus

Chromosome

DNA

IF YOU COULD **UNRAVEL** ALL THE **DNA** IN **ONE CELL,** IT WOULD BE ABOUT **6.6 FT (2 M) LONG!**

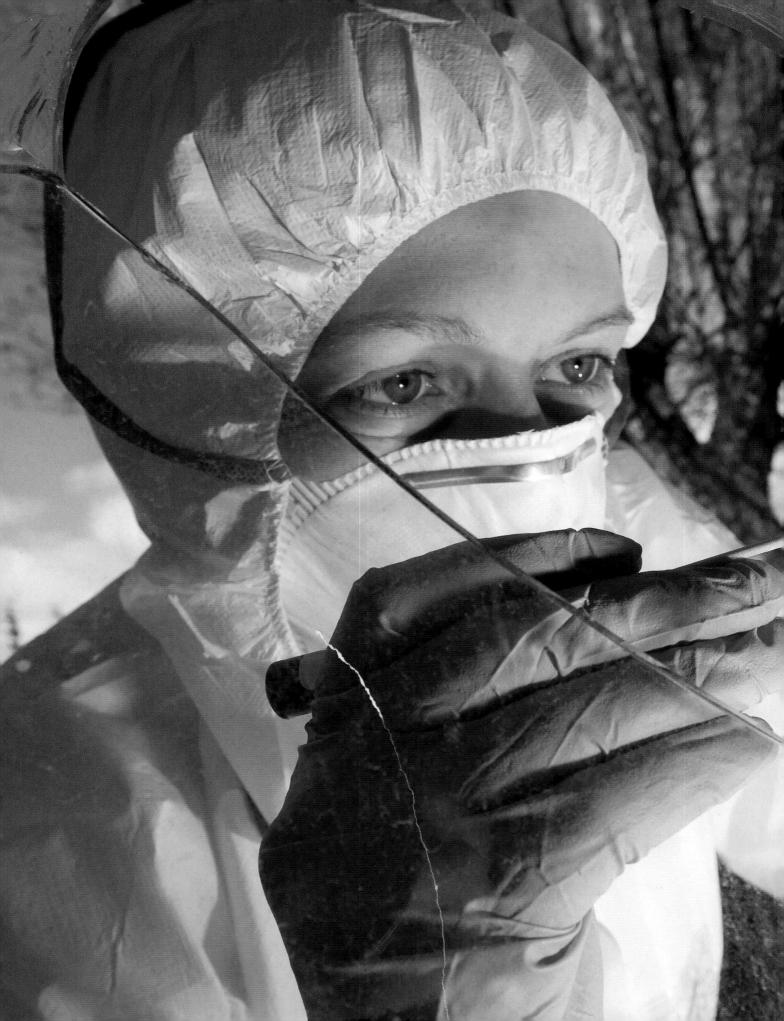

GATHERING
EVIDENCE

Crime scene investigators must scour every site for evidence that might provide information about the crime. They wear gloves and protective equipment to avoid disturbing the scene and each item they collect is carefully packaged in a separate container or bag to prevent it from being contaminated. Even the smallest samples can be useful, such as this swab of blood being taken from a broken window.

Leisa Nichols-Drew is an Associate Professor at De Montfort University, Leicester, UK, as well as a Chartered Forensic Practitioner. She teaches as well as works on cases.

Ask a... FORENSIC SCIENTIST

Q What is the most interesting part of your job?

A I love working with other experts and using scientific techniques to figure out who, what, where, when, and how—by doing so, solving crimes and keeping communities safe.

Q What different areas of forensic science are there?

A There are so many areas of forensic science, including toxicology (looking at medicines and poisons), technology (analyzing computers and cell phones), ecology (examining things such as soil and pollen), among many more!

Q What can you find at a crime scene?

A Crime scenes can contain many different types of evidence, such as footwear marks, tire marks, clothing fibers, fragments from glass and paint, documents, and human evidence such as hairs and saliva. Anything found is sent to a laboratory for examination.

Q How can DNA help solve crimes?

A DNA is present in every cell of the body (except red blood cells). DNA recovered from biological material at the crime scene, such as blood, can be examined by forensic scientists, which may help eliminate or identify people connected to a crime.

Q Do you have any special equipment to help you find evidence?

A Forensic scientists can now view evidence that was previously invisible. Ultraviolet light can be used to find who has handled an item by showing up cellular material from their skin. Infrared light can show if a person has washed away a message in pen ink from the back of their hand. Both kinds of light are also useful at determining if a document is genuine, such as passports and currency.

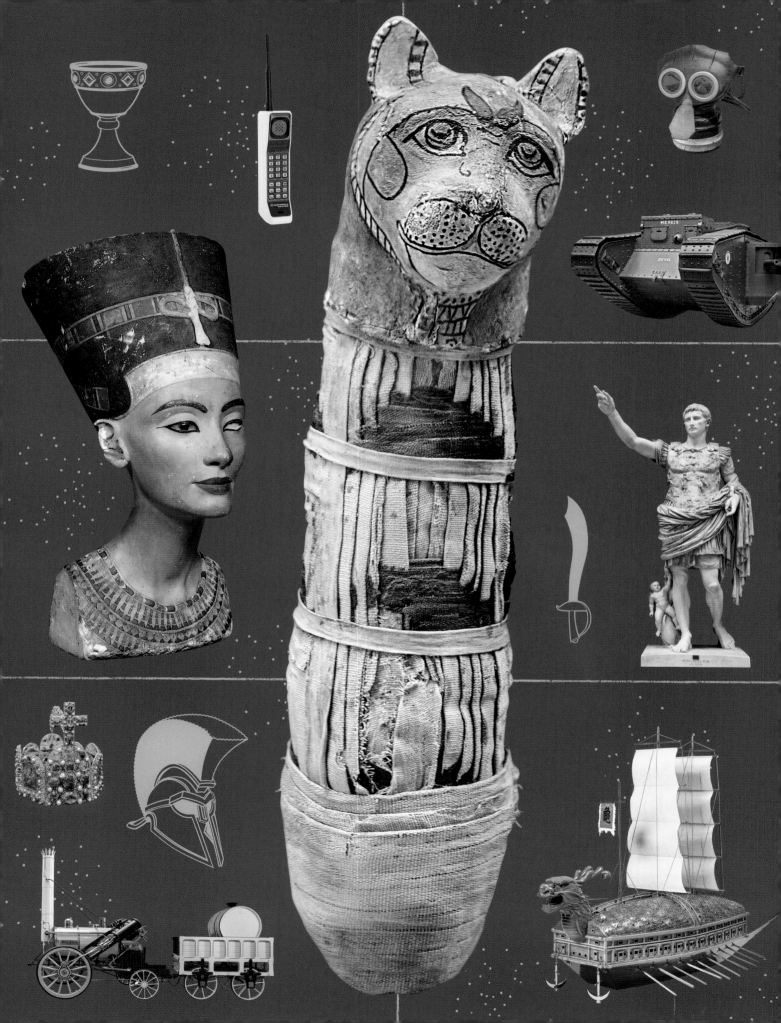

HISTORY

What is **history?**

Everything that has happened in the world so far makes up history. It can help us understand what is happening today and to appreciate the stories of different cultures.

SEEING **THE PAST**
From cave art to photographs, the ways in which people have created art, and the subjects they choose to depict, let us look into their worlds.

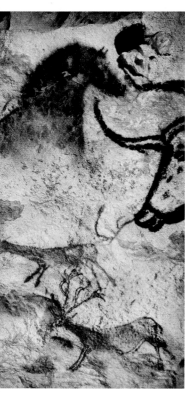

Animals
These bulls and horses were painted nearly 20,000 years ago in a cave in Lascaux, France, . Did the artist depict wildlife, or prey?

Power
Rulers have used art to boast of their wealth and power. The Standard of Ur, a 4,500-year-old mosaic, highlights Sumer's military strength.

Sports
Paintings, friezes, and sculptures from different times show that people have always enjoyed sports. This is a 7th-century Maya ballgame player.

Religion
Gods, holy people, and beliefs of many religions appear in art from all times. This medieval stained-glass window shows a Christian saint.

THE **ORAL HISTORY** OF THE **INDIGENOUS PEOPLES** OF AUSTRALIA GOES BACK **60,000 YEARS!**

WHOSE **HISTORY?**
Through history, people from different cultures have formed opinions about their own superiority, and dismissed other people's knowledge and traditions. In the past, a lack of written records was often treated as a lack of history—today we know that objects, art, and stories passed down generations also tell the tale.

Intricately decorated gold comb from Scythia, an ancient civilization that had no known written language

THE LAST PHARAOH, **CLEOPATRA**, IS CLOSER IN TIME TO THE **IPHONE** THAN THE **BUILDING** OF THE **PYRAMIDS OF GIZA!**

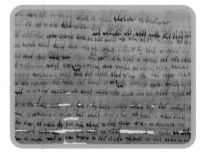

Indus script on a seal made around 5,000 years ago

MYSTERY **HISTORY**

Some of history's secrets remain unsolved. The language of the Indus Valley Civilization, which thrived in northwest India and Pakistan 5,000 years ago, is still impossible to read today. Historians are working to try and decipher it, but this may be one mystery that history keeps to itself.

HOW WE **KNOW**

Historical knowledge comes from lots of sources. Written records tell us how people saw the events they lived through, while archaeology reveals the material world of the past. Another source is oral history, the stories people tell of the past.

WRITTEN WORD

Firsthand records, such as diaries, letters, or documents such as this 2,500-year-old marriage certificate, tell us how people lived their lives. History books written later evaluate and analyze these original sources.

Everyday life
Art such as this 18th-century painting of two Indian girls flying kites gives a glimpse of daily life of people in the past.

Historic moments
Dramatic events can be shown in paintings glorifying those who took part, such as this work of the 1830 Revolution in France.

War
Battles have been painted through time. From the 1850s, their horrors were documented in photography. This photo is from World War I.

ARCHAEOLOGY

The objects that archaeologists find at historical sites can tell us a lot about how people used to live. This archaeologist is excavating an amphora from the ruined site of an ancient Greek trading center in present-day Bulgaria.

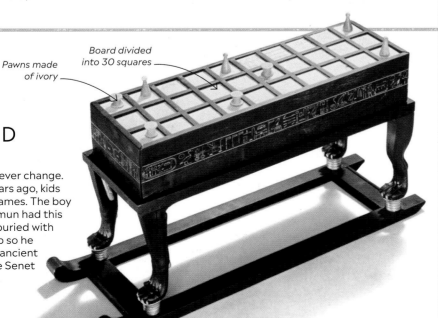

Board divided into 30 squares

Pawns made of ivory

FUN AND GAMES

Some things never change. Even 3,300 years ago, kids liked playing games. The boy king Tutankhamun had this gaming table buried with him in his tomb so he could play the ancient Egyptian game Senet in the afterlife.

ORAL HISTORY

Many cultures do not leave a written record, but their history is as rich and full of detail as those who do. Arvol Looking Horse is a Native American storyteller from the Cheyenne River Lakota tribe. He keeps his people's history alive and shares it with younger generations.

Food can be held above the fire to cook.

Flames provide light and warmth.

Human ancestors

The human story began millions of years ago, when one group of apes in Africa began to walk upright. Over time, these human-like apes evolved bigger brains until eventually our own species, *Homo sapiens*, emerged.

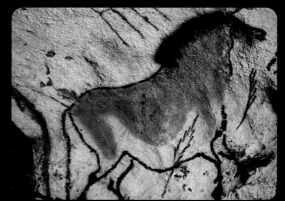

OLDEST **ART**

The earliest cave paintings date from about 45,000 years ago. This example, from Lascaux, France, is more recent—up to 20,000 years old. Cave art often depicted animals, in red, yellow, and brown pigments. It might have been a way of telling stories or it might have had a religious meaning.

MAKING **FIRE**

Around 1 million years ago, *Homo erectus* learned how to start and control a fire. This meant they could stay warm in harsh climates and scare off predators. Cooking food makes it easier to digest, and a diet of more nutritious food led humans to develop bigger brains.

CRAFTING **TOOLS**

Early humans became expert toolmakers. The flint hand ax (right) was invented 1.76 million years ago. It was made by chipping away flakes from a piece of flint. Tools like this were used for 1.5 million years. Much later, axe heads were tied to sticks or bones so that they could be swung with more force.

Broad base was left blunt so it was safe to hold.

Stone sharpened to a deadly point

Axe head securely joined to handle

Sturdy wood or bone handle, held at the lower end.

THIS ANCIENT **LION MAN** CARVED FROM A MAMMOTH TUSK IS **40,000 YEARS OLD!**

HOMO SAPIENS EVOLVED IN **AFRICA** AND SPREAD ACROSS THE **WORLD!**

Heavy brow ridge, like that of an ape

Large jaw with teeth adapted for chewing raw plants.

ANCIENT RELATIVE

Australopithecus africanus was one of the first human species to walk upright, over 3 million years ago. This reconstruction, based on a skeleton found in South Africa, shows a face with a mix of human and apelike features.

WE STILL DON'T KNOW WHY HUMANS FIRST BEGAN TO WALK UPRIGHT!

EXTENDED FAMILY

Around 20 human species have been discovered. Some of these existed at the same time as our species, but all of them died out. Here are five, with the dates they were around.

***Australopithecus africanus*, 3.2–2 million years ago**
This species walked mostly on two legs but still had the long arms of a tree-dweller. They were much smaller than modern humans.

***Homo habilis*, 2.4–1.7 million years ago**
One of the first species to use tools, their name means "handy man." Adapted to walk upright, they still had large jaws and thick hair like that of an ape.

***Homo erectus*, 1.9 million to 110,000 years ago**
With a name meaning "upright human," this species had a similar build to people today. They walked for miles to hunt and forage across Africa and Asia.

***Homo neanderthalensis*, 400,000 to 40,000 years ago**
Strong, large-brained, and well adapted to cold climates, Neanderthals lived alongside *Homo sapiens*.

***Homo sapiens* 300,000 years ago–today**
Modern humans first evolved in Africa around 300,000 years ago. A bigger brain allowed them to work together in groups and solve problems.

ON THE HUNT

The earliest humans were scavengers, but better tools meant they could become hunters. Stone-tipped spears were invented about 500,000 years ago and allowed humans to hunt large animals. Working together, they could overcome even the biggest prey.

First towns

The earliest humans hunted and foraged for food, moving from place to place to find fresh supplies. Then, around 12,000 years ago, people started farming crops and, for the first time, began to settle in one place.

Eyes were painted with black pigment.

A wig or a headdress would have topped the statue.

Face sculpted in more detail than the body

Statue has no arms, suggesting it might originally have been covered with clothes.

ANCIENT **STATUE**

'Ain Ghazal in modern-day Jordan was one of the world's first towns. People settled there some 9,000 years ago. Archaeologists have found more than 30 large human figures, sculpted from plaster, buried at the site. They may have been used for religious rituals, but no one knows for sure.

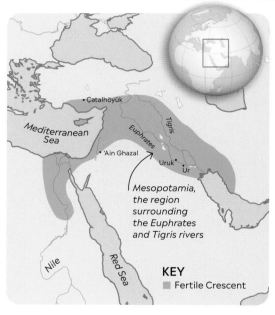

Mesopotamia, the region surrounding the Euphrates and Tigris rivers

KEY
◼ Fertile Crescent

FERTILE **FARMLAND**

The first farmers lived in an area known as the Fertile Crescent—a strip of fertile land around three great rivers. The world's first known settlements were built in the part of it called Mesopotamia.

Small feet with toes clearly marked

Reeds tightly bound with twine for stability

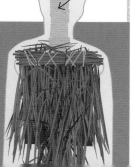

SCULPTED AROUND TIED REEDS, THE 'AIN GHAZAL STATUES ARE ABOUT 9,000 YEARS OLD!

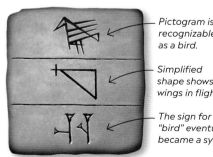

Pictogram is recognizable as a bird.

Simplified shape shows wings in flight.

The sign for "bird" eventually became a symbol.

FIRST **WRITING**

Writing was invented to keep track of food stores and legal agreements. Early script used in Mesopotamia used pictograms to represent physical objects. These gradually developed into simplified symbols.

THE **FIRST WHEEL** WAS INVENTED TO **MAKE POTTERY**, NOT FOR TRANSPORTATION!

ROYAL **UR**

In southern Mesopotamia, in a land called Sumer, the first cities arose. Ur was the capital, a center for trade ruled by great kings and queens. Inside its walls stood this mighty step pyramid, or ziggurat, used for religious rituals.

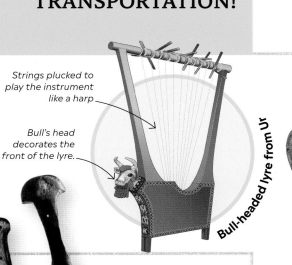

Strings plucked to play the instrument like a harp

Bull's head decorates the front of the lyre.

Bull-headed lyre from Ur

BRONZE AGE

Bronze was made by melting together copper and tin. It was stronger than bone or stone, and easily shaped. First developed around 3,500 BCE, this new technology led to much better tools and weapons.

Sharp edge formed by beating hot metal

Lapis lazuli, a blue stone once more precious than gold, is used for the eyes and beard.

A thin layer of gold covers the carved wooden head.

ROYAL **BULL**

In cities, specialist craftworkers created treasures using raw materials sourced from far-off lands. This gold bull's head was part of a lyre buried in a royal grave near Ur more than 4,000 years ago.

CROWDED ÇATALHÖYÜK

Founded more than 9,000 years ago, Çatalhöyük in modern-day Turkey had a unique form. There were no streets between the houses—people walked across the clay roofs. The town was inhabited for some 2,000 years.

Instead of a front door, there was a hole in the ceiling.

Buildings were packed closely together.

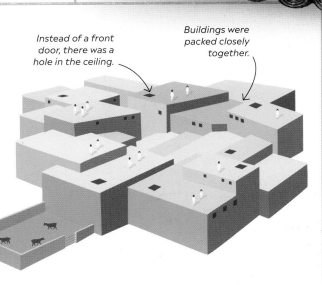

Domesticated animals were kept in pens nearby.

DOGS WERE THE **FIRST** ANIMALS TO BE **DOMESTICATED**, APPROXIMATELY **15,000 YEARS AGO!**

ALONG THE NILE

Much of Egypt was barren and inhospitable desert, but the banks of the Nile River were fertile for farming. This made Egypt wealthy and powerful enough to conquer the lands to the North. This map shows the kingdom of Egypt at its greatest extent.

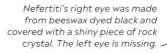

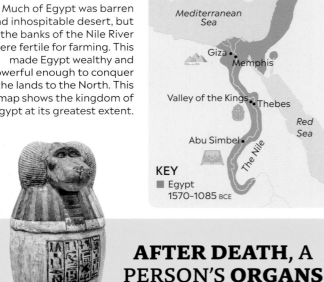

Mediterranean Sea

Giza
Memphis

Valley of the Kings
Thebes

Abu Simbel

Red Sea

The Nile

KEY
■ Egypt 1570–1085 BCE

FEMALE RULER

Although most pharaohs were men, Egyptian women could govern as regents on behalf of their children or with their husbands. Queen Nefertiti, shown here, reigned alongside her husband, Akhenaten. Although her exact role is unknown, she was clearly a powerful person, as artworks from the period depict her defeating Egypt's enemies.

Nefertiti's right eye was made from beeswax dyed black and covered with a shiny piece of rock crystal. The left eye is missing.

AFTER DEATH, A PERSON'S ORGANS WERE STORED IN CANOPIC JARS!

WRAPPING UP

Rich Egyptians were prepared for burial with great ceremony. Their bodies were mummified, wrapped, and then encased in a series of sarcophagi (coffins), ready for the afterlife.

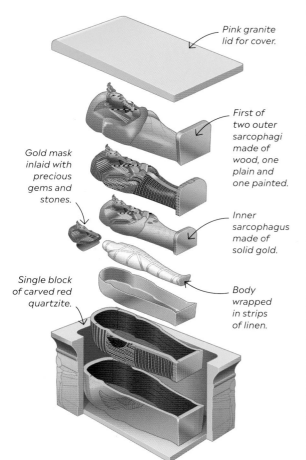

Pink granite lid for cover.

Gold mask inlaid with precious gems and stones.

First of two outer sarcophagi made of wood, one plain and one painted.

Inner sarcophagus made of solid gold.

Single block of carved red quartzite.

Body wrapped in strips of linen.

A lookout keeps an eye out for dangers.

This man is spear fishing.

The hunters have caught a huge fish.

HOLY CATS

Egyptians believed cats brought luck to the home: they were dressed in jewels and fed treats. When a cat died, it was mummified and its humans shaved off their eyebrows in mourning. Anyone who killed a cat was sentenced to death!

A cat mummy might be placed in the family tomb or a temple.

Kingdom of
the Nile

Around 3000 BCE a great civilization called Egypt arose along the Nile River in Africa. It became one of the wealthiest kingdoms the world had ever seen.

WONDER OF THE **WORLD!**

Some two million stone blocks, each weighing about 2.5 tons (2.3 metric tons), make up the Great Pyramid. Built as the tomb of Pharaoh Khufu, it is guarded by the Great Sphinx—a statue of a lion with a human head.

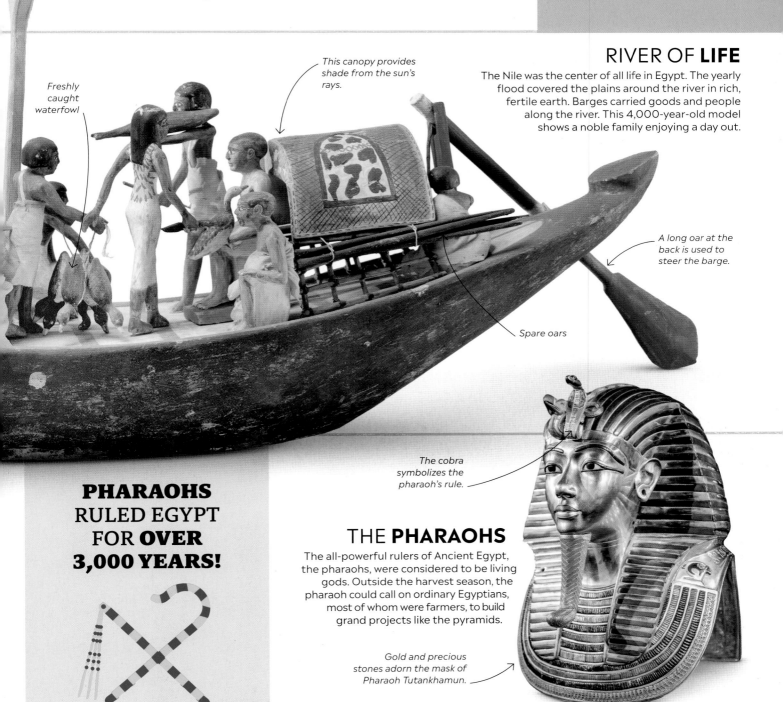

Freshly caught waterfowl

This canopy provides shade from the sun's rays.

RIVER OF **LIFE**

The Nile was the center of all life in Egypt. The yearly flood covered the plains around the river in rich, fertile earth. Barges carried goods and people along the river. This 4,000-year-old model shows a noble family enjoying a day out.

A long oar at the back is used to steer the barge.

Spare oars

The cobra symbolizes the pharaoh's rule.

PHARAOHS RULED EGYPT FOR **OVER 3,000 YEARS!**

THE **PHARAOHS**

The all-powerful rulers of Ancient Egypt, the pharaohs, were considered to be living gods. Outside the harvest season, the pharaoh could call on ordinary Egyptians, most of whom were farmers, to build grand projects like the pyramids.

Gold and precious stones adorn the mask of Pharaoh Tutankhamun.

Dr Mennat-Allah El Dorry is an Egyptian archaeologist specializing in plants. She uses the tools of her trade—like this microscope—as well as tomb paintings, to learn more about the foods her ancestors ate.

EGYPTOLOGIST

Q What do you do?

A I study ancient plants. Think about it: if you are preparing your favorite meal, you might remove the seeds and throw them away. If I come and look at your trash and spot the seeds, I can guess what you were making.

Q What were the ancient Egyptians' favorite foods?

A They ate a lot of bread, lentils, lettuce, and scallions as well as ducks, geese, pigs, and fish. They drank beer on a daily basis because it was a thick, nutritious drink. Wealthier people ate the same but had more beef and wine, which were more expensive.

Q Did they have sweet foods?

A Oh yes! They liked sweet things and used dried figs and dates to make cakelike sweet breads. The wealthy would have also used honey to make sweet cakes and pastries.

Q How did they keep food cool?

A We don't know exactly. They would have used different methods of drying, salting, or smoking foods in order to store them without having to cool them. They probably prepared food daily. Anything that needed to be kept cool would have been stored in dark cool corners of a house.

Q What is the most unusual place you have ever discovered something?

A In poop! Actually, both animal and human poop contain a lot of what they ate and can teach us a lot about ancient diets.

Q Why is it important to search for the traces of the past?

A As an Egyptian, as an Egyptologist, it is valuable for me to know who my ancestors were, and food is the perfect window to peer into to learn about their lives. I also want to study the history that led to the cuisine we eat today. I believe that as traditional foods around the world are disappearing, it is crucial that we document them.

FABULOUS FOOD

This tomb painting from 3,400 years ago shows the Egyptian scribe and astronomer Nakht and his wife Tawy receiving offerings of grain, grapes, fish, ducks, and figs, among other delicacies. Ancient Egypt was one of the most fertile places in the ancient world. Now, wall paintings like this provide evidence that Mennat-Allah and other Egyptologists can use to build a picture of the past.

THERE WERE MORE THAN 1,000 GREEK CITY-STATES, INCLUDING ATHENS AND SPARTA!

The chorus is a group of performers who comment on the action as it is happening.

Gods appear from above, lowered down by a machine.

Stone seats cut into the hillside

FABULOUS THEATER

Greek theater probably emerged out of the festival of the god Dionysos. Comedy plays poked fun at the rulers and gods, while tragedies depicted sad tales, often family dramas. Performers wore masks to help them play different roles.

Hercules is about to strike the serpent with a rock.

GRAND GODS

The Greeks had many gods, each in charge of a different area of life. People believed that if they made offerings to the gods, they would receive blessings in return.

HEROIC HERCULES

The Greeks had many myths. One of the most famous tells of the labors of Hercules, a man of incredible strength who had to complete 12 tasks as punishment for killing his family. Hercules has inspired many works of art, including this 19th-century sculpture of the hero battling a serpent.

Zeus
The king of the gods is armed with a lightning bolt.

Athena
The goddess of wisdom and warfare protects Athens.

Hermes
Messenger of the gods, he guides souls to the underworld.

GREEK STATUES MAY BE WHITE TODAY BUT THEY WERE ORIGINALLY PAINTED IN BRIGHT COLOURS!

Glorious
Greeks

2,500 years ago, the people of Greece created a unique, advanced, and influential civilization. Ancient Greece was not one country but hundreds of city-states that shared a common language and religion.

Hoplites wore bronze leg guards called greaves.

The serpent is in fact the river god Achelous, who has taken this form for the fight.

Sharp fangs can pierce human flesh.

Achelous strains to escape Hercules's grasp.

Hercules holds the serpent back with his iron grip.

HOPLITE **WARRIOR**

The Greek cities were often at war with each other. Their soldiers were named hoplites after *hoplon*, the Greek word for shield. Only the richest men could be hoplites as they had to pay for their own weapons and armor.

NUDE NOT **RUDE!**

The Greeks took off their clothes to work out. The word "gymnasium" means "naked exercise." Even runners at the Olympic Games competed wearing only their beards.

PEOPLE POWER

Early Greek states were ruled by kings like the one depicted in this Bronze Age mask. But in 507 BCE, the Athenians threw out their ruler and gave each free man the power to vote on important issues. They called this democracy, from the Greek words *demos*, people, and *kratos*, rule.

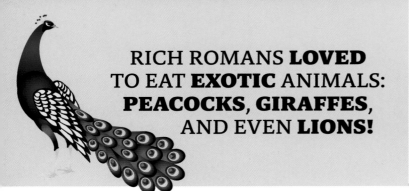

RICH ROMANS LOVED TO EAT EXOTIC ANIMALS: PEACOCKS, GIRAFFES, AND EVEN LIONS!

AN EDUCATION

The woman in this wall painting from the city of Pompeii poses with a stylus, a kind of pen used to make marks in the wax tablet she holds. Learning to read and write was a privilege only the wealthiest Romans could afford.

The rise of Rome

Around 2,000 years ago, the people of ancient Rome used disciplined armies and engineering skills to build one of the biggest empires the world had ever seen.

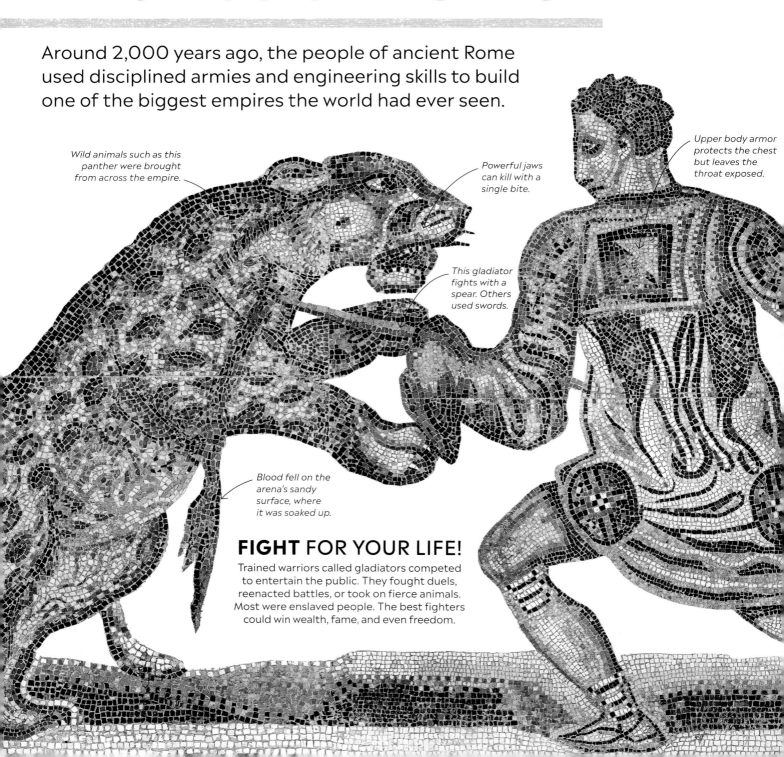

Wild animals such as this panther were brought from across the empire.

Powerful jaws can kill with a single bite.

Upper body armor protects the chest but leaves the throat exposed.

This gladiator fights with a spear. Others used swords.

Blood fell on the arena's sandy surface, where it was soaked up.

FIGHT FOR YOUR LIFE!

Trained warriors called gladiators competed to entertain the public. They fought duels, reenacted battles, or took on fierce animals. Most were enslaved people. The best fighters could win wealth, fame, and even freedom.

VAST EMPIRE

The Roman Empire grew steadily until, at its height in 117 CE, it stretched from Britain in the west to Iraq in the east, and had a population of 70 million people. To connect the far-flung corners of their empire, the Romans built 50,000 miles (80,000 km) of paved roads for troops, trade, and messages.

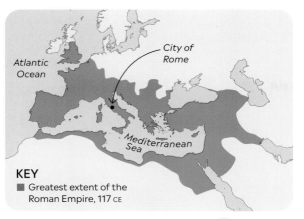

Atlantic Ocean

City of Rome

Mediterranean Sea

KEY
■ Greatest extent of the Roman Empire, 117 CE

TOILET HUMOR!

Most Roman homes had no toilet, so people used public latrines. These had no cubicles and became popular social spaces to chat and joke with others. Cleaning up was less fun; everyone shared a single sponge on a stick.

Shields form a protective cover.

Only the front row can see out.

Sturdy sandals for marching and fighting

Wings of the eagle, symbol of Rome

Curved shields wrap around the soldiers' bodies.

UNSTOPPABLE ARMY

The Roman army was divided into 30 legions, each with 4,800 soldiers, called legionaries. The legions made use of complex formations such as this one, called the tortoise, to protect themselves and gain the advantage in battle.

Augustus is depicted as a young man.

Augustus's outstretched arm means he is giving a speech.

Cupid, the Roman god of love, is shown close to the emperor.

Only gods were shown barefoot.

FIRST EMPEROR

For nearly 500 years, Rome was a republic, but in 49 BCE civil war broke out. Eventually, a general, Octavian, crowned himself emperor, took the name Augustus ("the revered one") and came to be worshipped as a god. Emperors ruled Rome for another 400 years.

ROMANS USED **URINE** TO WASH THEIR **LAUNDRY** BECAUSE THE AMMONIA IN IT CAN **REMOVE STAINS!**

AMAZING ENGINEERING

This bridge, known as the Pont du Gard, is part of an aqueduct carrying water 31 miles (50 km) from a spring to the city of Nîmes in France. It was built in the first century CE and is one of many Roman structures to have stood the test of time for more than 2,000 years.

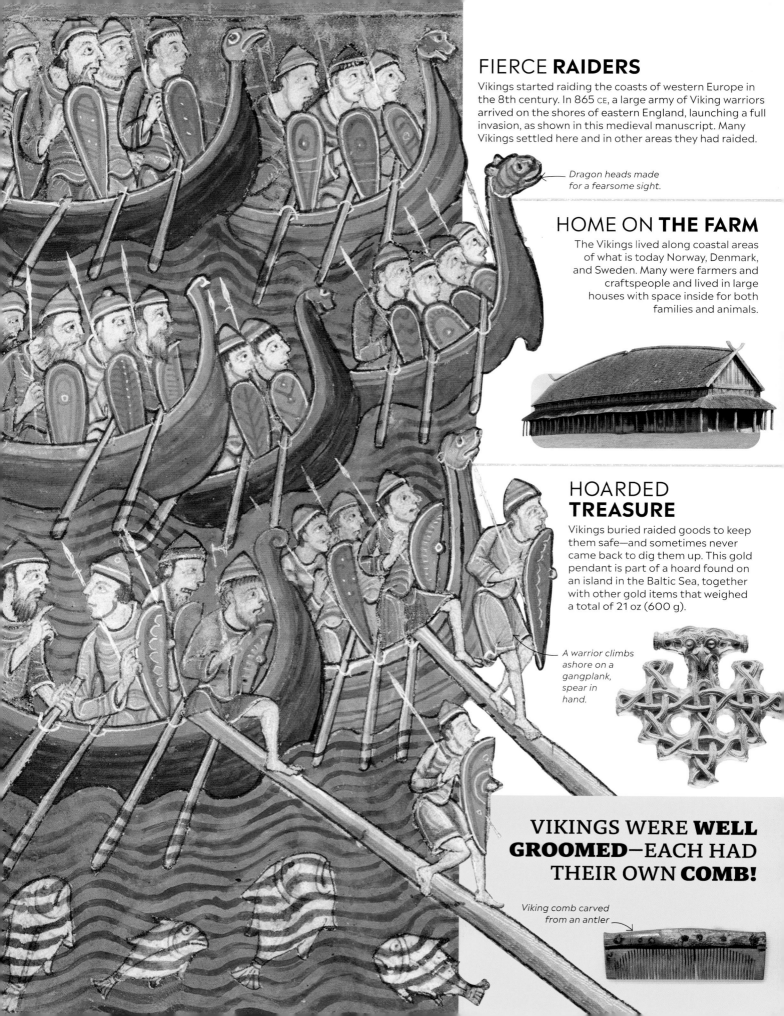

FIERCE **RAIDERS**

Vikings started raiding the coasts of western Europe in the 8th century. In 865 CE, a large army of Viking warriors arrived on the shores of eastern England, launching a full invasion, as shown in this medieval manuscript. Many Vikings settled here and in other areas they had raided.

Dragon heads made for a fearsome sight.

HOME ON **THE FARM**

The Vikings lived along coastal areas of what is today Norway, Denmark, and Sweden. Many were farmers and craftspeople and lived in large houses with space inside for both families and animals.

HOARDED **TREASURE**

Vikings buried raided goods to keep them safe—and sometimes never came back to dig them up. This gold pendant is part of a hoard found on an island in the Baltic Sea, together with other gold items that weighed a total of 21 oz (600 g).

A warrior climbs ashore on a gangplank, spear in hand.

VIKINGS WERE **WELL GROOMED**—EACH HAD THEIR OWN **COMB!**

Viking comb carved from an antler

Voyaging Vikings

Between the 8th and 11th centuries, Vikings set sail from Scandinavia. Their journeys led to land grabs but also to trade and cultural exchange.

Runes carved into wooden handle

BLUETOOTH IS NAMED AFTER A VIKING KING, **HARALD BLUETOOTH**. ITS **SYMBOL** SHOWS THE **RUNES** FOR HIS INITIALS!

VIKING WORLD

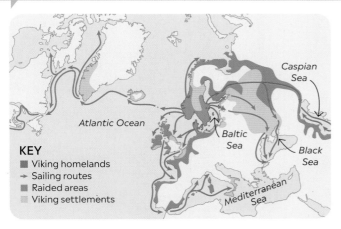

Caspian Sea

Atlantic Ocean

Baltic Sea

Black Sea

Mediterranean Sea

KEY
- Viking homelands
- → Sailing routes
- Raided areas
- Viking settlements

The Vikings set out from their homelands in Scandinavia, sailing east, west, and south. While some raided and killed to gain land and riches, others sailed far to explore new territories. Many were traders, establishing trade routes along rivers and seas in eastern Europe.

TRUSTY **WEAPONS**

Some Vikings owned valuable swords but axes and spears were more common, as less steel was needed to make them. Whatever the weapon, it was a treasured possession; some even had names carved in runes into their handles.

NORSE GODS

The Vikings had many gods, each with their own skills and personality. The gods lived in Asgard, at the top of the enormous tree Yggdrasil, above humans and giants.

Thor
A warrior and thunder god, Thor fights giants and serpents with his hammer.

TOP **TRANSPORT**

Vikings were skilled ship builders. They had different types of ships, but the most famous are their longboats. These fast, slender ships could be rowed or sailed. Their flat hull shape meant that they could get very close to shore and navigate shallow rivers.

Overlapping boards created a strong but light hull.

Cross-section showing the flat hull shape

The sail was lowered when the wind died down.

Steering oar

Oars were used when there was no wind.

The dragon head could be taken off when out at sea.

Odin
The chief god, Odin is wise and mighty. He rides an eight-legged horse.

Freyja
Goddess of love and fertility, Freyja has power over life and death.

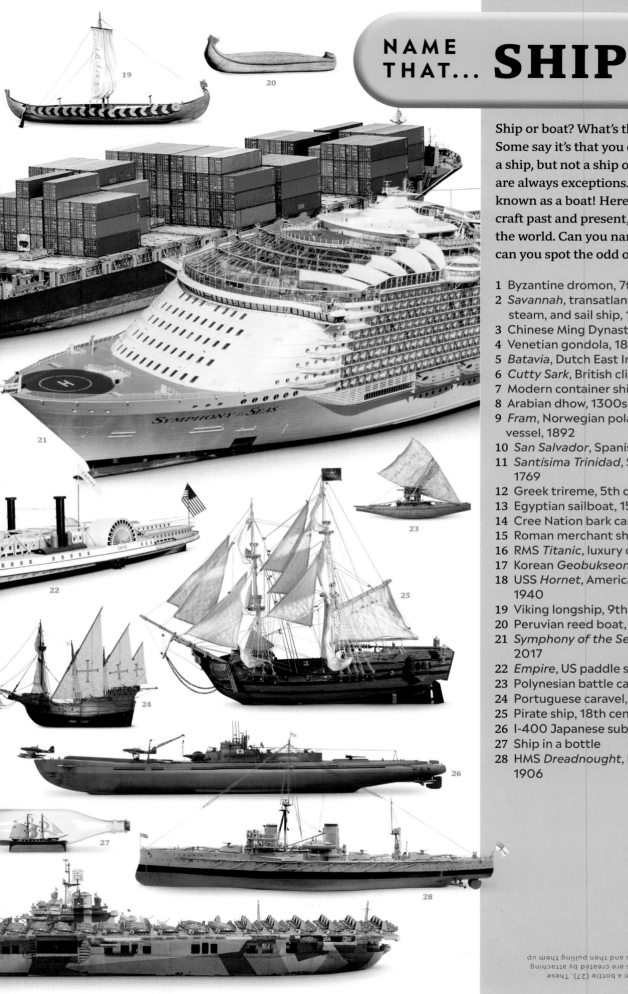

NAME THAT... SHIP

Ship or boat? What's the difference? Some say it's that you can put a boat on a ship, but not a ship on a boat, but there are always exceptions. A submarine is known as a boat! Here is a fleet of sea craft past and present, and from around the world. Can you name them all, and can you spot the odd one out?

1 Byzantine dromon, 7th century
2 *Savannah*, transatlantic sidewheel, steam, and sail ship, 1818
3 Chinese Ming Dynasty junk, c.1640
4 Venetian gondola, 18th century
5 *Batavia*, Dutch East Indiaman, 1628
6 *Cutty Sark*, British clipper ship, 1869
7 Modern container ship
8 Arabian dhow, 1300s onward
9 *Fram*, Norwegian polar exploration vessel, 1892
10 *San Salvador*, Spanish galleon, 1540
11 *Santísima Trinidad*, Spanish warship, 1769
12 Greek trireme, 5th century BCE
13 Egyptian sailboat, 1500 BCE
14 Cree Nation bark canoe, 17th century
15 Roman merchant ship, 3rd century CE
16 RMS *Titanic*, luxury ocean liner, 1912
17 Korean *Geobukseon* (turtle ship), 1590
18 USS *Hornet*, American aircraft carrier, 1940
19 Viking longship, 9th century
20 Peruvian reed boat, 13th century
21 *Symphony of the Seas*, cruise ship, 2017
22 *Empire*, US paddle steamer, 1843
23 Polynesian battle canoe, 5th century
24 Portuguese caravel, 1590s
25 Pirate ship, 18th century
26 I-400 Japanese submarine, 1944
27 Ship in a bottle
28 HMS *Dreadnought*, British warship, 1906

The odd one out is the ship in a bottle (27). These seemingly impossible models are created by attaching strings to the masts and sails and then pulling them up once inside the bottle.

Imperial
China

In 960, a general named Zhao Kuangyin united China's 10 states into a single empire. He established a new imperial dynasty, the Song, which ruled for over 300 years.

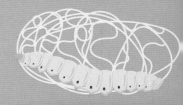

A **SILKWORM COCOON** CAN PRODUCE UP TO **2,953 FT (900 M)** OF SILK—IN **ONE LONG STRAND!**

An elephant would have been an exotic sight. Its presence is a display of the emperor's wealth.

BUILDING PAGODAS

The Song Dynasty saw the construction of many towering pagodas. These slender, multistory buildings were used to house sacred objects or act as lookout points. This is China's tallest surviving pagoda from the era, the 13-story Liaodi Pagoda. It was completed in 1055, and rises to 276 ft (84 m).

FORMAL EXAMS

To gain a job in the Song government people had to pass exams. Thousands of young men from all levels of society took the tests. Only the brightest passed. This meant that the government was staffed by the cleverest people in the country, not just the richest or best connected.

QUICK-FIRE CROSSBOW!

Handheld Chinese crossbows like this one had a range of over 1,200 ft (370 m). Some rapid-fire crossbows could shoot one bolt every two seconds.

SPLENDID SILK

These noble women are stretching and ironing silk. For many centuries, only the Chinese knew how to make silk, which came from the cocoons of mulberry silkworms. Traders carried the sought-after material from China all the way to Europe.

GUNPOWDER COULD BE STUFFED INTO **HOLLOW BAMBOO TUBES** TO MAKE EXPLOSIVE **FIRECRACKERS!**

SHADOW STORIES

These shadow puppets depict the grandeur of a Chinese emperor and his guards. Shadow puppetry became common during the Song Dynasty, and the tradition continued to flourish in later periods. This example was made during the Qing Dynasty, around 900 years after the end of the Song period. It comes from Gansu Province in the west of China.

The imperial guardsmen are armed with long-bladed weapons called guandao.

TECHNOLOGICAL ADVANCES

During the Song period, Chinese engineers and inventors developed many innovations that changed not just China but the entire world. Each of these inventions is still in use in some form today!

Compass
In the 1100s, the invention of a compass with a needle that always pointed south helped sailors navigate.

Paper money
The first paper money, called *jiaozi*, was first used by merchants and later became an official currency.

Movable type
Engineer Bi Sheng (990–1051) used ceramic blocks to create the first version of the printing press.

Canal locks
In 983, China began extending canals over hilly ground by creating locks that raised and lowered water levels.

Gunpowder
The Song made the first explosives from gunpowder, which was discovered just before they came to power.

This porcelain object in the shape of a baby could be used as a pillow or headrest.

PORCELAIN PILLOW

Vases, crockery, and ornaments made of Chinese porcelain—or "china"— were highly prized for their quality. Porcelain is made from white clay, called kaolin, mixed with ground petuntse, a stone containing glittering quartz and shiny mica.

Medieval Japan

From 1192, Japan was controlled by military leaders called shoguns. During their rule, an ordered society with a rich traditional culture emerged.

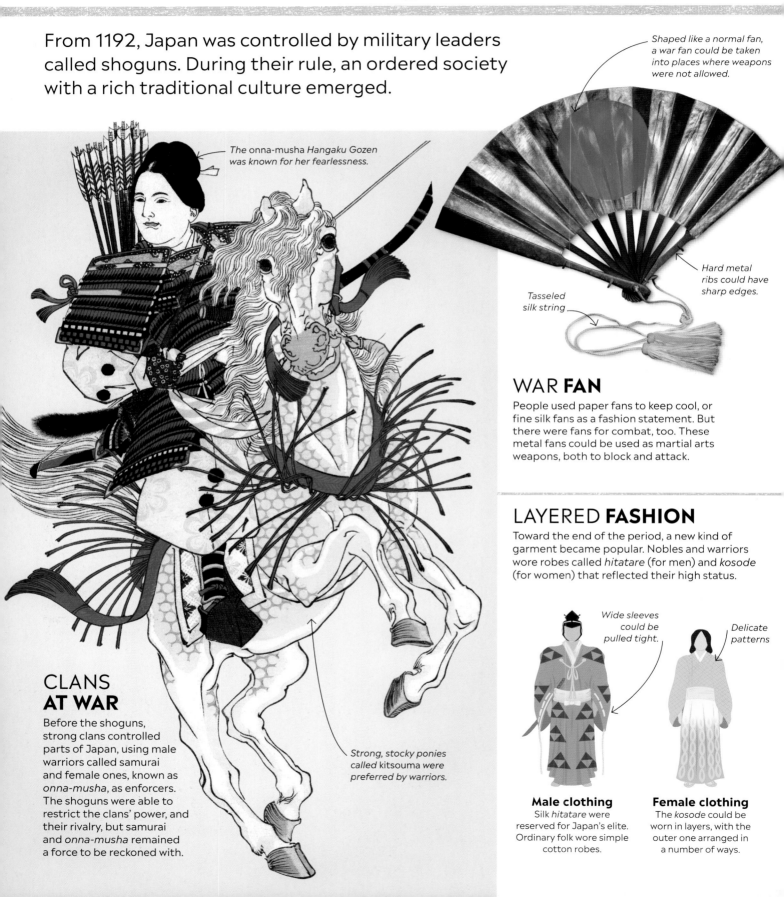

The onna-musha Hangaku Gozen *was known for her fearlessness.*

Shaped like a normal fan, a war fan could be taken into places where weapons were not allowed.

Hard metal ribs could have sharp edges.

Tasseled silk string

WAR **FAN**

People used paper fans to keep cool, or fine silk fans as a fashion statement. But there were fans for combat, too. These metal fans could be used as martial arts weapons, both to block and attack.

LAYERED **FASHION**

Toward the end of the period, a new kind of garment became popular. Nobles and warriors wore robes called *hitatare* (for men) and *kosode* (for women) that reflected their high status.

Wide sleeves could be pulled tight.

Delicate patterns

Male clothing
Silk *hitatare* were reserved for Japan's elite. Ordinary folk wore simple cotton robes.

Female clothing
The *kosode* could be worn in layers, with the outer one arranged in a number of ways.

CLANS **AT WAR**

Before the shoguns, strong clans controlled parts of Japan, using male warriors called samurai and female ones, known as *onna-musha*, as enforcers. The shoguns were able to restrict the clans' power, and their rivalry, but samurai and *onna-musha* remained a force to be reckoned with.

Strong, stocky ponies called kitsouma were preferred by warriors.

BETWEEN BATTLES, GENERALS RELAXED BY ARRANGING FLOWERS!

POWERFUL SHOGUN

In 1192, clan leader Minamoto no Yoritomo was made shogun by the emperor. He was the first shogun to take overall charge and hold more power than the emperor. Shoguns continued to rule Japan until 1868.

Mask worn by actor who plays the role of Hannya, a jealous demon.

BUDDHIST GUARDIAN

Buddhism was founded in 5th-century-BCE India. When it arrived in Japan, it took on new forms and became popular with the warrior clans—this Japanese sculpture of a guardian deity looks like a general.

SHINTO SPIRITS

Japan's traditional religion is called Shinto ("the way of the gods"). It teaches that all things can be inhabited by spirits called *kami*.

Statue of a magical fox spirit called a kitsune, one of the most popular kami.

NOH MASK

Noh theater flourished at this time, mixing drama, poetry, music, and dance in performances by masked actors. Plays featured the battles of gods, demons, and humans, in which good (usually) triumphed over evil.

The large, open mouth amplified the actor's voice.

THERE WERE 18 MARTIAL ARTS— ONE WAS SWIMMING FULLY ARMED UNDER WATER!

MIGHTY CASTLES

Despite the shogun's power, there were often clashes between rival clans, and some clans rebelled against the shogunate. Around 5,000 castles, including this one, at Himeji, were built by clans to fortify their lands.

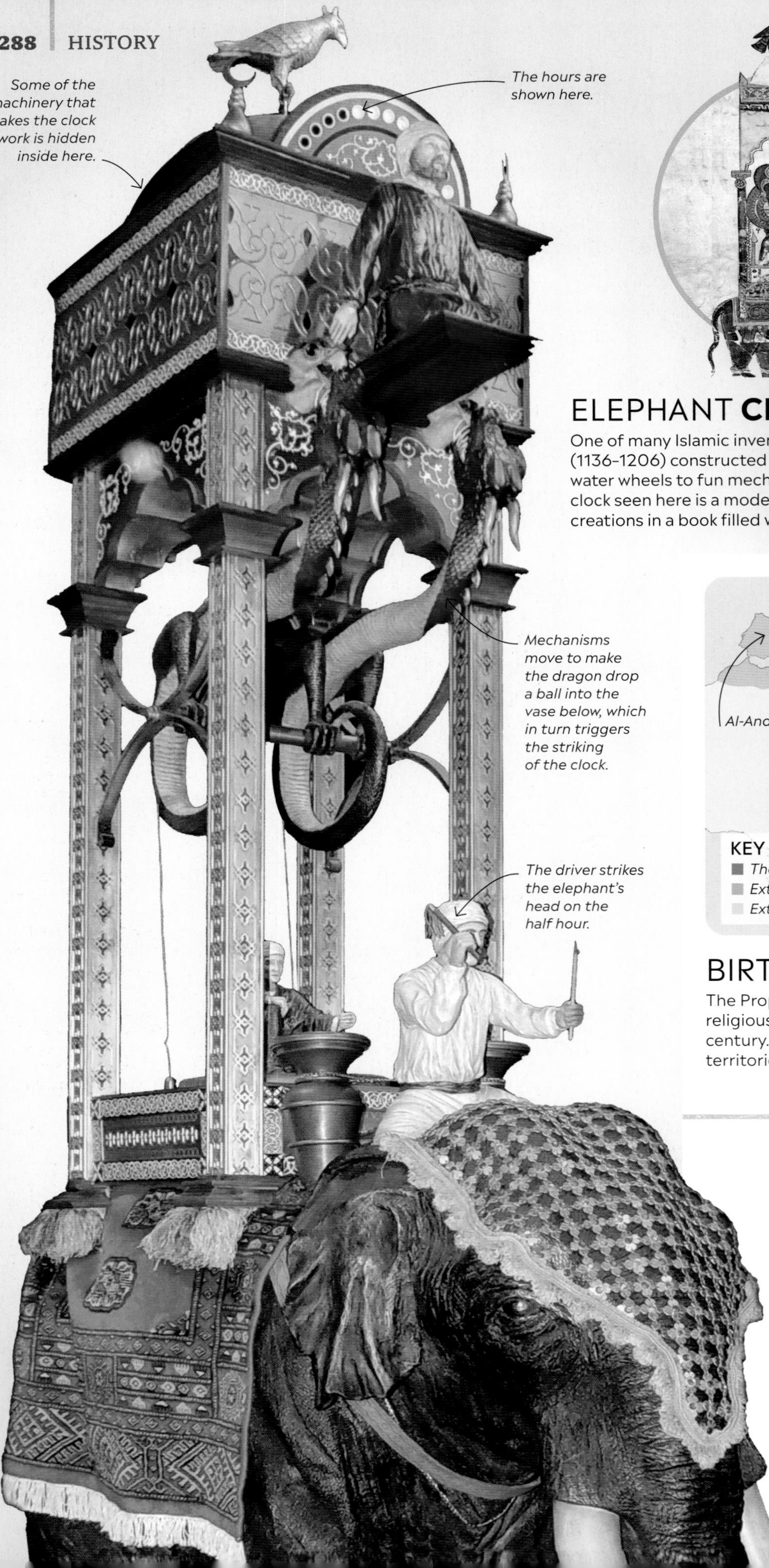

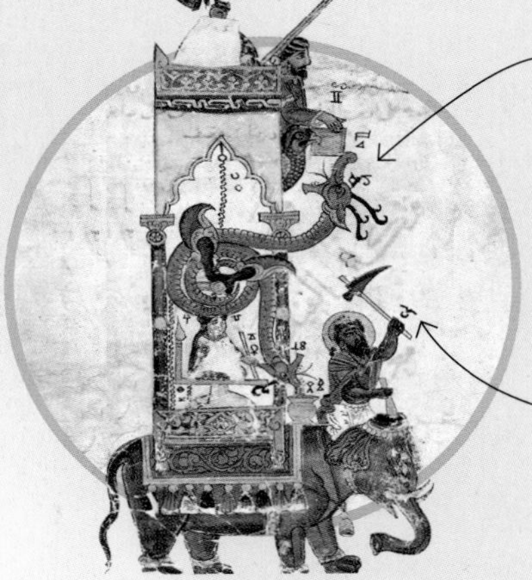

Some of the machinery that makes the clock work is hidden inside here.

The hours are shown here.

Illustration of the elephant clock in Al-Jazari's "Book of Knowledge of Ingenious Mechanical Devices"

The drawing is annotated in Arabic.

ELEPHANT **CLOCK**

One of many Islamic inventors, the engineer Al-Jazari (1136–1206) constructed all sorts of things, from practical water wheels to fun mechanical clocks—the elaborate clock seen here is a modern replica. He recorded his creations in a book filled with detailed illustrations.

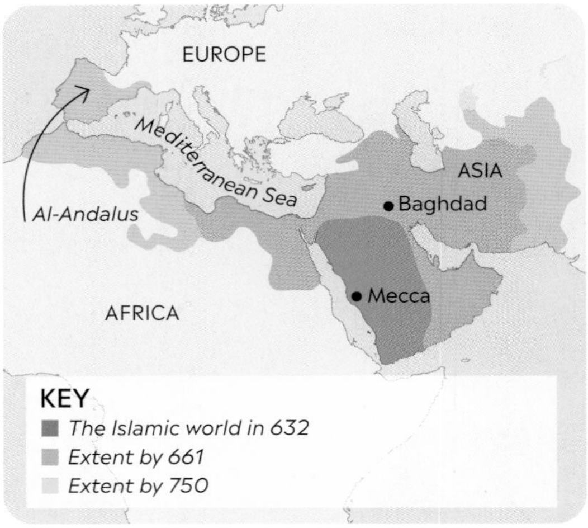

Mechanisms move to make the dragon drop a ball into the vase below, which in turn triggers the striking of the clock.

The driver strikes the elephant's head on the half hour.

EUROPE

Mediterranean Sea

Al-Andalus

ASIA

• Baghdad

AFRICA

• Mecca

KEY

■ The Islamic world in 632
■ Extent by 661
■ Extent by 750

BIRTH OF **ISLAM**

The Prophet Muhammad began spreading his religious message from Mecca in the early 7th century. As Islamic caliphs (rulers) expanded their territories, the new religion traveled with them.

KNOWLEDGE HUB

Baghdad's famous House of Wisdom housed thousands of books in different languages. Scientists, translators, and authors from all over the Islamic world gathered here to exchange ideas.

Islamic
Golden Age

The religion of Islam was founded in the 7th century in Arabia. As the teachings spread, a golden age of science and culture flourished across the Islamic world.

THE WORLD'S **OLDEST UNIVERSITY** WAS FOUNDED IN FEZ IN 859 CE BY **FATIMA AL-FIHRI!**

SUGAR FIRST ARRIVED IN **NORTH AFRICA** AND **EUROPE**, THANKS TO **ISLAMIC** TRADERS!

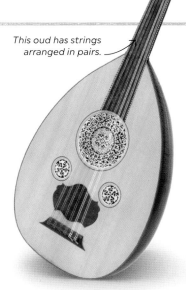

This oud has strings arranged in pairs.

SCIENCE **ADVANCES**

Islam encouraged scholars to invent and investigate. As well as preserving knowledge from ancient Greece and beyond, they made great scientific advances and many new discoveries.

Astronomy
Complex instruments known as astrolabes were developed to calculate the altitude of stars and the sun.

Chemistry
Alchemists worked with transforming and dissolving metals. They recorded their finds and also invented soap!

Instrument for healing an inflamed tooth

Medicine
Detailed descriptions of diseases and plants to use in medicines were published in big encyclopedias.

SWEET **MUSIC**

During much of the Golden Age, Islamic music flourished. Among the instruments of the time, the oud was a favorite. Many ouds were made in Al-Andalus, in what is now Spain. Traveling musicians took the oud to neighboring European kingdoms, where it became the lute.

Engineering
Water management was crucial in dry climates, and many clever irrigation devices were invented.

PIONEERING **DOCTORS**

Physicians were interested in finding new methods to cure people, from advanced surgical operations to everyday dental treatments, as seen in this illustration.

Camel caravans carried goods along the trade routes.

RICH **TRADE**

Busy trade routes between Asia, Africa, and Europe passed through the major trading centers of the Islamic world. Merchants grew wealthy as gold, salt, spices, foods, and textiles changed hands in the buzzing markets.

Architecture
Islamic architectural styles, such as fine tile work and horseshoe arches, were used in mosques and palaces.

ANCIENT WONDERS

There are grand structures on many continents that can be classed as "wonders of the world." But the first list was put together in ancient Greece, and included these seven monuments. They are commonly known as the "seven wonders of the ancient world."

Giza's **Great Pyramid** is the **only** one of the seven wonders that **still stands today!**

GREAT PYRAMID OF GIZA
Built 4,600 years ago, the oldest pyramid in Giza, Egypt, is made of some 2 million giant stone blocks.

HANGING GARDENS OF BABYLON
These legendary gardens, full of exotic plants, were built on terraces in the city of Babylon.

TEMPLE OF ARTEMIS AT EPHESUS
Built for worship of the Greek goddess of hunting, this was twice the size of the Parthenon in Athens.

MAUSOLEUM AT HALICARNASSUS
Up to 130 ft (40 m) tall, this huge tomb in Turkey was topped by a huge marble statue of a chariot.

COLOSSUS OF RHODES
This gigantic bronze and iron statue was toppled by an earthquake—it lay on the ground for 800 years.

LIGHTHOUSE OF ALEXANDRIA
Sailors relied on this 328 ft (100 m) beacon in Egypt until its collapse in the 14th century.

STATUE OF ZEUS AT OLYMPIA
This colossal gold and ivory statue stood in the city of the original Olympic Games, Greece.

PERFECT PYRAMIDS

The pyramid was a popular shape for monument builders. Here are five from different parts of the world.

1 **ZIGGURAT**
Chogha Zanbil, a terraced pyramid called a ziggurat, was built in Iran, 1250 BCE.

2 **EGYPTIAN STEP PYRAMID**
Made for Pharaoh Djoser, who died in 2648 BCE, this is Egypt's first pyramid.

3  **NUBIAN PYRAMID**
The Nubian kingdoms of Kush (Sudan) built their pyramids from 700 BCE.

4 **PYRAMID OF THE SUN**
Built in Mexico by 350 CE, the Aztecs named it when they took power here.

5 **MAYA PYRAMID**
The Temple of Kukulcan, Mexico, is a step pyramid built in the 11th century.

ROYAL CITY

The capital of the ancient kingdom of Great Zimbabwe was vast; up to 20,000 people lived here. At its core was the Great Enclosure, reconstructed above, with 33 ft (10 m) high walls.

LARGEST TEMPLE

The 12th-century temple complex of Angkor Wat in Cambodia is the world's largest religious monument. About 227 football fields could fit inside its walls.

NEW HEIGHTS

As engineering skills and techniques developed over time, the height of buildings increased. Each one of these monuments became the tallest in the world when it was built—the pyramid of Giza held its record for the longest time.

8000 BCE
Tower of Jericho, ancient Jericho: 28 ft (8.5 m)

2500 BCE
Great Pyramid of Giza, Egypt: 482 ft (147 m)

HIGH UP

Monasteries often sit in tall, rocky places, offering peace and seclusion. These four occupy some seemingly inaccessible spots.

Taung Kalat **monastery,** Myanmar, sits on a **volcanic** plug—the ancient **magma** core of an **eroded** volcano!

1 TAKTSANG PALPHUG MONASTERY
Perching on a cliff ledge, this monastery in Bhutan is 2,950 ft (900 m) above ground.

2 TAUNG KALAT MONASTERY
You need to climb 777 steps to reach this monastery that sits 2,415 ft (736 m) above ground.

3 MONASTERIES OF METEORA
These Greek monasteries crown sandstone pinnacles rising 1,310 ft (400 m).

4 XUANKONG SI HANGING TEMPLE
This temple in China rests on wooden beams drilled into the rock 164 ft (50 m) up a cliff.

BONE CHURCH

The Czech church of Sedlec has a very unusual chapel. It is decorated with thousands of human bones and skulls. This bone candelabra is the centerpiece.

STAT ATTACK!
MONUMENTS

Throughout history and across the world, people have built amazing monuments to show their power, honor their rulers, or proclaim their faith. These are some of the greatest, largest, or most intriguing.

14TH CENTURY
Lincoln Cathedral, UK: 525 ft (160 m)

The tall spire collapsed in 1548.

16TH CENTURY
Beauvais Cathedral, France: 502 ft (153 m)—it was the new tallest because Lincoln's spire had collapsed in 1548!

19TH CENTURY
Eiffel Tower, France: 984 ft (300 m)

20TH CENTURY
Petronas Towers, Malaysia: 1,483 ft (452 m)

Awesome
Aztecs

The Aztecs dominated a large region in what is now Mexico in 1400–1521. Their neighboring states, who shared much of their culture, were often made to pay them tribute.

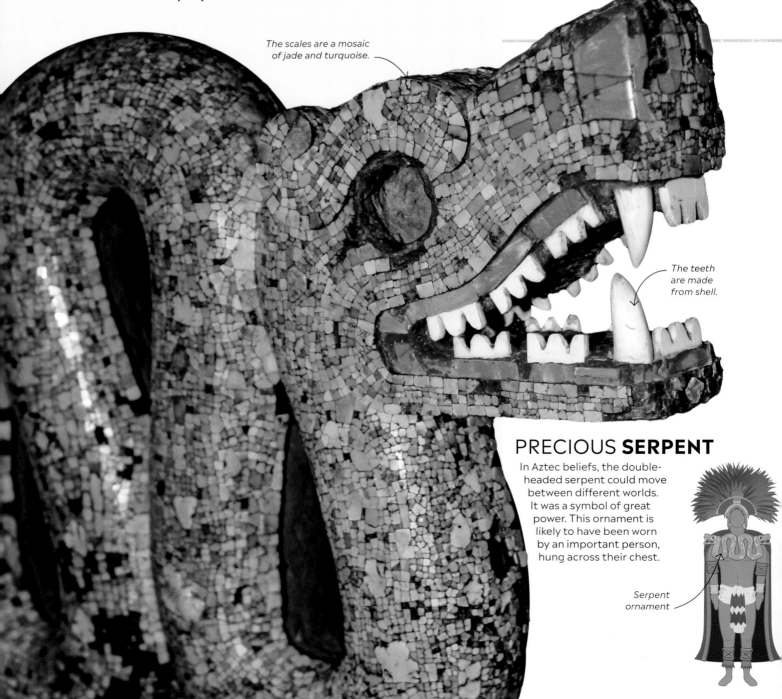

Handle in the shape of a kneeling eagle warrior

Flint blade

LETHAL **TOOLS**

The Aztecs made fine, extremely sharp knives from stone such as obsidian and flint. Their wooden handles were decorated with mineral and shell mosaics.

The scales are a mosaic of jade and turquoise.

The teeth are made from shell.

PRECIOUS **SERPENT**

In Aztec beliefs, the double-headed serpent could move between different worlds. It was a symbol of great power. This ornament is likely to have been worn by an important person, hung across their chest.

Serpent ornament

PAINTED RECORDS

Aztec accounts were recorded in books made of paper or deerskin. Their writing system was based on pictures representing a word, a phrase, an event, or a sound. This picture shows an important Aztec god, Tonacatecuhtli.

CONQUERED CITIES HAD TO PAY **TRIBUTE** TO THE AZTECS, WITH ANYTHING FROM **GOLD** TO **CACAO BEANS!**

These Maya ball players wear thick protective padding.

BALL GAME

The Mesoamerican ball game was played in many cultures. Teams used their bodies, except hands and feet, to keep a rubber ball in the air. If it dropped, they lost points.

FABULOUS FEATHERS

Colorful bird feathers were used to decorate everything from bags and head ornaments to ceremonial capes and shields. Many of the shimmering feathers came from the long tails of the brightly colored quetzal bird.

Ceremonial headdress

Feathers of more than 250 birds make up this headdress.

MOCTEZUMA II, ONE OF THE LAST AZTEC RULERS, HAD A WILD ANIMAL **ZOO** IN HIS **PALACE!**

OUTSTANDING ARCHITECTURE

The Aztecs were great builders. They constructed their capital Tenochtitlan on an artificial island in a lake. Official buildings such as temples, government buildings, and palaces were often built on terraced platforms, which were carefully faced with stone.

Ceremonies are conducted at the temples.

Residential area

A market sells goods and produce.

Goods come in and out of the city on boats.

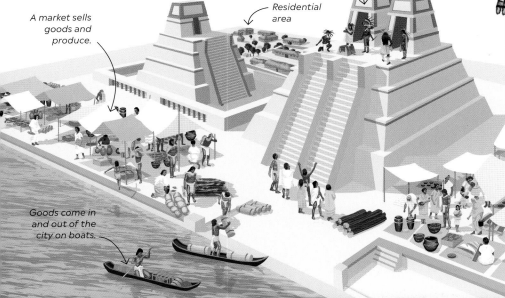

Wooden club with sharp obsidian shards

ELITE WARRIORS

The Aztecs used war and battles to gain wealth, rather than land, from their enemies. The fiercest fighters were the eagle and jaguar warriors, trained to capture enemy lords for ransom.

Inca Empire

In the 15th century, the Inca Empire was one of the largest in the world. It was ruled by a single, all-powerful man—the Sapa Inca. He controlled a well-organized society, with an extensive road network, tax system, and large army.

Feather headdress

VAST **EXPANSE**

The Inca Empire was long and narrow, stretching over 2,500 miles (4,000 km)—almost the full length of western South America. It covered a wide range of environments, including coasts, forests, and mountains.

THE **LONGEST** INCA **ROAD** RAN FOR OVER **2,200** **MILES** (3,600 KM)!

INCA **RUNNERS**

To send messages across their large empire, the Inca used a network of fleet-footed runners. Messages were relayed using knotted-string devices called *khipu*. The *khipu* was passed along from one runner to the next, moving quickly.

Runner one
Each runner carries a conch shell, which is blown like a trumpet to announce his arrival.

Relay
The next runner hears the conch and gets ready to run with the *khipu*.

Delivery
The last runner hands over the *khipu* at its final destination, and the message is read.

Made of silver and finely dressed, this figurine may represent an elite Inca woman.

The clothes are miniature versions of what a noble Inca woman would have worn, such as a tasseled llama wool cloak.

INCA **OFFERINGS**

The Inca worshipped a wide range of gods and built temples in their honor. At burial sites, they left offerings, such as these little silver and gold figurines.

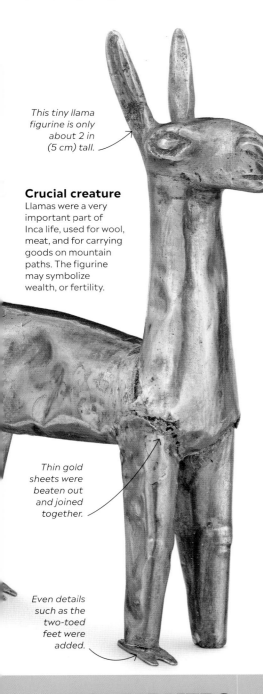

This tiny llama figurine is only about 2 in (5 cm) tall.

Crucial creature
Llamas were a very important part of Inca life, used for wool, meat, and for carrying goods on mountain paths. The figurine may symbolize wealth, or fertility.

Thin gold sheets were beaten out and joined together.

Even details such as the two-toed feet were added.

INCA **FARMERS** GREW OVER **3,000** VARIETIES OF **POTATOES!**

KNOTTED **RECORDS**

The Inca had no writing system, but they kept records using devices known as *khipu*. A *khipu* is a system of strings. Different colors and knots represent different information.

MOUNTAIN **FARMING**

There was little flat land available, so Inca farmers built stepped fields, called terraces, into the mountainsides. They grew a mixture of crops, including corn, beans, squash, and potatoes.

Corn

Farmer

Terrace built by hand

THE INCA BELIEVED THEIR **RULERS** WERE DESCENDED FROM **INTI**, THE **SUN GOD!**

ROPE **BRIDGES**

To cross rivers, the Inca built bridges from thick grasses. The grasses were twisted together into ropes, which were then woven to create a bridge. Similar bridges are still used today—they are renewed every year to keep them safe to use.

MACHU **PICCHU**

Cities were built from blocks of rock, which was cut to fit together perfectly. The city most famous today is Machu Picchu, with some 200 buildings and thousands of steps, high in the Andes mountains in Peru.

Kingdom of Benin

Benin City, in present-day Nigeria, was once at the heart of a powerful kingdom and trading nation. The walled capital was famous for its splendid palace and wide streets.

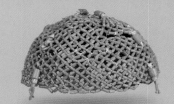

THE **OBA'S CROWN** WAS MADE OF **CORAL**, THOUGHT OF AS A GIFT FROM THE **GOD** OF THE **SEA!**

Finely dressed Oba

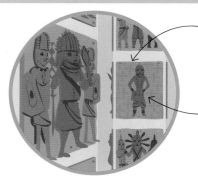

Hundreds of plaques decorated the palace walls and pillars.

Each plaque is a record of rulers and events in Benin's history.

MIGHTY **OBA**

The ruler of the Benin kingdom was known as the Oba. This plaque shows an Oba riding on a horse, supported by attendants. It is made of brass, an alloy of copper and zinc that was only allowed to be used for royal artifacts.

INTERNATIONAL **TRADE**

Benin traded products with other kingdoms, such as palm oil, pepper, and fine cloth. From the 15th century, they traded ivory with Portuguese merchants, who paid with brass bracelets, which were melted down and turned into art.

Oil palm fruit, from which palm oil is made

THE **WALLS** INSIDE AND AROUND **BENIN CITY** RAN FOR AN INCREDIBLE **10,000 MILES** (16,000 KM)!

SKILLFUL **GUILDS**

Artists, craftspeople, and the Oba's priests and musicians all belonged to guilds. Roles, skills, and knowledge were passed down through families. Metalworkers, for example, were all related.

Brass statue of a royal musician, a member of the hornblower guild

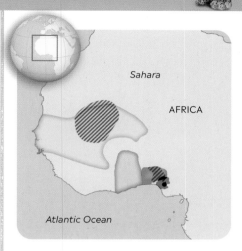

LEOPARDS WERE A SYMBOL OF **POWER**—THE OBA KEPT A FEW IN **HIS PALACE!**

Mudfish, which can live on land and in water, are a symbol of royal power.

Royal tiara

The collar is decorated with tiny faces of Portuguese traders.

QUEEN MOTHER

This ivory mask is thought to be a portrait of Idia, mother of the Oba Esigie. She helped him to make the kingdom strong again after a civil war in the late 15th century. Idia became the first official Iyoba (Queen Mother). She, and others after her, held a powerful position at court.

Sahara

AFRICA

Atlantic Ocean

HISTORIC KINGDOMS

Since ancient times, many different kingdoms have ruled different parts of Africa. These were just some of the most powerful ones in western Africa.

Wagadu (Ancient Ghana) c.300–1200
Emerging in 300 CE, this gold-rich empire became fabulously wealthy by controlling the trans-Saharan trade routes.

Ife c.700–1200
Founded by Yoruba people, this trading state was famous for its brass artifacts. Its metal-casting techniques inspired Benin's artists.

Kingdom of Benin c.1200–1897
With origins from the 10th century, Benin was at the height of its power in the 15th–18th centuries.

Mali Empire 1235–1899
Taking control of Wagadu's trade routes, this vast Islamic empire was at one point ruled by the famous Mansa Musa.

Oyo Empire c.1300–1900
This Yoruba state was at its height in the 17th–18th century. Militarily strong, it conquered many of its neighbors.

Asante Empire 1700–1901
Founded by descendants of the Akan people, this trading empire was ruled by a powerful Asantehene (king).

STOLEN **PROPERTY**

In 1897, British colonizers (see pages 308–309) attacked Benin City. Troops hacked off some 900 plaques from the royal palace walls. Together with other precious works of art, these ended up in foreign museums. Only recently, the slow process of returning some of them has begun.

Looted items ready for shipping off

GREAT WALL

Stretching for more than 13,000 miles (21,000 km), the Great Wall of China crosses coastland, desert, and misty mountains, as seen here, at Jinshanling. Along it rise sturdy guardhouses where soldiers would eat, sleep, and plan patrols. The Wall was built to defend the Chinese empire from attack by northern nomadic tribes. It served its purpose for many centuries until, in 1644, a group called the Manchus broke through and conquered China.

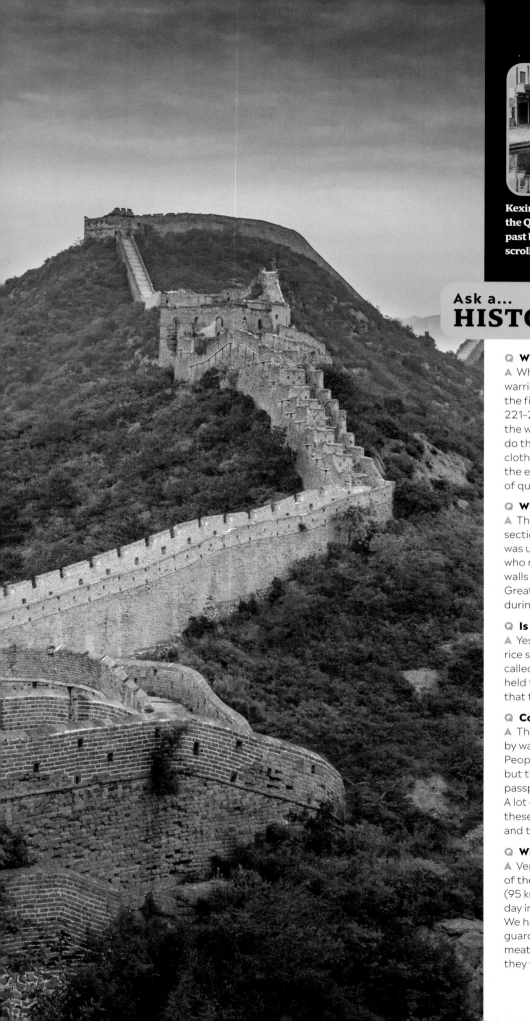

Kexin Ma is an art historian specializing in the Qing Dynasty of China. She explores the past by looking at pottery, porcelain, painted scrolls, and everything in between.

Ask a...
HISTORIAN

Q What made you become a historian?

A When I was a kid, I went to see the terracotta warriors found in the tomb of Qin Shi Huang, the first emperor of China, who reigned from 221–210 BCE. I was struck by the liveliness of the warriors and started to wonder: why do they have different faces, haircuts, and clothing? Why did they end up in the tomb of the emperor? Trying to answer these kinds of questions motivated me to study history.

Q Who built the Great Wall?

A The Wall was not built all at once but in sections, beginning in the 7th century BCE. It was under Qin Shi Huang, the same emperor who made those terracotta warriors, that the walls were connected and extended. The Great Wall we see today was mostly built during the Ming Dynasty (1368–1644).

Q Is it true the Wall has sticky rice in it?

A Yes! Chinese builders mixed sweet sticky rice soup with lime to make a special glue called "sticky rice mortar." The glue is what held the Great Wall together. It was so strong that the Wall even survived earthquakes.

Q Could people cross the Wall?

A They passed back and forth a lot, but not by walking on the Wall or climbing over it. People could travel through gates in the Wall, but they needed an entry document, like our passports with visas, to enter or leave China. A lot of markets were also established at these gates, where merchants from China and the northern regions would trade.

Q What was life like for the guards?

A Very busy. Each day, they patrolled portions of the Wall, covering a total of 59 miles (95 km). They also had to make 150 bricks a day in case any part of the Wall needed repair. We have discovered a daily menu for the guards, including chicken, fish, lamb, bison meat, pork, beans, barley, and wheat. I bet they would crave all that after a day of work!

DANCE **MANIA**

In 1347, a dancing disease broke out in the German town of Aachen and went on for several months. It later spread to other towns and cities in Germany and beyond!

CLEAN **HANDS**

Water jugs in the shape of animals like this lion were used for washing hands before formal meals. Cleanliness was important, as people often shared a plate and used their hands to eat.

The visor can be pushed up when not needed to protect the eyes.

Lance made of wood

Armored glove, known as a gauntlet.

MIGHTY **KNIGHT**

Knights were elite warriors who had trained since they were young. They pledged their service in times of war to powerful lords, who granted the knight land in return.

A chamfron protects the horse's face.

Knights and castles

From the 6th to the 15th century, Europe's rulers were often at war. Seeking protection, people pledged service to great lords. Although many new kingdoms arose, the greatest power of the era was the Catholic church.

PEPPER WAS SO **VALUABLE,** YOU COULD USE IT INSTEAD OF MONEY TO **PAY** THE **RENT!**

The lord's and lady's living quarter and Great Hall, where feasts were held.

Defensive towers called turrets

Multiple high, thick walls defend the castle from attack.

Archers can fire from narrow openings called arrow-slits.

The courtyard contains stables, laundry houses, and kitchens.

The moat slows down invaders trying to scale the walls.

Gatehouse, or barbican, reached by a drawbridge

WALLED IN
Stone castles had become common by the late 900s. They had thick, high walls and were situated in strategic places where they could defend the surrounding region from attack.

DOCTORS ATTEMPTED TO **CURE** ILLNESS BY **DRILLING HOLES** IN PATIENTS' **SKULLS**—TO RELEASE EVIL SPIRITS!

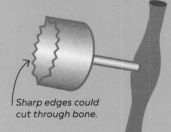

Sharp edges could cut through bone.

RELIGIOUS TOURISM
The dominant religion in Europe was Christianity. Many churches housed relics of saints in richly decorated containers. Pilgrims traveled to these shrines to pray for health, wealth, and the forgiveness of sins.

The mummified finger of St. Nicholas is visible through a window.

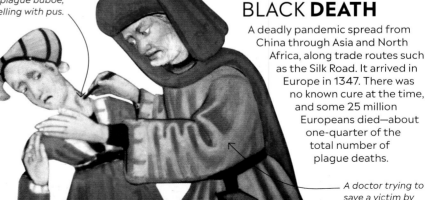

A plague buboe, swelling with pus.

BLACK **DEATH**
A deadly pandemic spread from China through Asia and North Africa, along trade routes such as the Silk Road. It arrived in Europe in 1347. There was no known cure at the time, and some 25 million Europeans died—about one-quarter of the total number of plague deaths.

A doctor trying to save a victim by letting out pus.

European Renaissance

European society underwent some dramatic changes in the 14th–16th centuries—a period now known as the Renaissance. New ways of thinking emerged from Italy's city-states, influencing culture, art, and science.

IN VENICE, SHOES GOT SO EXTRAVAGANT THAT LAWS WERE PASSED TO RESTRICT THEIR HEIGHT!

BEFORE THIS TIME, MOST EUROPEANS HAD NEVER SEEN A FORK!

INCREDIBLE INVENTIONS

Leonardo da Vinci was an Italian painter and inventor. He came up with many ideas that were far ahead of the technology of their time.

This is a modern model of an idea for a flying machine from Leonardo's sketch books.

PRINTING PRESS

In medieval Europe, books used to be copied out by hand. This was slow work, making books costly. In the 15th century, German inventor Johannes Gutenberg designed a press that used movable type to print a whole book page multiple times. This allowed ideas to be spread further and faster than ever before.

The paper is lowered down onto the type and slid under the press.

The handle is turned to squeeze together the paper and the inked type.

A sturdy wood frame supports the press.

This part presses down on the paper.

Letters cast in metal

Ink is spread across the type with a soaked leather-clad ink ball.

NEW OLD IDEAS

Greek and Roman myths were rediscovered in the Renaissance period and became popular topics for artists. This painting by the Italian artist Sandro Botticelli shows the Greek goddess Athena with a centaur (a creature that is half man and half horse).

WHAT WAS THE RENAISSANCE?

The Renaissance was a movement that spread across Europe. Similar changes happened everywhere, but at different times.

Art
Paintings and sculptures were often inspired by imagery from ancient Rome and Greece.

Architecture
New technologies and ideas were used to improve on ancient designs, such as large domes.

Learning
New universities opened, and nonreligious textbooks were printed.

Trade
Expanding trade meant more wealth. The rich had money to spend on building projects and the arts.

Astronomy
New telescopes allowed scientists to look to the skies and learn about the universe.

FABULOUS FLORENCE

The Renaissance began in the Italian city-states, and particularly in Florence. The dome of the cathedral in Florence was designed in 1418. It was, and still is, the largest brick-built dome ever constructed.

CRAZY CLAIMS!

People thought that the sun circled the Earth. But in 1543, the Polish astronomer Nicolaus Copernicus claimed that it was the other way around! Nobody believed him, and scientists who supported his ideas were jailed or burned at the stake.

All features are made up of fruit, flowers, and vegetables.

Corn was unknown in Europe until explorers brought it back from the Americas (see page 309).

(see page 309).

AMAZING ART

Before the Renaissance, European artists had spent their time painting images of Christ and the saints. Now, they began to expand their scope, trying out new subjects. Artists were often sponsored by the rich rulers of kingdoms and city-states.

This painting showing Vertumnus, Roman god of the seasons, is by an Italian artist, Giuseppe Arcimboldo.

1

2

3

4

5

6

7

8

9

10

11

12

13

14

15

16

WHO WORE THAT... HAT?

Do you know what you would wear on your head if you were a Mughal soldier? Or an ancient Mesopotamian queen? Put on your thinking cap and see if you can identify whose hat is whose—and spot the one that isn't headgear.

1 Mestizo cowboy, 15th century, Mexico
2 Chimu noble, 14th–15th centuries, Peru
3 Warrior, 5th–4th century BCE, Greece
4 Noblewoman, Ming Dynasty (1368–1644), China
5 Napoleon Bonaparte, 1799–1821, France
6 Mughal warrior, 16th–17th centuries, India
7 Soldier, 1st century CE, Roman Empire
8 Samurai, late 15th–16th centuries, Japan
9 Gladiator, 1st century BCE, Roman Empire
10 American revolutionary fighter, 1775–1783, US
11 Spanish soldier, 16th–17th centuries, Spain and South America
12 Yoruba king, 20th century, Nigeria
13 Queen Puabi, 2600 BCE, Mesopotamia
14 Apache warrior, 19th century, US
15 American infantry soldier, World War II
16 Pirate, 1650s–1720s, the Caribbean
17 Holy Roman Emperor, 10th century, Germany
18 Mongol warrior, 15th–17th centuries, Central Asia
19 High ranking military officer, 17th–18th centuries, China
20 German infantry soldier, World War I
21 Viking warrior, 8th–11th centuries, Europe
22 Cap shell, 200–145 million years ago
23 French revolutionary, 1789–1799
24 Puritan, 16th–17th centuries, England and US
25 Nubian king, 3rd–4th centuries, Kush, northeast Africa
26 Union infantry soldier, American Civil War, 1861–1865, US
27 Medieval knight, 14th–15th centuries, Europe
28 Soldier, 19th century, Bhutan

The odd one out is the cap shell (22), which is not a cap but a fossil of a prehistoric limpet.

Global explorers

As tales of foreign lands spread along trade networks, explorers from many continents set out to see for themselves. With better boats and navigation tools, they sailed across oceans. Some reached continents and islands previously unknown to them.

A giant moai stone figure, made by early Polynesian settlers on Rapa Nui

PACIFIC **ADVENTURE!**

Not all exploration was about trade. As early as 1500 BCE, Polynesians began exploring the Pacific Ocean, settling island after island. More than 2,000 years later, Polynesian ships first reached Rapa Nui, Hawaii, and Aotearoa/New Zealand.

REACHING **FARTHER**

Navigational tools such as the marine astrolabe, developed by Islamic scientists, made it easier for sailors to know roughly where they were and where they needed to go. This illustration from 1410 shows ships navigating in the Indian Ocean.

Marine astrolabe

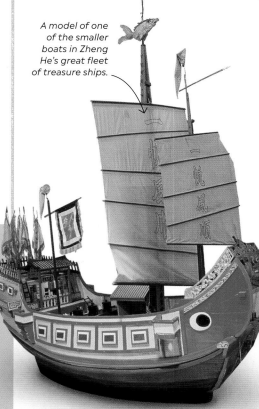

A model of one of the smaller boats in Zheng He's great fleet of treasure ships.

IN 1522, A **SPANISH SHIP** CALLED *VITTORIA* WAS THE FIRST TO SAIL **AROUND THE GLOBE!**

FIRST **ENCOUNTERS**

The first time people from different nations and continents came across each other, there was usually curiosity on both sides. But the arrival of European ships, such as this one observed by a Native American man in North America, often led to conflict.

ZHENG HE'S **TRAVELS**

The Chinese admiral Zheng He (1377–1433) led a huge fleet to visit ports in Southeast Asia, India, and the Swahili coast of Africa. He gifted Chinese goods, such as Ming vases, and in return brought back souvenirs for the Ming emperor, including a giraffe.

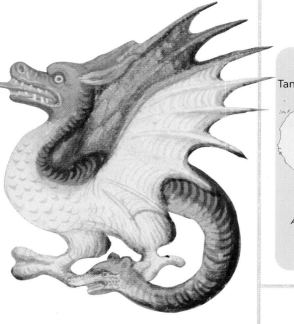

Tangier
Cairo
Mecca
Timbuktu
AFRICA
Kilwa
Beijing
Samarkand
ASIA
Indian Ocean
Atlantic Ocean

KEY
— First journey
— Second journey
— Third journey
— Fourth journey

CURIOUS **TOURIST**

The Moroccan explorer Ibn Battuta discovered his love of traveling during a customary Hajj (pilgrimage) to Mecca in 1325. His travels took him as far east as Beijing and as far south as Kilwa on Africa's Swahili coast. He retold all the amazing things he experienced in a book called *The Journey*.

TRAVELERS' **TALES**

Explorers often imagined that worlds unknown to them would be full of weird and wonderful things. They exaggerated their reports, too. This medieval drawing claims to show a dragon found in foreign lands.

The Caribbean region was already quite well known to Europeans at this point.

The shape of North America only shows the coastal parts known to Europeans at the time.

This island is meant to be Japan— but it is too big, and far too close to North America.

MAPPING THE WORLD

Maps had been produced since ancient times, but the more people traveled and observed, the more detailed maps became. They still only showed what each map maker knew, so many features were geographically incorrect or not there at all. This globe was made in Germany in 1522.

This map shows the actual size and shape of North, Central, and South America.

South America's yet unchartered west coast has been hidden by decorative clouds.

European
colonization

Soon after European explorers had reached other continents, stories of rich lands reached their rulers back home. Invaders were sent to take over these lands, making them into colonies from which raw materials would be extracted centuries.

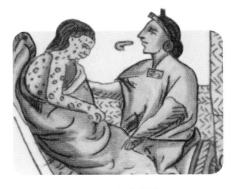

NEW **DISEASES**

In the Americas, the Europeans brought with them diseases that were new to the continent. The inhabitants had no resistance to them, and no cures, so millions died. This Aztec illustration shows a person seriously ill with smallpox.

LOCAL **KNOWLEDGE**

Indigenous people had well established societies and farming techniques. They would often teach their skills to newcomers. In North America, for example, Native Americans showed how to plant corn, beans, and squash together for the best possible yield. The colonizers, however, soon pushed people off their homelands.

Corn

THE PORTUGUESE COLONY IN BRAZIL WAS NEARLY 92 TIMES THE SIZE OF PORTUGAL.

STEALING SILVER

The first Spanish explorers arriving in the Americas were awestruck by the wealth of gold and silver objects made by the Inca and Aztec people. Artifacts were looted and shipped back to Spain, often to be melted down. The Spanish soon started mining for silver, forcing local people to work for them. Spanish coins were minted in Potosí, in present-day Colombia, and used worldwide.

A Spanish "piece-of-eight" silver coin, minted in South America

This coin might have been used as far away as China.

TRADE **INVASION**

In the 17th century, several European nations formed East India Companies to control the trade in Asian spices, tea, and fabrics. These became increasingly military and interfered with local rulers and politics. British merchants set up theirs in India in 1613. It expanded its power until 1858, when the British Crown took over the rule of India.

AMERICAN DELICACIES

Tomatoes, potatoes, pineapples, and cocoa had long been grown in the Americas. In the 1500s, they were seen in Europe for the first time.

LAND **GRABBING**

In the 1500s, Portugal and Spain started colonies in the Americas. Other European countries followed. Over the next 400 years, many parts of the world were colonized—some are shown in red on these globes.

Caribbean islands were fought over by many nations.

South America was divided between Spain and Portugal.

1770s

By the 1770s, almost all of the Americas was under colonial rule. There were a few small coastal colonies in Africa and Asia.

Most of Africa was occupied.

1914

In the 19th century, the focus shifted to Africa and Asia. By 1914, in Africa only Liberia and Ethiopia remained free, while Britain occupied the Indian subcontinent.

FIERCE **RESISTANCE**

On all continents, local people resisted the often brutal forms of colonization. In Dahomey (in present-day Benin), the French invaders encountered the Agojie— fierce female warrior units that the Europeans called Amazons.

This modern statue of an Agojie warrior stands in Cotonou, Benin's largest city.

Map of Africa, used by European leaders to split the continent and its resources, without any consideration for the people living there.

1884 **CARVE-UP**

European leaders competed to grab as many colonies as possible. But in 1884, they met to decide how to divide the African continent between themselves, in what they considered a more orderly manner. They did not invite local rulers, nor take existing kingdom borders into account.

Long rifles, as well as machetes, were the Agojie's weapons.

AT THE END OF WORLD WAR TWO, **750 MILLION PEOPLE** ACROSS THE WORLD STILL LIVED UNDER **COLONIAL RULE.**

Enslaved lives

From the 16th century, European nations—and later the newly founded US—grew rich by trading in enslaved people of African descent and using their forced, unpaid labor.

FORCED **LABOR**

Enslaved people were made to toil in the fields on plantations, or in steaming sugar factories, as shown in this painting from the Caribbean. Many were forced to work as unpaid servants.

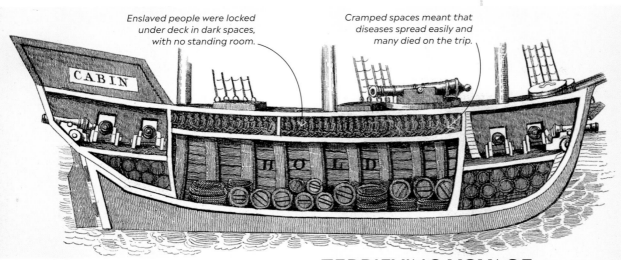

Enslaved people were locked under deck in dark spaces, with no standing room.

Cramped spaces meant that diseases spread easily and many died on the trip.

CABIN

HOLD

TERRIFYING **VOYAGE**

Snatched from friends and families, people from different African kingdoms were taken to the coast and then onto ships. They did not know where they were going. They were kept chained for months as the ship picked up more groups along the coast before setting out on the Atlantic crossing.

Map labels:
NORTH AMERICA
AFRICA
Caribbean
SOUTH AMERICA
Atlantic Ocean
Indian Ocean
KEY
← Ship routes

TRANSATLANTIC **TRADE**

European ships forcefully transported enslaved people from ports in Africa across the Atlantic. In the Americas, these people were sold and put to work.

AROUND **12.5 MILLION** ENSLAVED **PEOPLE** WERE **SHIPPED** ACROSS THE **ATLANTIC** OCEAN.

WHAT HAPPENED?

The ruthless use of enslaved people was legal for 400 years. Abolitionists worked to end it, but it took a long time, and the effects of it can still be felt even today.

Late 15th century
The Portuguese start using enslaved Africans for labor. In 1510, Spain sends enslaved Africans to Hispaniola in the Caribbean.

16th–17th centuries
Many more European nations get involved in the Transatlantic trade.

18th century
Enslaved labor is used in European colonies across the Americas.

1770s
Abolitionist movement begins. Black and white campaigners, many of them women, work to inform the white public and lobby politicians.

TAINTED CROPS

Plantations were farms that grew certain crops to meet the demand for them in Europe. Plantation owners and merchants grew rich on selling crops produced by unpaid, enslaved people.

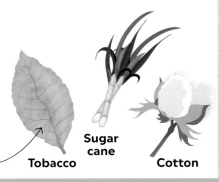

Tobacco became popular in Europe in the 1500s.

Tobacco

Sugar cane

Cotton

ESCAPE ROUTE!

In the US, a secret network of routes, helpers, and safe houses known as the Underground Railroad helped enslaved people escape to freedom. A lit lantern identified safe places, or "stations." Some 100,000 people got their freedom this way.

RISING RESISTANCE

Many enslaved people put up a fight on the ships, while others started plantation uprisings. Those who escaped formed rebel settlements and attacked plantations. One of the best-known communities was the Maroons in Jamaica, led by Queen Nanny. News of these rebellions made some people question the use of enslaved labor.

Queen Nanny

SPIRITUAL SURVIVAL

Life on the plantations was brutal, and often short. But enslaved people formed communities and sustained their own faith, traditions, and culture, gradually mixed with Christian customs. This painting shows an African American burial ceremony.

1777
The newly independent US join in on the trade.

1803
Denmark is the first nation to permanently outlaw the slave trade (but not slavery); other nations follow slowly. Britain abolishes the trade in 1807.

1834
Slavery is abolished in British colonies in the Caribbean. Slave owners are richly compensated for their "loss," but freed people get nothing.

1865
End of legal slavery is declared in the US after the end of the American Civil War (see pages 318–319).

1888
Brazil is the last nation in the Americas to abolish slavery. But freedom did not mean equal rights for Black people in the Americas or in Europe.

Age of **revolutions**

A series of revolutions erupted in the late 18th to mid-19th centuries. People rose up against their rulers to demand freedom, rights, fairer laws, and independence.

DURING THE **FRENCH REVOLUTION**, NEARLY **17,000** PEOPLE WERE TAKEN TO THE **GUILLOTINE.**

Toussaint l'Ouverture, leader of the Haiti Revolution

The blade fell fast, separating heads from bodies.

Haiti, 1791–1804
Starting with a revolt by enslaved people, by 1803 the island of Haiti had freed itself from its French colonizers. It became a republic in 1804.

France, 1789–1799
Demands for people's rights eventually led to the execution of King Louis XVI and the formation of a republic.

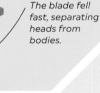

United States, 1775–1783
When 13 rebelling colonies declared independence from Britain in 1776, they had to fight a long war to defend their freedom as a new nation, the US.

POWER OF WORDS

New ways of thinking, inspired by French philosophers such as Voltaire, turned into calls for freedom and equality. People gathered to listen to speakers from all levels of society, and speeches led to action.

KEY **REVOLUTIONS**

Some revolutions led to the formation of new nations, while others led to better rights for ordinary people. Many took years, while others were short sparks followed by a backlash.

Battle of Lake Maracaibo, 1823

Bolívar's navy attacks a Spanish-held fort.

Latin America, 1808–1823
Spain's colonies fought several wars of independence. Revolutionary leader Simón Bolívar helped liberate Colombia, Ecuador, Panama, Peru, and Bolivia from Spanish rule.

German Confederation, 1848
People in the many German states wished to be part of one nation, but they did not want to be ruled by an all-powerful monarch. When citizens gathered to present their demands, troops attacked.

WOMEN **UNITE**

At this time, women weren't allowed to vote. But many, such as these women in Paris, joined political clubs. They discussed issues such as poverty caused by ever rising food prices, and how to make their voices heard in newspapers and politics.

Many small independent kingdoms were part of a confederation of German-speaking states.

EUROPE

KEY
- ☀ 1848 uprising
- State borders in 1848
- German Confederation

Italy was not yet a unified country.

1848 **FLASHPOINTS**

In one year, uprisings broke out across Europe. The reasons were many—food shortages led to riots; workers demanded rights; some wanted to be part of a unified nation; others wished to be free from imperial rule. Revolts were soon crushed, but the demands for change lived on.

THE WORLD'S **FIRST SUBMERSIBLE** WAS LAUNCHED IN AMERICA IN 1776 TO **ATTACK BRITISH BATTLESHIPS!**

CHRISTINE DE PIZAN

FIRST FEMINISTS

Women in many countries fought for and got the vote in the 20th century. But feminism didn't start with them!

CHRISTINE DE PIZAN
(1364–1430) This Italian French poet, one of the first women to make a living from writing, argued for women's rights.

OLYMPE DE GOUGES
(1748–1793) A French playwright and activist during the French Revolution, she wrote political articles on women's rights.

SOJOURNER TRUTH
(1793–1837) Born into slavery but set free, Sojourner toured the US to speak for abolition and women's right to vote.

MERI MANGAKĀHIA
(1868–1920) This influential Māori activist was part of the campaign that gave all women in Aotearoa/New Zealand the vote in 1893.

STAT ATTACK!
INFLUENCERS

Some individuals influence the course of history. Rulers can have impact through power, but others have blazed a trail by challenging prejudice or standing up to injustice. Here are some of history's greatest movers and shakers.

ROYAL CELEBS

Today we have famous movie stars and pop idols, but these powerful rulers were the international celebrities of their time.

CLEOPATRA Clever and beautiful, this Egyptian pharaoh made alliances with Roman rulers while trying to save her country.

MANSA MUSA The great 14th-century ruler of the Mali empire was famous for his wealth of gold.

NAPOLEON & JOSEPHINE During their rule of France in the early 18th century, they were the celebrity couple of their day.

TAKING PRIDE

Drag queen Marsha P. Johnson (1945–1992) was one of the best-known LGBTQ activists of the 1970s and '80s. Part of the 1969 Stonewall Uprising in New York and the first New York Pride march, Marsha cofounded two LGBTQ rights groups.

FREEDOM FIGHTERS

For thousands of years, people have stood up against invasions, colonialism, or racism—often thanks to leaders like these.

The country of Bolivia and its currency, the Boliviano, are named after Simón Bolívar!

VERCINGETORIX
This chieftain united tribes to stop the Roman invasion of Gaul (France). The Gauls fought bravely until their surrender in 52 BCE.

QUEEN NZINGA
The influential 17th-century ruler of Ndongo (in modern-day Angola) managed to keep her kingdom free from Portuguese invaders and the slave trade until the end of her reign.

SIMÓN BOLÍVAR
Inspired by the French and American revolutions, Bolívar led colonies in South America in rebellion against Spain. But his dream to unite them into one nation failed.

MIGHTY LEADERS

AMENHOTEP III (1391-1353 BCE)
This powerful pharaoh ruled Ancient Egypt at the height of its splendor.

SEJONG THE GREAT (1397-1450)
Encouraging science, art, and culture, Korea's greatest ruler created *hangul*, a new alphabet.

AKBAR (1542-1605)
Akbar used war and diplomacy to unite many Indian kingdoms into the mighty Mughal Empire.

LOUIS XIV (1638-1715)
The "Sun King" ruled France for 72 years and 110 days—the longest known reign ever.

CATHERINE II (1729-1786)
This German princess took power from her husband to rule as empress of Russia.

SEJONG THE GREAT

RADICAL THINKERS

CONFUCIUS (551-479 BCE)
This Chinese scholar believed that society would work better if people showed respect and discipline.

HYPATIA (370-415)
A philosopher and mathematician, Hypatia had her own school in Alexandria, Egypt.

KARL MARX (1818-1883)
Marx turned his thoughts about politics and economics into a radical philosophy that led to revolutions.

SIMONE DE BEAUVOIR (1908-1986) A French intellectual and writer, she is best known for her revolutionary feminist philosophy.

Philosophers through the ages have asked why the world is what it is and how we should live. The ideas of big thinkers such as these four have all led to significant changes in society.

ACCESS FOR ALL

From an early age, American disability advocate Judith Heumann (1947-2023) campaigned for equal rights to access, education, and work.

MODERN MOVERS

MALALA YOUSAFZAI
Shot for speaking for girls' right to go to school in Pakistan, she now campaigns for girls' education around the world.

GRETA THUNBERG
After starting her school strike for the environment in Sweden in 2018, Greta has inspired worldwide action.

AUTUMN PELTIER
This First Nation activist has worked for water preservation and Indigenous rights in Canada since she was eight years old.

PATRISSE CULLORS
A cofounder of Black Lives Matter in the US in 2013, she continues to speak against police brutality toward Black people.

GERONIMO
In the 19th century, this Apache warrior led a long guerrilla campaign to protect his people against Mexican and American soldiers.

NELSON MANDELA
Jailed for nearly 30 years for fighting against the racist system known as apartheid, he became South Africa's president in 1994.

CHE GUEVARA
Born in Argentina, this socialist rebel wanted to change poor people's lives. He took part in the Cuban Revolution, 1953-1959.

MALALA YOUSAFZAI

Industrial **Revolution**

Around 1750, the Industrial Revolution began in Britain, then spread across the world. Factories appeared, cities grew, economies expanded, and populations increased, transforming lives and lands.

HARD **WORK!**

Children worked long hours in factories. In 1833, a new law in the UK said that children could work only 8 hours per day, and not at all under the age of 9.

Rocket cross section

EARLY **RAILROADS**

Many inventors worked on developing steam locomotives. The most successful was the *Rocket*, designed by British engineer Robert Stephenson in 1829. The first railroads were used to transport goods, but soon passengers got on board.

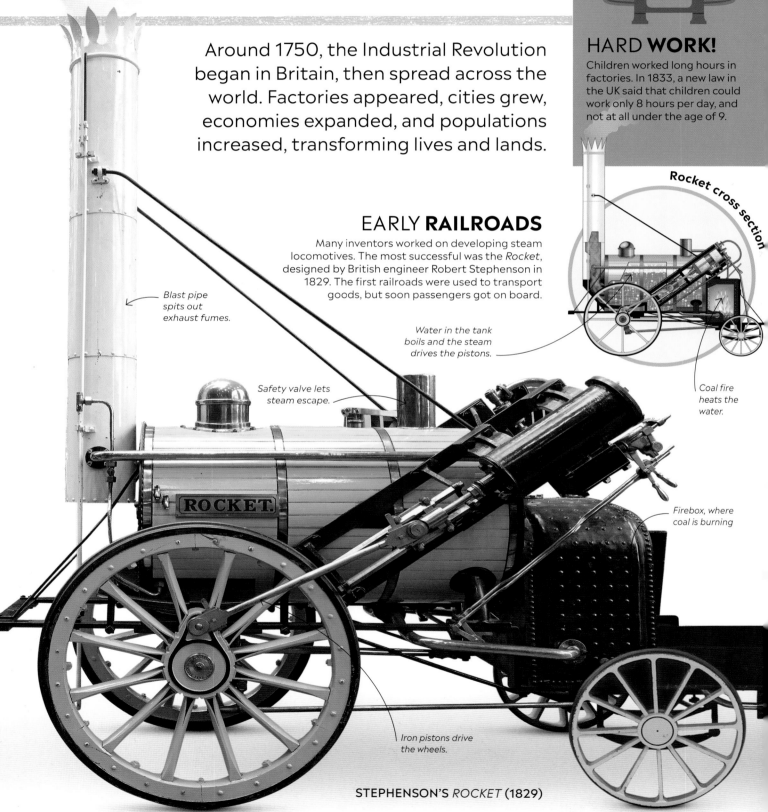

Blast pipe spits out exhaust fumes.

Water in the tank boils and the steam drives the pistons.

Coal fire heats the water.

Safety valve lets steam escape.

ROCKET

Firebox, where coal is burning

Iron pistons drive the wheels.

STEPHENSON'S *ROCKET* (1829)

NEW **MACHINES**

Clever innovations allowed machines to perform the jobs of humans and animals quickly and cheaply. A single machine could do the work of tens or hundreds of workers. Lots of ideas were developed and refined—these are just three of the most important of the time.

Up to 120 threads were spun at a time.

Steam-powered pistons drove the hammer.

Steam engine
This engine powered pumps in mines and machines in factories.

Spinning jenny
This device spun raw cotton into threads of yarn for textiles.

Steam hammer
Ironworks used this tool to beat metal into shape.

Fluffy cotton plant fibers

COTTON **SUPPLY**

The cotton that Britain used for its textile industries came from the Americas, where it was grown and harvested by enslaved people. This allowed Britain to outprice rival cloth producers, like India.

CHANGING **LANDS**

As industrialization accelerated, people left the countryside to work in factories. The cities they moved to were crowded and dirty. Poverty, disease, and social unrest were common.

GLOBAL **MOVEMENT**

Industrialization spread from Britain to Europe, America, and Asia. Large-scale mechanization, cheap labor, and mass-production became the norm. This image shows a silk factory in Japan.

THE FIRST **BICYCLE** WAS INVENTED IN 1817 – BUT YOU HAD TO **WALK IT!**

MORE THAN 400 WOMEN FOUGHT IN THE WAR, DISGUISED AS MEN!

FLYING **GRENADES**

Invented in 1861, Ketchum Grenades were used by the Union Army. They weighed up to 5 lb (2.3 kg) and soldiers threw them like darts. If they landed correctly, on their nose, the impact would make a plunger slide in, setting off the gunpowder inside.

American Civil War

In 1861–1865, the United States was locked in a bitter civil war. It erupted over the issue of enslaved labor, which was outlawed by the northern Union states but supported by the states in the south.

Plate triggering the plunger

The women living in the camps took in washing and laundry from other soldiers.

Whole families slept in small, basic tents.

The blue uniform shows that this man is part of the Union army.

CAMP **LIFE**

Combatants on both sides were volunteers rather than professional soldiers. Army camps were dirty, disease-ridden, uncomfortable, and sometimes violent places. Despite this, some soldiers' families lived with them on long campaigns.

Even babies and pets lived in army camps.

STATES AT WAR

In 1861, 11 states in the south broke away from the United States to form a separate government, known as the Confederacy. The northern states refused to recognize the new government and wanted them to rejoin the Union. After four years of war, the states were united again, but many divisions remained.

KEY
- Union states
- Confederate states
- Territories, not yet official states

Washington, DC, the Union capital

CLASHING SHIPS!

Resembling submarines more than ships, the USS *Monitor* and CSS *Virginia* fought to a draw in the Battle of Hampton Roads in 1862. This was the first-ever naval engagement between "Ironclad," or all-metal, ships.

IN BATTLE

In 1863, US President Abraham Lincoln declared that enslaved people should be freed and that Black men could enlist to fight. Some 180,000 African Americans from the north and south joined the Union army.

Black Union soldiers fighting in the Second Battle of Fort Wagner, 1863

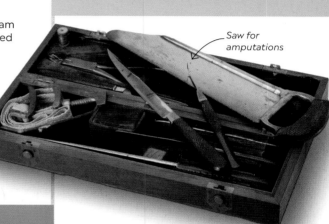

Saw for amputations

FIELD SURGERY

Of the men killed in the war, twice as many died from injuries and disease than in combat. Battlefield operations were often performed without anesthetic in dirty conditions, with unsterilized equipment.

OVER 3 MILLION HORSES AND MULES SERVED IN THE WAR!

GRIM BATTLEFIELDS

Bloody battles were fought with artillery, rifles, and bayonets, and casualties were high. There were about 50 major battles in the war, fought mainly in the states of Virginia and Tennessee, with thousands of smaller skirmishes. More than 620,000 people were killed.

The "Napoleon" howitzer was the most widely used cannon of the war.

SOCIAL CHANGE

The Union victory saw slavery abolished. In 1871, Josiah Walls (above) became one of the first African Americans elected to the US Congress. But Black people still had to fight for civil rights.

Mensun Bound is a British marine archaeologist who was Director of Exploration on the expedition team that discovered the wreck of *Endurance* in 2022.

Ask a... MARINE ARCHAEOLOGIST

Q How did you know where to look for *Endurance*?

A We followed the records of *Endurance's* captain, Frank Worsley, who identified the area where he thought the ship sank. It was a good estimate. We found the wreck just four nautical miles from where Worsley said it was.

Q How did it feel when you saw the wreck?

A Finding *Endurance* was the best moment of my life. I had never seen such a majestic shipwreck, we could even see the original paintwork. It was as if she had just been sitting there waiting to be discovered.

Q Why is Endurance so well preserved?

A Because Antarctica is so cold, ship worms cannot survive. When these creatures enter a ship's timbers, they are no bigger than a pinhead. But then they begin to eat and grow until they are about as long as a man's forearm and as thick as a thumb and no wood is left.

Q What were the biggest challenges you faced on the expedition?

A The ice. If a ship gets trapped in the ice, it can be crushed. This is just what happened to *Endurance*. We, too, were trapped by the ice many times, but we always managed to escape.

Q What technology did you use?

A The piece of equipment we used to find *Endurance* was called a "Sabertooth." This underwater robot can hunt the seabed automatically, but we can also use a remote control to direct it where we want it to go.

Q What is the hardest part of your job?

A I love diving underwater, but I never forget that it is a hostile environment. Over the years I, or those working for me, have run out of air, been attacked by sea lions, carried away by the current, trapped in fishing nets, or stung by poisonous fish. But as long as you have been properly trained, and are careful, you can explore an underwater world most people never get to see.

THE WRECK OF *ENDURANCE*

British explorer Ernest Shackleton set sail for Antarctica on *Endurance* in 1914. He planned to cross Antarctica on foot, a feat that had never been accomplished before. But *Endurance* became trapped in pack ice, which cracked the hull, allowing water to flood in. The crew escaped, but the ship sank to the bottom of the ocean. The wreck remains preserved deep under the Antarctic seas.

First World War

In 1914, long-standing tensions in Europe turned into a war. It spread like wildfire, with battles fought on several continents, and became the biggest, deadliest conflict the world had seen.

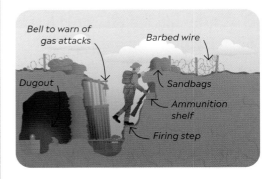

TRENCH WARFARE

Troops built long trenches to provide shelter from shell fire. As well as launching attacks from the trenches, soldiers also had to live, eat, and sleep in these filthy, dangerous conditions.

WESTERN FRONT

Many of the bloodiest and most drawn-out battles took place on the Western Front, across Belgium and France. In late 1917, the third Battle of Ypres claimed the lives of more than 800,000 men and left the landscape completely devastated.

WHAT HAPPENED?

In July 1914 when the war broke out, people believed it would end by Christmas. But it ground on for four long years.

June/July 1914: War breaks out
After Archduke Ferdinand is assassinated, Austria-Hungary declares war on Serbia. Russia sides with Serbia, and Germany declares war on Russia.

August 1914: Early battles
In the east, the Germans win a massive victory over the Russians at the Battle of Tannenberg.

September 1914: Digging in
The German advance across Western Europe is halted by Allied troops. Both sides dig trenches.

1915–1916: Eastern battles
Allied forces attack the Ottoman Empire at Gallipoli to help Russia on the Eastern Front.

Main Allies

Russia France Britain US

TAKING SIDES

The opposing nations formed two groups, the Allies and the Central Powers. By the end of 1914, most of Europe, the Ottoman Empire, and Japan, had taken sides. Bulgaria and Italy entered the war in 1915, and in 1917 the US and China joined, too.

Main Central Powers

Germany Austria-Hungary Ottoman Empire

65 MILLION TROOPS FOUGHT IN THE WAR, FROM 30 DIFFERENT COUNTRIES.

IN THE FOUR YEARS OF WAR, AN ESTIMATED 20 MILLION PEOPLE LOST THEIR LIVES.

NEW WEAPONS

Both sides developed new technology to get the better of the enemy. Armored tanks smashed through enemy lines defended by barbed wire and rapid-fire machine guns. These efficient, deadly weapons caused heavy casualties on both sides.

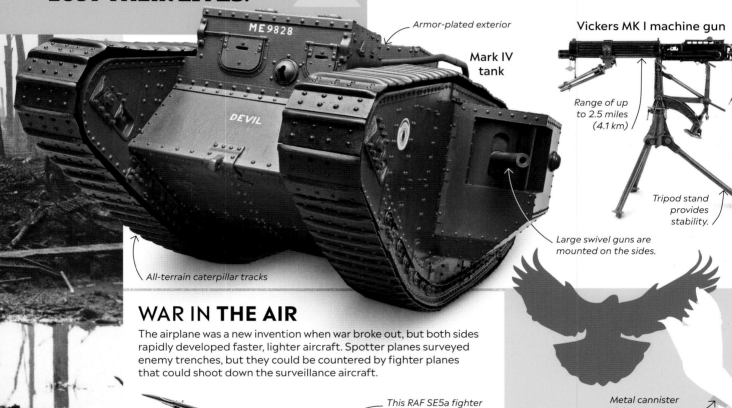

Armor-plated exterior

Mark IV tank

ME 9828

DEVIL

All-terrain caterpillar tracks

Vickers MK I machine gun

Range of up to 2.5 miles (4.1 km)

Tripod stand provides stability.

Large swivel guns are mounted on the sides.

WAR IN THE AIR

The airplane was a new invention when war broke out, but both sides rapidly developed faster, lighter aircraft. Spotter planes surveyed enemy trenches, but they could be countered by fighter planes that could shoot down the surveillance aircraft.

This RAF SE5a fighter has twin wings made of fabric-covered wood.

Metal cannister containing message

PIGEON POST!

At the front line, where there were no telephone lines, carrier pigeons were used to deliver secret information and orders. During the war, more than 500,000 pigeons carried important messages to and from the front lines.

May 31–June 1, 1916: Battle of Jutland
British and German naval forces fight the only major sea battle of the war, off the coast of Denmark.

1916: The big push
Allied forces launch a major offensive on the Western Front. More than one million men die.

April 1917: US joins the war
The sinking of US passenger ship *Lusitania* by a German submarine draws the US into the war.

November 11, 1918: Fighting ends
After losing several battles, the German forces agree to sign a truce.

1919: An uneasy peace
Germany signs a peace treaty with the Allies and is forced to agree to humiliating terms.

The war was fought between two groups: the Allies—led by Britain and, later, the USSR and the US—and the Axis powers led by Germany, Italy, and Japan.

September 1, 1939: War begins
Germany invades Poland. Britain and France declare war on Germany two days later.

May–June 1940: France falls
The German army sweeps through France and occupies Paris. Britain leads the resistance.

August– November 1940: Air war
"The Battle of Britain" sees German air attacks on England defeated by Allied fighter pilots.

June 22, 1941: Turning east
Germany invades the USSR, almost reaching Moscow before winter conditions halt the advance. Eventually, the Germans are forced to retreat, their army permanently weakened.

December 1941: Pacific onslaught
Japan attacks British colonies in Asia. The cities of Singapore and Hong Kong are forced to surrender.

Second World War

The largest conflict in history, World War II claimed at least 55 million lives. In total, more than 80 countries raised troops and fought in the war.

One of two 20 mm cannons

Engine exhaust pipes

RISE OF THE **NAZIS**

After the First World War, some European nations looked to dictators for leadership. In Germany, the Nazi party, led by Adolf Hitler, took power. The Nazis wanted to expand Germany by conquering other countries. When Germany invaded Poland, Britain and France declared war on Germany. Many European nations had colonies that joined the war, drawing more nations into the conflict.

BOMBED CITIES

For the first time, civilians far behind the front lines were vulnerable to attack. Bombing raids devastated cities on both sides. The German "Blitz" on London in 1940 killed 43,000 civilians. In 1943, Allied air raids destroyed Hamburg, Germany (above), killing 40,000 people.

The Nazi party held huge rallies to drum up support.

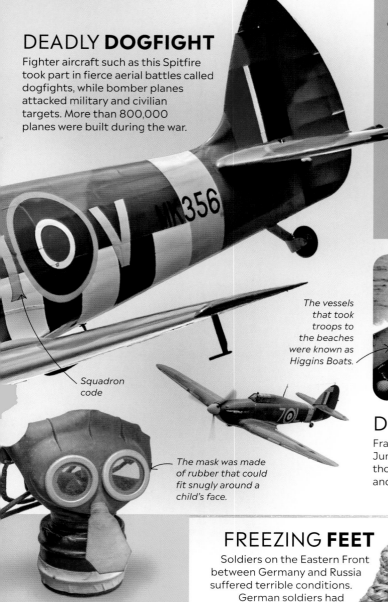

DEADLY **DOGFIGHT**

Fighter aircraft such as this Spitfire took part in fierce aerial battles called dogfights, while bomber planes attacked military and civilian targets. More than 800,000 planes were built during the war.

Squadron code

The mask was made of rubber that could fit snugly around a child's face.

GERMAN **SUBMARINES,** CALLED **U-BOATS,** SANK AROUND **3,000 ALLIED SHIPS.**

The vessels that took troops to the beaches were known as Higgins Boats.

D-DAY **LANDINGS**

France was occupied by Germany until, on June 6, 1944, in the largest sea invasion ever, thousands of boats landed on French beaches and the liberation of the country began.

GAS **MASK**

British children under four were given brightly colored "Mickey Mouse" masks to protect them from gas attacks.

FREEZING **FEET**

Soldiers on the Eastern Front between Germany and Russia suffered terrible conditions. German soldiers had to wear clumsy (but effective) straw overshoes to prevent frostbite while on guard duty.

Straw kept the heat in.

THE **HOLOCAUST**

The Nazis persecuted Jewish people, forcing them to live in separate areas called ghettos. Then, in 1942, the Nazis began to deport and kill Jews. At least six million Jews were murdered in prison camps, alongside other minority groups.

THE **END**

Japan was the last country to hold out against the Allies. On August 6 and 9, 1945, two US B-29 aircraft each dropped an atomic bomb over the Japanese cities of Hiroshima and Nagasaki. Both cities were destroyed and 200,000 civilians died. Japan surrendered shortly afterward.

December 7, 1941: Pearl Harbor
A surprise Japanese assault on the naval base at Pearl Harbor, Hawaii, brings the US into the war on the Allied side.

February 1943: Stalingrad
After eight months of bloody fighting, the German army suffers its worst defeat of the war so far at the Battle of Stalingrad in Russia.

June 6, 1944: D-Day
160,000 Allied troops land in Normandy in occupied France. Slowly, the German army is pushed back.

April 30, 1945: German defeat
With defeat certain, Hitler takes his own life. Germany surrenders a week later, but Japan continues fighting.

September 2, 1945: War ends
Japan surrenders after the US drops atomic bombs on the cities of Hiroshima and Nagasaki. The war is over.

When slavery was abolished, laws were passed to give African Americans equal rights. Racist violence continued, especially in the South, but the Civil Rights movement kept growing.

1868
The 14th amendment is passed, meant to grant full US-citizen rights to all African Americans.

1880s onward
The "Jim Crow" laws segregate Black citizens from white in Southern states; Black people perceived to break the rules are tortured and murdered by white mobs.

1955
The brutal murder of 14-year-old Emmett Till, accused of flirting with a white woman, sparks a wave of activism.

1960
Students in Greensboro, North Carolina, organize peaceful protests against segregation in diners.

1963
In May, teenagers march in Birmingham, Alabama. In September, four girls are killed when racists bomb the Sixteenth Street Baptist Church.

1964
Civil Rights act outlaws discrimination based on race, origin, and gender, as well as segregation and the "Jim Crow" laws.

1965
The Selma–Montgomery March leads to the Voting Rights Act. It is now illegal to make it harder for people to vote based on their race or ethnicity.

1968
Martin Luther King Jr. is assassinated in Memphis, Tennessee—a crime that shocks the world.

Civil Rights
movement

In the 1950s and '60s, African Americans gained ground in their long fight for equal rights. Activists achieved many goals, including making segregation illegal.

EARLY **CAMPAIGNER**

The struggle had been going on for a very long time. From the 1890s, journalist Ida B. Wells wrote articles against racist violence and campaigned with other early activists.

Replica of the Rosa Parks bus

FIGHTING **SEGREGATION**

In the US South, Black people could not sit in "white" sections on buses. Rosa Parks (opposite) challenged this. The Freedom Riders—Black and white people traveling together—continued the action on buses across the Southern states.

Martin Luther King Jr. leading the march for full voting rights in Selma, Alabama, in 1965.

MARCHING ON

Martin Luther King Jr., the main leader of peaceful protest, used marching as a means to gain attention for the cause. Despite often being attacked, marchers walked on.

MARTIN LUTHER KING JR. WAS **ARRESTED** FOR PEACEFUL PROTEST **29 TIMES!**

RACIAL SEGREGATION IN US PUBLIC SCHOOLS WAS MADE ILLEGAL ONLY IN 1954.

KEY ACTIVISTS

People of different backgrounds, professions, and religious beliefs engaged in the struggle for Black Civil Rights from the 1950s. These are just a few of the most influential.

Mamie Till-Mobley
The mother of teenager Emmett Till spoke out to make sure his brutal murder was not ignored.

Rosa Parks
Her arrest after refusing to give up her seat to a white person led to the 1955–1956 bus boycott.

Malcolm X
A Muslim minister, he believed that Black people in the US should form a separate nation.

Muhammad Ali
World-famous boxer Ali regularly spoke about Civil Rights in widely broadcast interviews.

Harry Belafonte
One of many artists involved, this popular singer spread the word in the US and abroad.

Huey Newton
Cofounder of the Black Panther movement, he campaigned for armed civil resistance.

Angela Davis
A radical political and feminist activist, this university professor has also written many books.

TAKING A STAND

At the 1968 Olympics, US medalists Tommie Smith (gold) and John Carlos (bronze) raised their fists in a Black Power salute against racial injustice. This protest meant the end of their Olympic careers, as well as that of the Australian silver medalist Peter Norman, who supported them.

MORE TO DO

Discrimination and racism have not gone away, not in the US nor in the rest of the world, so protests go on. Founded in 2013 against police brutality toward Black people, the Black Lives Matter movement went global after the murder of George Floyd by white police officers in 2020.

"BLACK IS BEAUTIFUL" FIRST BECAME A SLOGAN IN THE 1960s!

The Cold War

From 1945 until 1991, the US and communist Soviet Union (USSR) were rival "superpowers." The conflict between them was known as the Cold War because, while they threatened each other, they did not clash directly.

IN THE 1980S, **US** AND **SOVIET** LEADERS AGREED THEY WOULD **HALT** THE COLD WAR IF **ALIENS INVADED!**

CIA AGENTS TIED THEIR **SHOELACES** IN DIFFERENT PATTERNS TO SEND **SECRET MESSAGES!**

"Follow me"

Camera attaches to neck with strap.

BIRD'S-EYE VIEW

Each side spied on the other. The US spy agency, the CIA, used pigeons to observe bases in the Soviet Union. They also used ravens to drop listening devices on government building window ledges.

NUCLEAR **THREAT**

Between them, the superpowers had enough nuclear weapons to destroy the Earth. If one side launched a strike, the other would retaliate, triggering a global nuclear war. The fear of this kept the Cold War from turning into a "hot" war between the two countries.

ARMS **RACE**

After the end of the Second World War, the US was the only country in the world with nuclear weapons. But the Soviets began testing their own nuclear bomb in 1949. This led to an arms race, as both sides created bigger and more destructive weapons. The race finally slowed in the 21st century, and since the end of the Cold War the number of nuclear weapons has drastically reduced.

Number of nuclear missiles

US ■
USSR (Russia after 1991) ■

Increasing tension led the Soviets to build more missiles.

40,000
30,000
20,000
10,000
0

1950 1960 1965 1975 1986 2000 2010

VIETNAM **WAR**

The US and Soviet Union did not clash directly but still took sides against each other. For example, during the Vietnam War (1955–1975), the Soviet Union supplied arms to communist North Vietnam while the US sent 550,000 soldiers to fight on the side of South Vietnam.

SPACE **RACE**

The superpowers even competed in space. The Soviets took an early lead in the race to explore beyond Earth, launching the world's first satellite in 1957. Later that year, they sent a living creature into orbit, the dog Laika. The US however, was the first country to put a man on the moon, in 1969.

BERLIN **WALL**

At the end of the Second World War, Germany was divided between communist East and democratic West. Berlin was in the eastern zone, but it too was divided. In 1961 the communists built the Berlin Wall to keep East Berlin's citizens from leaving for the West.

CUBAN MISSILE **CRISIS**

The closest the world came to nuclear war was in October 1962 when the Soviet Union stationed nuclear missiles on Cuba, just 103 miles (166 km) off the US coast. After a tense 13 days, during which some American families sheltered in bunkers, the Soviets backed down and removed the missiles.

FOR YEARS, THE **TOP-SECRET** PASSCODE FOR LAUNCHING AMERICA'S **NUCLEAR** WEAPONS WAS **00000000!**

THE WALL **FALLS**

In the 1980s, a wave of unrest swept through the Soviet Union's allies in Eastern Europe as people called for greater democratic freedoms. Protesters tore down the Berlin Wall on November 9, 1989, and Germany was reunified into a single country. Two years later, the USSR itself broke apart into independent republics, no longer under Soviet rule.

ALGERIA'S INDEPENDENCE WAR MEMORIAL IS 302 FT (92 M) TALL!

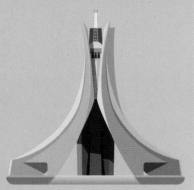

Claiming **independence**

After World War Two, independence movements gained ground, and colonial powers had to accept that the world was changing. Some struggles were violent; others took the form of negotiations. By the end of the 20th century, most—but not all—former colonies were independent.

YEARLY **CELEBRATION**

Many countries commemorate the date of their independence. Some mark the day with military parades and others with carnival-like festivities. In Kenya, Jamhuri Day is a national holiday. Crowds gather to celebrate the day in 1964 when the newly independent country became a republic.

Kwame Nkrumah, Ghana's first president

GHANA'S **DAY**

Ghana was one of the first countries in Africa to gain independence. The leader of Ghana's freedom movement was Kwame Nkrumah. In 1948, he supported Ghanaian veterans who had fought for Britain in World War Two but were unjustly treated. Their protests grew into an independence campaign, and in 1957 Nkrumah became leader of a free Ghana.

SPLIT **FREEDOM**

After many decades of campaigning by activists such as Mahatma Gandhi, Sarojini Naidu, and Muhammad Ali Jinnah, Britain left India in 1947. Upon independence, the country was divided, and a new country, Pakistan, was created. This event, known as the Partition, was marred by violence. Today, the two countries meet in a daily military ceremony at their joint border.

PAN-AFRICAN **MOVEMENT**

Pan-Africanism is a movement that began in the 19th century. Its aim was to unite Black people in their struggle against slavery and racism and celebrate their African roots. Later it played a part in the fight for independence and called for unity among African nations.

THERE ARE NOW **195** INDEPENDENT **COUNTRIES** IN THE **WORLD!**

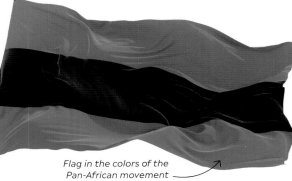

Flag in the colors of the Pan-African movement

Sandra Mason, flanked by Prime Minister Mia Mottley and R&B singer Rihanna, is sworn in as Barbados's President in 2021.

ISLAND INDEPENDENCE

A British colony since 1627, the Caribbean island of Barbados gained independence in 1966. Remaining part of the Commonwealth, it kept Queen Elizabeth II as head of state. But in 2021, Barbados became a republic.

AFRICAN **NATIONS**

This timeline shows when countries in Africa gained freedom from colonial rulers (in parentheses), since the 1950s.

1956
Tunisia, Morocco (France); Sudan (UK /Egypt)

1957
Ghana (UK)

1958
Guinea (France)

1960
Cameroon, Togo, Benin, Madagascar, Niger, Burkina Faso, Ivory Coast, Chad, Central African Republic, Congo-Brazzaville, Gabon, Senegal, Mali, Mauritania (France); Nigeria (UK); Somalia (UK/Italy); Congo Kinshasa/DRC (Belgium)

1961
Sierra Leone, Tanzania (UK)

1962
Algeria (France); Uganda (UK); Rwanda, Burundi (Belgium)

1963
Kenya (UK)

1964
Malawi, Zambia (UK)

1965
Rhodesia (as Zimbabwe from 1980), Gambia (UK)

1966
Botswana, Lesotho (UK)

1968
Eswatini/Swaziland (UK); Equatorial Guinea (Spain)

1973/1974
Guinea Bissau (Portugal)

1975
Mozambique, Cape Verde, Comoros, São Tomé & Príncipe, Angola (Portugal)

1976
Seychelles (UK)

1977
Djibouti (France)

FLOPPY DISKS, INVENTED IN THE 1970s, COULD ONLY HOLD 1MB OF DATA!

Going digital

In the early 20th century, the first computers were developed to carry out calculations. As their processing power increased, the machines themselves shrank and became available for more and more people to use.

EARLY **COMPUTERS**

The first electronic digital computers were created in the UK and US, for breaking German military codes in the Second World War. They took up entire rooms.

EARLY **INTERNET**

The forerunner of the internet was a network called ARPANET. In 1969, it connected computers at four US universities using telephone lines. By the 1970s, ARPANET stretched across the US. In the 1980s, it merged with other similar networks across the world and the internet as we know it was born.

USA

Each dot represents a separate connection.

PERSONAL **COMPUTERS**

By the 1970s, computers were used in businesses but not yet in people's homes. That changed when the first personal computers were produced in the early 1980s.

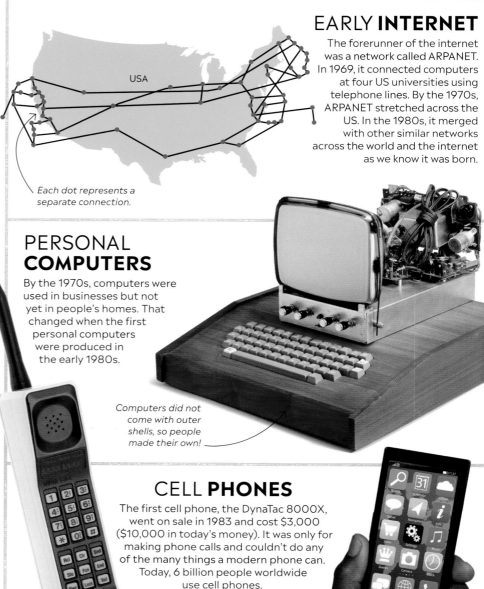

Computers did not come with outer shells, so people made their own!

FIRST **WEB PAGE**

The invention of the World Wide Web made information on the internet accessible, by linking documents together. The first-ever web page (above) went live in 1991. It was a list of instructions of how to use it!

CELL **PHONES**

The first cell phone, the DynaTac 8000X, went on sale in 1983 and cost $3,000 ($10,000 in today's money). It was only for making phone calls and couldn't do any of the many things a modern phone can. Today, 6 billion people worldwide use cell phones.

The DynaTac 8000X was the size of a house brick.

MOST MADE **ITEM!**

Tiny semiconductors, or microprocessors, are the "brains" of all digital devices. Around 1.5 trillion of them are manufactured each year.

Graphics in games such as Space Invaders were bold and colorful—but very basic.

The game screen is set back, behind a glass screen decorated with attention-grabbing graphics.

Early games were controlled by buttons, not joysticks.

Slot for putting in coins to pay for a game

EARLY **VIDEO GAMES**

In the 1970s, people played video games on large machines in special video game arcades. In the game Space Invaders, released in 1978, players had to fight off hordes of attacking aliens. The Atari 2600 released in 1977 was the first widely available home gaming console. Today, there are around 5 million different games.

TODAY, THERE ARE **1.98 BILLION** WEBSITES ON **THE INTERNET!**

ACROSS THE ATLANTIC

The time taken to cross the Atlantic Ocean has drastically decreased since the first voyages in sailing ships. The development of ships with motor engines sped things up significantly, and airplanes cut travel times from the UK to the US from days to hours.

66 DAYS
It took the *Mayflower* more than two months to reach North America in 1620.

15.5 DAYS
In 1838, the steamship *Great Western* crossed the Atlantic in just over two weeks.

4 DAYS
The *Queen Mary* ocean liner brought the trip down to a few days in 1936.

17 HOURS 40 MINUTES
The Douglas DC-4 flew from London to New York without stopping in 1945.

6 HOURS 12 MINUTES
In 1957 passenger jet planes cut travel times again.

2 HOURS 52 MINUTES
Supersonic Concorde hit its fastest speed on the London–New York route in 1996.

STAT ATTACK!
NETWORKS

People across the planet are more connected than ever before. Trips that once took months now last just a few hours, while with the help of the internet, people on opposite sides of the world can chat instantly.

TERRIFIC TRANSPORTATION

Moving millions of people and tons of cargo from one place to another is no small task. These are the busiest transport hubs in the world.

BUSIEST AIRPORT
More than 80 flights depart from Atlanta, Georgia, every hour.

BUSIEST SHIPPING PORT
The port of Shanghai, China shifts almost 130,000 shipping containers every day.

BUSIEST RAILROAD STATION
An average of 9 million passengers pass through Shinjuku station, Tokyo, Japan every hour.

SHINJUKU RAILROAD STATION

CRAMMED WITH CARGO

From camels to container ships, people have used many methods to transport goods around the world. Today's gigantic vessels carry far more than the merchants of the past could have imagined.

CAMEL
400–500 lb (180–226 kg)
Camels are strong and hardy enough to make long trips laden with goods.

SAILING SHIP
835,550 lb (379,000 kg)
17th-century wooden ships could carry 2,000 times more weight than a camel.

ANTONOV AN-225 MRIYA PLANE
551,150 lb (250,000 kg)
From 1988–2022, this aircraft transported heavy cargo, including a space shuttle.

EVER ALOT CONTAINER SHIP
1,344,224,000 lb (60,973,000 kg)
The world's biggest transport ship (below) can fit over 24,000 containers on board.

EVERGREEN

GOING ONLINE

The number of internet users has grown by 24 percent in just three years, with 1.1 billion people estimated to have come online since 2019. Approximately 5.3 billion people—or 66 percent of the world's population—were regular users of the internet in 2022.

2.7 billion people still have **no access** to the internet.

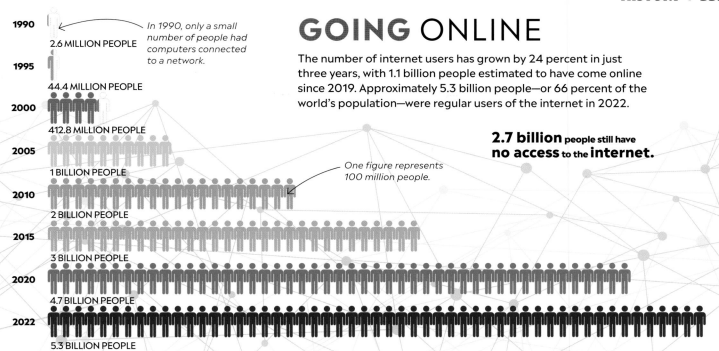

1990
2.6 MILLION PEOPLE

In 1990, only a small number of people had computers connected to a network.

1995
44.4 MILLION PEOPLE

2000
412.8 MILLION PEOPLE

2005
1 BILLION PEOPLE

2010
2 BILLION PEOPLE

One figure represents 100 million people.

2015
3 BILLION PEOPLE

2020
4.7 BILLION PEOPLE

2022
5.3 BILLION PEOPLE

DAILY COMMUNICATION

Huge numbers of digital messages are sent across the internet every single day.

AROUND 1 BILLION emails are sent and received.

500 MILLION tweets are published on Twitter.

AT LEAST 95 MILLION photos are posted on Instagram.

ADOPTING TECHNOLOGY

People have become very quick to begin using new technology, especially social media. It took more than three years for Netflix to reach one million users, but each of these technologies got there even faster.

 24 **MONTHS** Twitter had a million tweeters two years after it launched in 2006.

 10 **MONTHS** Facebook reached a million users soon after its 2004 launch.

 3 **MONTHS** Photo-sharing app Instagram took a few months to gather a million users.

 2 **WEEKS** A million people had interacted with AI chatbot ChatGPT after just two weeks.

ALWAYS ONLINE

The average user spent six hours and 37 minutes online every day in 2022—two hours and 28 minutes of that was on social media.

VIDEO VISION

Video calls surged in popularity during the COVID-19 lockdowns. Zoom, a video-calling website, saw a 535 percent increase in traffic in April 2020, just after stay-at-home orders were introduced.

CULTURE

What is **culture?**

Our culture is the way we live, both as individuals and in groups. We express our culture through art, literature, and music but in daily life, too. How we dress and speak, our beliefs and customs—even the buildings we live and work in, all reveal something about our culture.

GLOBAL VILLAGE

For centuries, most people had little access to people or places outside their own culture. Today, technology has made it much easier for us to discover how people all over the globe live.

Transportation
Transportation, especially by air, is faster than ever, which means that people, goods, and even ideas can travel much more easily than in the past.

Communication
New technologies allow us to talk and swap ideas with friends, family, or colleagues, no matter where they are.

News media
We can follow world events as they happen, as eyewitness reports are uploaded and instantly viewed on social media.

59% OF THE WORLD'S 8 BILLION PEOPLE LIVE ON THE CONTINENT OF ASIA!

OUR **WORLD**

Around the world, there is an amazing array of different cultures—from traditional communities whose way of life has not changed for thousands of years, to vast, fast-moving megacities. Here are some of the different ways in which inventive, creative humans contribute to the cultures we live in.

VISUAL ARTS
Drawing, painting, sculpture, photography, and graffiti are some of the visual ways in which people express their ideas and beliefs.

ENTERTAINMENT
From classical ballet to rock festivals and circuses to sporting events, people everywhere love to perform, or to watch others putting on a show!

COMING **TOGETHER**
Sydney, Australia, is a city with a large, diverse population made up of people from many different cultures. But some events bring everyone together to share in the celebrations. These crowds are welcoming in the new year at Sydney Harbour Bridge.

THE **WORLD'S MOST VISITED** MONUMENT IS THE **FORBIDDEN CITY** IN BEIJIING, **CHINA!**

Punk's influence on fashion lasted longer than it did on music—the "street punk" look still has fans today!

FASHION FADS

Cultures are often about traditions, but some, especially among young people, are short-lived. Punk music made a big impact in the late 1970s but burned out within a few years.

LIFESTYLE
Often without realizing it, we reflect our culture in our choice of clothes and hairstyles, the food we eat, and the products we buy.

SPEECH AND WRITING
The way we use words expresses our culture—both the literature we read and write and our language, dialect, or accent when we speak.

ACTIVITIES
Our favorite sports, hobbies, and groups, as well as traditional crafts are all activities that powerfully reflect our culture.

ARCHITECTURE
The design of cities, and of buildings such as homes, schools, and hospitals, can publicly express a cultural group's values and identity.

Living languages

We use language to communicate and convey our ideas, feelings, or knowledge. As the world has become more interconnected, some languages have become more widely spoken, while others have declined or even died out.

DO YOU SPEAK KLINGON?

Invented specially for the sci-fi TV series *Star Trek* the Klingon language even has its own dictionary! Other fictional languages include Na'vi, from the movie *Avatar*, and Lapine, spoken by the rabbits in the novel *Watership Down*.

Fans dressed as Klingons at a US comic convention.

TOP TONGUES

Some languages spread from their place of origin to become the main language in other countries, or a second language in areas with a lot of different languages. Here are the languages with the most speakers worldwide.

1 **English** 1.5 billion
2 **Mandarin** 1.1 billion
3 **Hindi** 602.2 million
4 **Spanish** 548.3 million
5 **French** 274.1 million

MULTIPLE LANGUAGES

Many countries have more than one official language. The top three are Zimbabwe with 16 languages, India with 23, and Bolivia, which has 37!

This railroad crossing in Israel has warnings in Hebrew, Arabic, and English.

ON AVERAGE, TWO LANGUAGES DIE OUT EVERY MONTH!

SAYING HELLO!

Every language has a word or phrase that people use to greet each other—here is "hello" in some of the world's most widely spoken languages. Different languages are written using a variety of alphabets and scripts, which are sets of symbols or characters.

xin chào
sin-chow, VIETNAMESE

Sampurasun
Sum-poo-rah-soon, SUNDANESE

Pronounce the word like this.

مرحبا
marr-hah-bah, ARABIC

ciao
chao, ITALIAN

नमस्ते
nuh-muh-stay, HINDI

السلام عليكم
as-salām-alaykum, URDU

helo
hello, MALAY

سلام
salaam, PERSIAN

hola
o-la, SPANISH

สวัสดี
sawasdee, THAI

TODAY, THERE ARE AROUND **7,100 LANGUAGES** SPOKEN IN THE **WORLD!**

Hand shapes, as well as body language and facial expressions, are used for letters, words, or phrases.

SYMBOLS AND **SIGNS**

Not all languages are spoken or written. Sign language is used by many deaf and hearing-impaired people. There are around 300 variations of sign language used today, by up to 70 million people.

STAYING **ALIVE**

A language can be lost if not enough people use it. When the Welsh language was in danger of dying out, efforts were made in Wales to keep it alive. Children learn Welsh in school, there are Welsh-language TV channels, and an annual festival called the Eisteddfod celebrates Welsh language and culture.

The Eisteddfod's winning poet sits in a specially made throne.

THERE ARE OVER **600,000 WORDS** IN **ENGLISH**—MORE THAN ANY **OTHER** LANGUAGE!

salam əleyküm
salām-alaykum, AZERBAIJANI

bawo ni
bah-wo nee, YORUBA

hallo
ha-low, GERMAN

నమస్కారం
namaskārām, TELUGU

bonjour
boh-zhoo, FRENCH

您好
nee-how, MANDARIN

cześć!
cheshch, POLISH

jambo
ja-m-boh, SWAHILI

Привіт
priveet, UKRANIAN

hello
Heh-low, ENGLISH

kumusta
coo-moos-tah, TAGALOG

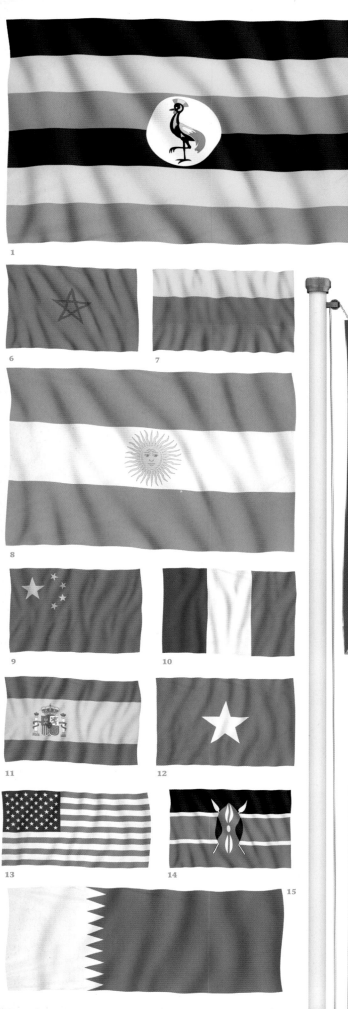

1

2

3

4

5

6

7

8

9

10

16

11

12

13

14

15

17

18

19

20

21

22

23

24

25

26

27

28

Every country has a national flag with its own unique design. Cover up the answers and see if you can name the country that flies each of these flags. Can you spot the one that doesn't belong to any nation?

1 Uganda
2 Belize
3 Ecuador
4 United Kingdom
5 Germany
6 Morocco
7 Lithuania
8 Argentina
9 China
10 France
11 Spain
12 Somalia
13 United States of America
14 Kenya
15 Qatar
16 Seychelles
17 Antigua and Barbuda
18 Saudi Arabia
19 South Korea
20 Chile
21 Papua New Guinea
22 Brazil
23 United Nations
24 Japan
25 Australia
26 Dominica
27 Nepal
28 Peru
29 South Africa
30 Kiribati
31 India
32 Sri Lanka
33 Italy
34 Colombia
35 Canada
36 Tonga
37 Jamaica

29

30

31

32

33

34

35

36

37

The odd one out is the flag of the United Nations (23).
The United Nations is an international organization
formed to uphold human rights and promote peace.

Religion and beliefs

How did we get here? What's the meaning of our lives? What happens to us when we die? Religions and belief systems are ways of exploring some of the big questions that humans have always wondered about.

 CHRISTIANITY
2.4 billion
Based on the life and teachings of Jesus Christ, born in c.4 BCE.

 BUDDHISM
506 million
Founded in India by the Buddha in the 5th century BCE.

 ISLAM
1.9 billion
Founded by the prophet Mohammed around 610 CE.

 SIKHISM
25 million
Founded by Guru Nanak in India in the 16th century.

 HINDUISM
1.1 billion
Originated in India 4,000 years ago.

 JUDAISM
14.6 million
Originated in the Middle East from the 8th century BCE.

A WORLD OF **BELIEFS**

This list shows some of the world's main religions and the estimated number of their followers. More than 1 billion people say they don't follow any religion, describing their beliefs as Humanist, agnostic, or atheist.

This totem pole was carved by an artist of the Kwakwaka'wakw people.

SACRED **NATURE**

Some First Nation cultures consider the land, the animals around them, and the ancestors that came before them as sacred. In North America's Pacific Northwest, wooden carvings called totem poles symbolize the beliefs, culture, or family history of nations or individuals.

THE STATUE OF **CHRIST THE REDEEMER** IN BRAZIL IS **98FT (30 M) HIGH!**

SPIRITUAL SITES

Most religions have holy buildings where people gather for prayers or ceremonies—these include Christian churches, Islamic mosques, and Jewish synagogues. Hindu temples, such as this one in Sri Lanka, are often large and ornate, featuring colorful carvings of Hindu deities (gods).

HOLY **JOURNEYS**

A pilgrimage is a journey, often long or difficult, that believers make to a holy site. They do this to strengthen their faith, give thanks for prayers answered, ask forgiveness, or seek a cure for illness.

The Ka'bah, the most sacred shrine in Islam, is the focus of the pilgrimage.

Every year, thousands of Muslims undertake the Hajj, a pilgrimage to the holy city of Mecca in Saudi Arabia.

WHAT IS A **RELIGION?**

There are many religions, but some features, called dimensions, are common to all of them. Four of these essential dimensions are listed below.

Ritual and practice
Actions carried out by believers may include prayer, baptism, or fasting for a set time.

Laws and teaching
Rules and guidance, either written or passed on orally, on how followers should live.

Stories and myths
Stories that give examples of how to live, or try to describe events such as the creation of the world.

Material things
Objects connected to the religion such as icons or art, or holy sites such as temples or shrines.

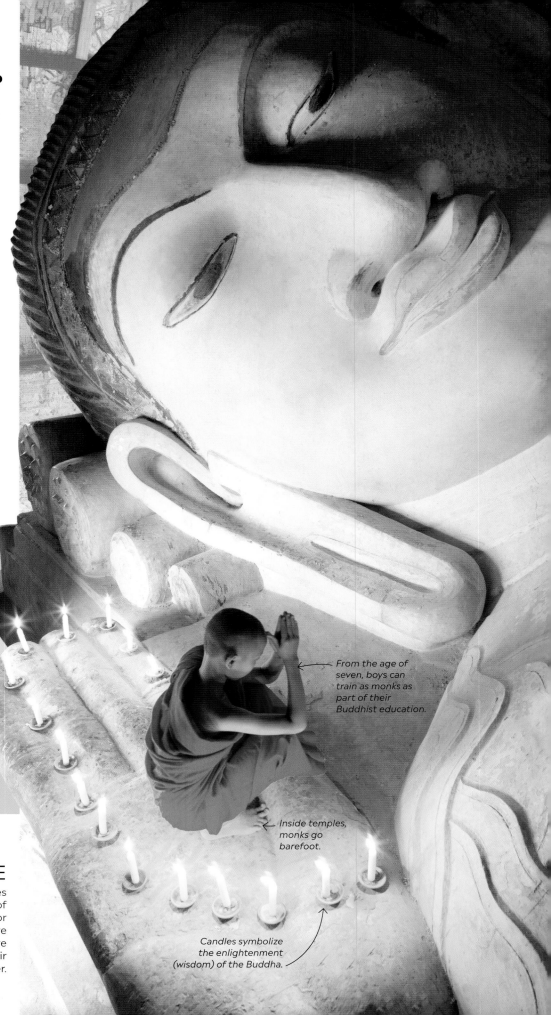

INDIAN PRINCE SIDDHARTHA GAUTAMA FOUNDED BUDDHISM AFTER MEDITATING UNDER A TREE FOR 49 DAYS!

From the age of seven, boys can train as monks as part of their Buddhist education.

Inside temples, monks go barefoot.

Candles symbolize the enlightenment (wisdom) of the Buddha.

MONASTIC LIFE

Some people devote themselves full-time to studying the teachings of their faith and living out its values. For example, Buddhist monks and nuns live simply; they wear plain robes, shave their heads, and spend much of their time in meditation and prayer.

Festival fun

In every community, there are special days when people gather to mark an important event or celebrate a tradition. Whether they feature food, parades, or gift-giving, festivals are often an opportunity to meet up and have fun.

TYPES OF **FESTIVALS**

There are many reasons why people may get together to celebrate; here are some of the main ones.

Sacred events
Marking significant dates in the religious year is a key part of many faiths.

Food and drink
In farming communities, harvest time is often marked by a big feast!

New year
Many cultures celebrate the chance to make a new start as the old year ends.

Changing seasons
Each season has a festival: in spring, people celebrate the rebirth of nature.

National days
These may mark the founding of a country or celebrate a national hero.

The "Green Man" leads the wassail.

WINTER **WASSAILS**

Wassailing is the ancient British custom of visiting apple orchards to sing to the trees to encourage a good harvest in the coming season. During the parade, the wassailers pass around the wassail bowl, which is filled with warm, spiced apple cider.

MASS MUSIC FEST

Music is always a good reason for people to get together. The *Donauinselfest* celebrates Austrian music and artists and attracts 3 million fans every year. The free festival is held on an island on the Danube River, in Austria's capital, Vienna.

Sky lanterns are made of paper and lit by candles.

Both tourists and local people take part in the ceremony.

Skeleton costumes and skull masks are popular parade costumes.

LIVING **DEAD**

The Mexican Day of the Dead is when people celebrate friends and family who have died. As well as holding colorful parades, families have picnics by the graves of their loved ones and decorate cemeteries with candles, flowers, and gifts.

THE **UP HELLY AA** FESTIVAL ON SHETLAND, UK, FEATURES THE **BURNING** OF A **VIKING LONGSHIP!**

Makeup emphasizes the eyes and teeth.

COMING **TOGETHER**

For people in remote places, festivals are a chance to get together with old friends, or even find romance. At the Gerewol festival in Chad, young men dress up and perform dances to impress potential partners.

FIERY FUN

Fire is a feature of many festivals all over the world. In parts of India, *Lohri* is a celebration of the end of winter. People sing and dance around a bonfire, then throw food into the flames to symbolize getting rid of the old year and starting afresh.

Students in Amritsar perform Giddha, a popular folk dance.

AT SPAIN'S **TOMATINA** FESTIVAL, PEOPLE FLING **165 TONS** (150,000 KG) OF **TOMATOES** AT EACH OTHER!

Temple lit by tea lights and hanging lanterns

FLOATING **LIGHTS**

In Chiang Mai, Thailand, at the festival of *Yi Peng*, the sky is lit up by thousands of lanterns. People release them to "make merit", which means that they offer them up as good deeds to make for a better life in the future.

Glorious food

Food is so much more than the fuel we need to survive. What we eat, as well as when and who we eat with, is part of who we are and also marks our belonging to a particular group or culture.

FLOATING **FRUIT**

Food markets have been around since ancient times, enabling people to buy fresh food daily. Markets such as this floating market in Banjarmasin, Indonesia, remain popular today. Women traders, in round hats called *tanggui*, travel to market in *jukung* (traditional boats), then sell fruits and vegetables directly from the boats.

Man grating a block of hard cheese

ANCIENT **CHEESE!**

Cheese is one of the oldest processed foods—turning milk into a nutritious, solid form that lasts for years. Traces of cheese have been found in pots up to 7,500 years old. The ancient Greeks were great cheese lovers, as this figurine from the 6th century BCE shows.

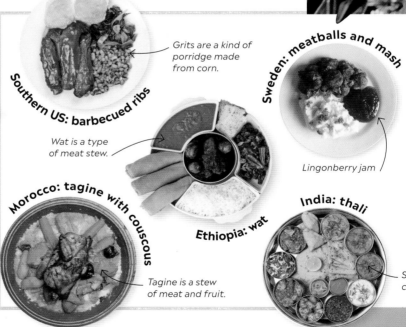

Grits are a kind of porridge made from corn.

Southern US: barbecued ribs

Wat is a type of meat stew.

Sweden: meatballs and mash

Lingonberry jam

Morocco: tagine with couscous

Ethiopia: wat

India: thali

Tagine is a stew of meat and fruit.

Small dishes of vegetable curries and bread

WORLD **CUISINES**

The traditional, typical food and recipes of a country or group of people is called its cuisine. A cuisine is influenced by many factors, including the available ingredients, the climate, different religious laws or beliefs, and how much time people have for cooking.

PRINT YOUR DINNER!

3-D digital technology can be used to design and create edible works of art. The food, such as sugar or chocolate, is built up layer by layer into a 3-D object. These sugar shapes have been 3-D-printed to be used as cake and dessert decorations.

ONE-THIRD OF ALL FOOD PRODUCED IS **WASTED** AND GOES STRAIGHT **IN THE TRASH!**

WHY WE EAT

We often assume our eating habits are shaped purely by our own personal taste, but there are lots of other things that play a part.

Cultural or national ties
Some foods have a strong link to one region, country, or culture—for example, we think of pizza as one of Italy's national dishes.

Health and fitness
Athletes eat to improve performance; for example, marathon runners may eat high-carbohydrate food for energy before a race.

Religion or belief
We may eat (or avoid) some foods because of our religious faith, or as a result of our beliefs about issues such as animal welfare.

Social occasions
Eating together as a family or group gives us a sense of being part of our community.

Celebrations
Getting together to eat special foods, such as birthday cake, helps us to mark important occasions in our lives.

HÁKARL IS AN ICELANDIC DISH OF SHARK MEAT LEFT TO ROT FOR UP TO SIX WEEKS!

GLOBAL APPEAL

In the last 50 years, "fast food" has spread all over the world. Fast food is cheap and easy to eat on the go but can contain more salt, sugar, or processed fats than we need to stay healthy. Global food companies often modify their menus to make them appeal to local cultures.

In some Arabic countries, McDonald's burger buns are replaced with flatbread.

Fried grasshopper is a popular street food in Thailand.

INSECT PROTEIN

Protein is essential for our bodies to grow and repair themselves. Insects are among the richest sources of protein. Around two billion people regularly eat insects, and some experts believe that this form of protein could feed even more people in the future.

SWEETEST
OF ALL

Sugars can be made from a variety of plants, including sugar cane and beet, but the sweetest taste of all comes from the agave plant. Agave syrup is around 1.5 times sweeter than white, granulated sugar.

Agave syrup is made from sap stored in the leaves of this desert plant.

Stigmas are dried to make saffron.

PRICEY
SPICE

Saffron, which comes from the saffron crocus, is the world's most expensive spice. The fragile stigmas of about 150,000 plants are needed to make just 2.2 lb (1 kg) of the richly flavored spice.

STAPLE
STARCHES

Most of the meals eaten worldwide are based on one of just four basic ingredients, known as staple foods. Together, these foods provide around 60 percent of all the energy we consume.

1 CORN
19.5 percent of energy consumed in the world comes from this ancient crop.

2 RICE
This is a staple for more than 3.5 billion people and accounts for 16.5 percent of the energy we eat.

3 WHEAT
Usually ground into flour to make bread, pasta, or cereal, wheat makes up 15 percent of energy consumed.

4 ROOTS AND TUBERS
Around 5.3 percent of the world's food energy come from starchy plants, including cassava, potatoes, and yams.

STAT ATTACK!
FOOD

Food is more than just fuel for survival. People worldwide really love to eat and drink—whether it's juicy tropical fruit; sweet, creamy chocolate; or eye-watering chilies. Here is a feast of facts about some of the fascinating foods we consume.

PASTA
FANATICS

Pasta is one of the world's favorite foods—around 18.6 million tons (16.9 million metric tons) of it is produced every year! Here are the most pasta-loving countries, based on the average amount eaten per person in 2021.

In Italy, there are **more than 350** different **pasta shapes** to choose from!

ITALY
51.8 lb (23.5 kg)

TUNISIA
37.4 lb (17 kg)

VENEZUELA
33 lb (15 kg)

GREECE
26.8 lb (12.2 kg)

PERU
21.8 lb (9.9 kg)

FEEL THE HEAT

Chilies get their tongue-burning heat from a chemical compound called capsaicin—the more of it, the hotter the pepper! Capsaicin content is measured in Scoville Heat Units (SHU). Here are the highest and lowest ranking chilies on the Scoville scale.

1 CAROLINA REAPER
1.5–2.2 million SHU

2 TRINIDAD MORUGA SCORPION
1.5–2 million SHU

3 BHUT JOLOKIA
855,000–1.5 million SHU

4 RED SAVINA HABANERO
350,000–580,000 SHU

5 SCOTCH BONNET PEPPER
100,000–350,000 SHU

6 BIRD'S EYE
50,000–100,000 SHU

7 CAYENNE PEPPER
30,000–50,000 SHU

8 SERRANO PEPPER
10,000–23,000 SHU

9 GREEN OR RED BELL PEPPER
0 SHU

Pure capsaicin contains 16 million Scoville Heat Units.

CHOC CHOMPERS

In 2022, Germany took the title of the world's most chocolate-loving nation. Germans munched 24.2 lb (11 kg) of chocolate per person, slightly ahead of Switzerland, which nibbled 21.4 lb (9.7 kg) per person.

FRUIT FEAST

More bananas are produced and eaten than any other fruit. Here is a list of the world's top five favorite fruits in 2021, ranked by the amount produced.

BANANAS 138 million tons (125 million metric tons)

WATERMELONS 112 million tons (102 million metric tons)

APPLES 103 million tons (93 million metric tons)

ORANGES 84 million tons (76 million metric tons)

GRAPES 82 million tons (74 million metric tons)

TEA OR COFFEE?

After water, tea and coffee are the most popular drinks in the world. Billions of pounds of each are brewed up and enjoyed every year.

TEA
13.9 billion lb
(6.3 billion kg)

COFFEE
21.6 billion lb
(9.8 billion kg)

MIGHTY JACKFRUIT

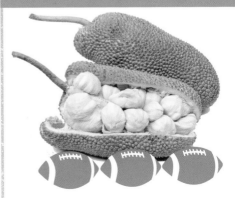

The tropical jackfruit can grow up to nearly 3 ft (90 cm) long. That's almost the length of three footballs!

WAYS OF **WINNING**

Whenever people compete against each other, there has to be an agreed way of finding a winner. Here are the four main types of sporting events, based on how they are contested.

Timed events
The competitor or team with the fastest completion time wins.

Distance events
These are decided based on the farthest distance achieved.

Scoring events
The number of goals or points scored decides the outcome.

Judged events
Performances are assessed and given marks by judges.

Spectacular **sports**

There are hundreds of different sports, each involving a specific physical skill and a set of rules. People play individually or as part of a team. Most sport is competitive, but for many people, the fun of sport is taking part, whatever the outcome.

OLYMPIC GLORY

Every four years, the world's best athletes compete for their country in the Summer, Winter, and Paralympic Olympic Games. At most Games, new sports are included: in 2020, surfing (left), karate, and sport climbing appeared for the first time.

Body stays upright. →

Legs and arms "cycle" rapidly to push the jumper forward. →

← *Explosive takeoff, to achieve as much lift as possible.*

TOP **TECHNIQUE**

In many sports, technique is key to achieving maximum performance—and victory. In events such as long jump, an athlete and their coach will use video to analyze every aspect of the jump and find ways to gain extra distance.

US SWIMMER TRISCHA ZORN, WITH **41 GOLD MEDALS**, IS THE MOST **SUCCESSFUL PARALYMPIAN** EVER!

EXTREME SPORT

Some sporting events are so long, demanding, or risky that they are done only by elite adult athletes. The *Marathon Des Sables* is a punishing 156-mile (250 km), six-day race in the Sahara Desert, Morocco.

Runners cover the distance of six marathons in temperatures of up to 122°F (50°C).

Decathlon events

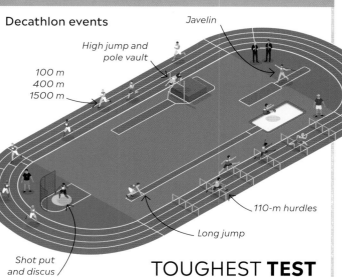

Javelin

High jump and pole vault

100 m
400 m
1500 m

110-m hurdles

Long jump

Shot put and discus

SOCCER FOR ALL

Soccer is the world's favorite sport, with 3.5 billion fans worldwide. More than 265 million people regularly play, including 29 million women and girls, making soccer one of the fastest-growing female sports.

In 2019, 1,000 girls and women took part in a soccer festival in London to raise the sport's profile.

TOUGHEST TEST

Athletics includes throwing, jumping, and running disciplines. The men's decathlon tests all these skills over 10 events. An Olympic decathlon champion can claim to be the world's best all-around athlete. The seven-event heptathlon is the women's equivalent competition.

THE MEN'S **LONG JUMP WORLD RECORD**, HELD BY AMERICAN **MIKE POWELL**, HAS **NOT BEEN BROKEN** SINCE 1991!

29 ft 4¼ in (8.95 m)

Torso and arms lean forward to maintain momentum.

Jumper lands feet first and throws body forward.

NAME THAT... SPORT

Do you know which sports use these balls, bats, and shoes? Cover up the answers below and find out! Can you spot the odd one out?

1 Badminton shuttlecock
2 Discus
3 Javelin
4 Handball
5 Squash ball
6 Kayak paddle
7 Surfboard
8 Croquet mallet
9 Darts
10 Australian football
11 Archery bow and arrow
12 Life buoy
13 Basketball
14 Pickleball paddle and ball
15 Shot put shot
16 Rhythmic gymnastics ribbon
17 Snowboard
18 Ski goggles
19 Karate helmet
20 Golf ball
21 Golf club
22 Hurling stick
23 Table tennis paddle
24 Ten-pin bowling pins
25 Ice hockey skates
26 Fencing mask
27 Inline roller skates
28 Field hockey stick
29 Soccer ball
30 Jianzi shuttlecock
31 Curling stone
32 Sepak Takraw ball
33 Cricket ball
34 Cricket bat
35 Sprint relay baton
36 Rugby ball
37 Soccer cleat
38 Baseball mitt and ball
39 Swimming goggles
40 Pool ball
41 Soccer goalkeeper's gloves
42 Baseball bat
43 Skateboard knee pads
44 F1 driver's helmet
45 Football helmet
46 Swimmer's nose clip
47 Tennis ball and racket
48 Basketball wheelchair
49 Ski boots
50 Road cyclist's helmet

The life buoy (12) is the odd one out. This life-saving device keeps someone afloat if they get into difficulty in the water.

MULTIPLE MEDALS

The only soccer player to win three World Cup winner's medals is Brazilian striker Pelé. The first came in 1958 when he was only 17 years old. Brazil lifted the cup again in 1962 and 1970.

1 SOCCER
3.5 billion fans

2 CRICKET
2.5 billion fans

STAT ATTACK!
SPORTS

On your marks, get set... GO! Elite athletes and top teams continually push themselves further to win medals, beat opponents, or set new records. Check out these sensational sports stats.

GOLF ON THE MOON!

In 1971, US astronaut Alan Shepard was the first human to play moon golf when he hit two golf balls off the lunar surface.

The moon's low gravity meant the balls went farther than they would have on Earth!

BADMINTON 260 mph (417 km/h)

GOLF 211 mph (339.6 km/h)

JAI ALAI 187.6 mph (302 km/h)

SQUASH 175 mph (281.6 km/h)

TENNIS 163.7 mph (263.4 km/h)

FASTEST MOVERS

Here is the league table of sport's five fastest-moving missiles! The winner is not a ball—it's the badminton shuttlecock. Its weight and conical shape enable the shuttlecock to move at great speed when hit in a smash, the most powerful shot in badminton.

QUIRKY QUIDDITCH

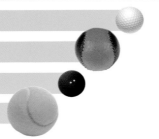

The fictional game played by wizard Harry Potter is now a real-life sport! Players astride broomsticks score points by shooting a ball through hoops.

FIRST OLYMPICS

Today's Olympic Games were inspired by games held in ancient Greece. The first modern Olympics was in Athens in 1896 and featured 14 nations competing in eight sports.

ATHLETICS

CYCLING

FENCING

SWIMMING

GYMNASTICS

SHOOTING

TENNIS

WEIGHTLIFTING

WATCHING SPORT

In this list of the six most popular spectator sports in the world, soccer is the clear winner. It is watched (and played) in virtually every country.

3 HOCKEY
2 billion fans

4 TENNIS
1 billion fans

5 VOLLEYBALL
900 million fans

6 TABLE TENNIS
850 million fans

TOP SPEEDS

How fast can a human go? Here are the fastest speeds achieved by people in four different sports.

RUNNING
The maximum speed a human runner has reached is just under 27.3 mph (44 km/h).

SWIMMING
A swimmer can achieve a speed of around 4.7 mph (7.6 km/h).

CYCLING
The record pedal-powered speed is a blistering 184 mph (296 km/h).

SKIIING
The quickest skiers on the slopes reach speeds of up to 158.5 mph (255 km/h).

AWESOME ARENA

The Narendra Modi stadium in Ahmedabad, India, is the world's largest cricket stadium. The vast venue can seat 132,000 spectators. Instead of having traditional floodlight towers, it was the first stadium to be lit by eco-friendly LED lights, which form a ring around the perimeter of its roof.

FIRST PARALYMPICS

The first official Paralympic Games took place in Rome, Italy, in 1960. 400 wheelchair-using athletes from 23 countries competed in eight sports.

Combination of darts and archery

ARCHERY

ATHLETICS

DARTCHERY

SWIMMING

SNOOKER

TABLE TENNIS

FENCING

BASKETBALL

TOUGHEST TESTS

Some sportspeople are always looking for new and more extreme ways to test their physical and mental strength and endurance. Here are five of the planet's most extreme sporting contests.

1 MONGOL DERBY
This 621-mile (1,000 km) endurance horse race is run on the steppe (plains) of Mongolia. Over the 7-day race, riders change horses every 25 miles (40 km).

2 VENDÉE GLOBE
This is the world's only nonstop, single-handed, around-the-world sailing race. Competitors are not allowed any assistance during the 25,000-mile (40,233 km) race.

3 IDITAROD TRAIL
In this 30-day race across Alaska, contenders trek, cycle, ski, or sled over 994 miles (1,600 km) of snow and ice. Sometimes, if conditions are especially harsh, there are no finishers!

4 BARKLEY MARATHONS
Held in the Frozen Head State Park in Tennessee, runners have only 60 hours to finish five 20-mile (32-km) stages. The routes are unmarked, and in most years, nobody completes all five stages.

5 TOUR DE FRANCE
One of the world's most grueling cycling races, the *Tour de France* (below) covers a distance of about 2,235 miles (3,600 km) in 21 stages over three weeks.

Telling stories

AROUND **4 MILLION BOOKS** ARE **PUBLISHED** WORLDWIDE **EVERY YEAR!**

Literature is writing that is valuable to people and their communities. It tells stories and offers insight into the world and other people. Literature lasts long after the writer's lifetime, often because it has themes that we can all still relate to.

TREASURE TROVE

In many countries, libraries are valued as places to discover literature, usually for free! This image is of the *Stadsbiblioteket* (public library) in Stockholm, Sweden. It holds around 4.4 million items, including printed books, CDs, and audio books.

Biography
Someone's life story. If it is written by that person, it's called an autobiography.

Fiction
This describes novels or short stories about imaginary events and people.

Drama
Stories written to be performed by actors on stage, radio, television, or film.

Myth and legend
Tales handed down through time of heroic figures, daring deeds, or magical events.

Poetry
Writing that uses vivid language to convey feelings. It often uses rhyme and rhythm.

TYPES OF LITERATURE

The different kinds of literature are called genres. Each genre has its own characteristics and style. Most works of literature fall into one of five categories.

FIRST AUTHOR

Published around 4,700 years ago, *The Teachings of Ptahhotep* is the earliest book we know about. The author, Ptahhotep, was an official at the court of Egypt's pharaoh, Izezi. However, no copy of his masterpiece has survived!

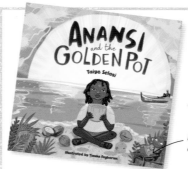

FOLK FABLES

Most cultures have their own folk and fairy tales—entertaining, exciting stories that teach important life lessons. Traditionally, these stories were spoken aloud and passed on to each new generation.

In West African folklore, Anansi is a cunning, creative, storytelling spider.

THE **BESTSELLING NOVEL** EVER IS *DON QUIXOTE* BY CERVANTES, WHICH HAS SOLD **500 MILLION COPIES!**

WORDS AND PICTURES

Comic books and graphic novels combine a series of illustrations, text, and speech bubbles to tell a story. Comic books come in installments, often weekly, whereas a graphic novel tells the whole story in book form.

Images tell the story, with text kept to a minimum.

Sound effects add drama to the story.

PLAY TIME!

From ancient times, drama has been one of the most popular forms of literature. In 16th-century London, plays by William Shakespeare were performed at the Globe Theatre (left). His works are still thought of as among the greatest works of literature ever.

The "hut" was a hidden space used for effects such as a ghostly voice.

Actors entered through doors in the back wall.

"Groundlings" paid a penny to stand and watch.

IN **SHAKESPEARE'S** TIME, IT WAS **ILLEGAL** FOR **WOMEN** TO BE **ACTORS!**

Amazing art

Almost as soon as there were humans, there was art. From stenciling their hands on prehistoric cave walls to making animations on a tablet, artists have continually looked for new and creative ways to express themselves.

The body is made from polyester resin.

Abstract shapes and recognizable bird features make up the form of an imaginary creature.

Strands of metal attach to the bird's body and coil to form a stable base.

Big Bird (1982)
Niki de Saint-Phalle

THE **MONA LISA** IN THE LOUVRE MUSEUM, PARIS, IS SEEN BY **10 MILLION VISITORS** A YEAR!

WAYS TO CREATE

Artists make their work using a vast range of techniques, media, and materials. Some artists work in traditional ways while others look for different or unusual methods and tools. Art can be made in 2-D, such as drawings, in 3-D, like sculptures, and digitally, such as film or animation.

Painting and drawing

Printmaking

Sculpture

Textiles

Digital animation

Photography

TAKING PART IN ART

Art can bring people together. Community art projects often see professional artists team up with local people to brighten up a space and help them express their own creativity.

Wall art project in Cape Town, South Africa

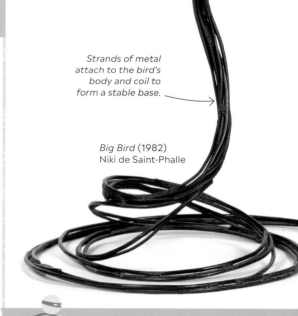

REMBRANDT'S PORTRAIT OF **JACOB DE GHEYN** HAS BEEN **STOLEN** AND **FOUND AGAIN** FOUR TIMES!

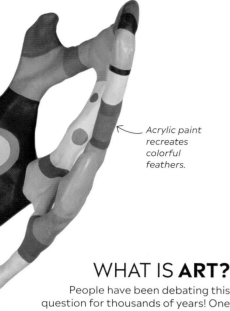

Acrylic paint recreates colorful feathers.

WHAT IS **ART?**

People have been debating this question for thousands of years! One definition is that art is an expression of an idea or feeling through a visual medium. In this sculpture, artist Niki de Saint-Phalle has combined color, shape, texture, and pattern to convey her playful interpretation of a bird.

Figurative
Also called representational art, this shows people, places, or things in a familiar and realistic way.

Sarumaru Dayu (1839)
Katsushika Hokusai

Abstract
This art doesn't try to be realistic. Instead shapes, colors, and marks convey an idea or feeling.

Artistic Architectonics (1916)
Lyubov Sergeevna Popova

Conceptual
Here, the idea is more important than materials or techniques. Some works are designed so viewers can participate.

The weather project (2003)
Olafur Eliasson

TYPES OF **ART**

Art can be made in all kinds of ways and in many styles, but most artists approach their work in one of three ways.

THE ART OF **CRAFT**

The design of everyday objects that turns them into works of art is sometimes called decorative art. Pottery, jewelry, glasswork, embroidery, and weaving are examples of decorative arts. This embroidered throw was made by craftspeople on the floating Uros Islands of Lake Titicaca, Peru.

Mythical creatures form the design.

PUBLIC **DISPLAYS**

Some artworks are made to be experienced in the outside world, not in galleries or museums. Many of these are large-scale and created for a specific place. Some artists design works that encourage people to touch or interact with them.

This giant vegetable sculpture sits on a pier in Naoshima, Japan.

Hunting with falcons was a popular royal pastime.

In Mughal portraits, sitters were painted in profile to signify their nobility.

PAINTING **PEOPLE**

A portrait has a person as its subject—before photography, it was the only way to record what someone looked like. Famous or powerful people often commissioned portraits of themselves or their families to claim their place in history or show how important they were. This 18th-century portrait is of the Mughal Emperor, Muhammad Shah.

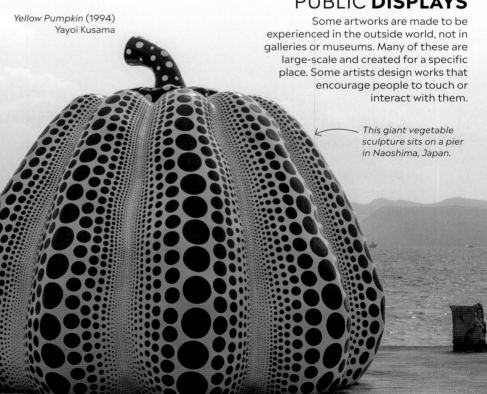

Yellow Pumpkin (1994)
Yayoi Kusama

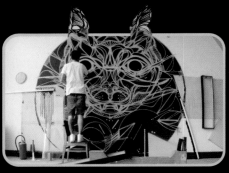

Dzia is a Belgian street artist whose unique wall paintings of animals can be seen in cities worldwide, including in China, Norway, France, and the US.

Ask a...
STREET ARTIST

Q How did you become an artist?

A I started drawing and painting when I was really young. My mom and dad, who were both very creative, encouraged me, and that motivated me even more. So I was born into being creative and went from there!

Q Why did you choose to paint on walls?

A I loved graffiti as a teenager, so after studying fine art at the Royal Academy of Antwerp, I decided I wanted to create artworks that were easy to access and had a positive impact on communities and environments. I wanted my artworks to be on the streets so people could enjoy them without going to galleries or art shows. I wanted to surprise people when they came across my work. Murals are there for everyone to discover—you just have to look for them!

Q Do you need special equipment?

A I mostly use spray paint and markers because they are fast-drying and easy to carry around. I also use mural paint, rollers, and brushes for backgrounds. I wear a safety harness for working on ladders, scaffolding, or cherrypickers, and a mask and gloves for protection from the paints.

Q How do you know where to start?

A I start with the background, from top to bottom, then I paint in the color areas. I finish by adding the black lines and highlights. I don't sketch too much in advance as I prefer to create the artwork on the spot. For me, it's easy to start but much more difficult to know when to stop!

Q What happens if you make a mistake?

A I just paint over it and try again. It's all part of the process and not a big deal!

Q Do you have a dream project?

A I would like to convert a factory building and create a beautiful gallery and studio to show my artworks, and for me to paint, create, breathe, eat, sleep—and repeat!

URBAN
NATURE

Dzia's mission is to inspire respect and wonder for the wildlife he loves, and to give animals their own place in urban settings. This hunting lynx is a detail of a painting created for an arts festival in the city of Saint-Dié-des-Vosges, France.

WHY WE DANCE

People dance for all kinds of reasons—or sometimes we do it simply to feel good!

Cultural identity
Folk dances, from the Polish mazurka to the Irish jig, express cultural or national pride.

Telling stories
Ballet is one type of dance in which traditional folk tales or myths are acted out.

Expressing faith
Religious dance, such as Islamic sufi whirling, help people feel closer to God.

Competition
Some dance forms, such as ballroom, can be professional sports.

Celebration
Dancing is key to many family or social events, such as weddings.

IN 2018, **BREAK DANCING** MADE ITS **DEBUT** AT THE **YOUTH OLYMPICS!**

FEELING **GOOD**

Science has confirmed what people have always known—that dance is good for us physically, mentally, and emotionally. Therapists use dance to help people recover from injury, or live with disabilities. It helps older people stay fit and may even help prevent dementia.

Costumes show off a dancer's grace while allowing free movement.

In the arabesque pose, one leg is lifted straight up behind the dancer.

BEAUTIFUL **BALLET**

One of the most graceful forms of classical dance, ballet is also one of the most physically demanding. Professional dancers start young and work hard to reach the highest levels of artistry.

Pointe shoe is reinforced so the dancer can balance on tiptoe.

SPORTING STEPS

In rugby, some teams do a prematch war dance to intimidate the opposition. Here, the Samoan national team is performing the traditional *Manu Siva Tau* dance.

THE **FIRST EVER BALLET** WAS PERFORMED IN 1581 FOR THE **QUEEN** OF **FRANCE!**

MAKING **MOVES**

Choreography is the art of creating dance moves and arranging them in a sequence. In Bollywood dance, dancers perform carefully choreographed steps and intricate hand gestures.

Dramatic
dance

Dancing might be the oldest art form—and there are as many ways to dance as there are humans. You can do it alone, with a partner, or in groups, and moves can be set down or made up on the spot. All you need to get moving is music, or even just a beat!

THE MASKED **ZAOULI DANCES** OF **CÔTE D'IVOIRE** ARE SO COMPLEX IT TAKES **SEVEN YEARS** TO LEARN **ONE DANCE!**

SOCIAL **SHOWTIME**

Some dances captivate a generation—even the waltz was once a craze! In recent years, social media has led to many short-lived, viral crazes, with millions of people joining in and uploading videos of their performances.

Performance
Seen mainly in musical theater and movies, this form includes tap, modern dance, and jazz (right).

Street
Street dances such as break dancing spring up spontaneously in response to new types of music.

TYPES OF DANCE

Worldwide, there are many different kinds of dance, old and new. Most dance forms fall into one of these four categories.

Folk
Often performed in traditional dress like this Ukrainian *Hopak*, folk dance is a fun way for people to keep their customs and culture alive.

Classical
Thai dance, like all classical forms, has strictly set movements. Performers are highly skilled.

Harmony
Different notes played together to make one sound

Melody
Pitch (how high or low notes are) and the order notes are played

Rhythm
How long notes are and the pattern in which they are played

WHAT IS **MUSIC?**

Music is made up of sounds, but what makes it different from the sound of reading aloud or of rainfall is that the sounds are organized and shaped by a musician to produce melody (or tune), harmony, and rhythm.

"IDOL," A MUSIC VIDEO BY BTS, WAS DOWNLOADED 45 MILLION TIMES IN ITS FIRST 24 HOURS!

MAKING **MUSIC**

There are many different musical instruments, but most can be put into one of five groups, depending on how they make their sound.

Sitar

Strings
The sound of stringed instruments is made by plucking the strings or moving a bow over them.

Electric piano

Keyboards
Pressing keys makes sounds either by hitting strings or by sending digital signals.

Magical **music**

Whether it is joining in the singing of a rousing anthem, hearing a tune that brings back happy memories, or simply strumming a guitar for fun, music is one of the most powerful ways we have to express our feelings and to connect to others.

THE BESTSELLING BAND EVER IS THE BEATLES, WITH OVER 300 MILLION RECORDS SOLD!

MUSICAL **MODES**

There is an incredible range of musical styles, and new types are constantly springing up or evolving from existing genres. Here are just a few of the most popular styles around the world.

Pop
Pop is short for popular—so pop is music that most people are listening to and buying at any time!

Pop often features vocal performances.

Cello

Jazz
A highly creative form, jazz was created by African American musicians in the early 20th century.

Classical
This type of music is written to be performed by trained musicians in a concert setting.

The trumpet is a key instrument in jazz.

Percussion
These instruments make sounds when they are struck, shaken, or clashed.

Drum

Woodwind
Sound is made by blowing through a hole in a hollow tube, making the air inside it vibrate.

Panpipes

Brass
These instruments are metal tubes that make sounds from vibrations of the player's lips against a mouthpiece.

Tuba

SING OUT

Singing plays a key part in many faiths. Gospel music is a joyful style that was first adopted by Black churchgoers in the US and has spread worldwide. South Africa's Soweto Gospel Choir (shown left) has won international awards for its high-energy performances and unique harmonies.

TAKING **NOTES**

Writing music down is helpful if you want others to play your compositions. The most common way of writing music was invented by monks in the 10th century. It uses dots and symbols on a five-line framework called a staff.

Time signature shows the rhythm.

The shape and color of the note shows how long to play it.

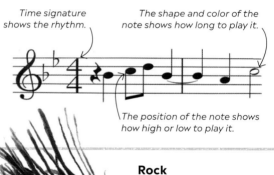

The position of the note shows how high or low to play it.

Fingerhole

ANCIENT TUNES!

Music is almost as old as humans. This fragment of a flute, made from the thigh bone of a bear, was found in a cave in Slovenia. It is thought to be more than 45,000 years old!

Violin is made from scrap metal and wood.

JUNKYARD HARMONY

You can play a tune on almost anything! The instruments played by the children of Paraguay's Recycled Orchestra are made out of objects salvaged from a large landfill site outside the country's capital, Asunción.

Rock
Rock is loud, with strong bass or drum rhythms and punchy lyrics (words).

Electric guitar is essential to the rock sound.

Folk
Many countries and cultures have their own unique style of music and dance, known as folk music.

Mongolian musician playing a type of lute.

Conga drum

Soul
This emotional, powerful genre grew out of two other Black music styles, gospel and blues.

Salsa
Cuba's best-known music style features rhythmic beats, perfect for dancing.

MUSICAL INSTRUMENT

Is that a trumpet, a trombone, or a triangle? Cover up the answers and see how many of these musical instruments you can identify. Then spot the odd one out!

1 Harmonica
2 Theremin
3 Violin and bow
4 DJ mixing deck
5 Congolese drum
6 Maracas
7 Trombone
8 Grand piano
9 Indian rattle drum

10 Bass guitar	19 Indian *tabla* drum	28 Ocarina	36 Chinese *erhu* fiddle
11 Cuban conga drum	20 Rock music drum kit	29 Cello and bow	37 Cuban claves
12 Japanese *koto*	21 Saxophone	30 Indonesian *angklung*	38 Accordion
13 Tuba	22 Acoustic guitar	31 Indian *dholak* drum	39 Harp
14 Xylophone	23 Mandolin	32 Korean *daegeum* flute	40 Australian Aboriginal
15 South American panpipes	24 French horn	33 West African	didgeridoo
16 Tam-tam (gong)	25 Tambourine	*djembe* drum	
17 Finger cymbals	26 Bagpipes	34 Trumpet	
18 Flute	27 Triangle	35 Indian *veena*	

The odd one out is the DJ mixing deck (4), which plays back music, but doesn't create musical notes.

City living

More than half of the planet—4.4 billion people—live in a city. This is a huge change compared to a century ago, when only 10 percent of us were city dwellers. The number of cities is still rising, and they are larger and more crowded than ever before.

MEGA**CITIES**

A city of 10 million or more people is classed as a megacity. In 1950, New York City was the only one but today there are more than 40. Here are the world's top five biggest cities.

Tokyo's Shibuya pedestrian crossing is the busiest in the world—up to 3,000 people cross the road at a time!

1 **Tokyo, Japan** 37.5 million

2 **Delhi, India** 29.4 million

3 **Shanghai, China** 26.3 million

4 **Sao Paulo, Brazil** 21.8 million

5 **Mexico City, Mexico** 21.6 million

WHAT IS **A CITY?**

A city is more than an extra-large town. It offers more facilities and often has zones for different purposes such as shopping, business, housing, and entertainment.

Government center
The city where a country's government is located is called a capital city.

Large population
A city provides homes, jobs, and education for thousands, or even millions of people.

Specialist services
Major hospitals, libraries, and cultural centers are some of the services cities offer.

IN COPENHAGEN, DENMARK, THERE ARE **FIVE BIKES** FOR **EVERY CAR** ON THE ROAD!

CHILLY CITY

Yakutsk in Siberia is the world's coldest city. It sits on permafrost (ground that is frozen all year round), so buildings have to be built on stilts or piles. In winter, the average temperature is –34.6°F (–37°C), and can go as low as –83.9°F (–64.4°C)!

URBAN **GREENERY**

Many cities are finding new ways to make urban life more sustainable and healthier. This rooftop city farm in Rotterdam, Netherlands, is one of the largest in Europe. The farm supplies organic vegetables, fruits, herbs, and honey to local stores and hotels.

IT TAKES **THREE MONTHS** TO CLEAN ALL **24,348 WINDOWS** OF THE **BURJ KHALIFA** BUILDING!

By 2007, half of the world was living in a city.

From 1960, the speed of the shift from rural to urban living increased.

URBAN POPULATION (in billions)

5
4
3
2
1

1920   1960   2000   2040

YEARS

MOVING TO **THE CITY**

For thousands of years, most people lived in the countryside and worked on farms. Today, more and more people are living in cities and towns. By 2050, it is expected that more than two-thirds of the world's people will live in urban areas.

The Burj Khalifa building is the world's tallest building at 2,717 ft (828 m).

The 57 elevators travel at 33 ft (10 m) per second!

There are 206 floors—more than any other building.

It is 10°F (6°C) warmer at the bottom of the building than at the top!

BUILDING **UPWARD**

When a city cannot grow outward, often because it is hemmed in by sea or mountains, the only way is up! Tall buildings make maximum use of every square foot of a city's space. However, Dubai's soaring skyscrapers were built for a different purpose— to put it on the map as one of the world's most modern, exciting destinations for tourists and businesses alike.

THE FUTURE OF **FLIGHT!**

Flying produces around 2 percent of the world's greenhouse gases (see pages 88–89), but a greener future may be possible. In 2009, this motor glider made the world's first crewed flight powered solely by electricity. Some predict electric planes could be common by 2035.

The propeller is powered by electricity generated from hydrogen stored under the wings.

On the move

For anything longer than the shortest trip, people use vehicles to get from one place to another. Buses, bicycles, and boats all form part of a transportation network that stretches around the entire world and is getting bigger all the time.

RAIL RECORD

The world's longest-ever passenger train snakes through the Swiss Alps on a special journey to mark the 175th anniversary of Switzerland's first railroad. In total, 25 electric locomotives, each pulling four train cars, made up the 1.2-mile (1.93 km) long train.

SELF-DRIVING CARS

Autonomous, or self-driving, vehicles use onboard sensors to scan their environment and maneuver safely. A human driver is still required for everything more than maintaining a steady speed, or staying in lane, but future advances may allow the cars to drive without any human input.

CLEANER TRANSPORTATION

Not every vehicle needs an engine. Some are people powered! Bicycles are a cheap and green way to travel short distances, making them perfect for cities. In some places, like Utrecht in the Netherlands, they are even the main means of transportation.

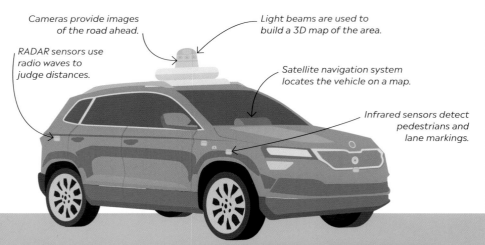

Cameras provide images of the road ahead.

Light beams are used to build a 3D map of the area.

RADAR sensors use radio waves to judge distances.

Satellite navigation system locates the vehicle on a map.

Infrared sensors detect pedestrians and lane markings.

THE WORLD'S LARGEST **RAIL NETWORK** IS IN THE **USA**. IT'S LONG ENOUGH TO GO **AROUND THE EQUATOR THREE TIMES!**

FAST FERRIES

Countries with long coastlines or a lot of islands rely on ferries as part of their transportation network. This ferry is called a trimaran. Its hull is divided into three so it can flow through the water swiftly and easily.

NORWAY HAS **81** **ELECTRIC VEHICLE CHARGERS** FOR EVERY **1,000** RESIDENTS!

ENERGY EFFICIENT?

The more energy a motor vehicle requires, the more of the greenhouse gases that accelerate climate change it produces. This chart shows how much energy (measured in kilowatt hours) different vehicles take to move a single passenger 0.6 miles (1 km). Those that carry more passengers are more efficient.

Bus	0.15 kWh
Train	0.31 kWh
Motorcycle	0.45 kWh
International flight	0.57 kWh
Car	0.83 kWh

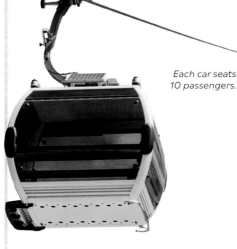

Each car seats 10 passengers.

COMMUTING ON CABLES

The neighboring cities of La Paz and El Alto in Bolivia are separated by a 1,300 ft (400 m) high hill. To make it easier to travel between them, a cable car line opened in 2014. The network has since expanded to include 7 lines, with cars departing every 12 seconds.

Captain Darryl Elliott flew commercial passenger aircraft across Europe in a career lasting 25 years. In total, he has flown 15,000 hours—that's 20 months in the air!

AIRLINE PILOT

Q How much do you fly the plane and how much is autopilot?

A Usually the pilot takes off and flies the airplane up to about 1,000 ft, then engages the autopilot. We then select altitudes (how high the plane is flying) and headings (the direction) by turning knobs on a control panel. The pilot usually lands the plane manually, but most modern airliners are capable of landing automatically when the pilot can't see the runway due to fog or low cloud.

Q How do you know where you are going?

A Before every flight, our Operations Department plans the best route. We as pilots then load the route into our onboard computers, and then much like a car's satnav, we have a map display that shows our position on that route.

Q How do you avoid all the other planes?

A Air Traffic Controllers on the ground give us altitudes and headings to fly to keep safe distances from other airplanes. Backing this up is a system where computers on our aircraft talk to all other nearby aircraft. If the computers calculate anything unsafe, they will instruct the pilot what to do to avoid it.

Q Have you ever flown in a storm?

A The simple answer is no! Pilots avoid storms by many miles. We have many ways to do this, from checking weather forecasts before we go flying, to onboard weather warning systems. Aircraft do, very rarely, get struck by lightning, but it's perfectly safe—aircraft designers spend many hours testing aircraft systems to withstand this sort of thing.

Q What's the view like?

A Pilots get to see fantastic sunrises and sunsets. When we fly to Iceland, we get to see the Northern Lights. In the months of June and July around midnight, we have the great privilege to see a phenomenon in the night skies called noctilucent clouds—wispy, white shining clouds high in the atmosphere.

FLIGHT CONTROL

On the flight deck of a passenger jet are hundreds of different instruments, as well as displays to show everything from the aircraft's altitude and speed to the temperature in the cabin, electrical power, and water and toilet waste quantities. There are always two pilots on big airliners. One flies the aircraft while the other monitors him or her and operates the radios, the wing flaps, and landing gear. Then on the next flight, the roles are reversed.

MONEY **MAKING**

Paper money is printed using special technology to add anti-counterfeit features such as holograms to the notes. In 2021, the US Bureau of Engraving and Printing printed 2.37 billion 100-dollar notes.

TYPES OF **MONEY**

The way we use money has changed a lot in the 21st century. For centuries, people mainly used cash, but today, most money changes hands via cashless payment methods.

Cash
This is the money in your pocket—coins and notes. Cash is designed to be durable and easy to use.

Tokens
Items such as amusement park tokens stand in for money and are used to obtain certain things or in specific places.

Cashless payment
A card or phone connects to a bank account so that money is moved from the buyer's account into the seller's.

The real ship in the Viking Ship Museum, Oslo, Norway

The Gokstad Viking ship is depicted on the 100-krone note.

NATIONAL PRIDE

Many countries put national leaders or famous figures on their currency—but Norway's notes celebrate its strong links with the sea. Different-value banknotes show a lighthouse, cod and herring, crashing waves, and a preserved Viking longship.

THE WORLD'S **LARGEST BANKNOTE**, AT 8.6 x 14.5 IN (22 x 37 CM), IS THE **MALAYSIAN 600 RINGGIT NOTE!**

Money matters

Whether you have lots or not enough, money affects all our lives. Money is a purely human invention and its set value means that it's worth the same to everyone who uses it. This is what makes it possible for us to buy or sell goods anywhere in the world.

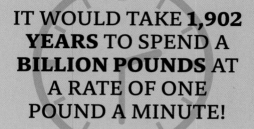

IT WOULD TAKE 1,902 YEARS TO SPEND A BILLION POUNDS AT A RATE OF ONE POUND A MINUTE!

SHELLING OUT

Before the invention of coins and notes, some ancient civilizations, including China, started using cowrie shells as money from around 1200 BCE. Shells are used today by communities in the Solomon Islands in the Pacific Ocean.

Exchangeable
When we buy something, we exchange an agreed sum of money for the thing we want.

Storable
Money can be saved, in a savings account or at home, until you want to spend it.

A TYPICAL UK £5 NOTE CHANGES HANDS 138 TIMES IN ONE YEAR!

Measurable
Money can be used to show something's value or to compare its value to something else.

WHAT IS **MONEY?**

Money is really three things in one: we use it to get what we need from sellers, we can store it for future use, and we can use it to measure how much a thing is worth.

 $
Dollar (US)
$2.9 trillion

€
Euro (EU)
$1.1 trillion

¥
Yen (Japan)
$554 billion

£
Pound (UK)
$422 billion

TOP **CURRENCIES**

Companies, investors, and traders often find it easier to do business in currencies different from the one in their home country. This list shows the world's top four currencies—the figures in US dollars show how much of them are traded every day!

The first cryptocurrency was Bitcoin, created in 2009.

RECYCLED CASH

When banknotes get old, worn, and torn, they have to be retired and disposed of safely. US dollar bills are made of biodegradable cotton and linen, so the notes are shredded, made into blocks, and used as compost on farms.

A 2.2 lb (1 kg) block contains 100,000 notes.

DIGITAL CURRENCY

Cryptocurrencies use cryptography (computer code breaking) to make money transactions easy and secure. Users don't need a bank account and can send or receive money from anywhere in the world without having to convert it into local currency.

Digital world

In the last two decades, almost every aspect of our lives has been transformed by digital technology. And things are set to change even more, as advances in artifical intelligence (AI) are sending the digital revolution into overdrive.

ESPORTS **EVENTS**

Competitive video gaming, or eSports, is a massive spectator sport, with millions of fans watching professional matches streamed online. Tournaments such as this 2022 event in Atlanta, USA, also attract huge live audiences.

More than 20,000 fans pack the arena to follow the action.

SMARTPHONE **STATS**

Smartphone technology means we can put a palm-sized computer in our pocket wherever we go. Here are the six activities that account for the most traffic on mobile phone networks.

 1 Streaming video and movies

 2 Social networking

 3 Messaging

 4 Web browsing

 5 Shopping

 6 Gaming

CONTENT **CREATION**

Digital technology has made it easy for anyone with a phone and something to say to upload content to social media. Some content creators make money by making their content pay-per-view, or attracting advertisements. Others do it just for fun and to collect "likes"!

As the headset user moves her head, she looks around the virtual world.

Sensors in controllers enable the user to interact with objects she "sees".

ENTER THE **METAVERSE**

The internet is moving from something we look at, to a 3D immersive world – the metaverse. Augmented reality (AR) enables users to interact with a virtual environment in the same way that they would if they were there in real life.

Fans view the game on huge, high-definition screens.

Competitors are seated in a circle under the big screens.

SOCIAL **SENSATIONS**

Here are the six most popular social media apps. The fastest growing is TikTok, which is especially popular with users under the age of 19.

1 **Facebook**   2.9 billion users

2 **YouTube**   2.5 billion users

3 **WhatsApp**   2 billion users

4 **Instagram**   2 billion users

5 **WeChat**   1.3 billion users

6 **TikTok**   1 billion users

VIRAL **SUPERSTAR!**

One of the first internet celebrities was a cat in the US called Tardar Sauce, known to her millions of fans as Grumpy Cat. Her distinctive "sad" face gained her millions of followers on social media before her fame spread to TV, books, and even a movie.

MEGA **MINECRAFT!**

The game that's most popular with children is 3-D construction game Minecraft. First released in 2011, Minecraft has sold 238 million copies and more than 176 million people worldwide regularly play!

SMART **HOMES**

Many household devices can be connected to the internet so they can share their data. With the use of apps, these devices can be controlled remotely by voice or via touch screen. For example, you can ask a smart speaker to play your favorite music or, when you're not at home, remotely operate a feeder to dispense a treat to your pet!

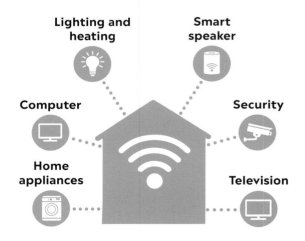

Lighting and heating

Smart speaker

Computer

Security

Home appliances

Television

THE **WORLD'S 22 RICHEST MEN** HAVE **MORE MONEY** THAN ALL THE **WOMEN IN AFRICA.**

ECONOMIC **INJUSTICE**

The divide between rich and poor is clear in the contrast between modern skyscrapers and makeshift shelters without sanitation in Jakarta, Indonesia. The victims of economic inequality are some of the world's most vulnerable people, yet they have the fewest means and opportunities to fight injustice.

LGBTQ+ **LIBERATION**

Lesbian, Gay, Bisexual, Transgender, and Queer (LGBTQ+) people have rights in many countries but are still fighting discrimination. The original rainbow flag was designed in 1978 as a symbol of hope. Each stripe had a different meaning.

FEMALE **EQUALITY**

Today, women are head of state or government in 31 countries, and make up just over one-quarter of lawmakers worldwide. There is a long way to go to equal representation. Here is a list of firsts and the dates they were achieved.

1893
New Zealand becomes the first country where women can vote.

1907
The first women are elected to a country's parliament, in Finland.

1917
Alexandra Kollontai is appointed a USSR government minister.

1960
In Sri Lanka, Sirimavo Bandaranaike is elected as head of government.

PEOPLE **POWER**

If those in power don't recognize the need for change, the people can try to make the agenda and call for action. Protests take many forms, from refusing to buy certain products to demonstrating in the street. This march was organized by the anti-racist movement Black Lives Matter.

Changing
the world

INDIGENOUS **PROTEST**

Indigenous people lead the way in campaigning to protect the natural environment against harmful policies. This photo shows a group in the Philippines protesting against the government's plan to build a new dam that would flood their land.

In many ways, our society is fairer than it was in the past, but positive change happens only when people take a stand. Despite the progress that has been made, there is still work to do to make the world a better place.

70% OF THE WORLD'S **476 MILLION** INDIGENOUS PEOPLE **LIVE IN ASIA!**

VOTE FOR **CHANGE**

In democratic countries, people have the right to vote for a government they hope will make the changes they want to see. The world's largest democracy is India, and counting every vote is a huge job. In some rural areas, voting machines have to be transported by elephant.

INDIA HAS AROUND **912 MILLION** VOTERS. THAT'S ALMOST **THREE TIMES THE** POPULATION OF **THE US!**

Glossary

abolitionist
A person campaigning for the end of slavery, especially relating to the Transatlantic trade and forced labor of enslaved people of African descent in the Americas in the 18th and 19th centuries.

accretion disc
A flattened ring of gas and other matter that forms around a massive object in space and orbits it at very high speed.

agnostic
A person who believes that it is not possible to know whether a god or gods exist.

AI (Artificial Intelligence)
Computer systems designed to think and learn in order to perform tasks typically requiring human intelligence. AI is also the branch of computer science that develops these systems.

alchemist
A person who practices alchemy: a medieval practice combining philosophy and early ideas of chemical science with the aim of turning base metals into gold and creating a substance to make humans immortal.

algae
Plantlike organisms that make food using energy from sunlight.

algorithm
A set of step-by-step instructions for a computer that describe how to perform a task. These steps are used to solve a problem or reach a result.

alloy
A mixture of two or more metals, or of a metal and a nonmetal.

ambush
A form of hunting used by many predators; a surprise attack by a hidden individual or group; a tactic used in warfare.

ancestor
A person who lived before us, in a direct line of descent.

aorta
The main artery that carries blood away from the heart to the rest of the body. It feeds almost all other arteries.

Aotearoa
The native name for New Zealand, meaning "Land of the Long White Cloud." The Indigenous Māori began using this name long before Europeans arrived.

aquatic
Living in water all or most of the time.

Arabia
Old term for the Arabian Peninsula: a large area in southwest Asia, surrounded by sea on three sides. It includes Saudi Arabia and several other countries.

archaeology
The study of the human past by analyzing remains left behind by previous generations; often through digging up objects, buildings, and bones.

asteroid
A small, rocky object that orbits the sun. It may contain metals such as nickel and iron.

atheist
A person who believes that no god exists.

atmosphere
The layer of gases that surround Earth and some other planets. Earth's contains nitrogen, oxygen, and other gases.

atom
The smallest unit of an element. The number of protons in the atom determine which element it is.

atomic bomb
An explosive device invented in the 1940s that releases energy by splitting atoms. Thousands of times more powerful than any previous weapon, a single bomb could destroy an entire city.

aurora
Patterns of light that appear near the poles of some planets. Solar wind particles are trapped by a planet's magnetic field and drawn into its atmosphere, where they collide with atoms, producing light.

bacteria
Microscopic organisms with a simple, single-celled form. There are billions of bacteria in our bodies and in the world around us, some good, some harmful.

biodegradable
Able to be broken down by natural processes in the environment.

biodiversity
The variety of all living things, on Earth or in a particular area, measured by the number of different species present.

black hole
An object in space with such strong gravitational pull that nothing, not even light, escapes.

blood clot
A knot of blood cells that have become solid. Clotting stops you from bleeding when cut.

book lungs
A form of lungs in which air is drawn through a layer of thin, stacked plates (like the pages of a half-open book) to exchange oxygen from the air for carbon dioxide from the blood.

botanist
A plant expert; a scientist who specializes in plant life.

bract
A specialized leaf with a single flower growing from the joint between bract and plant stem or branch.

brood
To sit on or hatch eggs; a family of young birds or other animals all born together.

bulbous
Unusually large and round, sometimes bulb-shaped.

buoy
A floating object that signals to ships or collects scientific information, for example, weather measurements.

cacao bean
The seed of the cacao tree, from which chocolate is made. It can also be eaten raw.

canopy
The main layer of overlapping tree branches in a forest.

caravan
A group of people traveling together, usually overland; often applied to traders.

carnivore
An animal that feeds on meat.

carrion
The rotting flesh of a dead animal, food for scavengers.

cartilage
A tough, flexible type of connective tissue that helps support the body and covers the ends of bones and joints.

cartilaginous fish
Fish with skeletons made not of bone but of cartilage.

cherrypicker
Equipment with a large basket mounted on an extendable arm, used to raise workers to high places that are difficult to reach, such as power lines or trees.

civil war
Conflict between two or more groups within the same country.

civilian
A person not in the armed forces or the police.

civilization
Culture and way of life of people living together in an organized and developed society.

climate change
Long-term shifts in the usual weather patterns of the Earth or a particular area. Often refers to the severe effects caused by human actions.

cold-blooded
Animals whose body temperature is the same as that of the environment. They cannot self-regulate that temperature.

colonization
Sending settlers to establish a colony in another country, often taking control over the people already living there and exploiting the natural resources. Many countries still suffer the effects of past colonization.

comet
An object made of dust and ice that travels around the sun in an elliptical orbit. As it nears the sun, the ice starts to vaporize, creating a tail of dust and gas.

communism
A political belief in a society based on common ownership of resources.

compound
A chemical substance in which two or more different elements are bonded together.

connective tissue
A type of tissue that supports and protects other tissues and organs in the body.

cosmonaut
The English term to describe a Russian astronaut.

Cretaceous
The period of Earth's geological history between 145 and 66 million years ago. The last period of the dinosaur eras.

crevasse
A deep, open crack in ice or rock.

crustaceans
A group of invertebrates with boneless bodies, armored shells, and jointed limbs.

data
Information that can be analyzed, often in the form of facts or statistics; in computing, information that can be processed by a computer.

decomposer
Bacteria, fungi, and other organisms that break down dead organisms in a process called decomposition or rotting.

democracy
A political system in which people have power to control their government, usually by electing politicians to represent their views.

dentine
Hard, bonelike material that shapes a tooth and forms its root.

dictator
A leader who rules a country alone, with no restrictions on the extent of their power.

domestication
The taming of wild animals to make them useful to humans.

dorsal fin
A fin on the back or top of a fish or aquatic mammal, which acts as a stabilizer.

drag
The resistance formed when an object pushes through a gas or liquid, such as air or water. Drag slows an object down.

dune
A large mound of sand, blown into place by the wind.

dwarf planet
A planet big enough to become spherical but much smaller than a full planet.

dynasty
A royal family ruling a country or empire for several generations.

eardrum
A structure in the middle ear, which vibrates in response to sound waves and helps transmit these to the brain.

electromagnetic radiation
Energy waves that can travel through space and matter. Types include visible light, X-rays, and infrared radiation.

electron
One of the tiny particles inside an atom. It has a negative electric charge. Moving electrons carry electricity.

element
A simple substance made of atoms that are all the same kind.

elliptical
Shaped like a regular oval—taking the form of a stretched, or elongated circle.

embryo
An unborn animal or plant in the very early stages of development.

empire
A group of different lands or peoples under the rule of a single person or government.

enamel
A hard, glossy substance that covers the visible part of a tooth and the scaly skin of a shark. It is the hardest substance in the human body.

enzyme
A substance that causes or speeds up a chemical reaction in a living organism.

equality
Ensuring that every person is fairly treated and has an equal opportunity to make the most of their lives and talents.

equation
A mathematical statement that two amounts are equal. It can be used to analyze data.

evaporation
The process by which a liquid turns into a gas, often due to an increase in temperature.

evolution
The process of gradual change in living things, including humans, over many generations.

exoskeleton
A hard outer layer that supports and protects soft-bodied animals without an internal skeleton. Many invertebrates have these.

extinction
The disappearance from Earth of all living members of a species.

filament
A very thin, flexible threadlike object, such as a hair or wire.

fjord
A narrow wedge of sea between high cliffs, especially in Norway.

flagellum
A long, whiplike growth from the body of an animal, often used for movement. Some animals have one, others many (plural flagella).

fossil
The remains or traces of an animal or plant from long ago, preserved in rock.

fossil fuel
Fuel burned for energy such as oil or gasoline. It is made/formed from long-dead plants or animals compressed underground over millions of years and cannot be replaced once used.

free diver
A person who dives deep underwater without the use of breathing equipment.

fungus
An organism that feeds on decaying matter and reproduces by releasing spores.

galaxy
A collection of gas, dust, and billions of stars held together by gravity.

galaxy cluster
A collection of hundreds or thousands of galaxies held together by gravity.

gamma ray
An electromagnetic energy wave that has a very short wavelength and very high energy.

gene
Units of DNA that control how cells behave and bodies grow and look. They are passed on from parents to children.

gills
An organ in fish for obtaining oxygen from water. Fish breathe using these instead of lungs.

glacier
A mass of compressed snow, turned to ice, that flows slowly downhill.

gorge
A deep, narrow valley with steep sides, usually formed by a waterfall or fast-moving river.

government
A country's system of rules and the people who make and implement them.

guild
A local association or group of people connected with a particular craft or skill, such as metal-working or weaving. It protects their interests and regulates their trade.

herbivore
An animal that feeds on plants.

hominin
A term meaning "human-like" that includes humans and our extinct ancestors.

hull
The main body of a ship: the bottom, sides, and deck.

humanist
A person who believes that humans, not gods, are responsible for human progress and well-being and that we should take action to improve our lives.

hurricane
A dangerous storm with extremely high wind and rainfall that begins over warm water then moves toward land.

hydropower
Energy derived from moving water, for example, by a water wheel to grind flour or a turbine to generate electricity.

hyphae
The thin strands that make up the mycelium, or network, of a fungus.

ice cap
A large area of frozen water that covers each of the Earth's poles.

icon
A piece of religious art: in Catholicism, a picture of Christ, his mother, or a saint.

Indigenous people
The first people to live in a particular place.

industrialization
A shift toward making products in factories using large-scale processes and heavy machinery. Also the move from a farming economy to an industrial, or factory-based, economy.

infrared
Electromagnetic radiation with wavelengths shorter than radio waves but longer than visible light. It is felt by humans as heat. Infrared is the main form of radiation emitted by many objects in space.

infrastructure
The basic features that enable a country or city to function: roads, buildings, water and power supply, communication networks, and more.

ingenious
Unusually clever and imaginative (as a solution to a problem).

invertebrate
An animal without a backbone.

iridescent
Showing luminous colors that seem to change when seen from different angles.

irrigation
A system of human-made channels or devices designed to water crops.

keratin
A tough, waterproof protein found in hair, nails, and skin.

lateral line
A row of sensory organs along the side of a fish. They detect movement, vibrations, and pressure.

lattice structure
A three-dimensional solid made up of many units arranged in a regular repeating pattern.

lava
Hot, liquid rock forced out of a volcano during an eruption.

lawmaker
A person who makes rules for a country's people to live by, such as a politician.

light-year
The distance light travels through space in one year: 5.88 trillion miles (9.46 trillion kilometers).

lime
A white mineral obtained by heating limestone. It is mixed with water to make cement to bind stones or bricks together in buildings.

limestone
A type of rock formed mostly from the crushed remains of ancient shells.

liquefy
To make or become liquid.

lord
In medieval times, a noble who owned land and had power over the people who lived there.

lymph
The liquid that flows through the lymphatic system, where it is filtered for germs and then returned to the blood.

magma
Hot, liquid rock found beneath the Earth's surface.

magnetic field
The area around a magnet or electric current where magnetic force is felt.

mass
A measure of the amount of matter in an object.

mastodon
A large, elephant-like mammal that became extinct around 11,000 years ago.

mechanization
The increased use of machines to do work that used to be done by people.

meditation
Remaining in a calm, quiet state for a period of time, often as part of religious practice. It may mean thinking deeply about a single subject, or emptying the mind completely.

meltwater
Liquid water formed when snow and ice melt.

menagerie
A collection of wild animals, usually for display.

merchant
A person who sells or trades goods for money or other goods, usually in large quantities.

Mesoamerica
A historic cultural area of present-day Mexico and Central America. Before the 16th-century Spanish invasion, Mesoamerica was home to civilizations such as the Maya and the Aztecs.

meteorologist
Someone who studies weather patterns, often in order to predict future conditions.

microgravity
Conditions of very low gravity, far from Earth or other planets, as experienced by astronauts in space.

microorganism
A creature too small to be seen without a microscope.

millennium
One thousand years (plural millennia).

mineral
A solid, inorganic (nonliving) material found in the Earth. Small amounts are found in food and drink, and some play important roles in our bodies.

mitochondrion
One of many tiny structures (mitochondria) in a living cell that release energy to power the cell's activity.

molecule
A group of atoms bonded together.

mollusks
A group of invertebrates that includes snails, clams, and squid. Most have a soft body with a hard shell, but a few, such as slugs, do not.

motor
A machine that converts electrical energy or fuel into movement.

movable type
A system of printing in which letters or words are created on individual blocks so that they can be moved into position to create a sentence.

mycelium
The network of thin strands by which a fungus grows and communicates with neighboring organisms.

Native American
Someone belonging to any of the many peoples who have lived in the Americas since before Europeans first arrived. Usually refers to the original inhabitants of the United States. Also used as an adjective for these peoples and cultures.

natural resources
Anything of value that exists independently in nature, without human intervention. What is considered valuable changes over time, but forests, lakes, oil, and even a beautiful view can all be natural resources.

nebula
A cloud of gas and dust in space.

nervous system
All the nerves in the human body, from the brain to the spinal cord to the tips of our toes. All animals except sea sponges have a nervous system.

neurology
The diagnosis and treatment of conditions and diseases of the nervous system.

neutron
One of the tiny particles in the nucleus of an atom. It has mass but no electrical charge.

neutron star
A dense collapsed star made mostly of neutrons.

nomad
A person who moves from place to place without establishing a permanent settlement.

novel
A book-length story about imaginary characters and events.

noxious
Harmful, poisonous, or very unpleasant. Usually used of substances or smells.

nuclear
Relating to the atomic nucleus. Can refer to forces within the nucleus, energy transfer from these forces, or weapons that harness this energy.

nuclear reaction
The splitting of an atom's nucleus or the fusing of two nuclei, releasing a huge amount of energy.

nucleus
In physics, the central part of an atom, composed of protons and neutrons. In biology, the control center found in most living cells.

nutrition
The balance and quantity of nutrients eaten by a person in their food and used for fuel, growth, and repair. Nutrition is also the process by which an organism uses food to support its life.

omnivore
An animal that eats both plants and meat.

opposable
A thumb or toe that can face and touch other digits on the same hand or foot. Humans and other apes have these, but so do many other species.

oral history
The collection of historical information by interviewing people about their past, or the past of their communities or cultures. Some stories have been passed on for generations yet never written down.

orbit
The path taken by one object around a heavier one due to gravity.

organelle
A tiny structure within a cell that does a specific job, such as a mitochondrion, which produces chemical energy to power the cell's reactions.

organic
Organic materials are made of carbon and other elements. All life on Earth is organic.

Ottoman Empire
An empire that extended from Turkey (Türkiye) across parts of Europe, West Asia, and North Africa between the 14th and early 20th centuries.

pack ice
A mass of ice floating in the sea, formed by many smaller pieces freezing or clustering together.

particle
An extremely small piece of matter, such as a speck of dust, part of an atom, or a photon.

pectoral fins
Paired fins located on both sides of a fish or marine mammal. In most fish, these help it steer up, down, or sideways. In rays, the flexible pectoral fins are used for movement and feeding.

pelvic fins
Paired fins located on the underside of a fish or marine mammal. They help change direction or stop.

philosopher
Someone who seeks wisdom or explores profound questions about how to live, who we are, and what really exists.

photon
The particle that makes up light. It is the fastest known particle.

photosynthesis
The process by which plants use the sun's energy to make food by converting carbon dioxide and water into oxygen and sugars in the presence of sunlight.

piston
A disc or short cylinder that fits closely within a tube and moves up and down against a liquid or gas. It is used in a steam or gas engine to move wheels.

plantation
A farm or estate on which cotton, tobacco, sugar, rice, or other crops are grown and where the workforce lives on site. Plantations were common in the Americas during the period of slavery, when enslaved people were forced to work on them.

plaque
A flat object made of metal or clay with images or writing on it, often attached to a wall.

plateau
Area of relatively flat ground, high above sea level.

pole
Each end of the Earth's axis (the straight line through the center of the Earth, from north to south, around which it spins). The two ends of a magnet are also called poles.

pollinator
Anything that carries pollen from the male anther to the female stigma of the same or another flower, helping to fertilize it. Examples include bees, bats, and wind.

pollution
The presence or release of harmful substances into the air, water, or soil. Most often refers to human-made pollution.

porous
A porous substance has many small holes in it, through which air and water can pass.

prey
An animal eaten by another animal is its prey.

protein
Vital nutrient that helps the body build new cells.

proton
One of the tiny particles in the nucleus of an atom; it has a positive charge. Different elements contain different numbers of protons.

protozoan
Microscopic, single-celled animal, which often lives inside larger animals.

pulsar
A neutron star that sends out beams of radiation as it spins.

radar
A system that detects objects by bouncing high-energy radio waves at them and measuring the reflected waves.

radiation
Waves or particles of energy that travel through space, such as radio waves, light, and heat. Nuclear radiation includes subatomic particles and fragments of atoms.

radioactive
Describes an unstable material whose nucleus may decay and emit nuclear radiation.

regenerate
Regrow part of the body. Also, to restore a natural environment or ecosystem.

renewables
Collective term for all renewable energy sources used to generate electrical power. Renewable energy is energy whose source will not run out, for example, wind and solar power. Energy made by burning fuel is called nonrenewable energy.

respiration
The process that converts glucose into energy in all living things.

Ring of Fire
The area around the edges of the Pacific Ocean, from New Zealand to Japan and Alaska to Chile, where the Pacific tectonic plate interacts with surrounding continental plates. Most of the world's volcanoes and earthquakes occur in the Ring of Fire.

rural
In or relating to the countryside and country life.

satellite
An object that orbits a larger body in space. These can be natural, such as the moon, or human-made.

sea stack
A pillar of rock left behind when the softer or more exposed rock around it has been worn away by the waves.

sediment
Small pieces of rock, sand, or mud that settle in layers, usually underwater.

segregation
A racist system in which Black people are prevented from using the same spaces and facilities as white people. Once common in the southern states of the US, as well as in South Africa, it is now outlawed but still occurs informally in some places.

seismic waves
Waves or vibrations that travel through the Earth. They are caused by sudden movements within the Earth, such as plates slipping during an earthquake.

shadow puppet
Flat shapes attached to thin sticks, held between a light source and a screen to cast shadows. The figures and the light are skillfully moved to tell stories.

shogun
A military commander in Japan. From 1192 to 1868, it was shoguns who ruled Japan, having more power than the emperor.

sinkhole
A large hole in the ground caused by erosion. In some cases, the underlying rock is eroded first, causing a dramatic collapse of the surface, as earth and rock sink into the hole beneath.

social media
Websites and apps that allow users to create and share content and information with other people online.

solar system
The sun and everything that orbits it, including planets.

Soviet Union (USSR)
After the Russian Revolution of 1917, the Russian Empire was succeeded by the Union of Soviet Socialist Republics (USSR for short). The Soviet Union broke apart in 1991.

spacewalk
Activity in which an astronaut leaves their spacecraft to work outside it while floating in space.

spiderling
Baby spider.

spinal cord
A bundle of nerves that runs down the middle of the spine and transmits messages between the brain and the rest of the body.

spore
A reproductive cell produced by a nonflowering plant or fungus. It is their equivalent of a seed.

spur
Small, pointed growth on an animal's body, often for a specific purpose such as fighting. Can also refer to a similar shape in a plant, rocky landscape, or road.

stalactite
Spike of rock hanging downward from the ceiling of a cave or rocky overhang, formed from minerals deposited by dripping water.

stalagmite
Spike of rock growing upward from the floor of a cave, formed from minerals deposited by dripping water.

state
An area of land ruled by a single government. This can be a whole country or one of the administrative regions that make up a country, for example, the US.

stellar
Relating to a star or stars.

subantarctic
The region just north of the Antarctic region, between 45 and 60 degrees south.

subatomic
Refers to particles, forces, and processes smaller than an atom, or to things within an atom.

supermassive black hole
The largest type of black hole, at least 100,000 times as heavy as the sun. The largest are billions of times heavier.

supernova
The violent explosion of a star—it is the most spectacular event in the universe, up to a billion times brighter than the sun.

synthetic
Human-made (of a material or compound).

tectonic plate
One of the large, interlocking chunks of rock that make up the Earth's outer layers.

thermogram
Image produced by measuring infrared radiation (heat) instead of visible light.

tornado
A violently spinning column of air that extends from storm clouds down to the ground. They are very destructive and can pick up and carry large objects.

torso
The core of the human body; the body except for the head, arms, and legs.

trade routes
Well-established routes on land or at sea along which merchants travel with goods between different countries and continents.

treaty
An agreement between countries, often about trade or borders.

turbine
Fanlike set of blades turned by air, water, or steam to do mechanical work (for example, turn an electricity generator).

typhoon
East Asian term for a hurricane: a dangerous storm with extremely high wind and rainfall that begins over warm water, then moves toward land.

ultraviolet light
A type of electromagnetic radiation with a wavelength shorter than visible light but longer than X-rays. Ultraviolet rays from the sun can cause sunburn.

upthrust
The upward force that a liquid or gas exerts on a body, such as a ship in water.

urban
In or relating to cities and city life.

USSR
See Soviet Union.

vertebrate
An animal with a backbone.

virus
A tiny, infectious nonliving agent that exists inside living organisms and uses them to reproduce. Some cause diseases, but others are essential to life.

visual impairment
A condition that makes a person unable to see as easily as other people.

warm-blooded
Warm-blooded animals can regulate their internal body temperature to maintain a stable level, even when the local environment is colder or hotter.

water vapor
Water in its gaseous form, when it has evaporated.

water wheel
A device used to gather up water from a river or canal for irrigation of farmland. Also a device for converting the energy of falling water to do work, for example, grind flour.

wavelength
The distance between wave crests, usually when referring to electromagnetic waves or sound waves. A longer wavelength carries less energy. See diagram in Science chapter, page 231.

weather balloon
A balloon that lifts measuring equipment high into the atmosphere to provide information about the weather.

weight
The force of gravity acting on an object. The weight depends on the mass of the object and the strength of gravity—an astronaut on the moon has the same mass as on Earth but less weight because the moon's gravity is weaker.

X-ray
Radiation with a wavelength shorter than ultraviolet but longer than gamma rays. Doctors use X-rays to check for broken bones, as they will pass through flesh but not bones or teeth.

Index

Page numbers in **bold** show the pages with the main information.

Acknowledgments

DK would like to thank:
Bharti Bedi, Michelle Crane, Priyanka Kharbanda, Ashwin Khurana, Zarak Rais, Steve Setford, and Alison Sturgeon for additional editorial help; Ray Bryant for MA picture research; Sumedha Chopra, Manpreet Kaur, and Vagisha Pushp for picture research assistance; Mrinmoy Mazumdar, Mohammad Rizwan, and Bimlesh Tiwary for DTP assistance; Simon Mumford for help with the maps; Hazel Beynon for proofreading; Chimaoge Itabor for providing the sensitivity read of the History and Culture chapters; Elizabeth Wise for the index; Maria Hademer and James Atkinson for help with the survey; and all of the experts who agreed to be interviewed for the Q&As.

The publisher would like to thank the following for their kind permission to reproduce their photographs:

(Key: a-above; b-below/bottom; c-center; f-far; l-left; r-right; t-top)

1 Getty Images: Yudik Pradnyana. **2 123RF.com:** costasz (cr/maracas). **Dorling Kindersley:** Ruth Jenkinson / RGB Research Limited (cla, bl/gold); Ruth Jenkinson / Holts Gems (bl). **Dreamstime.com:** 1evgeniya1 (fcr); Christos Georghiou (tl); Jakub Krechowicz (tc); µ € (fcla); Vlad3563 (ca); Kaiwut Niponkaew (fcl); Alexander Pokusay (cb); Nejron (clb); Elnur Amikishiyev (bc). **The Metropolitan Museum of Art:** Bequest of George C. Stone, 1935 (cr/Chinese helmet). **3 123RF.com:** Puripat Khummungkhoon (clb). **Dorling Kindersley:** Andy Crawford (bc); James Mann / Eagle E Types (bl); Colin Keates / Natural History Museum, London (br). **Dreamstime.com:** Karam Miri (crb); Martina Meyer (ftl); Yocamon (tl); Ekaterina Nikolaenko (ftr); Alexander Pokusay (cla); Natalya Manycheva (clb/Shell). **NASA:** Caltech (tc). **5 Dorling Kindersley:** Andy Crawford / Bob Gathany (tl/lunar module); Arran Lewis / NASA (c); Frank Greenaway / Natural History Museum, London (clb/Moth). **Dreamstime.com:** 1evgeniya1 (bl/rose); Macrovector (tl); Potysiev (cra/telescope); Alexander Pokusay (crb); Natalya Manycheva (ca); Alexander Pokusay (crb/Mushroom). **Getty Images / iStock:** Enrique Ramos Lopez (cb). **NASA:** Enhanced image by Kevin M. Gill (CC-BY) based on images provided courtesy of NASA / JPL-Caltech / SwRI / MSSS. (tr). **7 Alamy Stock Photo:** Granger - Historical Picture Archive (cb); Oleksiy Maksymenko Photography (ca); Sipa US (cb). **Dreamstime.com:** Christos Georghiou (crb); Alexander Pokusay (tc, cr, bc/camera, bl); Ilya Oktyabr (tr/kidneys); Lidiia Lykova (cla); Ivan Kotliar (cb/Quill). **Getty Images:** David Sacks (br). **Getty Images / iStock:** Yukosourov (cra/wires). **8 Dreamstime.com:** Aleks49 (cla); Karaevgen (tl); Alexander Pokusay (cla/Satellite); Macrovector (crb). **NASA:** (br); JPL (c); Joel Kowsky (bl). **Science Photo Library:** Gil Babin / EURELIOS (tr). **9 Alamy Stock Photo:** Sebastian Kaulitzki (cra/water bear); Stocktrek Images, Inc. (tc). **Dorling Kindersley:** Andy Crawford / Bob Gathany (ca). **Dreamstime.com:** Macrovector (cra, cla); Potysiev (clb/telescope). **ESA:** (tr). **Getty Images:** SSPL (clb); Stocktrek Images (cb). **NASA:** (br); JPL / University of Arizona (br/lo). **10 Dreamstime.com:** Anthony Heflin (br). **NASA:** (bl). **11 123RF.com:** Kittisak Taramas (cb/binoculars). **Dreamstime.com:** Firuz Buksayev (br/Hubble); Jekaterina Sahmanova (clb); Raphael Niederer / Astroniederer (bl). **NAOJ:** Harikane et al (cb). **NASA:** ESA, CSA, STScI, A Pagan (STScI) (bc). **12 NASA:** ESA, C SA, STScI. **13 ESA:** Hubble & NASA (ca/Proxima centauri); Planck Collaboration (c). **Getty Images:** Mark Garlick / Science Photo Library (cra). **NASA:** JPL-Caltech / SSC (tr); SDO (cla); JPL-Caltech / UCLA (ca). **14 ESO. NASA:** ESA and the Hubble Heritage Team (STScI / AURA); Acknowledgment: P. Cote (Herzberg Institute of Astrophysics) and E. Baltz (Stanford University) (c); JPL / Caltech / Harvard-Smithsonian Center for Astrophysics (cr); ESA / Laurent Drissen, Jean-Rene Roy and Carmelle Robert (Department de Physique and Observatoire du mont Megantic, Universite Laval) (br); ESA, CSA, STScI (l). **15 Dreamstime.com:** Biletskiy (l); DreamStockIcons (cr). **16 Dreamstime.com:** Vjanez (tr). **NASA:** JPL-Caltech / STScI / CXC / SAO (bl). **17 Dreamstime.com:** Torian Dixon / Mrincredible (bl/Neptune). **ESO:** S. Deiries (cr). **NASA:** JPL / DLR (tl, tl/callisto); JPL-Caltech / Space Science Institute (ftl); JPL / University of Arizona (tr); JPL / USGS (ftr). **18-19 NASA:** ESA, CSA, STScI (c). **18 ESA:** Hubble & NASA / Judy Schmidt (geckzilla.org) (bl).**ESO:** EHT Collaboration (tr). **NASA:** ESA, CSA, STScI (br). **20 The Royal Swedish Academy of Sciences:** (t). **Science Photo Library:** Miguel Claro (b). **21 NASA:** Jack Fischer (tl); Aubrey Gemignani (bl); JHU / APL (c). **22-23 NASA:** Enhanced image by Kevin M. Gill (CC-BY) based on images provided courtesy of NASA / JPL-Caltech / SwRI / MSSS. (c). **22 ESO. 23 BluePlanetArchive.com:** Jonathan Bird (tc). **NASA:** Aubrey Gemignani (bl); JPL-Caltech / ASU / MSSS (br). **24 Dr Katie Stack Morgan:** (tl). **24-25 NASA:** JPL-Caltech / MSSS. **26 American Museum of Natural History:** (r). **NASA:** Johns Hopkins University Applied Physics Laboratory / Southwest Research Institute (bl); JPL / MPS / DLR / IDA / Bjrn Jnsson (clb); JPL / DLR (crb); MSFC / Aaron Kingery (br). **27 Dreamstime.com:** Mario Savoia (b). **NASA:** ESA, STScI, Jian-Yang Li (PSI); Image Processing: Joseph DePasquale (cla); Johns Hopkins APL (t). **28 NASA:** Courtesy of the DSCOVR EPIC team (bl). **28-29 NASA:** (c). **29 Getty Images / iStock:** DieterMeyrl (bl). **NASA:** (tr). **Science Photo Library:** Miguel Claro (tl). **30 Alamy Stock Photo:** Richard Wainscoat (cb).**ESA:** (tc).**NASA:** ESA, J. Hester and A. Loll (Arizona State University) (tl); JPL (br). **Science Photo Library:** NRAO / AUI / NSF (cr). **31 ESO:** G. Hdepohl (bl). **NASA:** CfA, and J. DePasquale (STScI) (crb); JPL-Caltech / R. Gehrz (University of Minnesota) (c); DOE / Fermi LAT / R. Buehler (br/gamma rays). **32-33 Getty Images:** Kevin Dietsch (b). **32 ESA:** P. Carril (tc). **33 Alamy Stock Photo:** ZUMA Press, Inc. (br). **NASA:** Johns Hopkins University Applied Physics Laboratory / Southwest Research Institute / / Roman Tkachenko (cr); JPL-Caltech / UCLA / MPS / DLR / IDA (tr). **34 123RF.com:** archangel80889 (tr). **Alamy Stock Photo:** NASA Images (bl). **35 Alamy Stock Photo:** GK Images (clb/NASA logo); NASA Pictures (clb). **CNSA:** (cb/CNSA logo). **ESA. Shutterstock.com:** rvlsoft (crb); testing (cb/Roscosmos logo). **36 Alamy Stock Photo:** Sebastian Kaulitzki (tr). **NASA:** (bl). **37 NASA:** (b); DoubleTree by Hilton (tl). **38-39 NASA:** Michael Hopkins. **38 University of California, Los Angeles (UCLA):** (tl). **40 Dorling Kindersley:** Andy Crawford (3); James Stevenson / ESA (17). **Dreamstime.com:** Aleks49 (18). **ESA:** (1); ATG medialab (5/Philae, 5/Rosetta). **Getty Images:** Mike Cooper / Allsport; Adrian Mann / Future Publishing (12); Joe Raedle (10); Stocktrek Images (4). **NASA:** (7, 11); JPL-Caltech (2); Ames (15); ISRO, Robert Lea (8); GSFC / CIL / Adriana Manrique Gutierrez (9); JPL-Caltech / MSSS (16); JPL (13). **Science Photo Library:** Gil Babin / EURELIOS (6). **41 Alamy Stock Photo:** Stocktrek Images, Inc. (21). **Dorling Kindersley:** Andy Crawford / Bob Gathany (30). **Dreamstime.com:** Karaevgen (20). **Getty Images:** SSPL (28). **Getty Images / iStock:** Stocktrek Images (22). **NASA:** (24, 23); Joel Kowsky (27); McREL (25). **42 Dorling Kindersley:** Ruth Jenkinson / Holts Gems (tc); Ruth Jenkinson / Holts Gems (tr/sapphire, tr/ruby, br/aquamarine); Colin Keates / Natural History Museum, London (cra). **Dreamstime.com:** Luckypic (bl); Pleshko74 (cla); Vlad3563 (crb); Alexander Pokusay (crb/Coral, bl/coral); Ondej Prosick (br/caiman). **Science Photo Library:** Dirk Wiersma (c). **43 123RF.com:** Hapelena (cra/Red vanadinite). **Alamy Stock Photo:** Iryna Buryanska (tl); Susan E. Degginger (cra). **Dorling Kindersley:** Ruth Jenkinson / Holts Gems (tc); Colin Keates / Natural History Museum, London (crb); Arran Lewis / NASA (br). **Dreamstime.com:** Natalya Manycheva (tr/shell); Nataliya Pokrovska (clb); Bjrn Wylezich (cb); Vladimir Melnik (ca). **44-45 Dorling Kindersley:** Arran Lewis / NASA (c). **44 Science Photo Library:** Mark Garlick (cl). **46 Dreamstime.com:** Krajinar (bl). **46-47 Alamy Stock Photo:** Nature Picture Library (c). **47 Alamy Stock Photo:** Ammit (br). **Getty Images:** Fred Tanneau / AFP2 (28). **48 Alamy Stock Photo:** agefotostock (cl); Armands Pharyos (fcl); Susan E. Degginger (fcr). **Dorling Kindersley:** Colin Keates / Natural History Museum, London (cr). **49 Alamy Stock Photo:** Ralph Lee Hopkins (b). **Dreamstime.com:** Rodrigolab (cl); Willeye (tr). **Science Photo Library:** Steve Gschmeissner (ca). **50 Alamy Stock Photo:** E.R. Degginger (tr). **Dorling Kindersley:** Ruth Jenkinson / Holts Gems (c). **Getty Images:** Justin Tallis / AFP (tl). **Shutterstock.com:** Minakryn Ruslan (cr). **50-51 123RF.com:** Hapelena (c). **51 Dorling Kindersley:** Gary Ombler / Oxford University Museum of Natural History (c). **Getty Images / iStock:** Minakryn Ruslan (cr). **Courtesy of Smithsonian. ©2020 Smithsonian.:** National Gem Collection, Chip Clark (br). **52 123RF.com:** vvoennyy (21). **Alamy Stock Photo:** Panther Media GmbH (3). **Dorling Kindersley:** Ruth Jenkinson / Holts Gems (6, 8, 24, 27, 22); Tim Parmenter / Natural History Museum (2, 28); Colin Keates / Natural History Museum, London (12); Richard Leeney / Holts Gems, Hatton Garden (14). **Dreamstime.com:** Rob Kemp (16); Vlad3563 (17); Bjrn Wylezich (25). **Shutterstock.com:** Aleksandr Pobedimskiy (20). **53 Dorling Kindersley:** Ruth Jenkinson / Holts Gems (37); Tim Parmenter / Natural History Museum (42); Ruth Jenkinson / RGB Research Limited (44). **Dreamstime.com:** Phartisan (46); Siimsepp (39). **54 Royal Tyrrell Museum of Palaeontology:** (cr). **Shutterstock.com:** Soft Lighting (b). **55 Dreamstime.com:** Procyab (c); William Roberts (tl). **Getty Images:** Georges Gobet / AFP (tr). **Ryan McKellar:** Royal Saskatchewan Museum (cr). **Courtesy the Poozeum, Poozeum.com:** (crb). **Science Photo Library:** Dirk Wiersma (cl). **56 Dreamstime.com:** Pytyczech (bl). **Getty Images:** Octavio Passos (t). **57 Alamy Stock Photo:** BIOSPHOTO (tl). **Getty Images:** Kazuki Kimura / EyeEm (br); Westend61 (bl). **58-59 Dreamstime.com:** Oksana Byelikova (c). **58 Alamy Stock Photo:** Universal Images Group North America LLC (br). **Dreamstime.com:** Ondej Prosick (tc). **Shutterstock.com:** Lucas Leuzinger (tr). **59 Dreamstime.com:** Tampatra1 (br). **Getty Images / iStock:** JohnnyLye (bl). **Getty Images:** Twenty47studio (cb). **60 Alamy Stock Photo:** Jan Wlodarczyk (br). **Caleb Foster:** (cr). **naturepl.com:** Paul Souders / Worldfoto (bl). **Science Photo Library:** Kenneth Libbrecht (crb). **61 Alamy Stock Photo:** Nature Picture Library (tr). **Getty Images:** MAGNUS KRISTENSEN / Ritzau Scanpix / AFP (b). **naturepl.com:** Ben Cranke (c). **Shutterstock.com:** linear_design (cr). **62 Dreamstime.com:** Svitlana Belinska (b). **Shutterstock.com:** Amos Chapple (tl). **64 Dreamstime.com:** Znm (bc). **Getty Images:** Francesco Riccardo Iacomino (br). **Shutterstock.com:** Viktor Hladchenko (tr). **65 Alamy Stock Photo:** yorgil (crb). **Dorling Kindersley:** Malcolm Parchment (br, fbr). **66-67 Caters News Agency:** Martin Broen. **67 Alamy Stock Photo:** David Noton Photography (cr); Jukka Palm (t). **naturepl.com:** Wild Wonders of Europe / Hodalic (br). **Science Photo Library:** Javier Trueba / MSF (bc). **Shutterstock.com:** Rudmer Zwerver (tr). **68 Alamy Stock Photo:** robertharding (bc). **Getty Images:** Jim Sugar (cr). **Shutterstock.com:** Emilio Morenatti / AP (tr). **69 Caters News Agency:** Bradley White (tr/inset). **Brian Emfinger. 70-71 Alamy Stock Photo:** Media Drum World. **70 Dr Janine Krippner:** (tl). **72 Getty Images:** The Asahi Shimbun (l). **73 Dreamstime.com:** Sean Pavone (tr). **Getty Images:** Sadatsugu Tomizawa / Jiji Press (c). **Shutterstock.com:** Jack Hong (cr). **74 Alamy Stock Photo:** PA Images (br). **Stephen C Hummel:** (cr). **Science Photo Library:** NASA Goddard Space Flight Center (NASA-GSFC) (bl). **74-75 Dreamstime.com:** Rasica (c). **75 Getty Images / iStock:** lushik (br). **naturepl.com:** Phil Savoie (tr). **76 Dreamstime.com:** Maximus117 (bl). **NOAA. 77 Alamy Stock Photo:** Associated Press (tr); Image Professionals GmbH (tl); Cultura Creative RF (cra). **Dreamstime.com:** Martingraf (cla). **78-79 Marko Koroec. 78 Getty Images / iStock:** SpiffyJ (tl/Weather chart). **Chris Wright:** (tl). **80 Hamish Frost Photography. 81 Getty Images / iStock:** htrnr (br); Lysogor (cra). **82 Dreamstime.com:** Valentin M Armianu (clb); Kokhan (fbl). **Getty Images / iStock:** coolkengzz (fclb). **Shutterstock.com:** xamnesiacx84 (bl). **82-83 Alamy Stock Photo:** Nature Picture Library (bc). **83 Alamy Stock Photo:** John Sirlin (ca); Rich Wagner (cra). **Dreamstime.com:** David Hayes (tr). **84 naturepl.com:** Luciano Candisani (t). **85 Getty Images:** Craig Stennett (crb). **Getty Images / iStock:** Matthew J Thomas (clb); Philip Thurston (cra). **86 123RF.com:** joseelias (2/new); smileus (27/new). **Alamy Stock Photo:** Armands Pharyos (17/new); Rolf Richardson (16/new); Zoonar GmbH (21/new). **Dorling Kindersley:** Will Heap / Peter Chan (18/new). **Dreamstime.com:** Bignai (28/new); Luckypic (11/new); Vladimir Melnik (3/new); Eyeblink (26/new); Lev Kropotov (13); Ed8563 (15); Elena Butinova (19/new); Martin Schneiter (29/new). **Getty Images / iStock:** DigiTrees (12/new, 10/new); Sieboldianus (5/new). **Sanjay Tiwari:** (6). **87 123RF.com:** marigranula (24/new); Natalie Ruffing (7/new); Jaturon Ruaysoongnern (20/new). **Alamy Stock Photo:** BIOSPHOTO (15/new); imageBROKER (9/new, 30/new); blickwinkel (25/new); Genevieve Vallee (22/new). **Dreamstime.com:** Mikhail Dudarev (13/new); Karelgallas (4/new). **Getty Images / iStock:** DNY59 (23/new). **88 Shutterstock.com:** VLADJ55 (tl). **88-89**

Alamy Stock Photo: Reuters (b). **89 Dreamstime.com:** Shawn Goldberg (cra). **90 Dreamstime.com:** Molishka1988 (ca); Slowmotiongli (crb). **The Ocean Clean Up:** (b). **90-91 Dreamstime.com:** Francesco Ricciardi (tr). **91 Dreamstime.com:** Iryna Mylinska (bc). **Getty Images:** Loic Venance / AFP (bl). **92 Alamy Stock Photo:** ethangabito (c); Simon Knight (cr); Panther Media GmbH (fbr); www.pqpictures.co.uk (br). **Dreamstime.com:** Faunuslsd (cla); Nejron; Alexander Pokusay (ftl, tr, bl). **93 123RF.com:** alekss (cla). **Alamy Stock Photo:** Petlin Dmitry (crb); Minden Pictures (fbr); Peter Martin Rhind (br). **Dreamstime.com:** 1evgeniya1 (clb); Jakub Krechowicz (tr); Alexander Pokusay (tl); Natthapon M (cla/rabbit); Rudmer Zwerver. **Getty Images / iStock:** imv (ftr).**Getty Images:** Srinophan69 (cra). **94 Alamy Stock Photo:** Mediscan (tc); Science Photo Library (tr). **Science Photo Library:** Steve Gschmeissner (tl). **94-95 naturepl.com:** Gary Bell / Oceanwide (cb). **95 123RF.com:** wklzzz (cla). **Alamy Stock Photo:** BarzhDu (cr). **Dreamstime.com:** Heinz Peter Schwerin (cra). **Getty Images / iStock:** micro_photo (cl). **Science Photo Library:** Kateryna Kon (br). **96 naturepl.com:** Doug Perrine (cla). **97 Science Photo Library:** John Sibbick (clb). **Trustees of the National Museums Of Scotland:** Harry Taylor (t). **98-99 Dreamstime.com:** Crc711 (c). **98 Dreamstime.com:** Photomo (tr/Sky). **Science Photo Library:** Pascal Goetgheluck (c). **99 Getty Images:** Sergey Krasovskiy (tr). **100 Alamy Stock Photo:** dotted zebra (b). **Dorling Kindersley:** Lynton Gardiner / American Museum of Natural History (tc/Dinosaur tail). **Getty Images:** Mohamad Haghani / Stocktrek Images (clb). **101 Alamy Stock Photo:** Science Photo Library (br). **Getty Images:** Wang Dongming / China News Service (tr). **Velizar Simeonovski:** (cr). **Courtesy of Smithsonian. ©2020 Smithsonian.:** Courtesy U.S. Army Corps of Engineers, Omaha District and The Museum of the Rockies, Montana State University. Triceratops horridus, USNM PAL 500000 (composite cast), Smithsonian Institution. Photo courtesy Smithsonian Institution. (l). **102 123RF.com:** leonello calvetti (1). **Dorling Kindersley:** James Kuether (10, 12, 30, 24). **Getty Images:** Mark Garlick (15). **103 Dorling Kindersley:** James Kuether (28, 34, 37, 36). **104-105 Paul Sereno/University of Chicago:** Matthew Irving. **104 Paul Sereno/University of Chicago:** Michael Hettwer (bl). **106 Dorling Kindersley:** Mark Winwood / Lullingstone Castle, Kent (cr/Ferns). **Dreamstime.com:** Igor Dolgov (tr/Lichen); Feherlofia (tr/Club moss); Seroff (cr/Flower). **106-107 Shutterstock.com:** Jordan Pettitt / Solent News (bc). **107 Alamy Stock Photo:** Jeff Gilbert (cra). **Dreamstime.com:** Verastuchelova (tr). **108 Alamy Stock Photo:** Panther Media GmbH (r). **Dreamstime.com:** Bos11 (bl). **109 Alamy Stock Photo:** Giovanni Gagliardi (c); imageBROKER (bc). **Dreamstime.com:** Lenny7 (br). **Getty Images / iStock:** imv (cr). **naturepl.com:** Klein & Hubert (tr). **110 Dreamstime.com:** Dagobert1620 (cla); Sorsillo (tl); Cristina Dini (cl); Debu55y (clb); Zoran Milosavljevic (clb/Narcissus); Cathy Keifer (bl). **NASA:** Scott Kelly (tr). **111 123RF.com:** noppharat (cl/Water hyssop); nsdefender (c/Bark). **Alamy Stock Photo:** Jordana Meilleur (cr); Peter Yeeles (br). **Dorling Kindersley:** Paul Goff / Harry Tomlinson (tl). **Dreamstime.com:** Oleh Marchak (c/Snowdrops). **112 Alamy Stock Photo:** Peter Martin Rhind (clb). **naturepl.com:** Michael & Patricia Fogden (cla). **113 Alamy Stock Photo:** Simon Knight (crb); Minden Pictures (bl). **Getty Images:** Wokephoto17 (clb).**naturepl.com:** Juergen Freund (tr). **Science Photo Library:** Wim Van Egmond (br). **114 BluePlanetArchive.com:** Klaus Jost (tc); Andrew J. Martinez (tr). **114-115 Getty Images / iStock:** Alex Tsarfin (bc). **116 naturepl.com:** Alex Mustard.**NOAA:** (tr). **117 Alamy Stock Photo:** Mark Conlin / VWPics (br); Michael Greenfelder (tl). **Getty Images:** J.W.Alker (tr). **naturepl.com:** Alex Mustard (cl, cr). **118 pixoto.com:** Aizat Mustaqim (b). **119 Alamy Stock Photo:** Minden Pictures (bc). **Dreamstime.com:** Gary Webber (tr); Wirestock (ca). **Getty Images:** Sylvain Cordier / Gamma-Rapho (cra). **120 123RF.com:** paulrommer (4). **Alamy Stock Photo:** blickwinkel (18); Nature Photographers Ltd (14); HHelene (16, 16/ant); Don Mammoser (6); yod67 (25); www.pqpictures.co.uk (13); Henri Koskinen (2). **Dorling Kindersley:** Frank Greenaway / Natural History Museum, London (17, 20); Colin Keates / Natural History Museum, London (5, 9); Lynette Schimming (11). **Dreamstime.com:** Digitalimagined (28); Marcouliana (22); Galinasavina (26); Matee Nuserm (1); Faunuslsd (8); Pzaxe (27); Photobee (23). **Getty Images:** Jasius (21). **Getty Images / iStock:** ookawaphoto (15). **Thomas Marent:** (3). **naturepl.com:** MYN / Tim Hunt (12). **121 123RF.com:** alekss (43). **Dorling Kindersley:** Frank Greenaway / Natural History Museum, London (30, 38); Jerry Young (31); Frank Greenaway (36). **Dreamstime.com:** Alexeyleon (44); Digitalimagined (34); Matee Nuserm (46); Rozum (41); Stuart Andrews (29); Melinda Fawver (33). **Getty Images / iStock:** JanMiko (49). **Thomas Marent:** (39, 50). **naturepl.com:** John Abbott (45); Ingo Arndt (37); Chris Mattison (47). **122 Alamy Stock Photo:** Minden Pictures (tr); redbrickstock.com (tl). **Thomas Shahan:** (b). **123 Alamy Stock Photo:** Minden Pictures (crb); Nature Picture Library (tl); Emanuel Tanjala (cra). **Shutterstock.com:** Brett Hondow (cla). **Gil Wizn:** (tr). **124-5 Comedy Wildlife Photo:** Chi Han Lin (bc). **124 Alamy Stock Photo:** Minden Pictures (bc). **naturepl.com:** Gary Bell / Oceanwide (bl); Brandon Cole (cl). **125 BluePlanetArchive.com:** Steven Kovacs (tl). **Getty Images:** Srinophan69 (tr). **US Geological Survey:** Andrea L Miehls, PhD (crb). **126 BluePlanetArchive.com:** Franco Banfi (b). **127 Alamy Stock Photo:** Jeff Rotman (c). **BluePlanetArchive.com:** Phillip Colla (tl); Mark Conlin (br). **naturepl.com:** Ralph Pace (cl); Doug Perrine (cra). **OceanwideImages.com:** Rudie Kuiter (cb). **128 Brad Norman:** (tl). **128-129 Alamy Stock Photo:** Reinhard Dirscherl. **130-131 Robert Cinega:** (c). **130 Robert Cinega:** (cla). **naturepl.com:** Guy Edwardes (tc). **Santiago Ron:** (br). **131 Alamy Stock Photo:** Minden Pictures (br). **Getty Images / iStock:** AdrianHillman (cr/cat). **132 Dorling Kindersley:** Asia Orlando 2022 (c). **Dreamstime.com:** µ € (bl); Andrey Gudkov (cr). **naturepl.com:** Tui De Roy (br). **133 © Wei Fu:** (tr). **naturepl.com:** Enrique Lopez-Tapia (br). **Science Photo Library:** Nigel Downer (bc); Paul D Stewart (cb). **134-135 Andy Murch/BigFishExpeditions.com:** (bc). **134 Shutterstock.com:** Ibenk_88 (tr). **135 Dreamstime.com:** Tjkphotography (tr).**Shutterstock.com:** Charles HB Mercer (br). **136 Alamy Stock Photo:** All Canada Photos (bc). **naturepl.com:** Pete Oxford (t). **137 Alamy Stock Photo:** Petlin Dmitry (br); ethangabito (cr); Ariadne Van Zandbergen (clb). **Dreamstime.com:** Isselee (ca, cra/hatched). **Getty Images:** Paul Grace Photography Somersham (bl); Life On White (cla). **Science Photo Library:** Dante Fenolio (bc). **138 Dreamstime.com:** Lukas Blazek (clb/slow loris); Rudmer Zwerver (tl); Jxpfeer (cla/stonefish); Kcmatt (cl). **Getty Images:** by wildestanimal (bc). **naturepl.com:** Gary Bell / Oceanwide (cla). **Shutterstock.com:** RobJ808 (bl). **139 Alamy Stock Photo:** Panther Media GmbH (tc). **Getty Images:** Paul Starosta (cr). **140 Dreamstime.com:** Designua (crb). **Alberto Ghizzi Panizza**. **Science Photo Library:** Steve Gschmeissner (br). **141 Alamy Stock Photo:** Kevin Elsby (tc). **Dorling Kindersley:** Barnabas Kindersley (cr). **Dreamstime.com:** Pictac (tc/pencil); Pixworld (tr). **142 Alamy Stock Photo:** Minden Pictures (bl). **naturepl.com:** Stefan Christmann (cr). **143 Getty Images:** Auscape / Universal Images Group (tl). **Christopher Michel:** (b). **144 123RF.com:** irochka (19); Nico Smit / EcoSnap (18). **Dorling Kindersley:** Gary Ombler / Paradise Park, Cornwall (22). **Dreamstime.com:** Dndavis (10); Isselee (12); Erllre (15); Martinmark (23); Vasyl Helevachuk (20); Jocrebbin (4); Rudmer Zwerver (5). **Getty Images / iStock:** Film Studio Aves (11); johan64 (1); Enrique Ramos Lopez (16); PhanuwatNandee (24). **Shutterstock.com:** Andrey_Kuzmin (25); Jeffry Weymier (6). **145 123RF.com:** John Bailey / pictur123 (44). **Alamy Stock Photo:** Steve Bloom Images (33). **Dorling Kindersley:** Andrew Beckett (Illustration Ltd) (36). **Dreamstime.com:** Ben (27); Nejron (30); Henkbogaard (31); Isselee (35, 45, 47); Menno67 (17); Deaddogdodge (38); Taviphoto (34); Mikael Males (39); Ecophoto (41); Kotomiti_okuma (46); Ryan Rubino (50). **Getty Images / iStock:** drakuliren (40). **Getty Images:** Bob Smith (37). **Shutterstock.com:** phugunfire (42); Anton Rodionov (7). **146 Getty Images:** Michael Kappeler / DDP / AFP (cr); @Niladri Nath (cla). **146-147 Alamy Stock Photo:** Minden Pictures (b). **147 Alamy Stock Photo:** Design Pics Inc (cra); Minden Pictures (crb). **Dreamstime.com:** Anastasiya Aheyeva (tl); Passakorn Umpornmaha (tr); Hotshotsworldwide (cr). **148-149 Edgar Pacific Photography:** (br). **148 Alamy Stock Photo:** imageBROKER (tr); A & J Visage (c). **Getty Images / iStock:** Michel Viard (bl). **149 Ocean Alliance:** Christian Miller (tr). **150 Getty Images:** Yudik Pradnyana (tr). **151 Alamy Stock Photo:** blickwinkel (cla); Reuters (bl). **Brooklyn Museum:** Charles Edwin Wilbour Fund, 36.622. (tc). **Getty Images:** Fuse (clb, c, cr).**Magnus News Agency:** Haritri Goswami (br). **Shutterstock.com:** foxhound photos (tr). **152-153 Caters News Agency:** Yi Liu (t). **152 Sarah Durant:** (bl). **154 Dreamstime.com:** Petr Majek (tr). **naturepl.com:** Marion Vollborn / BIA (l). **155 Dreamstime.com:** Wirestock (crb). **Getty Images / iStock:** ???? ?????? (tr); GlobalP (cl). **naturepl.com:** Jami Tarris (br). **156-157 Will Burrard-Lucas:** (b). **156 123RF.com:** Andrei Samkov / satirus (cla). **Dorling Kindersley:** Jerry Young (c). **Dreamstime.com:** Mikelane45 (cr). **Getty Images:** Jurgen & Christine Sohns (tr). **157 Getty Images:** Jim Dyson (cla). **158 123RF.com:** Iakov Filimonov (bc). **Alamy Stock Photo:** Wirestock, Inc. (clb). **Dreamstime.com:** Isselee (crb, br). **naturepl.com:** Mark MacEwen (cra); Anup Shah (cla). **Shutterstock.com:** Eric Isselee (bl). **159 Alamy Stock Photo:** Fredrik Stenstrm (tl).**Depositphotos Inc:** odua (bl). **Dreamstime.com:** Isselee (cr); Natalia Volkova (bc). **Getty Images / iStock:** GlobalP (br). **SuperStock:** Cyril Ruoso / Biosphoto (tr/primates). **160 Alamy Stock Photo:** Amazon-Images (5); Blue Planet Archive (17); Oliver Thompson-Holmes (6). **Dreamstime.com:** Anankkml (12); Alfio Scisetti (tl); Isselee (2, 8, 4, 21, 23); Kobets (7); Atalvi (9); Saowakon Wichaichaleechon (tr); Dirk Ercken (15); Musat Christian (16); Nerthuz (25); Paul Vinten (26); Vladimir Melnik (27); Annaav (10); Vkilikov (18). **Fotolia:** Eric Isselee (1). **Getty Images / iStock:** 2630ben (3); GlobalP (20). **161 123RF.com:** Visarute Angkatavanich (30). **Alamy Stock Photo:** Nature Picture Library (32). **Dreamstime.com:** Anankkml (44); Natthapon M (29); Suriyaphoto (tc); Geerati (31); Jakub Krechowicz (35); David Steele (33); Lianquan Yu (34); Withgod (11); Nelikz (13); Isselee (40, 14, 42, 39); Arno Meintjes (22); Iakov Filimonov (41); Vasyl Helevachuk (43). **Getty Images / iStock:** linephoto (37). **Shutterstock.com:** Philippe Clement (19). **162 naturepl.com:** Juergen Freund (tl). **Scott Tuason:** (c). **163 Alamy Stock Photo:** steve bly (cl); Media Drum World (cra). **Getty Images:** Juan Carlos Vindas (tr, tr/detail). **naturepl.com:** Richard Du Toit (crb). **Science Photo Library:** Merlintuttle.org (bl). **164 Alamy Stock Photo:** Minden Pictures (t). **Dreamstime.com:** Dirk Ercken / Kikkerdirk (bl/frog); David Havel (bl); Jesse Kraft (clb). **Getty Images / iStock:** Enrique Ramos Lopez (cb). **165 Alamy Stock Photo:** imagegallery2 (cl); Dinesh kumar (ca). **Caters News Agency:** Em Gatland (tr). **Shutterstock.com:** jon lyall (bl). **Wondrous World Images:** Yvonne McKenzie (br). **166 Alamy Stock Photo:** dpa picture alliance (cl). **167 123RF.com:** Tristan Barrington (crb). **Dorling Kindersley:** Wildlife Heritage Foundation, Kent, UK (cra). **Dreamstime.com:** Herman Hermawan (tr). **Getty Images / iStock:** Alberto Carrera (br/Orangutan); leonello (tc); Christophe Sirabella (bl). **Shutterstock.com:** Takayuki Ohama (br/Porpoise); TigerStocks (cr). **168 Dreamstime.com:** Kaiwut Niponkaew (cra); Alexander Pokusay (tl/neurons); Ilya Oktyabr (br). **Getty Images:** Sebastian Kaulitzki / Science Photo Library (tr). **Getty Images / iStock:** VladimirFLoyd (tl). **169** Dreamstime.com: Lotophagi (crb). Getty Images / iStock: djiledesign (ca); FuatKose (br). Shutterstock / Alex Mit (cra). **170 Dreamstime.com:** Alona Stepaniuk (br). **171 Dreamstime.com:** Radub85 (tr). **Getty Images / iStock:** stock_colors (cr). **172 123RF.com:** Watchara Khamphonsaeng (tr). **Getty Images / iStock:** Firstsignal (bl). **Science Photo Library:** Steve Gschmeissner (cl, crb/Skin cells, br/Fat cells); Ziad M. El-Zaatari (cr/Muscle cells); Kevin Mackenzie / University of Aberdeen (cr/Bone cells); Power and Syred (crb/Blood cells); Lennart Nilsson, TT (br/Nerve cells). **173 Dreamstime.com:** Achmat Jappie (cr). **Science Photo Library:** (tr); Dr Gopal Murti (tl); Dennis Kunkel Miscroscopy (crb); Dr Yorgos Nikas (br). **174 Alamy Stock Photo:** Science Photo Library (r). **Getty Images / iStock:** fizkes (cl). **178 Alamy Stock Photo:** Johan Siebke (cb). **Getty Images:** Joseph Giacomin (tr). **Getty Images / iStock:** VladimirFLoyd (cl). **Science Photo Library:** Martin Oeggerli (bl). **179 ArenaPAL:** Johan Persson (bl). **Getty Images:** Sebastian Kaulitzki / Science Photo Library (tl). **Science Photo Library:** Martin Dohrn (tr); Steve Gschmeissner (crb/Smooth muscle, crb/Cardia muscle, br/Skeletal muscle). **180 Science Photo Library:** Alain Pol, ISM. **181 Getty Images / iStock:** FuatKose (bl). **Shutterstock.com:** Alex Mit (br). **182 Getty Images:** Science Photo Library (crb). **183 Alamy Stock Photo:** Agencja Fotograficzna Caro (tl). **184 123RF.com:** langstrup (ca). **Getty Images / iStock:** bymuratdeniz (clb); knape (cra); FreshSplash (bl). **185 Getty Images / iStock:** jhorrocks (cr); RuthBlack (R/bl). **186-187 Getty Images / iStock:** technotr (t). **187 Dreamstime.com:** Xavier Gallego Morell (br). **Getty Images / iStock:** Zzvet (bc). **188 Getty Images:** Jamie Grill (clb); imageBROKER / Helmut Meyer zur Capellen (bl). **Science Photo Library:** Hank Morgan (cra). **189 123RF.com:** phive2015 (tr). **190-191 Science Photo Library:** Zephyr. **190 Dr Zeller:** (tl). **193 Getty Images / iStock:** djiledesign (tr); Vicu9 (tl). **Jonathan Stephen Harris. 194 Science Photo Library:** D. Phillips (tr). **195 Dreamstime.com:** Jose Manuel Gelpi Diaz (c). **Getty Images:** Nazar Abbas Photography (br). **196 Getty Images:** Giordano Cipriani (bl). **Guinness World Records Limited:** (r). **197 Getty Images / iStock:** SeanShot (cl); YakobchukOlena (cr). **Science Photo Library:** (tr). **198-199 Getty Images / iStock:** technotr. **198 Allan Williams:** (tl). **200 Getty Images:** KoldoyChris (crb). **Science Photo Library:** (bl). **201 Alamy Stock Photo:** Science Photo Library (cb). **Andrew Davidhazy:** (t). **Science Photo Library:** Kateryna Kon (bl). **202 123RF.com:** andreykuzmin (c); Puripat Khummungkhoon (tr); greyjj (clb). **Alamy Stock Photo:** Maurice Savage (br). **Dorling Kindersley:** Ruth Jenkinson / RGB

Research Limited (cl). **Dreamstime.com:** Ekaterina Nikolaenko (cra); Alexander Pokusay (bl, fbr). **Getty Images / iStock:** AnatolyM (ftr). **203 Alamy Stock Photo:** Blue Planet Archive (cr). **Dorling Kindersley:** Ruth Jenkinson / RGB Research Limited (ca). **Dreamstime.com:** Kseniia Gorova (tr); Lidiia Lykova (tl). **Getty Images / iStock:** tridland (ftr); Yukosourov (cra/wires). **Science Photo Library:** Kateryna Kon (br). **Shutterstock.com:** Salavat Fidai (ca/pencil).
204 Alamy Stock Photo: Reuters (cl). **Dreamstime.com:** Rdonar (tl). **Science Photo Library:** Martyn F Chillmaid (tr). **204-205 Alamy Stock Photo:** dpa picture alliance (b). **205 Alamy Stock Photo:** Everett Collection Inc (tl); M I (Spike) Walker (cl). **Dreamstime.com:** Angellodeco (tr); Tawat Lamphoosri (ca); Heysues23 (cra). **206 Alamy Stock Photo:** David Wall (tl). **Dreamstime.com:** Haveseen (cl). **206-207 Getty Images:** Joshua Bozarth (b). **207 Dreamstime.com:** Toxitz (tr). **208 Alamy Stock Photo:** Granger - Historical Picture Archive (c). **Science Photo Library:** NASA (tr). **Shutterstock.com:** SaveJungle (cr). **209 Alamy Stock Photo:** Album. **210 Dorling Kindersley:** Ruth Jenkinson / RGB Research Limited (4, 3, 12, 11, 19, 20, 21, 22, 23, 24, 25, 37, 38, 41, 42, 43, 44, 55, 56, 72, 73, 74, 75, 57, 58, 91, 60, 89, 90, 59, 92, 93); Gary Ombler / Oxford University Museum of Natural History (39). **211 Dorling Kindersley:** Ruth Jenkinson / RGB Research Limited (20, 5, 9, 13, 14, 15, 17, 27, 28, 29, 30, 31, 32, 34, 35, 46, 48, 49, 50, 51, 52, 77, 81, 82, 85, 86, 62, 94, 63, 64, 65, 66, 67, 68, 69, 70, 71); Colin Keates / Natural History Museum, London (78). **Dreamstime.com:** (6); Bjrn Wylezich (16); Marcel Clemens (80). **212 Dorling Kindersley:** Ruth Jenkinson / RGB Research Limited (9, 7, 11, 15, 1, 16, 2, 8, 6, 14); Colin Keates / Natural History Museum, London (10). **213 Dorling Kindersley:** Ruth Jenkinson / RGB Research Limited (27, 31, 20, 29, 26, 35, 5, 19, 21, 25, 23, 39, 37, 17, 32, 30); Tim Parmenter / Natural History Museum (18); Colin Keates / Natural History Museum, London (28). **Dreamstime.com:** Roberto Junior (36); Bjrn Wylezich (22). **US Department of Energy:** (34). **214 Alamy Stock Photo:** WidStock (cl/coal). **Dorling Kindersley:** Colin Keates / Natural History Museum, London (cl). **Dreamstime.com:** Geografika (clb/Coal). **Shutterstock.com:** Salavat Fidai (bc, br). **215 Alamy Stock Photo:** Maurice Savage (br).**Ardea:** Scott Linstead / Science Source (tr). **Getty Images / iStock:** AnatolyM (bc). **Shutterstock.com:** Salavat Fidai (bl). **216 Alamy Stock Photo:** Cultura Creative RF (clb). **Science Photo Library:** Turtle Rock Scientific (tl). **216-217 Alamy Stock Photo:** Andrey Radchenko (c). **217 Alamy Stock Photo:** Tewin Kijthamrongworakul (bl). **218 Dorling Kindersley:** Ruth Jenkinson / RGB Research Limited (br/Hydrogen). **Dreamstime.com:** (br/Carbon); Gjs (tc). **218-219 Shutterstock.com:** Albert Russ (c). **219 Dreamstime.com:** Bruno Ismael Da Silva Alves (crb); Ianlangley (br). **220 Alamy Stock Photo:** H.S. Photos (fcl); Science History Images (crb); Science Photo Library (cb). **Dreamstime.com:** Christian Wei (cra, bc); Scol22 (cl); Winai Tepsuttinun (ca); Radzh Dzhabbarov (fbl). **Getty Images / iStock:** Sorawat Sunthornthaweechot (clb). **221 Dreamstime.com:** Martin Brayley (cb); Krischam (tl); Newlight (tr); Adam Nowak (bl). **Science Photo Library:** Eye of Science (cl); Steve Gschmeissner (cr). **222 Dreamstime.com:** Microvone (b). **Getty Images:** Jonas Gratzer / LightRocket (tl). **Science Photo Library:** Pascal Goetgheluck (cb). **223 Dorling Kindersley:** Dan Crisp (tl/house icon). **Dreamstime.com:** Macrovector (tl/phone); Vectorikart (tl/lizard). **Science Photo Library:** M I Walker / Science Source (tr). **Shutterstock.com:** Sebw (cl). **224 Dreamstime.com:** David Carillet (bl). **225 Alamy Stock Photo:** Andrey Armyagov (bc). **Science Photo Library:** Tony McConnell (tl). **226 Getty Images:** Geert Vanden Wijngaert (bl). **227 Dreamstime.com:** Steve Allen (cb); Liorpt (cl); Jarcosa (t); Ssuaphoto (ca). **228 Alamy Stock Photo:** robertharding (t). **Sam Hardy:** (bl). **229 Alamy Stock Photo:** Hilda Weges. **230 Alamy Stock Photo:** Blue Planet Archive (tl); Yossef (Maksym) Zilberman (Duboshko) (tr). **Science Photo Library:** Giphotostock (c). **231 Getty Images / iStock:** Mumemories (t). **232-233 Matthew Drinkall:** (c). **232 Getty Images:** Jose Luis Pelaez Inc (bc). **233 Dreamstime.com:** 7xpert (cb). **Getty Images / iStock:** Yukosourov (cra). **234 Science Photo Library:** David Parker (bc). **235 123RF.com:** greyjj (clb); Puripat Khummungkhoon (cb). **Alamy Stock Photo:** Lenscap (bl); Mouse in the House (cla). **Dreamstime.com:** Satyr (cra). **Fotolia:** Alex Staroseltsev (c). **236 Dorling Kindersley:** Stephen Oliver (cb). **237 123RF.com:** andreykuzmin (ca). **Getty Images:** Zhang Jingang / VCG (b). **Science Photo Library:** Juan Carlos Casado (STARRYEARTH.COM) (cr). **238 Alamy Stock Photo:** Mark Harris (tc); Daniel Teetor (cl). **238-39 Alamy Stock Photo:** picturesbyrob (c). **240 Alamy Stock Photo:** Heritage Image Partnership Ltd (10); Oleksiy Maksymenko Photography (2); Stan Rohrer (3); Motoring Picture Library (15). **Dorling Kindersley:** James Mann / Joe Mason (11); Matthew Ward / Derek E.J. Fisher and Citroen (1); Gary Ombler / Keystone Tractor Works (13). **Dreamstime.com:** Artzzz (6); Felix Mizioznikov (7); Casfotoarda (8); © Konstantinos Moraitis (12); Margojh (14); Hupeng (9); Benjamin Sibuet (17); Imaengine (18). **241 Alamy Stock Photo:** Everett Collection Inc (28); Oleksiy Maksymenko Photography (22); Matthew Richardson (27). **Dorling Kindersley:** James Mann / Eagle E Types (25); Gary Ombler / R. Florio (19); Matthew Ward / 1959 Isetta (Plus model) owned and restored by Dave Watson (20). **Dreamstime.com:** Artzzz (26); Daria Trefilova (16); Brian Sullivan (23); Valerio Bianchi (24); Aleksandr Kondratov (30). **Getty Images:** John Keeble (21). **242-243 Noah Bahnson**. **242 Alamy Stock Photo:** Joo Miranda (br). **Dreamstime.com:** Peter Jurik (bl); Razihusin (cra). **244-245 Getty Images:** Josh Edelson / AFP (c). **245 Alamy Stock Photo:** Aviation Images Ltd (cra). **Getty Images:** NASA (crb). **Getty Images / iStock:** tridland (br). **246 Alamy Stock Photo:** Aviation Images Ltd (12); JSM Historical (1); David Gowans (3); The Print Collector (4); Jonathan Ayres (8). **Dorling Kindersley:** Peter Cook / Planes of Fame Air Museum, Chino, California (9); Gary Ombler / Nationaal Luchtvaart Themapark (2); Gary Ombler / RAF Museum, Cosford (7); Gary Ombler / Fleet Air Arm Museum (10); Gary Ombler / Gatwick Aviation Museum (13). **Dreamstime.com:** Ajdibilio (11); Franzisca Guedel (6). **Getty Images:** (5). **247 Smithsonian National Air and Space Museum:** Eric Long (14). **Alamy Stock Photo:** IanDagnall Computing (16). **Dorling Kindersley:** Gary Ombler / Model Exhibition, Telford (15). **Dreamstime.com:** David Bautista (24); Rui Matos (17); Ryan Fletcher (18, 29); VanderWolfImages (20); Ansar Kyzylaliyeu (23); Shawn Edlund (22); Nadezda Murmakova (26); Craig Russell (27). **Getty Images:** Chris Weeks / WireImage (21). **248-249 Gilles Martin-Raget:** (c). **249 Alamy Stock Photo:** Nature Picture Library (cb). **Dreamstime.com:** Sabelskaya (crb). **250 Dreamstime.com:** VectorMine (bl). **250-251 Getty Images:** Posnov (c). **251 Alamy Stock Photo:** Stocktrek Images, Inc. (tr). **252 Alamy Stock Photo:** SFL Travel (bl). **253 123RF.com:** lamtaira (fcr). **Alamy Stock Photo:** Cameron Hilker (c); MYANMAR (Burma) landmards and people by VISION (cr). **Getty Images:** Taro Hama @ e-kamakura (tl). **Shutterstock.com:** Kunal Mahto (fcl); Sagittarius Pro (cl). **254 Alamy Stock Photo:** Cristina Ionescu (cra). **Dreamstime.com:** Artushfoto (clb); Dmytro Zinkevych (cla); Christian Delbert (ca); Natalia Siverina (cb). **Shutterstock.com:** Gorodenkoff (br). **255 Dreamstime.com:** Rawpixelimages (crb). **Getty Images:** Jens Khler / ullstein bild (bl). **Chris Harrison:** Carnegie Mellon University (t). **Shutterstock.com:** PHOTOCREO Michal Bednarek (cl). **257 Alamy Stock Photo:** Reuters (tr). **Getty Images:** Patrick T Fallon (l); Pascal Pochard-Casabianca / AFP (crb). **258 Science Photo Library:** Biophoto Associates (fbr); Frank Fox (tl); Robert Brook (bl); Kateryna Kon (fbl). **259 Dreamstime.com:** Pavel Chagochkin (bc). **Science Photo Library:** Eye of Science (tl); Science Picture Co. (bl). **260 Science Photo Library:** Power and Syred (bl). **260-261 Getty Images / iStock:** BorupFoto (cb). **261 Alamy Stock Photo:** Konstantin Nechaev (tr). **Getty Images / iStock:** CBCK-Christine (cr). **262-263 Courtesy of Greater Manchester Police Museum & Archive**. **263 Leisa Nichols-Drew, De Montfort University, Leicester:** (tr). **264 Alamy Stock Photo:** Erin Babnik (fcr); Chris Willson (tl); Maurice Savage (tr); funkyfood London - Paul Williams (c); Granger - Historical Picture Archive (cl); Newscom (br). **Dorling Kindersley:** Gary Ombler / National Railway Museum, York / Science Museum Group (bl). **Dreamstime.com:** Christos Georghiou (clb); Alexander Pokusay (ftl); Potysiev (cr); Zim235 (fclb). **265 Alamy Stock Photo:** steeve. e. flowers (fbr); Granger- Historical Picture Archive (cb); Suzuki Kaku (clb); Rick Lewis (br). **© The Trustees of the British Museum. All rights reserved:** Tim Parmenter (cra). **Dorling Kindersley:** Richard Leeney / Maidstone Museum and Bentliff Art Gallery (ca); Gary Ombler / University of Pennsylvania Museum of Archaeology and Anthropology (bl). **Dreamstime.com:** Hel080808 (tr); Potysiev (tl); Ivan Kotliar (fbl). **The Metropolitan Museum of Art:** The Michael C. Rockefeller Memorial Collection, Gift of Nelson A. Rockefeller, 1972 (ftl). **266 Alamy Stock Photo:** Heritage Image Partnership Ltd (bc). **Bridgeman Images. Dreamstime.com:** Kmiragaya (cl); Nm0915 (bl). **267 akg-images:** De Agostini Picture Lib. / G. Nimatallah (tc). **Alamy Stock Photo:** Anton Chalakov (fcr); ZUMA Press, Inc. (br); The Print Collector (bc); Shawshots (cr). **Bridgeman Images. 268 Alamy Stock Photo:** Oleksandr Fediuk (tl); Glasshouse Images (tr). **Dreamstime.com:** Neil Harrison (bl); Alain Lacroix / Icefields (br). **269 Alamy Stock Photo:** The Natural History Museum (bl). **John Gurche:** (tl). **270 Alamy Stock Photo:** Dmitriy Moroz (tl). **271 Alamy Stock Photo:** Zev Radovan (cl). **Dorling Kindersley:** Gary Ombler / University of Pennsylvania Museum of Archaeology and Anthropology (c). **Dreamstime.com:** Sergey Mayorov (tr). **272 Alamy Stock Photo:** funkyfood London - Paul Williams (cla, bc, crb, br); Granger - Historical Picture Archive (tr). **272-273 The Metropolitan Museum of Art:** (c). **273 Alamy Stock Photo:** Jaroslav Moravk (br). **Dreamstime.com:** Anton Aleksenko (tr). **274 Courtesy Mennat-allah El Dorry:** M Gamil (tl). **274-275 The Metropolitan Museum of Art. 276-277 Alamy Stock Photo:** H-AB (bc). **276 © Vinzenz Brinkmann / Ulrike Koch-Brinkman:** (bl). **277 © The Trustees of the British Museum. All rights reserved:** (tr). **Dreamstime.com:** Sergio Bertino (br). **Getty Images:** Grant Faint (cr). **278 Bridgeman Images:** Alinari Archives, Florence - Reproduced with the permission of Ministero per i Beni e le Attivit Culturali (b). **Dreamstime.com:** Ievgen Melamud (tl). **Getty Images:** DEA / G. Nimatallah (tr). **279 Alamy Stock Photo:** Erin Babnik (cr); Photiconix (tr). **Dreamstime.com:** Pavel Naumov (clb, crb). **Getty Images / iStock:** kavram (br). **280 Alamy Stock Photo:** Album (l); imageBROKER (cr); dpa picture alliance (crb); World History Archive (br). **281 Dorling Kindersley:** Gary Ombler / Vikings of Middle England (tr). **282 123RF.com:** (3). **Alamy Stock Photo:** Art of Travel (8); Eye Ubiquitous; Tony Cunningham (5); ZUMA Press, Inc. (10); gary warnimont (14).**Dorling Kindersley:** Clive Streeter / Science Museum, London (13). **Dreamstime.com:** Thomas Jurkowski (11); Nerthuz (16).**Getty Images:** Photo 12 (9); SSPL (2, 6, 15, 12). **283 123RF.com:** Arunas Gabalis (27). **Alamy Stock Photo:** Newscom (17); Universal Images Group North America LLC / DeAgostini (25).**Dorling Kindersley:** Richard Leeney / Maidstone Museum and Bentliff Art Gallery (23); Gary Ombler / Scale Model World, Allan Toyne (26); Gary Ombler / Fleet Air Arm Museum (28); Gary Ombler / Fleet Air Arm Museum, Richard Stewart (18).**Dreamstime.com:** Enanuchit (7); Libux77 (20). **Getty Images:** SSPL (19, 22). **Shutterstock.com:** Janice Carlson (21). **284 Alamy Stock Photo:** Chronicle of World History (bc); ZUMA Press, Inc. (bl). **284-285 akg-images:** Pictures From History (c). **285 Alamy Stock Photo:** (bc). **Getty Images:** Pictures From History / Universal Images Group (tl). **286 Alamy Stock Photo:** B. David Cathell (tr); Science History Images (l). **287 Alamy Stock Photo:** B Christopher (cla); Danvis Collection (cr); Alex Ramsay (clb). **Dreamstime.com:** Bubkatya (br); Mast3r (tl); Danilo Sanino (bl). **Getty Images:** Pictures From History / Universal Images Group (tr). **288 Alamy Stock Photo:** World History Archive (l). **Getty Images:** Pictures From History / Universal Images Group (tr, br). **289 Alamy Stock Photo:** Tom McGahan (c). **Bridgeman Images:** Archives Charmet (clb). **Dreamstime.com:** Artisticco Llc (tr); Pavel Naumov (cla); Shtirlitc (crb). **Getty Images:** Pictures From History / Universal Images Group (bc). **290 Alamy Stock Photo:** Alexander Ludwig (cl); Roland Brack (clb/Nubian). **Dorling Kindersley:** Barry Croucher - Wildlife Art Agency (c). **Dreamstime.com:** Kguzel (bl/Maya pyramid); Martin Molcan (clb/Pyramid of the Sun). **Getty Images / iStock:** leezsnow (crb). **291 Alamy Stock Photo:** Zdenk Mal (tr); Sean Pavone (tl). **292 Alamy Stock Photo:** World History Archive (bl). **© The Trustees of the British Museum. All rights reserved:** Tim Parmenter (tr). **293 Alamy Stock Photo:** IanDagnall Computing (br); The History Collection (tl). **Dorling Kindersley:** Vicky Read (ca); Michel Zabe (c). **294 123RF.com:** Alejandro Bernal (tr). **Dreamstime.com:** Yevheniia Rodina (bl). **Museo Nacional de Historia Natural de Chile:** (cr, r). **295 Alamy Stock Photo:** Hemis (c); Suzuki Kaku (tc). **Dorling Kindersley:** Gary Ombler / University of Pennsylvania Museum of Archaeology and Anthropology (cl). **Dreamstime.com:** Jarnogz (br). **296 © The Trustees of the British Museum. All rights reserved:** (tr). **Getty Images:** Pictures From History / Universal Images Group (cl); Werner Forman / Universal Images Group (br). **297 Alamy Stock Photo:** CPA Media Pte Ltd (b). **Getty Images / iStock:** GlobalP (tr). **The Metropolitan Museum of Art:** The Michael C. Rockefeller Memorial Collection, Gift of Nelson A. Rockefeller, 1972 (tl). **298-299 Alamy Stock Photo:** View Stock. **299 Kexin Ma:** (tr). **300 Shutterstock.com:** kontrymphoto (b); truhelen (tl). **301 123RF.com:** Aleksandra Sabelskaia (tl). **Alamy Stock Photo:** Granger - Historical Picture Archive (bl). **Bridgeman Images:** (br). **302 Alamy Stock Photo:** Sipa US (cr). **Bridgeman Images:** (br). **Dreamstime.com:** Neizu03 (cl). **303 Alamy Stock Photo:** steeve. e. flowers (br); funkyfood London - Paul Williams (tc). **Dreamstime.com:** Nemetse (tl); Sentavio (cla). **304 Alamy Stock Photo:** Matteo Omied (12). **Dorling Kindersley:** Gary Ombler / 4hoplites (3); Gary Ombler / Board of Trustees of the Royal Armouries (6); Gary Ombler / University of Pennsylvania Museum of Archaeology and Anthropology (13). **Dreamstime.com:** Hel080808 (4); Zim235 (11); Rcpphoto (15). **Getty Images / iStock:** kkant1937 (7). **Getty Images:** Patrick Kovarik / AFP (5). **The Metropolitan Museum of Art:** Bequest of Jane Costello Goldberg, from the Collection of Arnold I. Goldberg, 1986 (2);

Rogers Fund, 1913 (8). **305 Alamy Stock Photo:** Roland Bouvier (23). **Bridgeman Images:** (25). **Dorling Kindersley:** Peter Anderson / Universitets Oldsaksamling, Oslo (21). **Dreamstime.com:** Viacheslav Baranov (27); Nikolai Sorokin (17); Bjorn Hovdal (26). **The Metropolitan Museum of Art:** Bequest of George C. Stone, 1935 (19, 28); Purchase, Gift of William H. Riggs, by exchange, 1999 (18). **PunchStock:** Photodisc (24). **Collection of Jean-Pierre Verney:** Gary Ombler (20). **306 Alamy Stock Photo:** Image Gap (tr). **Bridgeman Images:** (cl); North Wind Pictures (bl); Pictures from History / David Henley (br). **307 Bridgeman Images:** (tl, br). **308 Alamy Stock Photo:** North Wind Picture Archives (c). **Bridgeman Images:** (br). **© The Trustees of the British Museum. All rights reserved:** Alan Hills (bl). **Shutterstock.com:** Everett Collection (tr). **309 123RF.com:** Dusan Loncar (br). **Alamy Stock Photo:** Photo 12 (tr). **Dreamstime.com:** Annzabella (tl). **Getty Images:** Yanick Folly / AFP) (bc). **310 Alamy Stock Photo:** Science History Images (tr). **Dreamstime.com:** Ahmad Safarudin (bc). **Getty Images:** Pictures From History / Universal Images Group (ca). **Shutterstock.com:** Dzm1try (crb, br). **311 Alamy Stock Photo:** Karol Kozlowski Premium RM Collection (tr). **Bridgeman Images:** Historic New Orleans Collection (c). **Dreamstime.com:** Cookamoto (tc); Kristina Samoilova (tl); Gamegfx (cla); Stefan Malesevic (bl); Oaties (br). **312 Alamy Stock Photo:** Everett Collection Historical (bl); Photo 12 (c). **Bridgeman Images:** Archives Charmet (tr); Photo Josse (br). **Dreamstime.com:** Alexander Pokusay (cl). **313 Alamy Stock Photo:** Niday Picture Library (tr). **Bridgeman Images:** Archives Charmet (tl); Leonard de Selva (clb). **314 Bridgeman Images:** Leonard de Selva (tl).**Getty Images:** Barbara Alper (tr). **315 Alamy Stock Photo:** Associated Press (c). **Dreamstime.com:** Jackbluee (clb). **Getty Images:** Kate Green / Getty Images for BoF (br). **316-317 Dorling Kindersley:** Gary Ombler / National Railway Museum, York / Science Museum Group (b). **317 Alamy Stock Photo:** Chronicle of World History (cr). **Bridgeman Images:** Stefano Bianchetti (cl). **Dreamstime.com:** Mahira (c). **318 Bridgeman Images:** Civil War Archive (tr). **Library of Congress, Washington, D.C.:** (b). **319 Alamy Stock Photo:** GL Archive (br); Niday Picture Library (tr). **Bridgeman Images:** Chicago History Museum (cr). **Dorling Kindersley:** Dave King / Gettysburg National Military Park, PA (bl). **Getty Images:** Universal History Archive / UIG (cla). **320 Mensun Bound:** Pierre Le Gall (tl). **320-321 Falklands Maritime Heritage:** National Geographic. **322 Alamy Stock Photo:** Granger-Historical Picture Archive (c). **Dorling Kinde sley:** Gary Ombler / Board of Trustees of the Royal Armouries (c). **323 Getty Images / iStock:** gsmudger (clb). **324-325 Shutterstock.com:** Andrew Harker (tc). **324 Alamy Stock Photo:** Shawshots (bc). **Getty Images:** Keystone (br). **325 Alamy Stock Photo:** Maurice Savage (cl). **Dreamstime.com:** Jonatan Stockton (cr/Surrendering soldier, cr/Soldier with gun). **Getty Images:** Apic (bc); Galerie Bilderwelt (cra). **Imperial War Museum:** (crb). **Shutterstock.com:** FAawRay (tc); Fotogenix (c). **www.mediadrumworld.com:** Tom Marshall (bl). **326 Alamy Stock Photo:** Alpha Historica (cl); Rick Lewis (cr). **Dreamstime.com:** Ianisme28 (br). **Getty Images:** Steve Schapiro / Corbis (cb). **327 Alamy Stock Photo:** David Grossman (bc).**Dreamstime.com:** Rank Sol (br). **Getty Images:** Angelo Cozzi / Archivio Angelo Cozzi / Mondadori (tr). **328 Alamy Stock Photo:** Reuters (cr). **Dreamstime.com:** Maksym Kapliuk (cb/US flag); VectorHome (cl). **Getty Images:** Dirck Halstead (br). **329 Alamy Stock Photo:** dpa picture alliance (tl); Michael Seleznev (tr); Granger - Historical Picture Archive (cr); Sueddeutsche Zeitung Photo (br). **Dreamstime.com:** Anastasiia Nevestenko (bl). **330 Getty Images:** Luis Tato / Bloomberg (b).**Shutterstock.com:** Sentavio (tl). **331 Dreamstime.com:** Info633933 (cb); Oaties (clb/Chain). **Getty Images:** Toby Melville - Pool (bc); Narinder Nanu / AFP (ca). **Shutterstock.com:** Mark Kauffman / The LIFE Picture Collection (tl). **332 123RF.com:** Sergey Peterman (br/screen). **Alamy Stock Photo:** Science History Images (cl); Chris Willson (bc). **© CERN:** (bl). **Dreamstime.com:** Andrii Arkhipov (tl); Photka (br). **Getty Images:** SSPL (crb). **333 Alamy Stock Photo:** Rick Crane (tr); Maurice Savage (c). **Dreamstime.com:** Branchecarica (br); Nexusby (tl). **334 Alamy Stock Photo:** mauritius images GmbH (tr). **Getty Images:** Thierry Monasse (br). **335 Alamy Stock Photo:** ifeelstock (c). **Dreamstime.com:** Arbaz Khan (fbr); Vitalii Krasnoselskyi (br). **336 123RF.com:** costasz (tl). **Dreamstime.com:** AlyaBigJoy (cr); Potysiev; Verdateo (ftr); Alexis Belec (cra); Suttiwat Phokaiautjima (bc); Ivan Kotliar (clb). **Getty Images:** DEA / G. Dagli Orti / De Agostini (tc); Lawrence Manning (tr). **Getty Images / iStock:** inarik (c); staticnak1983 (bl). **337 Alamy Stock Photo:** Evelyn Orea (bl). **Dreamstime.com:** Jiri Hera (br); Alexander Pokusay (ca, crb). **Getty Images / iStock:** Anastasia Dobrusina (ftl); toktak_kondesign (fbl). **Getty Images:** Martin Puddy (ftr). **338 Dreamstime.com:** Michael Bush (cra). **Getty Images / iStock:** dino4 (ca). **338-339 Getty Images:** James D. Morgan (bc). **339 Alamy Stock Photo:** Image Source (cl). **Dreamstime.com:** Xzotica (cr). **Getty Images / iStock:** Asurobson (fcr). **Getty Images:** Christopher Furlong (tr); Plume Creative (fcl). **340-341 Alamy Stock Photo:** melita (b). **340 Alamy Stock Photo:** Oleg Zaslavsky (c). **Getty Images:** Monica Morgan / WireImage (tr). **341 Alamy Stock Photo:** Jeff Morgan 13 (cl); Zoonar GmbH (tr). **342 Dorling Kindersley:** (12); Simon Mumford / The Flag Institute (1, 2, 3, 4, 5, 8, 9, 10, 11, 13, 14, 15, 16, 18, 19, 20, 22, 21). **Dreamstime.com:** Kanpisut Chaichalor (23). **343 Dorling Kindersley:** Simon Mumford / The Flag Institute (24, 26, 25, 27, 28, 29, 30, 31, 32, 33, 34, 35, 37, 36). **344 Alamy Stock Photo:** Dan Breckwoldt (tl); Images & Stories (b). **Dreamstime.com:** Alexey Pushkin (c). **345 Getty Images:** Martin Puddy (r). **346 Alamy Stock Photo:** Ruby (cl). **Donauinselfest, Vienna:** Photo Alexander Mller (c). **346-347 Getty Images / iStock:** Toa55 (b, t). **347 Alamy Stock Photo:** Evelyn Orea (tl). **Getty Images:** Hindustan Times (c).**naturepl.com:** Enrique Lopez-Tapia (tr). **348 Alamy Stock Photo:** John D. Ivanko (bl). **Getty Images / iStock:** ALLEKO (cra/Sweden); Anastasia Dobrusina (crb). **Getty Images:** DEA / G. Dagli Orti / De Agostini (cl). **348-349 Shutterstock.com:** adiwijayanto (t). **349 Getty Images:** Todd Maisel / NY Daily News Archive (bc). **Shutterstock.com:** nontarith songrerk (crb). **350 123RF.com:** lumaso (cl). **Getty Images / iStock:** toktak_kondesign (cla). **351 Dreamstime.com:** Jiri Hera (tr/Chocolate); Vlad Ivantcov (tr); Niceregionpics (bl/Jackfruit). **352 Alamy Stock Photo:** Hans Kristian Olsen (cla); PCN Photography (c).**Getty Images:** Mauro Ujetto / NurPhoto (tl); George Wood / Getty Images for RLWC (cl). **Getty Images / iStock:** Windzepher (cr). **352-353 Getty Images / iStock:** PeopleImages (b). **353 Alamy Stock Photo:** Hemis (tr). **Getty Images:** Kate McShane / Getty Images for Nike (cr). **354 123RF.com:** Sergii Kolesnyk / givaga (27). **Alamy Stock Photo:** Miran Buri (11). **Dreamstime.com:** Albund (3); Glen Edwards (14); Alexis Belec (8); Zagorskid (1); John Kasawa (2); Oleksii Terpugov (5); Tatjana Zvirblinska (16); Skypixel (13); Aleksandar Kosev (18); Lim Seng Kui (7); Pincarel (20); Phasinphoto (19); Vladvitek (21); Suljo (26); Marek Uliasz (6). **Fotolia:** Claudio Divizia (12). **Getty Images / iStock:** allanswart (15); stuartbur (4); Stockbyte (17). **Getty Images:** Lawrence Manning (24). **355 Dreamstime.com:** (45); Kuremo (48); Yocamon (30); Jan Pokorn (35); Carolina K. Smith M.d. (36); Elnur Amikishiyev (37); Viktoriya Kuzmenkova (44); Les Cunliffe (40); Ronniechua (42); Eduard Antonian (46); Sergeyoch (47/ball); Akwitps (32). **Fotolia:** robynmac (33). **356 Dreamstime.com:** Pincarel (cb/Golf ball); Olaf Speier (cb); Oleksii Terpugov (cb/Squash ball); Sergeyoch (cb/tennis ball); Thomas Vieth (bl); Zagorskid (crb, crb/Shuttlecock). **357 Alamy Stock Photo:** Associated Press (c). **Dreamstime.com:** Razvanjp (br). **358-359 Dreamstime.com:** Travellingtobeprecise (c). **358 123RF.com:** Hong Li (crb). **Alamy Stock Photo:** Magica (bl). **360 Alamy Stock Photo:** PG Arphexad (bl). **Bridgeman Images:** Dublin City Gallery, the Hugh Lane / © Niki de Saint Phalle Charitable Art Foundation / ADAGP, Paris and DACS, London 2023 (r). **361 Alamy Stock Photo:** Krys Bailey (tr); Niday Picture Library (bl); Kat Davis (br). **Bridgeman Images:** (cla); Fitzwilliam Museum (tl); Olafur Eliasson , The weather project, 2003. Monofrequency lights, projection foil, haze machines, mirror foil, aluminium, scaffolding, 26.7 x 22.3 x 155.44 metres. Installation view: Tate Modern, London. Photo Bridgeman Art Library / Richard Haughton. Courtesy the artist; neugerriemschneider, Berlin; Tanya Bonakdar Gallery, New York / Los Angeles . © 2003 Olafur Eliasson / Courtesy of the artist; neugerriemschneider, Berlin; Tanya Bonakdar Gallery, New York / Los Angeles © Olafur Eliasson (cl). **362 Dzia:** (tl). **362-363 Dzia. 364 Getty Images / iStock:** CasarsaGuru (bl); inarik (r). **365 Dreamstime.com:** Jannoon028 (br/Phone); Stepanov (bl). **Getty Images / iStock:** JackF (br); southtownboy (crb). **Getty Images:** Alex Livesey / Getty Images for RLWC (tl). **366 Alamy Stock Photo:** LJSphotography (br) **Dreamstime.com:** Featureflash (cr). **Getty Images / iStock:** baona (bc); Denisfilm (bl). **367 Alamy Stock Photo:** Ian Georgeson (tr); Tjasa Janovljak (c). **Getty Images / iStock:** lisegagne (bl). **Getty Images:** Valerie Macon / AFP (cr); Hugh Sitton (crb); David Sacks (br). **Shutterstock.com:** Ljupco Smokovski (clb). **368 123RF.com:** costasz (6). **Alamy Stock Photo:** Ablestock / Hemera Technologies (1). **Dorling Kindersley:** Ray Moller / Powell-Cotton Museum, Kent (5); Gary Ombler / Bate Collection (18). **Dreamstime.com:** Furtseff (7); Sergiy1975 (4); Worldshots (19); Martina Meyer (17). **Getty Images:** C Squared Studios (2). **369 Dorling Kindersley:** Mattel INC (25); Gary Ombler (22); Gary Ombler / National Music Museum (35, 23); Gary Ombler / Bate Collection (21). **Dreamstime.com:** Karam Miri (38); Suttiwat Phokaiautjima (28); Verdateo (33). **Getty Images / iStock:** JUN2 (32). **370 Alamy Stock Photo:** Kawee Wateesatogkij (tr). **Shutterstock.com:** Anastasia Gruzdeva / AP (bl). **370-371 Alamy Stock Photo:** MQ Naufal (b). **371 Dakakker:** Karin Oppelland (tl). **372 Alamy Stock Photo:** Reuters (tc); Jochen Tack (br). **372-373 Philipp Schmidli:** (tc). **373 123RF.com:** Nikola Roglic (bl). **Alamy Stock Photo:** Andrey Khrobostov (br). **Dreamstime.com:** Typhoonski (tr). **374-375 Dreamstime.com:** Alexey Petrov (c/Cockpit); Tacettin Ulas / Photofactoryulas (ca/clouds). **374 Captain Darryl Elliott:** (tl). **376 Alamy Stock Photo:** Roland Magnusson (cr); Nerthuz (t); robertharding (cb). **377 Alamy Stock Photo:** Hero Images Inc. (tr). **Getty Images / iStock:** Nikada (crb). **Getty Images:** Thitiphat Khuankaew / EyeEm (cr).**SchimiAlf:** (bc). **378 Getty Images / iStock:** martin-dm (bl); staticnak1983 (br). **378-379 Getty Images:** Elijah Nouvelage / AFP (tc). **379 Alamy Stock Photo:** Amlan Mathur (bl). **Dreamstime.com:** Josefkubes (cra). **Getty Images:** Robin Marchant (crb). **380-381 Alamy Stock Photo:** Michele D'Ottavio (b). **380 Dreamstime.com:** Leremy (fcr). **Getty Images:** Jefri Tarigan / Anadolu Agency (tr). **381 Getty Images:** Dante Diosina Jr / Anadolu Agency (tl); STR / AFP (cr). **393 Alamy Stock Photo:** Granger - Historical Picture Archive (tr)

Data credits: 35 Space Exploration Data: **Radio Free Europe/Radio Liberty © RFE/RL** – https://www.rferl.org/a/space-agencies-and-their-budgets/29766044.html; **166** Endangered species Data: **The IUCN Red List of Threatened Species version 2022-2.** Retrieved from https://www.iucnredlist.org/ (Accessed, 30 Mar 2023); **335** Going Global Data: **© ITU 2023** – https://www.itu.int/en/ITU-D/Statistics/Pages/stat/default.aspx; **350** Pasta consumption: **I.P.O. International Pasta Organisation Secretariat General c/o Unione Italiana Food** – https://internationalpasta.org/annual-report/; **351** Global fruit production figures: **Food and Agriculture Organization of the United Nations:** FAOSTAT. Crops and livestock products. Accessed: 24 Mar 2023. https://fenix.fao.org/faostat/internal/en/#data/QCL/visualize / Global fruit production figures; **356-357** Sports Data: **WorldAtlas** – https://www.worldatlas.com/articles/what-are-the-most-popular-sports-in-the-world.html

Cover images: *Front:* **123RF.com:** eshved clb/ (heart), scanrail bc, thelightwriter cb; **Alamy Stock Photo:** Iryna Buryanska (x4), Mechanik cra, Panther Media GmbH / niki crb, Steppenwolf c; **Dorling Kindersley:** Gary Ombler / Shuttleworth Collection cra/ (aircraft); **Dreamstime.com:** Dragoneye cla, Kolestamas cla/ (Tyrannosaurus), Peterfactors ca; **Getty Images / iStock:** FGorgun clb; **Robert Harding Picture Library:** TUNS clb/ (Macaw); **Science Photo Library:** Miguel Claro bl, Power and Syred clb/ (Halobacterium); **Shutterstock.com:** Arthur Balitskii crb/ (Hand), KsanaGraphica, Dotted Yeti cra/ (astronaut); *Back:* **123RF.com:** Denis Barbulat crb/ (Lily), solarseven cra; **Alamy Stock Photo:** Iryna Buryanska (x3), imageBROKER / J.W.Alker crb/ (turtle), Alexandr Mitiuc cl; **Dorling Kindersley:** Gary Ombler / University of Pennsylvania Museum of Archaeology and Anthropology cla/ (boat), Arran Lewis(science3) / Rajeev Doshi (medi-mation) / Zygote cr; **Dreamstime.com:** Feathercollector clb, Patrick Guenette bc, Nerthuz c, Lynda Dobbin Turner cla/ (Jellyfish); **Getty Images:** Tim Flach clb/ (ants), Gerhard Schulz / The Image Bank bl; **Getty Images / iStock:** GlobalP cla/ (snake), Anton_Sokolov cb/ (car), Vladayoung cb; **NASA:** GSFC / Arizona State University cla; **Science Photo Library:** Wim Van Egmond crb, Steve Gschmeissner br; **Shutterstock.com:** Sebastian Janicki ca, KsanaGraphica; *Spine:* **Shutterstock.com:** Sebastian Janicki b

All other images © Dorling Kindersley

DK WHAT WILL YOU EYEWITNESS NEXT?

THE AMAZON

AMERICAN REVOLUTION

ANCIENT GREECE

ANCIENT EGYPT

ANCIENT ROME

CAT

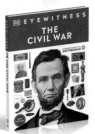
THE CIVIL WAR

CLIMATE CHANGE

CRYSTAL & GEM

DINOSAUR

THE ELEMENTS

FISH

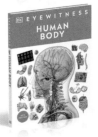
HUMAN BODY

HURRICANE & TORNADO

INSECT

NATIONAL PARKS

NATURAL DISASTERS

OCEAN

PLANETS

ROCKS & MINERALS

SHARK

SOCCER

TITANIC

TRAIN

VOLCANO & EARTHQUAKE

WEATHER

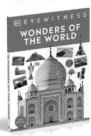
WONDERS OF THE WORLD

WORLD WAR II

DK For the curious